Visual C# .NET
Programming

Visual C#™ .NET Programming

Harold Davis

SYBEX

San Francisco · London

Associate Publisher: Richard Mills
Acquisitions Editor: Denise Santoro Lincoln
Developmental Editor: Tom Cirtin
Editor: Pete Gaughan
Production Editor: Mae Lum
Technical Editor: Matt Tagliaferri
Electronic Publishing Specialists: Rozi Harris, Bill Clark, Interactive Composition Corporation
Proofreaders: Amey Garber, Nelson Kim, David Nash, Laurie O'Connell, Yariv Rabinovitch, Nancy Riddiough
Indexer: Lynnzee Elze
Cover Designer: Caryl Gorska, Gorska Design
Cover Photographer: Carlog Navajas, Image Bank

Library of Congress Card Number: 2002106412

ISBN: 0-7821-4046-7

For Phyllis, who makes the music in my life

Acknowledgments

When the music stops, an author alone is responsible for the book he or she has created. That said, a book such as this is produced through the efforts of many people. Richard Mills and Denise Santoro Lincoln originated this project and brought me into it. Tom Cirtin did a great job of helping to birth this book, and contributed from his vast store of musical knowledge. Mae Lum masterfully handled the logistics as the book became a full-fledged project. Pete Gaughan copyedited this book and has substantially helped to make it something we can all be proud of. Matt Tagliaferri provided technical review and helped save me from myself.

In addition to team Sybex, I would like to thank my friend and agent, Matt Wagner, and Bill Gladstone, both of Waterside Productions.

I am thankful to Phyllis Davis, who contributed beyond the call of duty in a number of ways, and to Martin Davis, who read several chapters in "manuscript," as they quaintly say, and made many useful suggestions. And thanks to Chris Hopper, who helped with hardware.

Last, but not least, a standing ovation for Anders Hejlsberg and Scott Wiltamuth, without whom there would be no C# to write about.

Contents at a Glance

Contents

Introduction

I dreamed that black-clad horsemen pursued me down a lonely road. The hoofs of their steeds rang with urgent clanks on the paving stones. I turned to look at my pursuers and saw fiery red-rimmed eyes fixed within deathly pale faces. A sword was raised, and as it swept down...

No, that's not the way it goes at all.

I dreamed of a city far in the future. Sentient machines performed all menial labor, so there was plenty of time for science and art. But all was not well in paradise. Regimentation begat alienation, and alienation begat a class of cyber-hackers who had dropped out of known society and lived in caves far from the city.

That's a little closer, but we're not quite there yet! Let's try again.

I dreamed of a pure programming language, so sweet and tender, yet flexible and strong. This language, named after a musical note, incorporated the best features of other languages and also made available an extremely potent library of classes. You guessed it: the language is C#, and the library of classes the .NET Framework. This dream is true!

This is a different kind of book about a programming language. The conventional thing is to begin with syntax and semantics, proceed through user interfaces and object orientation, and end with various applications. But why be conventional? This book does not do the standard thing.

To some degree, a book is a compact between writer and reader. The reader will rightly be disappointed if what they expected to find is missing. At the same time, no book can be everything for everybody.

In this sense, the compact between writer and reader is analogous to the implementation of an interface in a class. Everything is spelled out in the interface, so that there is no misunderstanding about how to use an implementation of it.

I expect readers of this book to have some experience with programming, or at least be highly intelligent. This is not a book for dummies. (Or, as Mel Brooks exhorted in a different context, "Be a smarty!")

However, your programming experience need not be with a language in the "C" family—or even with Java. C# represents a wonderful "next step" for Visual Basic programmers. If you are a VB programmer looking for new horizons, this book was written for you.

By the way, the one area that seems to trip VB programmers new to C# is type conversion. So if you are a VB programmer new to C#, you might want to start with a look at the material explaining type conversion in Chapter 6, "Zen and Now: The C# Language."

I do not promise to be comprehensive or encyclopedic in my coverage of C# or the .NET Framework. For one thing, no single book could ever keep this promise, as the field is so vast. For another, online help is the best place for detailed answers to many questions—so, as appropriate in this book, I refer you to help topics.

Internal tools such as the Object Browser reveal more information than any documentation could—I show you how to make the best use of the Object Browser in Chapter 5, "Reflecting on Classes."

Finally, most serious programmers—or students of a programming language—have multiple books about the language on their shelves: In other words, comprehensiveness is found in libraries, and in online compendiums, not individual books.

So if I don't promise to be comprehensive, what commitments am I making?

First, regarding the code in the book: I've tried to provide examples that you will be able to use in the real world, based on my experience as a developer. I've run and tested every example in the book. Many of the examples should be usable in whole or part as they are written.

C# is a graceful language. I've tried to write about it in an intelligent, elegant, and humorous way.

I hope you enjoy this book. C# .NET is a powerful, exciting, easy-to-use programming language. The primary goals of my book are to:

- Share my excitement and joy in this aesthetically pleasing and productive tool.
- Help you to understand the concepts involved in programming with C# and the .NET Framework.
- Help you easily produce the code that you need for real projects.

If you read through this book and follow the examples, you will learn a lot. In contrast to the conventional structure of the programming language book, described earlier in this introduction, the narrative structure of this book involves immersion. You'll learn by doing—starting with creating a web service in the first few pages. It's only later that the nitty-gritty of language syntax is covered in detail. The idea is that you'll be having so much fun by then that the pain of mastering the details will be muted.

While we're on the subject of narrative structure—and, yes, Virginia, even computer books do have narrative structure—let's talk about the musical part names of this book.

The Structure of This Book: About the Musical Part Names

Since C# is a programming language named after a musical note, I thought it appropriate to involve musical concepts when structuring this book. In keeping with this, I've named each of the four parts of the book after movements in a classical composition. These movements—prelude, allemande, courante, and gigue—primarily are found in Baroque music. Musical scholars should note that I have not been compulsive about the accuracy or consistency of the musical metaphor. The point really is the metaphor and how it relates to the structure of this book and to programming in C#.

The structure of the book is essentially spiral, like a chambered nautilus shell or the pattern in this volume's cover photograph of a Zen garden. By the end of the book, readers will be able to comprehend and accomplish things that seemed shadowy and mysterious when they plunged in at the beginning. Each of the four parts represents a different stage in this quest for skills and understanding.

Part 1: Prelude—Service with a Smile

In classical music, the prelude introduces the work. Often composed in a free-flowing style, it sets the mood and mode for the rest of the work and is designed to pique the interest of the audience. It can contain references to ideas that are delivered later—foreshadowings, a taste of things to come. The themes in the prelude are not whole ideas but snippets, *motifs*—just enough to whet the appetite and make the listener want more. These motifs are pre-echoes—not déjà vu, which are vague memories of things already seen, but rather premonitions of things to come. If you listen to the composition more than once, then in the prelude you should be able to begin to hear the pattern of the entire piece.

At the same time that a prelude introduces the larger work; it is an organic unit in and of itself, with a beginning, middle, and end. This cohesive mini-composition exists within the larger whole and has its own sense of narrative conflict and resolution, point and counterpoint, all reconciling in a conclusion that serves as an introduction.

Our prelude introduces the theme of the web service. Web services have been hailed by some as revolutionary: a brand new kind of unit of executable code, fit for the distributed environments of the Internet age.

A web service is not an end in and of itself. To actually do anything as a part of a program, it must be used—or, put another way, "consumed."

It is also the case that this book is not "about" web services; it is about programming in the C# language and the .NET Framework.

Our prelude explores creating a web service, in Chapter 1, "Creating a Web Service," and coding ASP.NET web applications to consume the web service, in Chapter 2, "Consuming the Service on the Web," as a dramatic way to jump into the topics that will form the pattern of the composition that is this book. Keep your eyes and ears open for premonitions that reveal this book's real themes: the best way to write C# code for clarity, and patterns and practice of communication between objects.

Part II: Allemande—Striding Forward

The allemande is a movement of great substance that directly follows the prelude of a musical suite and picks up where the prelude leaves off. It is stately in manner and can be highly stylized. The allemande carries forward the mood prefigured in the prelude and introduces gravity into the suite; but the prelude's free style gives way to the processional-like regularity of the allemande.

The sentiments casually introduced in the prelude have become a stepping dance with reality—and the allemande keeps it all moving. The meter is steady and so is the progress. The allemande is striding forward without hesitation into the future, and the future is now.

Early allemandes come in three sections, or strains, that are related but not the same. The second strain contrasts with the first strain. They resolve in the third and final section, which paves the way for the next movement in the composition.

You can't have an application without a user interface. Chapter 3, "Windows Uses Web Services, Too!," is an introduction to programming the Windows user interface—while carrying on the web services motif explicitly introduced in the first part of the book. The allemande also keeps one of the underlying themes of this book moving, with an explanation of the asynchronous communication design pattern.

Chapter 4, "Building a Better Windows Interface," is about the hard-core plumbing of a Windows interface. Services have been left behind. This is the territory of displaying lists of items, menus, common dialogs, and such. This strain of the allemande may be concerned with conventional Windows development, and it may be a little dissonant, but it has a sense of humor. For example, you'll start this chapter by making round buttons dance.

The allemande is complete with Chapter 5, "Reflecting on Classes." We've taken strides forward and are now past Windows, in the realm of objects and classes. This chapter fits C# code in with the .NET Framework. Once again, it's about communication. Classes are not islands, and they must be instantiated to be used. It is a time for reflection, for understanding of ourselves and our environment, and also to soar the peaks of what is possible—knowing that soon we must return to the humble arenas of language and syntax that make it all possible.

Part III: Courante—The Dance of the Language

The courante is a dance movement of vigor and complexity. It is rhythmically interesting and exciting, but capable of hard work. A courante combines playfulness and movement with heart, soul, and substance.

Courantes were used for dancing in court and in theater, and later as stylized movements in instrumental music. The form combines rhythmic and metrical fluidity with a complicated texture.

This part, the courante, is in many ways the heart and soul of this book.

We start with Chapter 6, "Zen and Now: The C# Language." What could be more important than a good understanding and grasp of syntax of the beautiful C# language?

Moving on, Chapter 7, "Arrays, Indexers, and Collections," shows you how to work with groups of objects—and make them dance.

Chapter 8, "The Life of the Object in C#," is all about classes and object-oriented programming. Since all programming in C# is class-based and object-oriented—the only question is whether the programming is good object-oriented code or bad object-oriented code—the material in that chapter is important. I think the running example in Chapter 8 is quite a bit of fun. This program is a simulation based on the ideas of Pulitzer Prize–winning author Jared Diamond. As you'll see, the program allows users to track the rise (and fall) of tribes and civilizations.

Strings are everything, and everything is string. If you know how to manipulate strings, you know lots of things—and you'll find out how in Chapter 9, "Everything Is String Manipulation."

Our courante has proceeded from language and syntax, and onward through arrays, collections, objects, and classes. Coming back to the beginning, it has explained the sophisticated manipulation of language elements. This is a complex dance, a spiral within a spiral. As the courante winds down, we're ready to move onward—by looking outwards instead of inwards.

Part IV: Gigue—Leaping to Success

The gigue—which became a popular Baroque movement—probably originated in Great Britain as the "jig" or "jigg" (although note that the Old French verb *giguer* means "to leap" or "to gambol"). Whatever the derivation of the word, it's clear that in Elizabethan times a jig was a dance—notably performed by Scottish lairds—that involved a great deal of jumping (or, as one contemporary put it, the dance is "full of leapings").

In the context of our gigue, this remains true: the movement is full of leapings. It is happy, exuberant, full of life, and extroverted.

It's time to turn the knowledge we've learned in the early movements outwards—and use the gigue to interact with the world.

Chapter 10, "Working with Streams and Files," shows you how to work with files—and, generally, how to serialize objects.

Chapter 11, "Messaging," explains how to program messaging applications. Using message queues, as you'll see in Chapter 11, it's possible to build families of applications that divide workloads and start and stop each other.

Chapter 12, "Working with XML and ADO.NET," covers interacting with XML and databases.

Chapter 13, "Web Services as Architecture," wraps it all up. Coming back to the beginning—after all, Chapter 1 started with a web service—we can use the sophisticated tools and techniques that we've learned in order to build web services that are truly exciting! The chapter concludes with an example showing how to use the TerraServer web service and display aerial photos or topographic maps of almost anywhere in the U.S. at a variety of magnifications.

And, finally, the gigue is up! Now programming in C# is up to you...

How to Download the Code

Most of the code samples in this book are not very long, since they emphasize the principles of how to do something rather than full implementation details or production software. I encourage you to follow the examples in this book by re-creating the objects in the projects and by using your keyboard to enter the source code. You will learn the most by doing this!

Alternatively, you can download projects containing the source code used in this book. (One reason to do so is for comparison if the code you entered manually doesn't work.) Sybex has published all the code used in this book on their website at www.sybex.com. Search for this book (using the title, the author, or the ISBN number 4046), and click the Downloads button. Once you have accepted the license agreement, you'll be able to download any of the code listed in this book, organized in zipped projects by chapter.

How to Contact the Author

I've made every effort to make this book as useful and accurate as possible. Please let me know what you think; I would love to hear from you. I have set up a special e-mail address for this book: csharp@bearhome.com. I would greatly appreciate any suggestions or information about problems that you have with the text.

PART I

Prelude: Service with a Smile

Chapter 1: Creating a Web Service

Chapter 2: Consuming the Service on the Web

CHAPTER 1

Creating a Web Service

- Understanding web services

- Creating a web service using Notepad

- Creating an ASP.NET web service using Visual Studio

- Adding a class module

- XML documentation tags

I believe that the best way to learn something is to plunge in. Of course, that leaves the question of where it's best to plunge. This book is, of course, about a programming language—C#—and a programming environment—Visual Studio .NET. It would be natural—and typical—to start with one or the other. Another conventional possibility would be to start by creating a Windows application.

But let's not be conventional! C# is a brand new language, and web services are a genuinely new programming concept. New languages and revolutionary programming architectures don't come along very often. Why not plunge in in a way that keeps things interesting and isn't the "same old, same old"? This chapter will show you how to create a very simple ASP.NET web service by hand using Notepad (it will be automatically compiled when the service is opened the first time). You'll also learn how to build somewhat more complex ASP.NET web services using Visual Studio. Along the way you'll learn (of course) about web services—and also C# language concepts, and how to work with the Visual Studio environment.

When all is said and done, this is a book about programming in C#, and web services are only one of the exciting things you can create using C#. In this chapter, I'll use web services as a launch pad for helping you to understand class-based programming in C#—a truism, since all C# programming is working with classes. Before we get there, you do need to understand a bit about web services.

Understanding Web Services

A web service is a mechanism for making components available across the Internet using open standards, including HTTP (Hypertext Transfer Protocol) and XML (Extensible Markup Language). The idea is to create "black box" components that can communicate with each other, regardless of the operating system or programming language. A little more precisely, a web service is a component, or module, of executable code with a special interface that makes its methods available for use (also called "consumption") by other programs using an HTTP-based request. This request is made using HTTP GET or using HTTP POST and Simple Object Access Protocol (SOAP). (You are probably familiar with GETs and POSTs from working with HTML web forms; SOAP is discussed further in this section.)

Component-Based Distributed Architectures

Web services are by no means the only architectural technology used for component-based distributed computing; for example, you are probably somewhat familiar with Common Object Request Broker Architecture (CORBA) and Distributed Component Object Model (DCOM).

Table 1.1 compares some of the characteristics of CORBA, DCOM, and web services. The protocols listed under the Web Service column are described throughout the subsequent sections of this chapter.

TABLE 1.1: CORBA, DCOM, and Web Services Compared

Characteristic	CORBA	DCOM	Web Service
Mechanism for remote procedure call (RPC)	Internet Inter-ORB Protocol (IIOP)	Distributed Computing Environment Remote Procedure Call (DCE-RPC)	HTTP
Encoding	Common Data Representation (CDR)	Network Data Representation (NDR)	XML and SOAP
Interface description	Interface Definition Language (IDL)	IDL	WSDL
Discovery	Naming service and trading service	System Registry	UDDI repositories
Works through firewall?	No	No	Yes
Complexity of protocols?	High	High	Low
Cross-platform?	Somewhat	No	Yes

As you can see from Table 1.1, web services have some significant advantages over CORBA and DCOM: web services are less complex, can get through firewalls, and are accessible from any client platform. Note that this, of course, does not mean that web services are always a good replacement for CORBA and DCOM—these other protocols have their place in homogenous systems behind a firewall in which the platform is the same and the servers are directly connected, and where performance is an important concern.

Ways to Create Web Services

Essentially, a web service is implemented as a SOAP XML document. There are many ways to create this document. For example, IBM provides a Web Services Toolkit, as does the Apache project. You can also hand-format the SOAP XML. Even within the Microsoft universe, there are several different ways of implementing SOAP-based XML web services. These include

- Microsoft's SOAP Toolkit, which lets you expose COM components as web services (and does not require the .NET Framework for deployment). To download the SOAP Toolkit, go to http://msdn.microsoft.com and search for **SOAP Toolkit**.

- Office XP Web Services Toolkit.

- An ATL Server implementation written in C++. ATL Server is part of Visual Studio .NET but does not require the .NET Framework for deployment.

- .NET Remoting, which lets classes inherited from a base class named `MarshalByRefObject` be exposed as web services using SOAP.

- ASP.NET.

You probably will not be surprised to learn that ASP.NET—using either Visual Basic or C# ("see sharp")—is the easiest way on this list to create web services. As I'll show you shortly, you can write an ASP.NET web service by hand in a text editor such as Notepad and let ASP.NET compile and deploy it for you, or you can take advantage of Visual Studio .NET's rich integrated development environment.

NOTE   In this book, I'll use the term "web service" to mean an ASP.NET web service rather than any of the other kinds of web services described above.

Simple Object Access Protocol (SOAP)

The SOAP specification can be found at www.w3.org/TR/SOAP/. According to the specification abstract,

> *SOAP is a lightweight protocol for exchange of information in a decentralized, distributed environment. It is an XML based protocol that consists of three parts: an envelope that defines a framework for describing what is in a message and how to process it, a set of encoding rules for expressing instances of application-defined datatypes, and a convention for representing remote procedure calls and responses.*

It's worth noting that:

- While SOAP can be used as a remote procedure invocation mechanism, it can also be used to exchange XML documents.

- SOAP uses XML namespaces.

- The SOAP envelope mentioned in the specification contains the actual message in the body of the envelope. It also contains SOAP headers, which can be used programmatically (see Chapter 13, "Web Services as Architecture," for an example).

- When you want to invoke a method remotely, you're sending a SOAP request and getting a SOAP response.

Web Services Description Language (WSDL)

Web Services Description Language (WSDL) describes the methods supported by a web service, the parameters the methods take, and what the web service returns. You can find the specification, sponsored by a cross-industry group that includes IBM and Microsoft, at www.w3.org/TR/wsdl.

A WSDL document is an XML schema that provides the required information about a web service—methods, data types, and response—so that a proxy can be created (you'll see how to create and use a proxy in Chapter 2, "Consuming the Service on the Web").

Generally, creators of ASP.NET web services do not have to worry themselves about WSDL; a WSDL document is automatically generated at runtime on the fly by the ASP.NET runtime using a process called reflection. (Reflection is a mechanism that allows metadata about a program to be examined at runtime.)

Universal Description, Discovery, and Integration (UDDI)

How do you find a web service that you might want to consume? Conversely, how do you publish a web service so that others can find it?

One answer is word of mouth. I might tell you about a web service, or you might tell me. Similarly, it's no problem for us to find the web services that we'll create in the remainder of this chapter. When we want to consume them, we'll know what we named them, and what URL to use.

Universal Description, Discovery, and Integration (UDDI) is a more general, cross-industry effort at creating a repository for publishing and finding web services. The UDDI project (www.uddi.org) consists of a registry and a set of APIs for accessing the registry. IBM and Microsoft maintain cross-synchronized UDDI registries that can be browsed. The Microsoft registry can also be accessed from the Visual Studio Start page, as explained in Chapter 2.

In addition to UDDI, there are websites that provide directories of web services you can consume. You'll find more information about this in the "UDDI" section of Chapter 2.

One If by Hand

You have enough background about web services to get started with creating one. We'll start with a text editor and the simple "Hello, Web Service!" program shown in Listing 1.1 and in Notepad in Figure 1.1.

Listing 1.1	"Hello, Web Service!"

```
<%@ WebService Language="C#" class="Helloweb" %>

using System.Web.Services;

[WebService (Namespace="http://sybex.com/webservices")]
public class Helloweb {
    [WebMethod]
```

```
    public string HelloWebService() {
        return "Hello, Web Service!";
    }
}
```

FIGURE 1.1:

A web service can be created using Notepad.

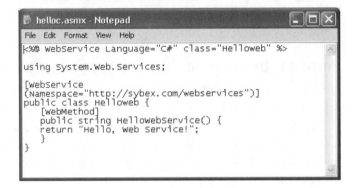

Let's have a look at this web service line by line. The directive at the top of the code

```
<%@ WebService Language="C#" class="Helloweb" %>
```

tells the compiler that this is a web service written in C# and implemented in the `Helloweb` class. The next line,

```
using System.Web.Services;
```

allows the program to use the types in the `System.Web.Services` namespace. (For more on the .NET Framework and namespaces, see Chapter 5, "Reflecting on Classes".)

TIP   The Visual Basic equivalent to `using` in C# is `import`.

The next line of code adds an optional attribute to the class that implements the service:

```
[WebService (Namespace="http://sybex.com/webservices")]
```

The `WebService` attribute allows you to set the default namespace for the web service. If you don't set this, ASP.NET will default the namespace to the URI `http://tempuri.org` and will display a message when you open the web service test page suggesting that you rename the default namespace.

URIs and URLs

You should know that the default namespace is a URI (Uniform Resource Identifier) rather than a URL (Uniform Resource Locator). There's no expectation that a user can click the URI and gain access to a resource (as opposed to a URL, which does work this way), but it should a unique string and—if it's a domain—be under your control. In other words, a URI is for identification, not navigation (although if the URI is a URL, it can also be navigated to).

Next comes the Helloweb class declaration. Everything within the curly braces will be part of the class:

```
public class Helloweb {

}
```

The [WebMethod] directive says that the method coming next is exposed as a web service. The C# method declaration names the method and says that its return is a string (once again, everything within the curly braces is part of the method):

```
public string HelloWebService() {

}
```

The string literal following the return keyword is, of course, the value returned by the method. Here's the complete Helloweb class:

```
public class Helloweb {
    [WebMethod]
    public string HelloWebService() {
    return "Hello, Web Service!";
    }
}
```

The Battle of the Curly Braces

As you probably know, although C# is case sensitive, it is not white-space sensitive, meaning you can lay your programming statements out any way you'd like, even across multiple lines. A statement of code is ended when you reach the delimiter, a semicolon (;), no matter how many physical lines it takes. Similarly, curly braces ({}) are used to mark the beginning and end of constructs such as namespaces, classes, and methods.

Since you are allowed to position these curly braces any way you'd like, you should aim to do so for readability. Which brings us to one of the greatest controversies of modern life: do you place the opening brace on the same line as the declaration, like so:

```
public class Class1 {
    // blah blah
}
```

or do you position it below the initial character of the declaration, like this:

```
public class Class1
{
    // blah blah
}
```

Continued on next page

The two are syntactically equivalent, and you'll find both styles in the code examples in this book. My personal preference is to do it the first way, as I think it helps to make really clear what is inside the construct—but Visual Studio, and .NET auto-generated code, position the opening brace on a new line.

Deploying the Web Service

Deploying the web service is a simple matter of making sure that the file it is in has an extension of `.asmx`—the file extension for ASP.NET web services—and opening it in Internet Information Services (IIS). ASP.NET will automatically take care of compiling it.

NOTE   As you may know, you can also use the C# command-line compiler to compile C# programs created in a text editor. The C# compiler, `csc.exe`, which ships as part of the .NET Framework, can be found in a folder beneath `\Windows\Microsoft.NET\Framework`. C# command-line compiler options can be found by searching Visual Studio .NET's online help for **C# Compiler Options**.

With our sample text editor web service in a file named `helloc.asmx`, the next step is to use the IIS administrative tools to create a virtual directory that points to it.

It's pretty standard—but not required—to put ASP.NET (and ASP.NET web service) application files in directories below `\Inetpub\wwwroot`. In this example, I'll put `helloc.asmx` in `C:\Inetput\wwwroot\SybexC1`.

The next step is to configure IIS to provide a virtual directory to point to this location. To do this, open the IIS administrative application (which is shown in Figure 1.2) by using the Start menu to select Control Panel ➢ Administrative Tools ➢ Internet Information Services. Click to expand the local computer and Web Sites icons, shown in the left pane of Figure 1.2, and select Default Web Site.

NOTE   Internet Information Services is called "Internet Services Manager" in Windows 2000.

Choose Action ➢ New ➢ Virtual Directory, and the Virtual Directory Creation Wizard will open. You must designate the virtual directory with an alias (Figure 1.3)—for example, SybexC1. The alias is used as part of the URL to access the web application—for example, `http://localhost/SybexC1/helloc.asmx`.

FIGURE 1.2:

The IIS administrative application is used to configure your local instance of IIS.

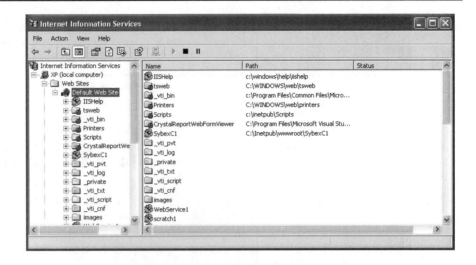

FIGURE 1.3:

A virtual directory is given an alias.

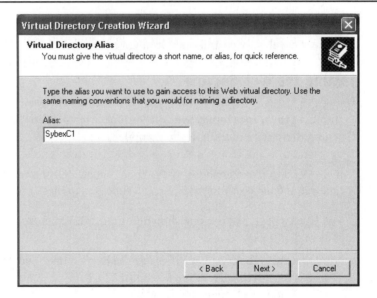

The next panel of the wizard is used to point at the path to the actual content referenced by the virtual directory (Figure 1.4).

FIGURE 1.4:
The directory that contains the contents is selected in the wizard.

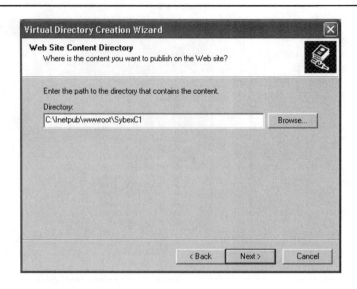

When the wizard is complete, and the virtual directory has been created, you are ready to compile the web service and open it in your browser.

Testing the Web Service

Using the virtual directory you created, and the web service file name, as the URL—for example, `http://localhost/SybexC1/helloc.asmx`—open the web service in your browser. Opening the service automatically compiles it.

> **NOTE**   If you need to make changes to the code, simply edit the text file and save it. The next time you reopen it in your browser, it will be automatically recompiled.

You'll see a page like the one shown in Figure 1.5, displaying the web service class and the members that it exposes.

Note that the web service, itself, is just a class with members (here, the only member of class `Helloweb` is the `HelloWebService` method). The pages displayed in Figures 1.5 through 1.7 are created around this class on the fly by ASP.NET.

Click the HelloWebService link shown in Figure 1.5 (which, of course, corresponds to the `HelloWebService` method in the class). The next page (shown in Figure 1.6) allows you to test the web service method using HTTP GET by clicking Invoke.

FIGURE 1.5:

A page for the web service is displayed in the browser.

FIGURE 1.6:

You can test the web service method by clicking Invoke.

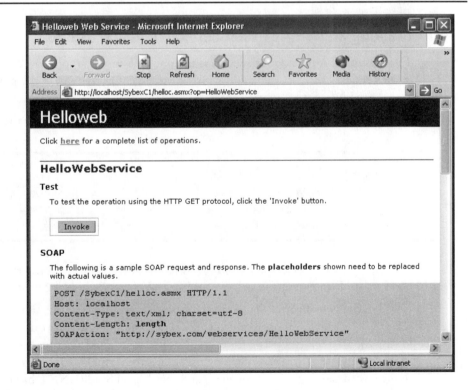

A new browser window will open that displays the XML response to the HTTP GET (Figure 1.7). You'll see that the appropriate string—"Hello, Web Service!"—has been returned.

FIGURE 1.7:

A new window displays the web service response to the HTTP GET.

NOTE   Obviously, when the consumption of a web service is embedded in a web or Windows application (as explained in Chapter 2 and in Chapter 3, "Windows Uses Web Services, Too!"), users don't get to see the raw XML returned from these test pages.

Creating an ASP.NET Web Service in Visual Studio

The example in the previous section is the one and only example you'll see in this book that creates code by hand in a text editor. It's so much easier to unleash the power of .NET using Visual Studio—so why not go for it?

To create a web services project in Visual Studio .NET using C#, open the New Project dialog.

Opening the New Project Dialog

To open the New Project dialog, select File ➣ New ➣ Project. Alternatively, click the New Project button on the Get Started tab of the Visual Studio Start page. If the Start page is not displayed, select Help ➣ Show Start Page.

With the New Project dialog open, select Visual C# Projects in the Project Types pane. Next, in the Templates pane, select ASP.NET Web Service as the project type (see Figure 1.8).

Still in the New Project dialog, in the Location box, delete everything following the web server URL (which is most likely `http://localhost/`). Now add your own project name following the web server URL—for example, SybexC2. The Location box should now contain `http://localhost/SybexC2`, meaning that this is the virtual URL that will be used to open the service (with the `.asmx` file appended) and that Visual Studio .NET has created a folder for the project under the default website location, most likely `\Inetpub\wwwroot`.

FIGURE 1.8:

To start a new web services project, select ASP.NET Web Service as the project type.

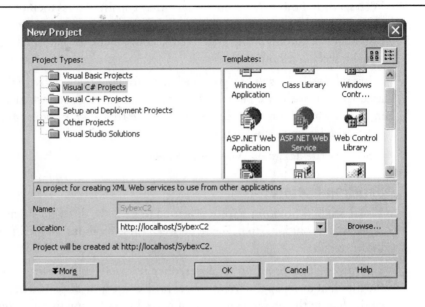

Click OK to create the project. When the new project opens, the designer for the web service (ASMX) module will be displayed (Figure 1.9).

FIGURE 1.9:

When the new project is opened, the designer for the web service module is displayed.

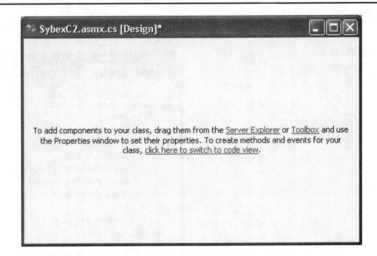

When you are building a Windows or web application, the designer for the Windows or web form is a very handy-dandy thing indeed, because you can visually drag and drop controls from the Toolbox onto the designer and have an instance of the control automatically instantiated.

Web services, however, are not visual—they consist of class members created in code. It's true that you can drag a component, such as a Timer, onto the designer and have the code that instantiates it automatically generated (a component, as opposed to a control, not having a visual interface at runtime).

But this really doesn't buy you much bang for your buck. Most of the time the designer is not used with web services, because the act of creating a web service means the creation of classes in code—which is one of the reasons why I started a book about programming C# with web services: it lets me focus on the coding.

So close the designer. We won't be needing it.

Solution Explorer

Visual Studio's Solution Explorer is used to view the different modules that are parts of projects and solutions, to navigate between these modules, and to open tools that interact with these modules.

If you don't see Solution Explorer, open it by selecting View ➢ Solution Explorer. Many of the files that make up the web services project are now displayed in Solution Explorer. To see all the files in the project, click the Show All Files button in the Solution Explorer toolbar (Figure 1.10). You may also need to expand the nodes in Solution Explorer that are denoted with a plus icon.

FIGURE 1.10:

The files that make up a project are displayed in Solution Explorer.

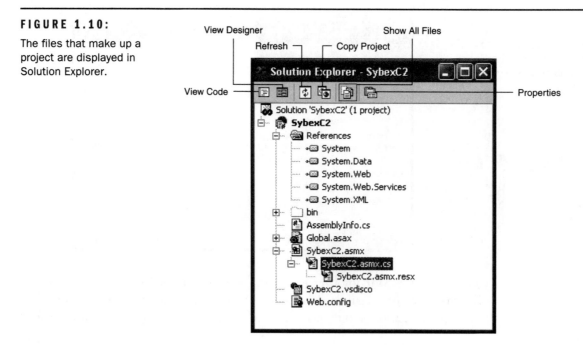

WARNING The buttons displayed on the Solution Explorer toolbar depend on the project module selected.

We're primarily interested in the SybexC2.asmx.cs code module, which is the "out of the box" web service that this project will deploy. To view the code contained in this file, select it and click the View Code button in Solution Explorer. Alternatively, you can right-click the file and choose View Code from its context menu, or just hit the F7 key.

Listing 1.2 shows what you'll find in the ready-made web service code module.

Listing 1.2   **An "Out of the Box" ASP.NET Web Service Code Module**

```
using System;
using System.Collections;
using System.ComponentModel;
using System.Data;
using System.Diagnostics;
using System.Web;
using System.Web.Services;

namespace SybexC2
{
    /// <summary>
    /// Summary description for Service1.
    /// </summary>
    public class Service1 : System.Web.Services.WebService
    {
        public Service1()
        {
//CODEGEN: This call is required by the ASP.NET Web Services Designer
            InitializeComponent();
        }

        #region Component Designer generated code

        //Required by the Web Services Designer
        private IContainer components = null;

        /// <summary>
        /// Required method for Designer support - do not modify
        /// the contents of this method with the code editor.
        /// </summary>
        private void InitializeComponent()
        {
        }

        /// <summary>
        /// Clean up any resources being used.
```

```
    /// </summary>
    protected override void Dispose( bool disposing )
    {
       if(disposing && components != null)
       {
          components.Dispose();
       }
       base.Dispose(disposing);
    }

    #endregion

    // WEB SERVICE EXAMPLE
    // The HelloWorld() example service returns the string Hello World
    // To build, uncomment the following lines then save and build the
    // project. To test this web service, press F5

//    [WebMethod]
//    public string HelloWorld()
//    {
//       return "Hello World";
//    }
    }
}
```

We're not going to go through this in detail, although you should have a general idea of what you are likely to find when you open one of these modules.

If you are not familiar with C# at all, you should know that lines beginning with two forward slash marks (//) are comments (this is sometimes known as C++ comment style).

Lines beginning with *three* forward slash marks (///) are also comments—but of a special sort. They are designed to contain XML documentation of the code, which can be automatically rendered into documentation for programs. I'll provide an overview of how this works towards the end of this chapter.

C# also supports so-called C-style comments, not shown in Listing 1.2, which begin with /* and end with */. Everything between the begin and end marks is a comment, which can span multiple lines. For example:

```
/* I am a comment! */
```

You should also know that the code between #region and #endregion directives does not display in the Code Editor (unless the region is expanded by clicking on the plus icon at the left side). As you can see in Figure 1.11, the code on the line of the #region directive,

```
#region Component Designer generated code
```

is displayed, but any subsequent code up to #endregion is hidden in the collapsed block.

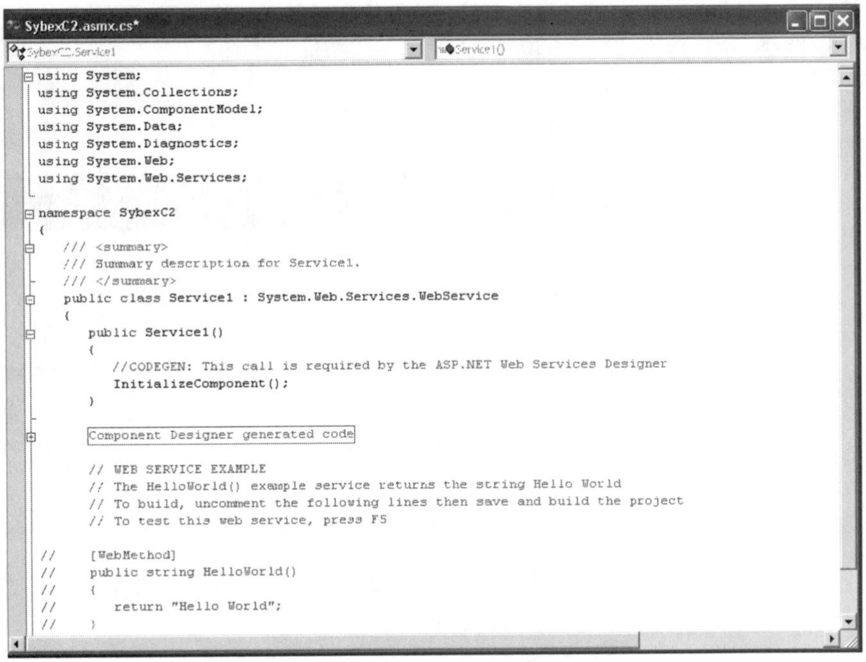

FIGURE 1.11:

The Code Editor doesn't display code within a `#region` / `#endregion` block unless it is expanded.

```
using System;
using System.Collections;
using System.ComponentModel;
using System.Data;
using System.Diagnostics;
using System.Web;
using System.Web.Services;

namespace SybexC2
{
    /// <summary>
    /// Summary description for Service1.
    /// </summary>
    public class Service1 : System.Web.Services.WebService
    {
        public Service1()
        {
            //CODEGEN: This call is required by the ASP.NET Web Services Designer
            InitializeComponent();
        }

        Component Designer generated code

        // WEB SERVICE EXAMPLE
        // The HelloWorld() example service returns the string Hello World
        // To build, uncomment the following lines then save and build the project
        // To test this web service, press F5

//        [WebMethod]
//        public string HelloWorld()
//        {
//            return "Hello World";
//        }
```

Let's go ahead and replace the commented-out "Hello World" web service shown in Listing 1.2 with our own "Hello, Web Service!" The replacement boilerplate web service looks like this:

```
[WebMethod]
public string HelloWebService()
{
        return "Hello, Web Service!";
}
```

Now let's view the test pages for the web service we've created. To do this, start the project in the development environment by choosing Debug ➢ Start (you can, alternatively, choose F5 on the keyboard).

NOTE   If you're not planning on doing any debugging, you can select Debug ➢ Start Without Debugging (Ctrl+F5 is the keyboard shortcut) and the page will load faster than in debug mode.

The project will be built, and the ASMX file opened in Internet Explorer, as shown in Figure 1.12.

FIGURE 1.12:

The test page for the web service is displayed in Internet Explorer.

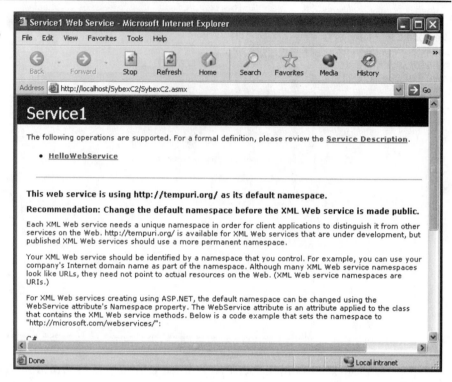

NOTE   You can also build the project by selecting Build ➤ Build Solution. The test page can then be opened by URL—in this case, `http://localhost/SybexC2/SybexC2.asmx`—in your browser.

As you can see in Figure 1.12, the name of the service is defaulted to Service1. It would be nice to give it a custom name. We can also add a description of the web service, and we should also change `http://tempuri.org/` to a URI under our control. To do this, add a `WebService` directive within the namespace and before the class declaration:

```
...
namespace SybexC2
{
    [WebService (Description="Chapter 1 demo program",
        Name="SybexC2Service",
        Namespace="http://www.bearhome.com/webservices")]
    ...
    public class Service1  : System.Web.Services.WebService
    {
```

```
    ...
    [WebMethod]
    public string HelloWebService()
    {
        return "Hello, Web Service!";
    }
    ...
  }
}
```

While we're having a look at this, you should make note of the declaration for Service1:

```
public class Service1  : System.Web.Services.WebService
```

The colon in the middle of the statement says that Service1 inherits from the `System` `.Web.Services.WebService` class.

TIP   The Visual Basic equivalent of the C# colon operator (:) is the `Inherits` keyword.

As you'll see shortly, you can add multiple methods to a single web service. Each method is denoted using a `WebMethod` directive.

OK. Let's run the revised web service and view its test page (shown in Figure 1.13). You'll see that it now displays a custom service name and description, and that annoying message about `http://tempuri.org/` is gone.

FIGURE 1.13:

The test page now shows the service name and description.

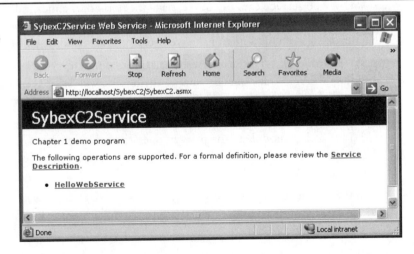

As a clean-up step, let's get rid of the auto-generated code added by Visual Studio that we don't really need, and delete the references to namespaces—which were also automatically added—that we don't really need. There's no overwhelming reason to do this, other than for clarity—although, of course, the unneeded code and references do consume some resources. Listing 1.3 shows the complete web service code module.

Listing 1.3   **The Cleaned-Up "Hello, Web Service!" Code Module**

```
using System.Web.Services;

namespace SybexC2
{
    [WebService (Description="Chapter 1 demo program",
        Name="SybexC2Service",
        Namespace="http://www.bearhome.com/webservices")]
    /// <summary>
    /// Service1 contains demo methods!
    /// </summary>
    public class Service1  : System.Web.Services.WebService
    {
        [WebMethod]
        public string HelloWebService()
        {
            return "Hello, Web Service!";
        }
    }
}
```

Adding a Class Module

A single web service can, of course, have more than one method—each web method being represented by a method that is a member of the web service class. In addition, you can add whatever classes you'd like to the web service code module to support its web methods.

We're going to add three new web methods to our demonstration web service, but we'll take a slightly different tack in constructing them. The web service code module and class will be used only for the actual web method calls—the supporting code will be placed in classes in a separate class module that has been added to the project.

To add a class module to the project, open the Add New Item dialog by selecting Project ≻ Add Class. (You can also right-click in Solution Explorer, and select Add ≻ Add Class from the context menu.)

In the dialog (shown in Figure 1.14), make sure that Class is selected as the kind of object to add in the Templates pane. You can accept the default name for the class module, Class1.cs, or change it if you'd like.

FIGURE 1.14:

The Add New Item dialog is used to add a class module.

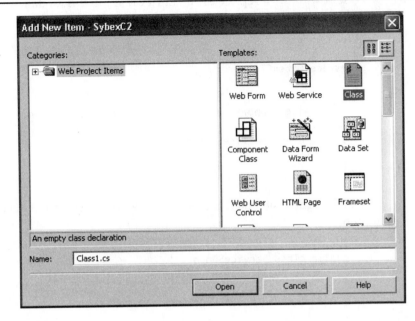

When the new class module is added to the project, it will come "out of the box" with the code shown in Listing 1.4. Specifically, note that the namespace used in the web service code module has been carried across to the class code module.

Listing 1.4   A Boilerplate Class Code Module

```csharp
using System;

namespace SybexC2
{
   /// <summary>
   /// Summary description for Class1.
   /// </summary>
   public class Class1
   {
      public Class1()
      {
         //
         // TODO: Add constructor logic here
         //
      }
   }
}
```

To start with, we'll replace the nominal Class1 in this module with a class designed to support the web service, named—logically enough—ServiceSupport:

```
using System;

namespace SybexC2
{
   /// <summary>
   ///Service Support supports the web services module
   /// </summary>
   public class ServiceSupport {

   }
}
```

Next, let's add a method that uses a get property accessor to return the string "Web services are cool!":

```
...
public class ServiceSupport {
   static public string ReturnText {
      get {
         return "Web services are cool!";
      }
   }
...
```

There's no earthly reason you'd want to do this in the real world, in two respects:

- A straight method that returns the string makes just as much sense as returning it as a property.

- You don't need a support class to return a string—why not just return it in the web method as in the earlier example?

We've done it this way to easily demonstrate using the get property accessor. Note that the property as it appears here is read-only; there is no way to set it.

It's also important to know that you can invoke the members of another class from a web method class. In this regard, you should note the use of the static keyword—which means that the member is shared so that an object based on the class doesn't have to be instantiated to use the member.

TIP   The Visual Basic equivalent to C#'s static is the Shared keyword.

Let's go back to the web service module, and invoke the ServiceSupport ReturnText property in a new web method named HelloWS2:

```
[WebMethod]
public string HelloWS2()
```

```
{
    return ServiceSupport.ReturnText;
}
```

You know you are on the right track when you type the class name in the Code Editor, and the IntelliSense auto-completion facility supplies the name of the member you'd like to use.

```
[WebMethod]
public string HelloWS2()
{
    return ServiceSupport.|
                          ┌──────────────────────┐
                          │ ◈ Equals             │
                          │ ◈ ReferenceEquals    │
                          │ ⌂ ReturnText         │
                          └──────────────────────┘
}
```

Running and Testing the Service

To test the new service method, run the project in the development environment. As you can see in Figure 1.15, the new test page that is generated has both web service methods listed.

FIGURE 1.15:

The new test page that is generated has two web service methods.

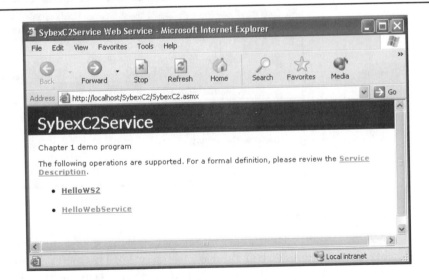

Click the HelloWS2 link. You can now invoke the method and verify that the specified text string is returned, as seen in Figure 1.16.

FIGURE 1.16:

Clicking the Invoke button (top) produces the appropriate string return (bottom).

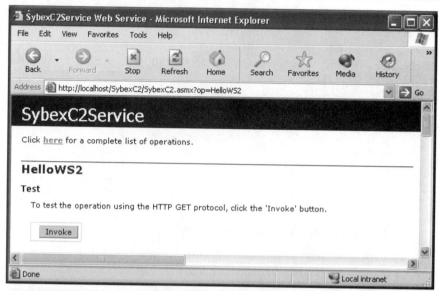

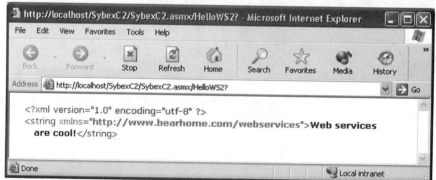

Doing the Math

Let's add a method to the ServiceSupport class that does something a little more complicated (we can then expose the method as a web service). This method uses the mod operator (%) and the square root method of the System.Math object (Math.Sqrt) to determine whether an input is a prime number, something that is potentially useful in cryptography and encryption.

> **NOTE**   Note that you can leave the System namespace off when referencing its members: Math.Sqrt is the equivalent of System.Math.Sqrt.

Here's the method:

```
static public bool IsPrime (long NumToCheck) {
    for (long i = 2; i <= Math.Sqrt(NumToCheck); i++) {
        if (NumToCheck%i == 0) {
```

```
        return false;
    }
  }
  return true;
}
```

Unlike the previous example, this method takes an input—the number to check—which is typed as a long integer. (You'll see in a minute where the input shows up on the test page.) The method returns a Boolean value of true or false, as indicated using the bool keyword, depending upon whether the input is a prime number or not.

> **TIP** The Boolean values True and False are always lowercase within C# code: true and false. The capped versions appear in the Visual Studio Properties window and are acceptable in Visual Basic, since VB is case insensitive; but attempting to use "True" or "False" in C# code will cause the compiler to generate a syntax error.

A for loop is used to check the potential divisors of the input number up to the square root of the number. If any potential divisor goes into the number evenly (as tested by the mod 0 result), then it is not a prime, and the method returns false. Otherwise, if there are no even divisors, it returns true.

Turning to the web service module, here's the web method wrapper that invokes the ServiceSupport.IsPrime method:

```
[WebMethod]
public bool IsPrime (long NumToCheck) {
    return ServiceSupport.IsPrime(NumToCheck);
}
```

If you run the project, you'll see that the IsPrime web method has been added to the list of methods available in the service (Figure 1.17).

FIGURE 1.17:

The IsPrime web method has been added to the web service.

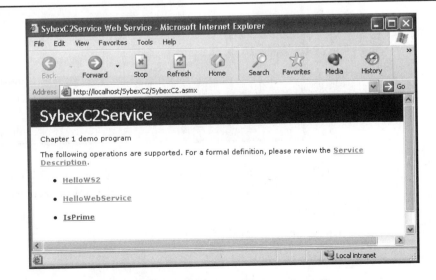

If you click the IsPrime link shown in Figure 1.17, the test page for the method opens (Figure 1.18). This is a little different from the previous test pages because it allows you to input a value.

The IsPrime test page lets you input a value to be checked and then displays the value returned by the method.

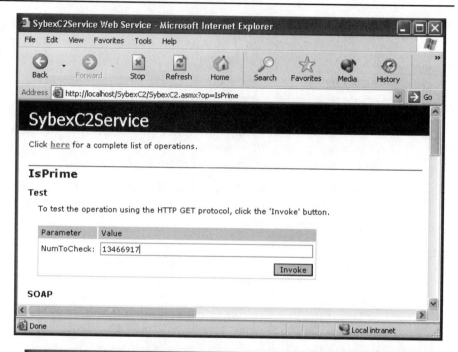

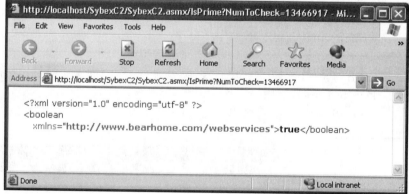

In Figure 1.18, a relatively large prime number is shown input for testing. When the Invoke button is clicked, the return value of true indicates that it is a prime and that the method is working.

Reversal of Fortune

We'll implement a final web method in the service, one that reverses a string that is input. The implementation of this in the class module will be a bit different from the previous two examples. First, it will be implemented in a class of its own named StringManipulation, rather than as part of the ServiceSupport class. Next, the StringManipulation class members will not be declared using the static keyword, meaning that they won't be shared, so an object based on the class will have to be instantiated to use the class members in the web service module.

The StringManipulation class implements a read-write property, Text, and a method, ReverseString. To use these members, the Text property must first be set with the value to be reversed. The Text property is then operated on by the ReverseString method, which takes no arguments. The changed string value is then retrieved from the Text property.

Here's the class declaration and the implementation of the Text property:

```
public class StringManipulation {
    private string m_text = "";

    public string Text {
        get {
            return m_text;
        }
        set {
            m_text = value;
        }
    }
    ...
}
```

The value of the property is stored internally in a private variable, *m_text*, which is read and written with the get and set accessors associated with the public Text property.

The ReverseString method doesn't return a value; this is indicated by the void keyword. The method starts by declaring, and initializing, a new string variable, *strNew*. The keyword this is used to refer to the current instance of the object, so that this.Text is the value of the Text property.

TIP   The Visual Basic equivalent of the C# keyword this is the Me keyword.

Some built-in methods of the string class, Length and Substring, are used within a for loop that is iterated as many times as there are characters in the Text property. As each character at the front of the string is peeled off, it is added to the end of *strNew* using the concatenation operator (+). (For more on string manipulation in C#, see Chapter 9, "Everything Is String Manipulation.")

Finally, after the loop is complete, *strNew* is assigned as the new value of the Text property:

```
public void ReverseString() {
    string strNew = "";
    for (int i = 0; i < this.Text.Length; i++) {
        strNew = this.Text.Substring(i,1) + strNew;
    }
    this.Text = strNew;
}
```

Let's use the StringManipulation class within the web service module to create a new web method. The first step is to declare and instantiate a StringManipulation object using the new keyword, stored in the variable *SM*:

```
StringManipulation SM  = new StringManipulation();
```

The rest is straightforward. Following the [WebMethod] directive, declare a method ReverseString that takes a string as input and returns a string. Within ReverseString, using the string input, set SM.Text and invoke the parameter-less SM.ReverseString method. Finally, return the value of SM.Text:

```
[WebMethod]
public string ReverseString (string inString) {
    SM.Text = inString;
    SM.ReverseString();
    return SM.Text;
}
```

If you run the project, you'll see that the ReverseString method has been added to the Web service.

If you click the ReverseString link, you can enter text and verify that is returned reversed, as shown in Figure 1.19—that is, as long as you don't enter a palindrome (which is the same backward and forward)!

FIGURE 1.19:

The ReverseString method has been added to the web service.

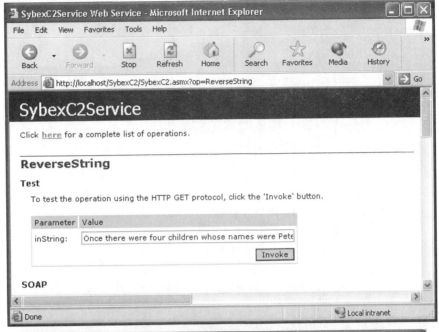

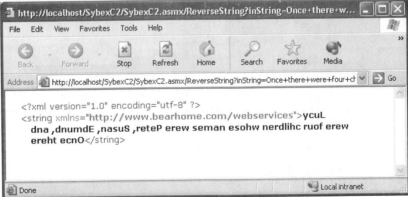

To wrap this all up, you'll find the complete code for the web service module in Listing 1.5, and the code for the class in module in Listing 1.6.

Listing 1.5   The Complete Web Service Code Module

```
using System.Web.Services;

namespace SybexC2
```

```
{
    [WebService (Description="Chapter 1 demo program",
        Name="SybexC2Service",
        Namespace="http://www.bearhome.com/webservices")]
    /// <summary>
    /// Service1 contains demo methods!
    /// </summary>
    public class Service1  : System.Web.Services.WebService
    {
        [WebMethod]
        public string HelloWebService()
        {
            return "Hello, Web Service!";
        }
        [WebMethod]
        public string HelloWS2()
        {
            return ServiceSupport.ReturnText;
        }
        [WebMethod]
        public bool IsPrime (long NumToCheck) {
            return ServiceSupport.IsPrime(NumToCheck);
        }
        StringManipulation SM  = new StringManipulation();
        [WebMethod]
        public string ReverseString (string inString) {
            SM.Text = inString;
            SM.ReverseString();
            return SM.Text;
        }
    }
}
```

Listing 1.6   **The Complete Class Module**

```
using System;

namespace SybexC2
{
    public class ServiceSupport {
        static public string ReturnText {
            get {
                return "Web services are cool!";
            }
        }

        static public bool IsPrime (long NumToCheck) {
            for (long i =2; i <= Math.Sqrt(NumToCheck); i++) {
                if (NumToCheck%i == 0 ) {
                    return false;
                }
            }
            return true;
```

```
        }
    }

    public class StringManipulation {
        private string m_text = "";

        public string Text {
            get {
                return m_text;
            }
            set {
                m_text = value;
            }
        }

        public void ReverseString() {
            string strNew = "";
            for (int i = 0; i < this.Text.Length; i++) {
                strNew = this.Text.Substring(i,1) + strNew;
            }
            this.Text = strNew;
        }
    }
}
```

XML Comments

I mentioned earlier in this chapter that a special kind of comment is indicated with C# code by three forward slashes at the beginning of the line (///). These comments can be used to automatically generate XML documentation for a program, provided the XML used in the tags is well-formed.

This is the answer to a common problem: no one ever has time to document code until it is too late. If you insert some simple XML documentation tags as you go along, you won't have to worry about this.

Two of the most commonly used tags are <summary></summary> and <remarks> </remarks>. For a complete list, see "Tags for Documentation Comments" in online help.

For example, you could comment the ReverseString method discussed in the preceding section as follows:

```
/// <summary>
/// The ReverseString Method of the StringManipulation class
/// reads the class instance Text property value, reverses it,
/// and writes it back to the Text property
/// </summary>
```

This summary will then appear in the generated documentation file, along with listings of classes and members.

To generate an XML documentation file from these tags, select the project in Solution Explorer, right-click, and choose Properties from the context menu. With the property pages for the project open, select Configuration Properties. On the Build page, provide a value for the XML Documentation File property (Figure 1.20). The next time the project is built, an XML documentation file with the name specified will be created.

FIGURE 1.20:

You can easily auto-generate an XML documentation file in the location specified.

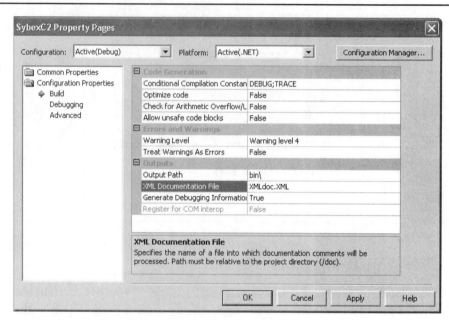

You can also easily generate a Code Comment Web Report based on the XML tags in your project. To do this, select Tools ➢ Build Comment Web Pages. The result is a set of HTML files viewable from within Visual Studio or from a browser (Figure 1.21).

FIGURE 1.21:

You can generate a Code Comment Web Report based on the XML tags.

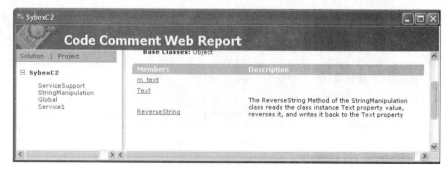

Conclusion

As you've seen in this chapter, it's fun—and very easy—to create ASP.NET web services using C#. Along the way, I've introduced you to some important concepts involved with class-based programming in C#.

But the web services in this chapter haven't been used—consumed—in any way. The only thing done with them has been to verify that they work using the test pages generated on the fly by the .NET Framework. Let's move on to web service consumption—both synchronous and asynchronous—in the context of ASP.NET web applications.

CHAPTER 2

Consuming the Service on the Web

- Understanding ASP.NET

- Creating ASP.NET applications

- Consuming web methods

- Synchronous consumption

- Asynchronous consumption

- Finding services

This chapter is a tale of two themes. The first theme is using Visual Studio and C# to create ASP.NET web applications (sometimes called "web forms" projects). The chapter introduces you to the key concepts you need to create an ASP.NET web application.

The second theme picks up where Chapter 1 left off: How do you consume a web service in a web application? Specifically, how are the web services that were created in Chapter 1— reversing a string and determining whether a number is a prime—consumed? Since these web services are implemented as methods, this boils down to the question of how to remotely invoke a web service method.

Along the way, we'll examine the difference between synchronous and asynchronous calls to the service method IsPrime developed in Chapter 1, which checks to see if a number is prime. A synchronous call to this method waits for the response back before the calling program can do anything else. In contrast, an asynchronous call to the web service method allows other programming tasks to be performed while waiting for the response.

The final part of the chapter is concerned with discovering and using web services created by others.

Understanding ASP.NET

Let's start with the basic question of how server-side web applications work. When anything beyond static HTML is required, the typical web scenario uses custom tags and script commands embedded in server-side HTML pages. (There are many examples of this approach, such as Cold Fusion, JSP, and earlier versions of ASP [Active Server Pages].) A web browser uses HTTP, normally via a form POST or GET, to request the server-side "page" that includes the custom tags.

These custom tags and server-side scripts perform many functions. For example, they may allow database connectivity or invoke a server-side code module such as a control. Software—sometimes called an application server—that is connected with (or part of) the web server expands these custom tags on the server side, reads and writes to the database, and returns straight HTML via HTTP to the web browser. The general arrangement is shown in Figure 2.1.

Processing of the server-side "page" generally occurs in a top-down linear fashion. When it is complete, a new set of "straight" HTML—probably including client-side programs written in a scripting language such as JavaScript—is sent back to the browser. This means that if you look at the source code in a browser, you will not see the server-side scripting tags or language, although you will probably see form POSTs and GETs to server-side pages.

FIGURE 2.1:

Generically, a server-side page that includes custom tags and programmatic commands is invoked using an HTTP request and returns straight HTML over HTTP to the browser.

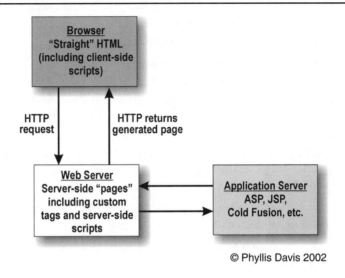

The ASP.NET approach is, in some respects, radically different from this traditional approach. In other respects, nothing has changed.

It's still the case that all the real action happens on the server side and that plain, old HTML that gets sent to the browser. You can verify this by viewing the sources in a browser such as Internet Explorer or Netscape Navigator.

An ASP.NET application is invoked by opening an ASP.NET web form page—which has an .aspx file extension—over HTTP. Internally, the ASP.NET page interacts programmatically with the server—Internet Information Services (IIS)—by using an HTTP form GET or POST to request an .aspx page (which might be itself). This is all, *mutatis mutandi*, the same as it ever was.

The radical difference is in the way ASP.NET programs are created using Visual Studio .NET and the .NET Framework:

- A compiled program is created, which is actually an executable that outputs HTML to the client. Essentially, what happens is that by invoking an .aspx file, the HTML form commands in the original project are processed on the server by a custom application.

- Within the compiled program, flow control is organized around an event model, and not limited to top-down page processing.

- A complete separation of the HTML (and other client-side) content from the server-side programming has been effected, with the HTML placed in the ASPX file and the server-side code in the related code-behind module, as I'll explain later in this chapter.

The last point is extremely important to creating applications that are maintainable. In the past, the client-side interface has been mixed up with the server-side programming logic in a way that made maintenance a nightmare.

ASP.NET web applications are built around web forms in the same way that Windows applications are built around Windows forms. A web form represents a web page in the browser in the same way that a Windows form represents an application window on the Desktop. (If you don't already know, I'll show you how to use Visual Studio to build a Windows application in Chapter 3, "Windows Uses Web Services, Too!")

Just like Windows forms, web forms have properties, methods, and events that can be used to modify the appearance and behavior of the page in the browser. By default, an ASP.NET Web Application project has one web form, which becomes a web page in the Internet Explorer browser when the compiled project is run—although you can add as many pages as you'd like to a project.

The development of an ASP.NET web application can be represented as shown in Figure 2.2.

Requirements for Running an ASP.NET Application

In order to run web forms (ASP.NET) applications, you'll need to have Internet Information Services (IIS) version 5 (or later) and the FrontPage Server Extensions. (In order to install Visual Studio .NET, you should be running Windows 2000 Server or Professional, or Windows XP Professional.) The Windows 2000 and Windows XP software ship with current versions of IIS, and your installation of Visual Studio .NET should have automatically configured it correctly to work with ASP.NET applications. You should have no problems running web forms applications from the Visual Studio .NET development environment (the default web server is designated using the URL `http://localhost/`.)

Note that if your web forms application is deployed on an external server running IIS—in other words, is not running locally—the server needs to have the .NET Framework installed and the FrontPage Server Extensions configured.

As you'll see later in this chapter, you don't *have* to use Visual Studio to create an ASP.NET application. While it is a great development environment, there are sometimes reasons to hand-craft ASP.NET applications. Just as with the web service created in Notepad shown in Chapter 1, which was saved in a file with an `.asmx` extension, a properly formed file that is named using the `.aspx` suffix will be compiled when it is first opened in a browser, and the resulting ASP.NET application will generate HTML to be rendered in the browser.

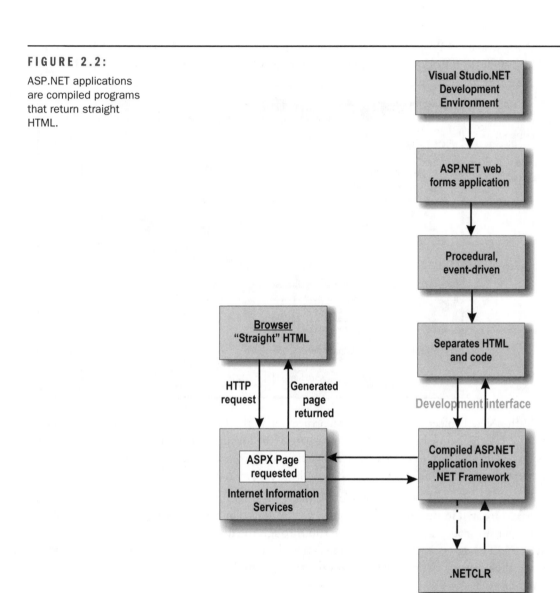

ASP.NET applications
are compiled programs
that return straight
HTML.

© Phyllis Davis 2002

Creating an ASP.NET Web Application

To start a new web application, open the New Project dialog either by selecting File ➢ New ➢ Project or by clicking the New Project button on the Visual Studio Start Page. If you don't see the Start page, you can always open it by choosing Help ➢ Show Start Page.

With Visual C# Projects selected in the left pane as the Project Type, choose ASP.NET Web Application from the right pane as the project template, as shown in Figure 2.3.

FIGURE 2.3:

To create a web application, choose ASP.NET Web Application in the New Project dialog.

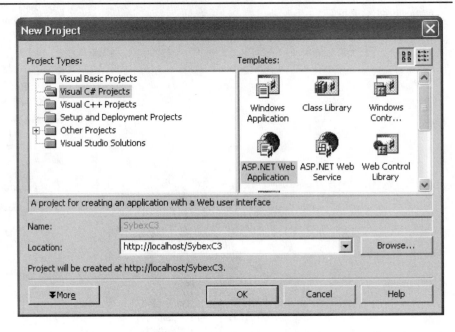

In the New Project dialog, name the project using the Location box. As you'll notice in Figure 2.3, the Name box is disabled. The part of the location entry following the server name (which is typically `http://localhost/`) becomes the project name. In Figure 2.3, the location is shown as `http://localhost/SybexC3`, and the project name becomes SybexC3.

When you click OK, your new Web Application project will be created in a folder named SybexC3 located in the virtual root folder for the `localhost` web server, which is normally \Inetpub\wwwroot. The project can be run through the development environment—by selecting Debug ➢ Start, or F5 on the keyboard—or by invoking a web form (ASPX page) using the project's virtual URL in a browser: for example, `http://localhost/SybexC3` `/WebForm1.aspx`.

NOTE   Note that if you rename WebForm1.aspx to Default.aspx, it can be opened using the URL `http://localhost/SybexC3/` (without mentioning the page name explicitly). The Default Document feature is set using the Documents tab of the website properties dialog in the Internet Information Services administrative utility.

Depending on how you have set your development environment preferences, it will look more or less like Figure 2.4, which shows both a web form and the project files in Solution

Explorer. (If Solution Explorer does not appear, you can open it by selecting View ≻ Solution Explorer.)

Web Forms

What has happened so far? First, a Visual Studio project containing a web form has been created. By default, this is named WebForm1 and is saved with an .aspx suffix (WebForm1.aspx). This web form provides a precise layout grid that can be used to host controls (as you'll see in the "Adding Controls to a Web Form" section later in this chapter) as well as an integrated HTML editor (click the HTML tab shown in the lower-left of the designer in Figure 2.4 to open the HTML editor).

In addition, you can place C# code related to the form in the connected code module, which is a file with the same name as the web form and an additional .cs suffix (WebForm1.aspx.cs). The connected code file, for reasons you'll see shortly, is also called the *code-behind* file.

NOTE   By default, a web form's code-behind file does not appear in the Solution Explorer. To display the code-behind file in the Solution Explorer, click the Show All Files button in the Solution Explorer's Toolbar and expand the .aspx file node. The code-behind files then appear "under" the ASPX file in the hierarchal view in the Solution Explorer.

Listing 2.1 shows what you get "out of the box" in the code-behind module for a C# web form. (Note that the hidden code in the Web Form Designer–generated region has been expanded and included in the listing.)

Listing 2.1   **"Out of the Box" Web Form Code-Behind Module**

```
using System;
using System.Collections;
using System.ComponentModel;
using System.Data;
using System.Drawing;
using System.Web;
```

```
using System.Web.SessionState;
using System.Web.UI;
using System.Web.UI.WebControls;
using System.Web.UI.HtmlControls;

namespace SybexC3
{
    /// <summary>
    /// Summary description for WebForm1.
    /// </summary>
    public class WebForm1 : System.Web.UI.Page
    {
        private void Page_Load(object sender, System.EventArgs e)
        {
            // Put user code to initialize the page here
        }

        #region Web Form Designer generated code
        override protected void OnInit(EventArgs e)
        {
//
// CODEGEN: This call is required by the ASP.NET Web Form Designer.
//
            InitializeComponent();
            base.OnInit(e);
        }

        /// <summary>
        /// Required method for Designer support - do not modify
        /// the contents of this method with the code editor.
        /// </summary>
        private void InitializeComponent()
        {
            this.Load += new System.EventHandler(this.Page_Load);
        }
        #endregion
    }
}
```

Once again, we are not going to go through this in detail, although you may find it instructive to compare this "out of the box" web form with the equivalent default web service (Listing 1.2) and default Windows form module (Listing 3.1).

The SybexC3 project is intended to demonstrate invoking the string-reversal web method created in Chapter 1. It will provide a web interface that will reverse a string entered by the user. To start setting this up, let's first click the HTML tab of the WebForm1 designer and have a look at the server-side HTML (Figure 2.5). You can use this tab of the designer to add a custom title to the web page that will be created:

```
<title>Reverse those strings today!</title>
```

and a header in the body of the HTML:

```
<h1>Reverse your strings today!><br>
</h1>
```

FIGURE 2.5:

You can add HTML to your
ASP.NET web form using
the HTML tab of the
designer.

```
WebForm1.aspx
Client Objects & Events                          (No Events)
<%@ Page language="c#" Codebehind="WebForm1.aspx.cs" AutoEventWireup="false" Inherits=
<!DOCTYPE HTML PUBLIC "-//W3C//DTD HTML 4.0 Transitional//EN" >
<HTML>
    <HEAD>
        <title>Reverse those strings today!</title>
        <meta name="GENERATOR" Content="Microsoft Visual Studio 7.0">
        <meta name="CODE_LANGUAGE" Content="C#">
        <meta name="vs_defaultClientScript" content="JavaScript">
        <meta name="vs_targetSchema" content="http://schemas.microsoft.com/intellisens
    </HEAD>
    <body MS_POSITIONING="GridLayout">
        <h1>Reverse your strings today!<br>
        </h1>
        <br>
        <form id="Form1" method="post" runat="server">
            <asp:TextBox id="txtInString" style="Z-INDEX: 101; LEFT: 198px; POSITION:
            <asp:RequiredFieldValidator id="RequiredFieldValidator1" style="Z-INDEX: 1
            <asp:Button id="btnRev" style="Z-INDEX: 102; LEFT: 200px; POSITION: absolu
            <asp:Label id="lblResult" style="Z-INDEX: 103; LEFT: 211px; POSITION: absc
            <asp:Label id="Label2" style="Z-INDEX: 104; LEFT: 15px; POSITION: absolute
        </form>
 Design   HTML
```

You should also note the @Page directive at the top of the designer. The attributes of this
directive have important implications to the ASP.NET page parser and compiler—designating,
for example, the language used and the name of the code-behind module.

Going back to the Design tab, you'll see that the HTML header appears.

Adding Controls

Now it's time to add the user interface, which we'll create using five controls. As you likely know, the Toolbox, shown in Figure 2.6, is used to add controls to a form (if the Toolbox is not displayed, you can open it by selecting View ➤ Toolbox).

FIGURE 2.6:

The Toolbox is used to add controls to a web form.

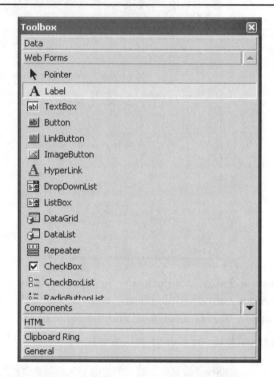

Use the Web Forms tab of the Toolbox to add the controls shown in Table 2.1 with their intended purpose.

TABLE 2.1: Controls on the SybexC3 Web Form and Their Purpose

Control Type	ID	Purpose
Label	Label1	Displays static text (no functional purpose).
Label	lblResult	Displays the results of the string reversal.
TextBox	txtInString	Area to input the string to be reversed.
Button	btnRev	Starts the reversal process when the user clicks.
RequiredFieldValidator	RequiredFieldValidator1	Makes sure that the user inputs something.

As you most likely know, the Properties window is used to set the properties of objects such as controls (and forms). Open the Properties window (by selecting View ➢ Properties window), shown in Figure 2.7, and set the Text property of Label1 (the default ID for the first Label) to "Enter text to reverse:".

FIGURE 2.7:

Set the Text property of the Label control.

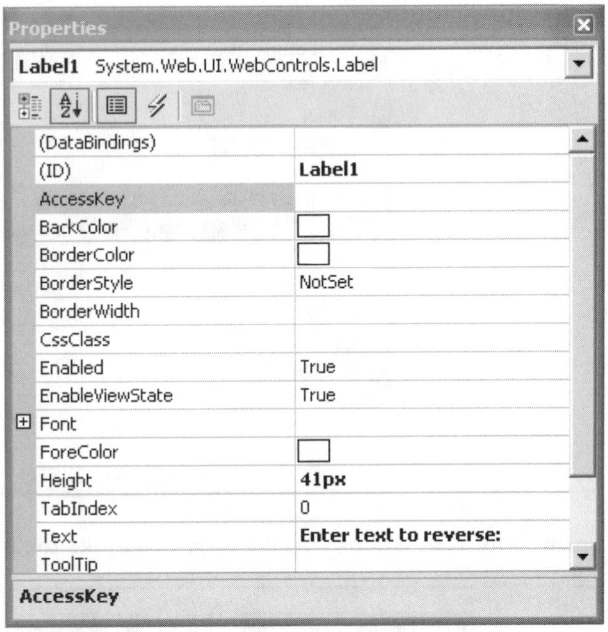

Properties	
Label1 System.Web.UI.WebControls.Label	▼
(DataBindings)	
(ID)	**Label1**
AccessKey	
BackColor	
BorderColor	
BorderStyle	NotSet
BorderWidth	
CssClass	
Enabled	True
EnableViewState	True
⊞ Font	
ForeColor	
Height	**41px**
TabIndex	0
Text	**Enter text to reverse:**
ToolTip	
AccessKey	

NOTE Web form controls are identified by their ID property, rather than the Name property used with Windows form controls.

Using the Properties window, set the ID of the remaining controls as indicated in Table 2.1. Clear the Text properties of lblResult and txtInString. Change the Text property of btnRev to "Click to reverse!".

The RequiredFieldValidator is one of several controls that can easily be used to validate user input, meaning that you don't have to write client-side scripts to do this. With RequiredFieldValidator1 selected in the Properties window, use the drop-down list to set the ControlToValidate property to txtInString and supply some text for the ErrorMessage property (Figure 2.8).

FIGURE 2.8:

The RequiredFieldValidator control makes it a snap to make sure that the user has entered something in the TextBox.

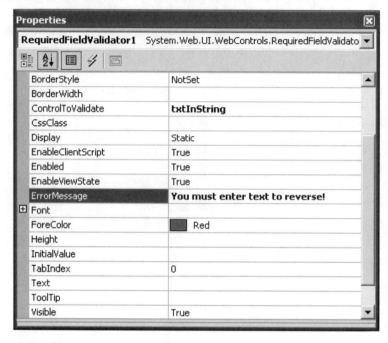

Your web form should now look pretty much like the one shown in Figure 2.9.

FIGURE 2.9:

The finished web form

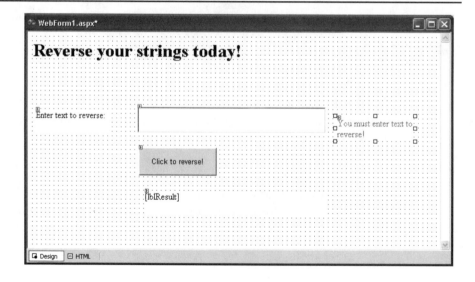

Adding a Proxy to the Web Method

A *proxy* is a program that does something on behalf of another program. In order for our ASP.NET web application to consume the ReverseString web method, we need to create a proxy program that handles the job of communicating with the web service containing the web method (Figure 2.10).

FIGURE 2.10:

The Visual Studio program invokes a proxy, which communicates with the web service.

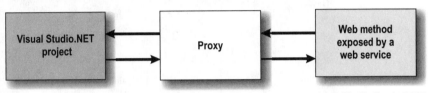

© Phyllis Davis 2002

There are several ways of auto-generating this proxy, including using the Web Services Description Language (WSDL) command-line utility and adding a web reference to a project (you could also write one from scratch—not necessarily a huge job once you've looked at a few of them).

Whichever one of the auto-generation techniques you choose, a code module will be created by parsing the WSDL file that describes the interface provided by the web service. The code module provides classes that enable both synchronous and asynchronous calls to the methods exposed by the web service. Calling the web method synchronously is more straightforward, so that's what we'll do with the string-reversal web method. (Later in this chapter, I'll show you how to call the IsPrime web method both synchronously and asynchronously. Additionally, in Chapter 3, I'll show you the general design pattern favored by Visual Studio .NET for asynchronous invocations.)

You should know about wsdl.exe (you'll certainly see it described, rather confusingly, in books about web services). But both techniques accomplish the same thing, and adding web references is somewhat easier, so that's what we'll be using in the remainder of this book when it's necessary to auto-generate a web service proxy.

Using the WSDL Utility

To invoke the WSDL utility, wsdl.exe, first open the Visual Studio .NET Command Prompt window. (You'll find it on your Windows Start menu under Microsoft Visual Studio .NET ≻ Visual Studio .NET Tools.)

To see all the command-line switches available with the utility, at the prompt type **wsdl /?** and press Enter.

To create a proxy, enter **wsdl**, followed by the language choice (**CS** for C# and **VB** for Visual Basic), and then the URL of the web service with **?WSDL** appended. For example:

```
wsdl /language:CS http://localhost/Sybexc2/SybexC2.asmx?WSDL
```

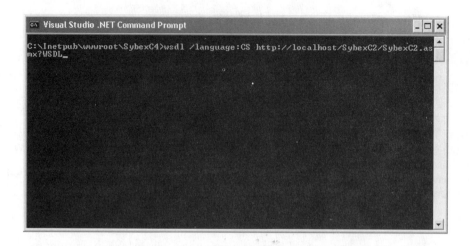

If you don't specify a file name and location, the file name is created based on the web service at the current location.

If the proxy has been successfully created, a banner is returned by the WSDL utility containing the name of the file.

One step remains if you want to use this auto-generated proxy code module with a Visual Studio project: you must add it to the project. Select Project ➢ Add Existing Item, choose the proxy file from the file system, and click Open. The code module will now appear in Solution Explorer. Since the contents of the proxy module are the same whether it is created this way or by adding a web reference to a project, we'll wait until a little later to have a look at its contents.

Adding a Web Reference

The other way of adding a proxy to a project is to select Add Web Reference from the Project menu. The Add Web Reference dialog will open (note that the Add Reference button is disabled). In the Address box at the top of the dialog, you can enter the URL for a remote web service—or, in our case, the local web service created in Chapter 1,

```
http://localhost/SybexC2/SybexC2.asmx
```

With the URL entered, the Visual Studio–generated documentation for the service appears in the dialog, and the Add Reference button is enabled (Figure 2.11).

FIGURE 2.11:

To add a web reference, enter the URL for the web service in the Address box at the top of the Add Web Reference dialog.

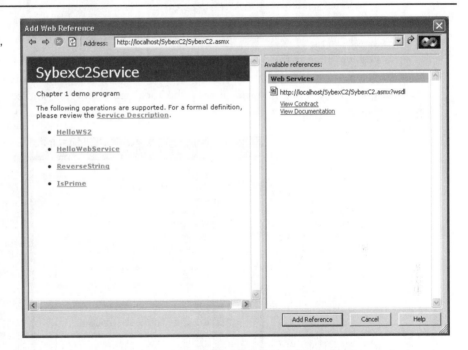

Click the Add Reference button to add the auto-generated proxy code module to the current project. If you look in Solution Explorer, you'll see that a new Web References section has been added to the project. (There was no need to specify a language to use—Visual Studio used the language of the current project by default.)

You'll have to expand the Web References section to really see what's going on. The web reference that was just added has been named localhost by default.

It's easy to change the name of the web reference to something that might be more to one's taste (or more specific) than `localhost`. Go ahead and change its name to the ever-popular sobriquet `theService` by right-clicking the `localhost` reference and selecting Rename from the context menu.

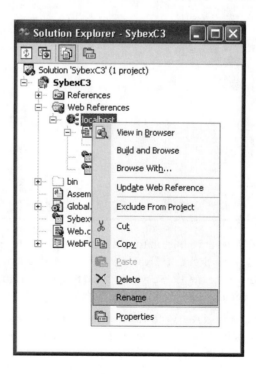

NOTE   It's important to know about the Update Web Reference choice, which is also available on the context menu for the reference. Use this when the web service has changed and you want to update the proxy.

The proxy code module itself is kind of buried, but if you expand a level below the reference now named theService you'll see a module named Reference.map. One node below Reference .Map is Reference.cs, the proxy code module file.

Listing 2.2 shows the portions of this proxy code module that are relevant to the ReverseString web method. Primarily, note that in addition to the ReverseString method, which we'll be using in this example, there are BeginReverseString and EndReverseString methods designed for asynchronous calls.

Listing 2.2   **Selected Portions of the Auto-Generated Proxy Code Module**

```
//------------------------------------------------------------------
// <autogenerated>
//      This code was generated by a tool.
//      Runtime Version: 1.0.3705.0
//
//      Changes to this file may cause incorrect behavior and will be
//      lost if the code is regenerated.
// </autogenerated>
//------------------------------------------------------------------

//
// This source code was auto-generated by Microsoft.VSDesigner,
// Version 1.0.3705.0.

namespace SybexC3.theService {
    using System.Diagnostics;
    using System.Xml.Serialization;
    using System;
    using System.Web.Services.Protocols;
    using System.ComponentModel;
    using System.Web.Services;
```

```
/// <remarks/>
[System.Diagnostics.DebuggerStepThroughAttribute()]
[System.ComponentModel.DesignerCategoryAttribute("code")]
[System.Web.Services.WebServiceBindingAttribute(Name="SybexC2ServiceSoap",
    Namespace="http://www.bearhome.com/webservices")]

public class SybexC2Service :
    System.Web.Services.Protocols.SoapHttpClientProtocol {

    /// <remarks/>
    public SybexC2Service() {
        this.Url = "http://localhost/SybexC2/SybexC2.asmx";
    }

    /// <remarks/>
    [System.Web.Services.Protocols.SoapDocumentMethodAttribute
        ("http://www.bearhome.com/webservices/HelloWebService",
        RequestNamespace="http://www.bearhome.com/webservices",
        ResponseNamespace="http://www.bearhome.com/webservices",
        Use=System.Web.Services.Description.SoapBindingUse.Literal,
        ParameterStyle =
            System.Web.Services.Protocols.SoapParameterStyle.Wrapped)]
     ...

        [System.Web.Services.Protocols.SoapDocumentMethodAttribute
            ("http://www.bearhome.com/webservices/ReverseString",
            RequestNamespace="http://www.bearhome.com/webservices",
            ResponseNamespace="http://www.bearhome.com/webservices",
            Use=System.Web.Services.Description.SoapBindingUse.Literal,
            ParameterStyle =
                System.Web.Services.Protocols.SoapParameterStyle.Wrapped)]
    public string ReverseString(string inString) {
        object[] results = this.Invoke("ReverseString", new object[] {
                                        inString});
        return ((string)(results[0]));
    }

    /// <remarks/>
    public System.IAsyncResult BeginReverseString(string inString,
        System.AsyncCallback callback, object asyncState) {
            return this.BeginInvoke("ReverseString", new object[]
                                    {inString}, callback, asyncState);
    }

    /// <remarks/>
    public string EndReverseString(System.IAsyncResult asyncResult) {
        object[] results = this.EndInvoke(asyncResult);
        return ((string)(results[0]));
    }
    }
}
```

The Code Behind

It always comes down to the code behind—at least in this book, since this is a book about programming. In other words, let's get on with it and wire up that form already! To do so, we need to open the code-behind module in the Code Editor and create the method that handles the click event for the Button control—because the code in the application will respond to the user's click to process the string that is to be reversed.

The easiest way to do this is to double-click the Button in the Web Form Designer. Not only does this open the code-behind module in the Code Editor, it also creates the scaffolding for the method that handles the Button's click event. (Of course, if you prefer, you can open the code-behind module in the Code Editor in other ways, and manually create the event handler.)

NOTE   If the web form is named WebForm1.aspx, the default name for the code-behind module is WebForm1.aspx.cs. You can change the related code-behind module by changing the value of the Codebehind attribute in the <%@ Page ... %> directive on the HTML tab of the Web Form Designer.

When you double-click the Button control, the following method is created, and you are taken to it in the Code Editor:

```
private void btnRev_Click(object sender, System.EventArgs e) {

}
```

By the way, you'll also find a line of code added to the hidden region of the module that registers the event handler:

```
private void InitializeComponent()
{
    this.btnRev.Click += new System.EventHandler(this.btnRev_Click);
    this.Load += new System.EventHandler(this.Page_Load);
}
```

NOTE   The += operator allows new event handlers to be added to the Button's click event without destroying methods that have already subscribed to an event.

Within the event handler, create an instance of the web service stored in the variable theService by referring to the class contained in the proxy code module:

```
private void btnRev_Click(object sender, System.EventArgs e) {
    theService.SybexC2Service theService = new theService.SybexC2Service();
}
```

Next, return the reversed value of the string entered by the user in a new string variable, *result*:

```
string result = theService.ReverseString(txtInString.Text);
```

Just to make things a little more interesting, in case some user wants to make fun of this application, we're going to check to see whether a palindrome—an expression that is the same backward and forward—has been entered. Here's the function that checks whether the input is a palindrome:

```
public bool Palindrome(string String1, string String2) {
    if (!(String1.ToUpper() == String2.ToUpper())) {
        return false;
    }
    if (String1.Length == 1) {
        return false;
    }
    return true;
}
```

As you can see, this `Palindrome` function is pretty basic stuff—it compares the two strings input, both converted to uppercase to side-step differences between uppercase and lowercase letters, and returns `false` if they are not equal. It also returns `false` if the first string is only one character long. It's possible that a true palindrome check might want to get more elaborate— for example, stripping out punctuation and white space from consideration. You'll find more information on relevant techniques in Chapter 9, "Everything Is String Manipulation!"

If you check Listing 2.3, you'll note that the `Palindrome` function is placed within the same class (`WebForm1`) as the click event handler.

Back in the click handler, the `Palindrome` function is called with the return value from the web service and the input text as the arguments. If it is a palindrome, an admonition is displayed, and if it's not a palindrome, the reversed text is displayed using `lblResult`'s `Text` property:

```
if (Palindrome(result,txtInString.Text)) {
    lblResult.Text = "Don't even think of giving me a palindrome!";
}
else {
    lblResult.Text = result;
}
```

That's it! It's time to build and run the project by selecting Debug ➤ Start or by building it (Build ➤ Solution) and opening it by URL in your browser (`http://localhost/SybexC3 /WebForm1.aspx`).

With the web application running, you can enter a string, as shown in Figure 2.12, and verify that it gets reversed.

FIGURE 2.12:

The application invokes
the web service in the
code-behind module to
reverse the string.

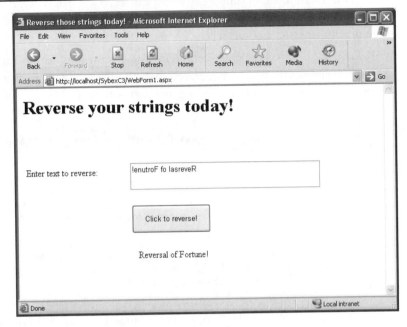

You can also try entering a palindrome to see whether it gets past the Palindrome function
(Figure 2.13).

FIGURE 2.13:

The palindrome filter
seems to work.

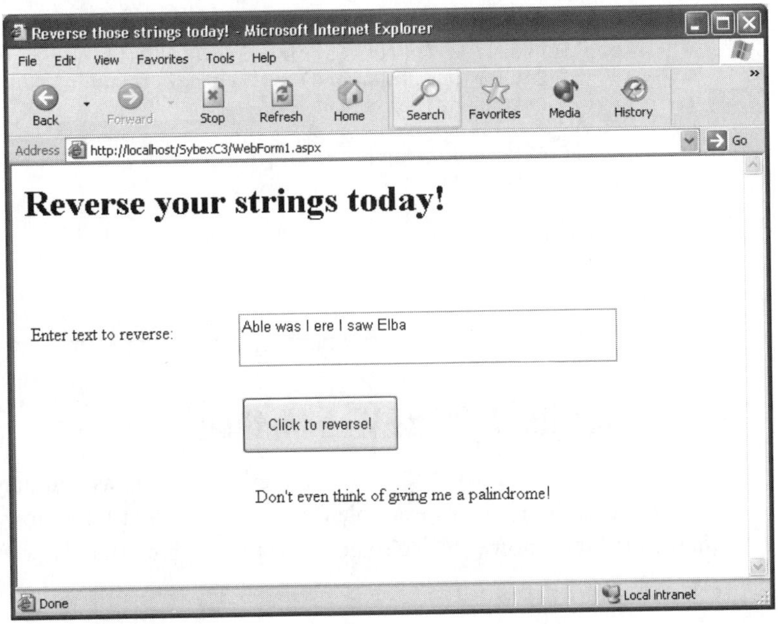

With the application running in your browser, it's worth viewing the source that the browser is rendering to verify that it is straight HTML (and some client-side JavaScript). To view the source in Internet Explorer, select View ➤ Source.

Listing 2.3 shows the code-behind module for the application, complete except for the portions of code that are auto-generated—which is how I normally intend to present code in this book, after first showing the auto-generated portions.

Listing 2.3   **Non-Auto-Generated Portions of the Code-Behind Module for *ReverseString***

```
...
namespace SybexC3
{
    ...
    public class WebForm1 : System.Web.UI.Page
    {
        ...
        private void btnRev_Click(object sender, System.EventArgs e) {
            theService.SybexC2Service theService = new
                theService.SybexC2Service();
            string result = theService.ReverseString(txtInString.Text);
            if (Palindrome(result,txtInString.Text)) {
                lblResult.Text = "Don't even think of giving me a palindrome!";
            }
            else {
                lblResult.Text = result;
            }
        }

        public bool Palindrome(string String1, string String2) {
            if (!(String1.ToUpper() == String2.ToUpper())) {
                return false;
            }
            if (String1.Length == 1) {
                return false;
            }
            return true;
        }
    }
}
```

Consuming the *IsPrime* Web Method

Next on our agenda is the IsPrime web method, which, as you may recall, is part of the same web service as the previous example (SybexC2Service) that I showed you how to create in Chapter 1. Here, however, we're going to play a game that's a wee bit different.

Once you have the proxy built and added to the project, calling a web method is just like calling any other method, as you saw in the ReverseString example. In the same fashion, there should be no particular problem in calling the IsPrime web method synchronously, passing it a long integer to evaluate for primality (that is, its primeness—whether it's a prime number), and displaying an appropriate message depending on the result of the method call. I'll show you how to do this (it doesn't particularly differ from working with the ReverseString method). More interestingly, I'll show you how to call the IsPrime web method asynchronously, so that your program can do other things while waiting to learn whether the number passed to IsPrime is or isn't a prime.

Before we can get to the asynchronous call to the web method, there's a tangent we have to take (actually, one of several tangents). Well, it's what you learn along the way that counts, not the destination, right?

Given the efficient nature of the algorithm for determining primality used in the IsPrime web method (at most, it needs to iterate up to the square root of the number), it just doesn't take very long to determine whether a number is a prime, at least if the number is within the bounds of the long data type (–9,223,372,036,854,775,808 to 9,223,372,036,854,775,808). Of course, if the number input is out of bounds, it will throw an error. In order to actually witness any asynchronous behavior, we're going to add code to the IsPrime web method that will slow it down on demand.

Extending the Service Interface

Going back to the web service developed in Chapter 1, we're going to add a parameter to the IsPrime web service that delays the method's return by the designated number of seconds. Here's a function that can be added to the class module behind the SybexC2 web service that sends the thread being executed to sleep for the designated number of seconds:

```
static public void GoToSleep(int DelayInSec) {
    if (DelayInSec > 0) {
        System.Threading.Thread.Sleep(DelayInSec * 1000);
    }
}
```

NOTE The Thread.Sleep method takes an argument in milliseconds, so the multiplication by 1000 is needed to convert the delay into seconds. It's important to make sure that the method is not passed an argument of zero (0), which would suspend the thread indefinitely; avoiding this is achieved with the conditional check that DelayInSec > 0.

The web method needs to be changed to invoke the new function:

```
[WebMethod (BufferResponse = false, CacheDuration = 0)]
public bool IsPrime(long NumToCheck, int DelayInSec) {
```

```
        ServiceSupport.GoToSleep(DelayInSec);
        return ServiceSupport.IsPrime(NumToCheck);
    }
```

Note that I've added attributes to the WebMethod directive to make sure that the IsPrime web method is neither buffering nor caching its response to a call.

Listing 2.4 shows the entire revised web method. If you go back to the SybexC2 project developed in Chapter 1 and run it with the revisions, you'll see that the test page for the web method generated by Visual Studio now includes input fields for the *DelayInSec* argument as well as *NumToCheck* (Figure 2.14).

FIGURE 2.14:

The generated test page for the revised web service now shows two parameters.

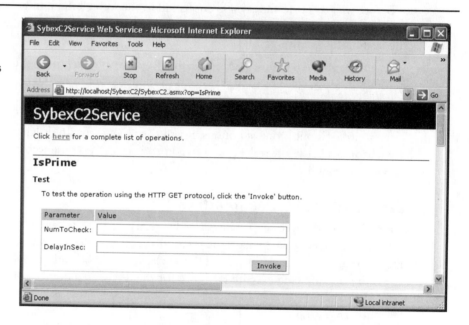

NOTE   If you've already generated a proxy that references this method in a project, you should update it by selecting the web reference in Solution Explorer, right-clicking, and selecting Update Web Reference from the context menu. If you used wsdl.exe to create the proxy module, you should delete the current module, run wsdl.exe again, and add the newly generated module.

Listing 2.4   **The Extended *IsPrime* Web Method**

```
// SybexC2.SybexC2Service
using System.Web.Services;
```

```
namespace SybexC2 {
   [WebService (Description="Chapter 1 demo program",
      Name="SybexC2Service",
      Namespace="http://www.bearhome.com/webservices")]

   public class SybexC2Service  : System.Web.Services.WebService
   {
      ...
      [WebMethod (BufferResponse = false, CacheDuration = 0)]
      public bool IsPrime(long NumToCheck, int DelayInSec) {
         ServiceSupport.GoToSleep(DelayInSec);
         return ServiceSupport.IsPrime(NumToCheck);
      }
      ...
   }
}

// Class1.cs
...
namespace SybexC2 {
   public class ServiceSupport {

      ...
      static public bool IsPrime(long NumToCheck ) {
         for (long i =2; i <= Math.Sqrt(NumToCheck); i++) {
            if (NumToCheck%i == 0 ) {
               return false;
            }
         }
      return true;
      }

      static public void GoToSleep(int DelayInSec) {
         if (DelayInSec > 0) {
            System.Threading.Thread.Sleep(DelayInSec * 1000);
         }
      }
   }
}
```

Synchronous Consumption

As we've already said, synchronous consumption is easy. Assuming you've added a web reference to the SybexC2Service, you can create a user interface consisting primarily of a TextBox (for the number to be checked), a Button (to do the checking when the users clicks), and a Label to display the results. Figure 2.15 shows a web forms interface in its designer along these lines, with the addition of a Button to perform asynchronous consumption and a second TextBox that will be used later on for the results of the asynchronous call.

FIGURE 2.15:

It's easy to create an interface that can be used to check synchronous and asynchronous consumption of the IsPrime web method.

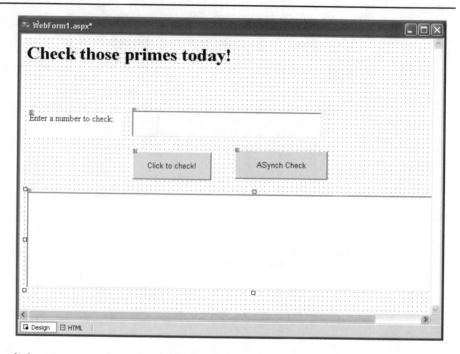

Here's the click event procedure that calls the web method synchronously to check whether the number input is a prime, and displays the appropriate message based on the method return value:

```
private void btnCheck_Click(object sender, System.EventArgs e) {
    theService.SybexC2Service theService = new
        theService.SybexC2Service();
    if (theService.IsPrime(Convert.ToInt64(txtInNum.Text),0)) {
        txtStatus.Text = "Is a prime!";
    }
    else {
        txtStatus.Text = "Not prime!";
    }
}
```

Of course, since we want this call to return as soon as possible, the second parameter of the call to the IsPrime method is 0—meaning, no extra delay.

If you run the program, you can see that it puts a nice front end on the web service (Figure 2.16).

FIGURE 2.16:

A synchronous call to
the web method easily
determines whether a
number is a prime.

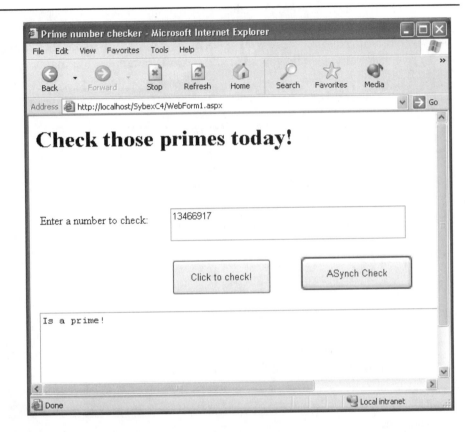

Asynchronous Consumption

If you looked at the code for the auto-generated proxy module back in Listing 2.2, you'll see
that it created three methods for each web method that might be invoked. The general pattern
is that for each NamedWebServiceMethod included in the web service, the proxy class includes
three methods:

- NamedWebServiceMethod

- BeginNamedWebServiceMethod

- EndNamedWebServiceMethod

The Named... method is used synchronously, whereas the BeginNamed... and EndNamed...
methods are intended for use with asynchronous calls.

In the proxy class for the SybexC2 service, in addition to IsPrime, you'll find a BeginIsPrime
and an EndIsPrime.

Here's the click event procedure code that invokes `BeginIsPrime` asynchronously. The point of the example is to demonstrate something else happening while the web method call is waiting to return. This procedure writes periods (...) into the TextBox that displays the status message while it waits (what do you do to idle away the time while waiting for something to happen?).

```
private void btnASynchCheck_Click(object sender, System.EventArgs e) {
    theService.SybexC2Service theService = new theService.SybexC2Service();
    IAsyncResult ar =
        theService.BeginIsPrime(Convert.ToInt64(txtInNum.Text), 1, null, null);
    // do something until call returns
    txtStatus.Text = "Not blocked, don't have to wait...\r\n";
    while (ar.IsCompleted == false) {
        txtStatus.Text = txtStatus.Text + ".";
    }
    txtStatus.Text = txtStatus.Text + " I'm back! ";
    if (theService.EndIsPrime(ar)) {
        txtStatus.Text = txtStatus.Text + " Is a prime!";
    }
    else {
        txtStatus.Text = txtStatus.Text +  " Not prime!";
    }
}
```

If you run the project, enter a number to check, and click the ASynch Check button, you'll get a display like that shown in Figure 2.17 (although there may be a great many more periods when you run this in real life, particularly if you put in a larger delay).

FIGURE 2.17:

Periods are added to the TextBox while the asynchronous web method call does its thing.

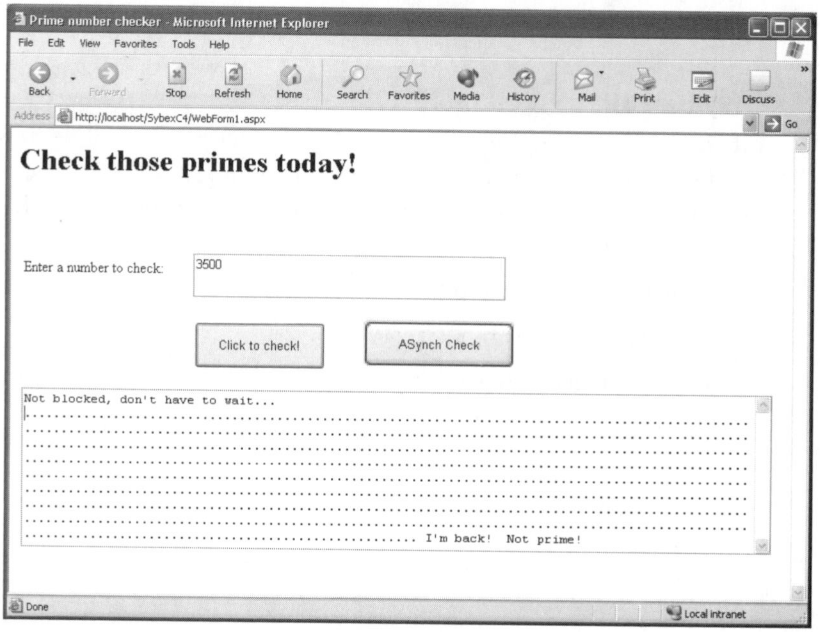

Now that you've seen the asynchronous call in action, let's go through the code a little more carefully.

The first line instantiates an instance of the web service class, named `theService`, based on the class defined in the proxy module in the normal fashion:

```
theService.SybexC2Service theService = new theService.SybexC2Service();
```

The next line,

```
IAsyncResult ar =
    theService.BeginIsPrime(Convert.ToInt64(txtInNum.Text), 1, null, null);
```

stores state information for the asynchronous call in a variable named *ar*. The first two arguments of the call to `BeginIsPrime` are, of course, the parameters required by the `IsPrime` method—the number to be checked and the delay in seconds. The third and fourth arguments are each represented here by `null`, a keyword that means a null reference, one that does not refer to any object.

You'll see an example in Chapter 3 of an asynchronous call that uses these parameters. As a preview, the third parameter is for a *delegate* of type `System.AsyncCallback`. A delegate is one method standing in for another. The fourth parameter is for a *callback* method—the method that is called when the asynchronous call is complete.

Next, a line of text is displayed in the TextBox:

```
txtStatus.Text = "Not blocked, don't have to wait...\r\n";
```

NOTE   The backslash indicates that \r and \n are escape characters—two-character tokens with special meanings. \r means carriage return, and \n means line feed (new line).

Finally, the `IsComplete` property of the `IAsyncResult` variable is polled using a `while` loop. As long as its value is `false`—meaning the asynchronous call has not completed—a period is added to the TextBox:

```
while (ar.IsCompleted == false) {
    txtStatus.Text = txtStatus.Text + ".";
}
```

In theory, of course, you could do all kinds of things in this loop, not just display periods on the screen.

When the loop completes (because the `IsCompleted` property of the `IAsyncResult` object has become `true`), the procedure goes on in a normal fashion:

```
txtStatus.Text = txtStatus.Text + " I'm back! ";
if (theService.EndIsPrime(ar)) {
    txtStatus.Text = txtStatus.Text + " Is a prime!";
}
else {
    txtStatus.Text = txtStatus.Text + " Not prime!";
}
```

I think you'll find if you set this program up and run it that there is a fly in the ointment, or a serpent in paradise. (See, I told you there would be tangents!) The problem is the observable behavior of the program. While it is true that a great many periods get written to the screen before the results of the asynchronous call are delivered, what happens is that it seems like there is a fairly long pause, and then everything is written all at once—first the periods, then the asynchronous call completion. It would be much more satisfying to actually see something being done *while* the call is being processed. The problem here is the way ASP.NET processes web forms—it waits for the entire response to the HTTP request before displaying anything. We can get around this by "rolling our own" HTML.

Doing It Without Web Forms

As you may remember from Chapter 1, a web service can be created by hand in a text editor if the file is saved with an .asmx file extension, the file includes appropriate directives, and the file is played in an Internet Information Services virtual path accessible via URL. (For details, see Listing 1.1 and related text.) The file is compiled into an ASP.NET web service the first time it is opened.

In a similar fashion, we can create an ASP.NET web application by hand, provided it contains appropriate directives and is saved with an .aspx file extension in an accessible virtual directory. The advantage of this is that we can use the Page.Response object to hand-code HTML that is sent directly back to the browser—bypassing the Visual Studio .NET web forms page-generation process.

Note that the page still has to reference a proxy to the web service. For convenience sake, I simply imported the proxy class created for the SybexC4 example in this chapter, hard-coded in a small value (23) to check for primality, named the file async.aspx, and placed it in the virtual directory created for this chapter's example.

Here's the way the file initially looked:

```
<%@ Page language="C#" %>
<%@ Import namespace="SybexC4.theService" %>
<%Response.BufferOutput=false;
Response.Write("<html><body>\r\n");
SybexC4.theService.SybexC2Service theService = new
    SybexC4.theService.SybexC2Service();
IAsyncResult ar = theService.BeginIsPrime(23, 0, null, null);
// do something until call returns
Response.Write("Not blocked, don't have to wait...<h3>");
while (ar.IsCompleted == false) {
    Response.Write("<b>W</b><br>");
    Response.Flush();
}
Response.Write("I can do stuff while I wait!");
Response.Write("<br></h3> I'm back! ");
```

```
if (theService.EndIsPrime(ar)) {
   Response.Write("<br> Is a prime!");
}
else {
   Response.Write("<br> Not prime!");
}
Response.Flush();
Response.Write("</body></html>");
Response.Flush();
%>
```

The intention was to open it with the URL http://localhost/SybexC4/async.aspx and to have the page display the letter *W* down a page until the asynchronous call completed. To my dismay, this did not happen, and in fact the browser would not render a page at all—not even the initial "Not blocked, don't have to wait," let alone displaying *W*s or returning from the web method. I eventually realized that the browser was hanging in infinite limbo because it was being overwhelmed by the sheer number of *W*s generated, so I added a for loop that uses iteration and modulo arithmetic to greatly cut down the *W*s and break out of the asynchronous while statement when the loop completes:

```
while (ar.IsCompleted == false) {
   for (long i = 1; i <= 100000000; i++) {
      if (i%10000000 == 0 ) {
         Response.Write("<b>W</b><br>");
         Response.Flush();
      }
   }
break;
}
```

When I ran it with this addition, which you can see incorporated in Listing 2.5, I was able to watch ten *W*s gently plop onto my screen and then observe the completion of the asynchronous call (Figure 2.18).

Listing 2.5   Displaying Asynchronous Behavior in a Hand-Coded ASP.NET Page

```
<%@ Page language="C#" %>
<%@ Import namespace="SybexC4.theService" %>
<%Response.BufferOutput=false;
Response.Write("<html><body>\r\n");
SybexC4.theService.SybexC2Service theService = new
   SybexC4.theService.SybexC2Service();
IAsyncResult ar = theService.BeginIsPrime(23, 0, null, null);
// do something until call returns
Response.Write("Not blocked, don't have to wait...<h3>");
while (ar.IsCompleted == false) {
   for (long i = 1; i <= 100000000; i++) {
```

```
      if (i%10000000 == 0 ) {
          Response.Write("<b>W</b><br>");
          Response.Flush();
      }
   }
break;
}
Response.Write("I can do stuff while I wait!");
Response.Write("<br></h3> I'm back! ");
if (theService.EndIsPrime(ar)) {
   Response.Write("<br> Is a prime!");
}
else {
   Response.Write("<br> Not prime!");
}
Response.Flush();
Response.Write("</body></html>");
Response.Flush();
%>
```

FIGURE 2.18:

The Ws are written one
after another to the
screen, then the
asynchronous call
completes.

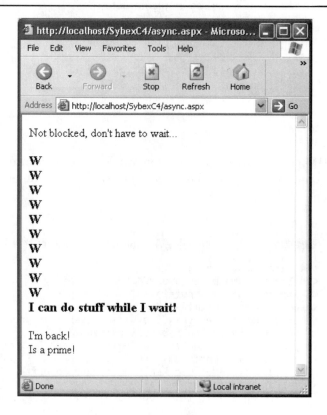

NOTE   You may have to fiddle with the numbers in the loop depending on the speed of your system. One might think that one could loop to 100 using modulo 10 and have the same impact as the code in the listing—namely writing ten Ws to the screen—but it worked better for me with the larger numbers.

Finding Services to Consume

Doing it by oneself may be satisfying and useful, but it is ultimately much more fun to do it with others. If you could only consume services you yourself had written, it might be an interesting, novel, and handy way to extend the architectures of your applications across the web—but hardly revolutionary. The real point of web services is the ability to remotely use code methods provided by others on the basis of the WSDL interface description provided (or to provide web methods that other people can access).

So how do you find web services to consume? Here are a few places to start...

Passport

Passport is probably the premier and best-known of the Microsoft .NET My Services. It's used as a one-stop authentication and sign-in mechanism by a great many websites (and it can also be used as a digital wallet to store credit card information for e-commerce purchases).

As web services go, Passport is non-trivial to implement. You'll find a software development kit (SDK) available for download and much information at www.passport.com.

UDDI

The Universal Description, Discovery, and Integration (UDDI) directory service, conceptually introduced in Chapter 1, is not intended to be easily readable by humans. While you could write your own UDDI client to browse UDDI repositories, there's no need to go to this kind of trouble. Visual Studio .NET provides a UDDI interface that allows you to register your web services and to search for web services you can use by category. To open this interface, shown in Figure 2.19, choose XML Web Services from the Start page (you can also display the Start page by selecting Help ➢ Show Start Page).

FIGURE 2.19:

The XML Web Services tab of the Visual Studio Start page allows you to register web services and to search for web services by category.

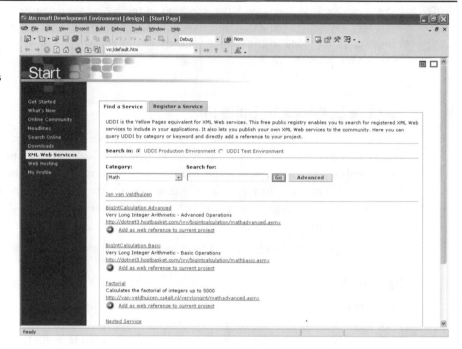

Directories

Several websites have extensive directories of web services you can use. Some of the best of these include:

Got Dot Net	www.gotdotnet.com
Salcentral	www.salcentral.com
XMethods	www.xmethods.com

Conclusion

This chapter has been fun! In it, I showed you how to create ASP.NET web applications and how to consume the web service methods created in Chapter 1. Along the way, you've seen how to work with web server controls, learned how to put a thread to sleep, and explored the difference between calling a web method synchronously and asynchronously.

Let's move on to Chapter 3, which explores the creation of Windows applications using C# .NET—and revisits invoking our web service asynchronously in the context of a generalized asynchronous design pattern.

PART II

Allemande: Striding Forward

CHAPTER 3

Windows Uses Web Services, Too!

- Windows application projects

- Forms

- Form properties, events, and methods

- The MessageBox.Show method

- Changing the shape of a window

- Asynchronous design pattern (used in web service consumption)

For all the fun and glory of web services and web applications, the roots of Visual Studio are deeply entwined with Windows application development. (You could say that Windows development is Visual Studio "classic.")

No tool is better suited to Windows development than Visual Studio .NET—and no language more appropriate than C#. In addition, even considering web services and the Web, Windows application development is likely to be where the vast bulk of programmers spend their time for the foreseeable future—particularly considering .NET's no-touch deployment, which allows a .NET Windows executable program to be opened and run from within Internet Explorer.

This chapter begins the exploration of Windows application projects with information about forms, message boxes, and more. It concludes with an asynchronous invocation of the web service developed in Part I, and shows the preferred general design pattern to use when making asynchronous calls in .NET.

Creating a Windows Application Project

To create a new Windows application project, open the New Project dialog (File ➤ New ➤ Project). In the New Project dialog, select Visual C# Projects in the Project Types pane, Windows Application in the Templates pane, and give the project a name and location ➤ Figure 3.1).

FIGURE 3.1:

To create a Windows application project, select Visual C# Projects and Windows Application, and provide a name and location for the project files.

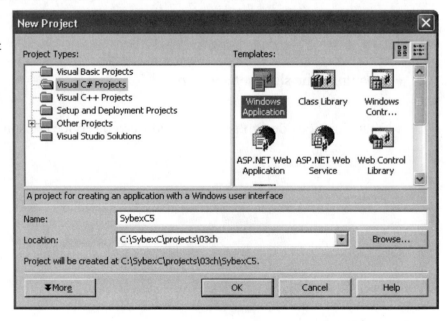

Visual Studio will create a new project based around a Windows form named Form1. The Windows form will be displayed in its designer, and the project files will appear in Solution Explorer, as shown in Figure 3.2.

FIGURE 3.2:

A form is created in its designer, along with the various other files required to run a Windows project (shown in Solution Explorer).

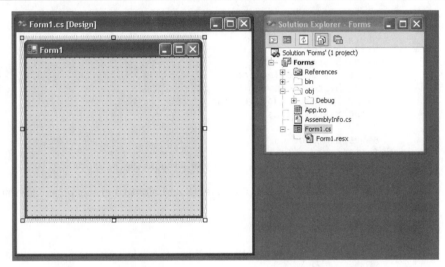

NOTE   Depending on your Visual Studio configuration, to see the form's designer, you may have to select View ➤ Designer. If Solution Explorer is not displayed, select View ➤ Solution Explorer. To view all the project's files (as shown in Figure 3.2), click the Show All Files button on the Solution Explorer toolbar.

The basic project shown in Solution Explorer contains one form. You can add new forms, class modules, and other objects to it using the Add New Item dialog (Project ➤ Add New Item). You can add existing items using the Add Existing Item dialog (Project ➤ Add Existing Item). For that matter, if you want, you can remove Form1 from the project (although in that case, you will have to supply an entry point for the project if you want it to run as an executable).

Forms

The project module named by default Form1.cs contains the code required to instantiate the form object as well as a Main() procedure that serves as the entry point, or starting place, for the application.

To view the code for the form module in the Code Editor, right-click the form in its designer or Solution Explorer and select View Code from the context menu. Alternatively, double-click the form in its designer.

Listing 3.1 shows the auto-generated "out of the box" form code. You may be interested in comparing this with Listing 1.2 (a default web service) and Listing 2.1 (a default ASP.NET web forms application).

Listing 3.1   **"Out of the Box" Windows Form Code, with Hidden Region Expanded**

```
using System;
using System.Drawing;
using System.Collections;
using System.ComponentModel;
using System.Windows.Forms;
using System.Data;

namespace SybexC5
{
    public class Form1 : System.Windows.Forms.Form
    {
        private System.ComponentModel.Container components = null;

        public Form1()
        {
            //
            // Required for Windows Form Designer support
            //
            InitializeComponent();

            //
            // TODO: Add any constructor code after
            // InitializeComponent call
        }

        protected override void Dispose(bool disposing)
        {
            if (disposing)
            {
                if (components != null)
                {
                    components.Dispose();
                }
            }
            base.Dispose(disposing);
        }

        #region Windows Form Designer generated code
        /// <summary>
        /// Required method for Designer support - do not modify
        /// the contents of this method with the code editor.
        /// </summary>
        private void InitializeComponent()
```

```
    {
        this.components = new System.ComponentModel.Container();
        this.Size = new System.Drawing.Size(300,300);
        this.Text = "Form1";
    }
    #endregion

    /// <summary>
    /// The main entry point for the application.
    /// </summary>
    [STAThread]
    static void Main()
    {
        Application.Run(new Form1());
    }
  }
}
```

As you can see in the class declaration in the form code, the newly minted `Form1` object inherits from `System.Windows.Forms.Form`. The form class itself represents a window or dialog box that is part of an application's user interface and inherits from `Component` by way of `Control`, which is the base class for all controls. `Form`'s immediate parent is `ContainerControl`, a class that provides functionality for controls that can function as a container for other controls.

NOTE   A *control* is a component with visual representation. Controls (and components) in the Toolbox are instantiated without additional code when added to a form and run.

We're going to quickly waltz through some Form properties, events, and methods. After having a look at them, I'm sure you'll agree that forms are powerful objects with a great deal of functionality—even before you do anything to them.

Form Properties

A *property* is a setting that describes something about an object such as a form. Properties can be set at design time using the Properties window and at run time in a code assignment.

NOTE   Some form properties, such as `Region` (explained later in this chapter), can only be set in code.

In other words, using the Properties window to set the form's `Text` property to "I am the form's text!" (Figure 3.3) has the same consequences—namely, setting the `Text` property to the designated string when the form is displayed—as executing

```
this.Text = "I am the form's text!";
```

in the form constructor (the procedure that creates the instance of the form object; see the "Constructors" sidebar later in this chapter) or the form load event.

FIGURE 3.3:

The form's Text property is set in the Properties window. (Here, the Properties window is set to categorize rather than alphabetize properties.)

NOTE   Using the first two buttons on the Properties window toolbar, the window can be set to display properties alphabetically or by category.

A great many form properties can be set in the Properties window, ranging from setting the form icon, its background color, its behavior, appearance, and more. You need to play with form properties in the Properties window to get to know them and understand what they do. In this section we'll just have a look at a few properties.

NOTE   When you select a property in the Properties window, you'll find a brief description of what it does in the pane at the bottom of the Properties window.

The *FormBorderStyle* Property

Windows forms come in various styles, which are set using the FormBorderStyle property. Styles change the basic appearance of the window when the form is run, and also its behavior in significant ways. For example, depending on the FormBorderStyle setting, an icon will (or will not) be displayed in the Windows Taskbar. This setting also determines whether a running window is resizable. We tend to take these things for granted, but the reality is that a Windows form buys one a great deal of "scaffolding" in terms of behaving as users expect windows to behave. The good news for the programmer is that you don't need to do any work to get this scaffolding—just select a FormBorderStyle setting.

To select a FormBorderStyle, open a form in its designer. In the Properties window, highlight FormBorderStyle and click the arrow in the right column to display a drop-down list of possible settings (Figure 3.4). Table 3.1 describes the windows that result from the seven different FormBorderStyle choices.

FIGURE 3.4:

The Properties window can be used to set form properties such as FormBorderStyle.

TABLE 3.1: Members of the *FormBorderStyle* Enumeration

Constant	Resulting Window
None	A window without a border or border-related elements. This is the setting to use for introductory "splash" screens.
FixedSingle	A nearly normal window with a single-line border that is only resizable using its Minimize and Maximize buttons. You cannot drag the window's borders to resize it while it is running.
Fixed3D	Like FixedSingle, except that the borders are created with a raised, 3D effect.
FixedDialog	Like FixedSingle, except that the borders appear recessed. This setting is commonly used for dialog boxes.
Sizable	A normal, resizable window, with Minimize and Maximize buttons if desired. This is the default and most commonly used setting.
FixedToolWindow	A non-resizable window with a Close button and small-size text in the title bar. Unlike the preceding settings, this kind of window does not display an icon in the Windows Taskbar.
SizableToolWindow	Like FixedToolWindow, but sizable.

You can set the FormBorderStyle property dynamically at run time in code by assigning a member of the FormBorderStyle enumeration constants (shown in Table 3.1) to the property. For example,

```
this.FormBorderStyle = FormBorderStyle.None;
```

turns the form into a borderless window when it is executed (although it is unusual to execute this code, since most programs do not change window styles at run time).

The *Anchor* and *Dock* Properties

Anchor and Dock are two properties that greatly help with positioning controls on a form and save us from writing code to take care of things when the user resizes a running form.

The Dock property "docks" the border of a control to its container (such as a form). Dock can be set visually (Figure 3.5) or by assigning a value of DockStyle.Left, DockStyle.Right, DockStyle.Top, DockStyle.Bottom, or DockStyle.Fill to the Dock property.

DockStyle.Fill means that the control takes up all unused space in the center of the form, and DockStyle.None means that the control is not docked.

The Anchor property describes which edge of the container, such as a form, the control is bound to. The distance between the form edge and the closest edge of the control will remain constant no matter how the form is resized.

FIGURE 3.5:

The Dock property simplifies managing the run-time position of controls.

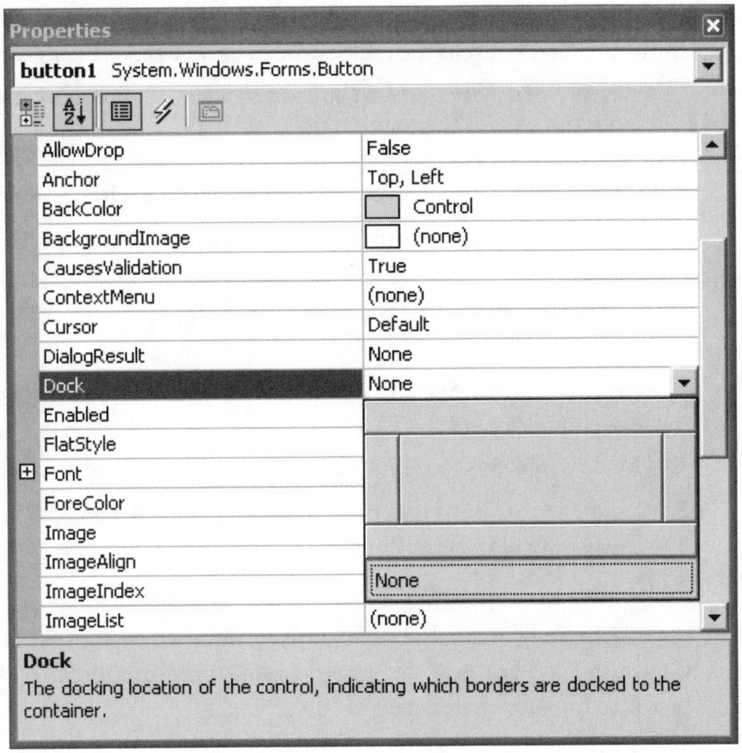

Form Events

Event methods are placeholders for code that is only processed when the event is fired—triggered—by a user action, program code, or the system.

An *event* is a procedure with a name, such as button1_Click, followed by parameters (also called arguments) within parentheses. The event method must also be hooked up as a delegate to handle the event using the += operator (you'll find this in the hidden region of the form code). One event method can be used by many events (each event can be assigned the same delegate).

Here's the general form:

```
this.Click += new System.EventHandler(this.Form1_Click);
...
private void Form1_Click(object sender, System.EventArgs e) {

}
```

You probably know that it is easy to call an event procedure in code. You must be sure to pass to the event procedure the number and type of arguments it expects. For example, to call a Button named button1's Click event in code from a Form click event:

```
private void Form1_Click(object sender, System.EventArgs e) {
    button1_Click(sender, e);
}
```

Now, when Form1's click event is fired, button1's will be, as well.

If you're not already within an event, you can create your own System.EventArgs to invoke an event:

```
System.EventArgs g = new System.EventArgs();
Form1_Click(this, g);
```

So far in this discussion, I've introduced one way to create an event handler, which is strictly in code. The steps are:

1. Create a new System.EventHandler.

2. Assign it to an event and provide a delegate (the name of the method that will handle it) to register the new event handler.

3. Create the framework for the event procedure.

You can find out more about creating your own custom events in Chapter 8, "The Life of the Object in C#." For now, let's have a look at the support that the Visual Studio interface provides for auto-generating events.

Events in the Properties Window

In most ways, the development tools for Visual Basic .NET and C# .NET are the same, but they differ greatly when it comes to events. In VB, the auto-generation of event scaffolding is done using the Objects and Procedures drop-down lists in the Code Editor.

In contrast, C# has its own interface for auto-generating event scaffolding, which is accessed via the Properties window. To open this interface, click the lightning bolt icon (the lightning bolt means an event, get it?) on the Properties window toolbar (Figure 3.6).

Using the Events tab of the Properties window, you can select an object event from the list in the left column and type in a name on the right (you do not have to name it conforming to the *object_event* convention). The IDE will generate a new procedure with the proper arguments and register it as an event handler. You can now put code within the event procedure.

It's really useful to know that if you double-click an event in the left column, an event procedure, named in the standard way (e.g., Form1_Click), will be created.

FIGURE 3.6:

FIGURE 3.6:

You can use the Events tab of the Properties window to name event procedures and have their scaffolding auto-generated.

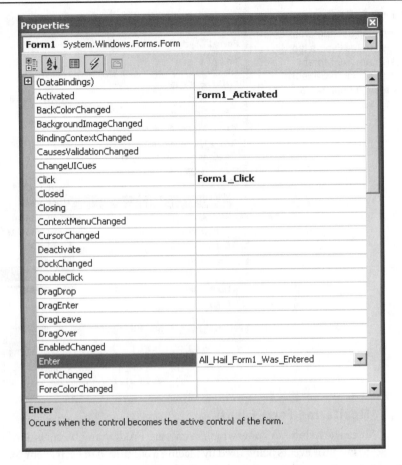

Besides typing in the same of an event procedure, you can select an existing event handler from the drop-down list (Figure 3.7). In this case, a new event procedure will not be created, only the code wiring the event to the existing procedure:

```
this.Closed += new System.EventHandler(this.OneForAll);
```

You'll often find that you want to wire multiple events to one handler, possibly generated by more than one object, perhaps determining within the handler which object invoked the event. I'll show you an example, in a little while, of how this works.

I've shown in this section how to write the code that adds event handlers to form events, and how to use the Properties window to do the same thing. Choose whichever way you like better!

FIGURE 3.7:

You can also use the drop-down list on the Events tab to assign an event to an existing handler, provided it has the right number of arguments.

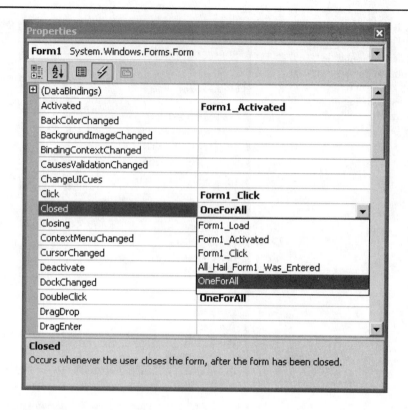

Monitoring Form Events

It can be helpful to know which events are fired by an object, and in precisely what order. It's easy to monitor events being fired by placing a command in each event that uses the `WriteLine` method of the `Debug` object to display a notification in the Output window that the event has been fired.

To monitor the form event sequence, you first should add a `using` directive to the top of the form code so that you can access the `System.Diagnostics` namespace easily:

```
using System.Diagnostics;
```

Next, in each event you'd like to monitor, add a call to the `Debug.WriteLine` method. For example:

```
private void Form1_Load(object sender, System.EventArgs e) {
    Debug.WriteLine("Form Load Event Fired");
}
```

Run the project in debug mode in the development environment (Debug ➢ Start, or F5 on the keyboard). With the project running, open the Output window (View ➢ Other Windows ➢ Output). You can now watch the progress of events being fired (Figure 3.8). Listing 3.2 shows several form events being monitored.

FIGURE 3.8:

You can use the WriteLine method of the Debug object to follow the progress of form events in the Output window.

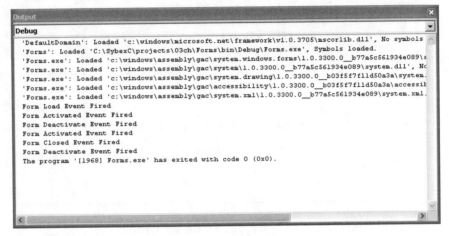

Listing 3.2   Monitoring Form Events

```
...
using System.Diagnostics;

namespace SybexC5
{
    public class Form1 : System.Windows.Forms.Form
    {
        ...
        #region Windows Form Designer generated code

        private void InitializeComponent()
        {
            ...
            this.Load += new System.EventHandler(this.Form1_Load);
            this.Closed += new System.EventHandler(this.Form1_Closed);
            this.Activated += new system.EventHandler(this.Form1_Activated);
            this.Enter += new
                System.EventHandler(this.All_Hail_Form1_Was_Entered);
            this.Deactivate += new System.EventHandler(this.Form1_Deactivate);
            ...
        }
        #endregion

        ...

        private void Form1_Load(object sender, System.EventArgs e) {
            Debug.WriteLine("Form Load Event Fired");
        }

        private void Form1_Activated(object sender, System.EventArgs e) {
            Debug.WriteLine("Form Activated Event Fired");
        }
```

```
private void All_Hail_Form1_Was_Entered(object sender,
    System.EventArgs e) {
    Debug.WriteLine
       ("Form Enter Event a/k/a All_Hail_Form1_Was_Entered Fired");
}

private void Form1_Closed(object sender, System.EventArgs e) {
    Debug.WriteLine("Form Closed Event Fired");
}

private void Form1_Deactivate(object sender, System.EventArgs e)
{
    Debug.WriteLine("Form Deactivate Event Fired");
}
    }
}
```

Determining Which Object Fired an Event

As I mentioned earlier, a common pattern is to have one handler that handles events for multiple objects—likely, but not necessarily, the same event, for example, Click. The code in the handler then uses the Sender parameter to determine which object's Click event fired—and provides different code accordingly.

To see how this might work, I'll show you a single handler for a Click event that determines whether a Button or Form fired it.

First, assign the handler, named EventHandler, to both the Form and Button click events either in code or using the Events tab of the Properties window:

```
this.button1.Click += new System.EventHandler(this.which_object);
...
this.Click += new System.EventHandler(this.which_object);
```

Next, explicitly cast the sender parameter, declared simply as object, to an object of type Control:

```
System.Windows.Forms.Control ctrl = (System.Windows.Forms.Control) sender;
```

Let's examine this statement carefully, because it is very important. The part before the equal sign declares a variable *ctrl* of type System.Windows.Forms.Control, or more simply, Control.

Control means System.Windows.Forms.Control

I could have simply used the Control object without the qualifying namespaces in the statement. This abbreviated statement

```
Control ctrl = (Control) sender;
```

Continued on next page

is the equivalent of the longer version because the `System.Windows.Forms` namespace is included with a `using` directive at the beginning of the auto-generated form code (see Listing 3.1). In order to keep things really clear, I used the long form of the statement.

The part of the statement to the right of the equal sign,

`(System.Windows.Forms.Control) sender`

casts, or converts, the `sender` object to an object of the type within the parentheses, namely a control. If you didn't cast `sender` to a control, you'd get a syntax error due to strong typing when you tried to use `sender.Name` to determine the kind of control that fired the event. I chose `Control` as the type to cast into because it is a common ancestor of all controls, and almost certainly an ancestor of anything that can fire a click event.

TIP By way of comparison, in Visual Basic, you'd use a function such as CType() to explicitly cast, or convert, from one type to another. Note that C# is *always* strongly typed; it's as if Option Strict could not be turned off in VB.

With the event's sender now stored in a variable of type `Control`, it's easy to access it to determine which object it is. The information can be displayed in the Output window, as shown in Figure 3.9 and Listing 3.3, or used in a more practical way.

FIGURE 3.9:

The generalized click event handler can determine which object invoked it.

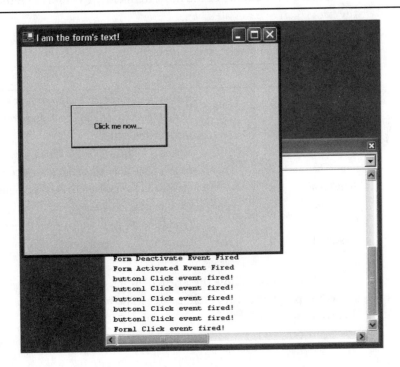

Listing 3.3	Casting the *sender* Parameter to Determine Which Object Invoked the Click Event

```
...
this.button1.Click += new System.EventHandler(this.which_object);
...
this.Click += new System.EventHandler(this.which_object);
...
private void which_object(object sender, System.EventArgs e) {
    System.Windows.Forms.Control ctrl = (System.Windows.Forms.Control) sender;
    Debug.WriteLine(ctrl.Name + " Click event fired!");
}
...
```

Form Methods

Methods are a way to tell an object to do something. In just the way that a property is a *variable* tied to an object, a method is a *procedure* or *function* tied to an object.

Methods are implemented using functions, and invoked by calling an object instance followed by the dot operator followed by the method:

```
Object.Method;
```

Table 3.2 shows some of the most frequently used form methods and describes what they do.

TABLE 3.2: Commonly Used Form Methods

Method	Purpose
Activate	Moves the focus to the form and makes it active.
BringToFront	Moves the form on top of all other forms. See also SendToBack.
Close	Unloads the form.
Hide	Makes a form invisible, or hides it, without unloading the form.
Refresh	Updates the appearance of a form by repainting the form.
SendToBack	Moves the form beneath all other forms. See also BringToFront.
SetBounds	Used to position a form.
Show	Loads and displays a modeless form (a normal window).
ShowDialog	Loads and displays a modal form, such as a dialog box.

Let's have a look at how the Form Closing event works, which is interesting, because it allows the programmer to build in an escape hatch. Maybe the user really didn't want to close that window...

To see how this works, add a Button to a form, and name it btnClose. In the Click event for the Button, invoke the form's Close method:

```
private void btnClose_Click(object sender, System.EventArgs e) {
    this.Close();
}
```

Next, in the form's Closing event, display a message box that asks whether the user is sure (message boxes are discussed in considerable detail in the next section):

```
DialogResult answer = MessageBox.Show("Do you really want to close me?",
    "A second chance...", MessageBoxButtons.YesNo);
```

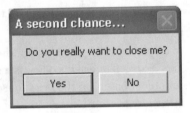

If the user answers "No," then set the Cancel property of the passed System.EventArgs property to true:

```
if (answer == DialogResult.No) {
    e.Cancel = true;
}
```

The window will now stay open.

NOTE   You can use the Form Closing event for cleanup code of various kinds—not just to query whether the user really wants to close the window.

Listing 3.4 shows a Close method and the related Closing event procedure with an included query about whether to close.

Listing 3.4   Closing, and Querying Whether to Close, a Form

```
private void btnClose_Click(object sender, System.EventArgs e) {
    this.Close();
}

private void Form1_Closing(object sender,
    System.ComponentModel.CancelEventArgs e) {
    DialogResult answer = MessageBox.Show("Do you really want to close me?",
        "A second chance...", MessageBoxButtons.YesNo);
```

```
    if (answer == DialogResult.No) {
        // Cancel the closure
        e.Cancel = true;
    }
}
```

The Lowly Message Box

We just used a message box in the previous example to query the user (did she really want to close the form?). You've undoubtedly seen hundreds, if not thousands, of message boxes in your time. This lowly dialog window gets no respect but is always ready to shoulder the burden and do more work!

Message boxes are displayed using the Show method of the MessageBox object, which is part of the System.Windows.Forms namespace. Show is a static method, meaning that you do not have to instantiate an object based on the MessageBox class to use the method. It's also overloaded—meaning that there are various versions of Show you can use with different argument lists. Essentially, you have to include a string to be the text of the message box displayed, but additional arguments after that are optional.

I'm going to spend a little time going over the message box syntax, because it is so useful and easy. Then I'm going to use the message box as a jumping-off place for some variations on a theme: If you allow the user to create their own message box, and enter their own text, and display a set of radio buttons that allow them to choose the buttons for the message box, how do you know which radio button is selected—and how can the information easily be used?

MessageBox.Show Syntax

MessageBox.Show has the following format:

```
DialogResult = MessageBox.Show(text, caption, buttons, icon, defaultbutton,
    options)
```

Here are the meanings of the arguments, which must be entered in the order shown above:

text   Contains the text that will be displayed in the message box. The contents of a variable in the *text* position must evaluate to a *string*, meaning that it must be alphanumeric. One way to do this is with *string literals*. To create a string literal, enclose an alphanumeric sequence in quotation marks, as in, "I am a string!".

caption   Optional; contains the text that will go in the message box caption bar. Like the *text* argument, the *caption* argument must be of string type.

buttons   Optional; tells C# .NET which buttons will be displayed.

icon   Optional; tells C# .NET which icon will be displayed.

defaultbutton   Optional; tells C# .NET which button is activated by default (when the user presses the Enter key).

options   Optional; allows you to select some special options for the message box. These include things like making the text right-aligned, specifying a right-to-left reading order, or writing an entry in the system logs (see example below).

To use `MessageBox.Show` to display a message box without returning a value, just use it in a statement without an equal sign:

```
MessageBox.Show(text, caption, buttons, icon);
```

The following sections describe how to use the `MessageBox.Show` arguments.

So where do you find the values to use for buttons and icons? The Code Editor's IntelliSense feature will generally supply this information, called *member* information. In other words, when you type `MessageBoxButtons` and enter the dot operator that follows it, IntelliSense will automatically pop up a list of the members, or enumeration constants, that you can use as a `MessageBoxButton` value. I've also included these values here for your easy reference.

Table 3.3 shows the `MessageBoxButtons` members, and Table 3.4 shows the `MessageBoxIcon` set of values.

TABLE 3.3: The *MessageBoxButtons* Enumeration

Constant	Description
AbortRetryIgnore	Displays Abort, Retry, and Ignore buttons
OK	Displays an OK button only
OKCancel	Displays OK and Cancel buttons
RetryCancel	Displays Retry and Cancel buttons
YesNo	Displays Yes and No buttons
YesNoCancel	Displays Yes, No, and Cancel buttons

TABLE 3.4: The *MessageBoxIcon* Enumeration

Constant	Description
Asterisk	Displays an information icon
Error	Displays an error icon
Exclamation	Displays an exclamation icon
Hand	Displays an error icon
Information	Displays an information icon

Continued on next page

TABLE 3.4 CONTINUED: The *MessageBoxIcon* Enumeration

Constant	Description
None	Does not display an icon
Question	Displays a question icon
Stop	Displays an error icon
Warning	Displays an exclamation icon

You also need to know what the possible return values are for `MessageBox.Show`. These values are the members of `System.Windows.Forms.DialogResult`, or `DialogResult` for short, shown in Table 3.5.

TABLE 3.5: The *DialogResult* Enumeration

Constant	Description
Abort	The Abort button was clicked.
Cancel	The Cancel button was clicked.
Ignore	The Ignore button was clicked.
No	The No button was clicked.
None	The user did not click a button.
OK	The OK button was clicked.
Retry	The Retry button was clicked.
Yes	The Yes button was clicked.

Writing an Event Log Entry

As an example of how `MessageBox.Show` works, let's use it to write an entry to the system logs.

First, add a Button named `btnService` to a form. The `Click` event of `btnService` will be used to display the message box. The elements of the message box will be placed in variables and then displayed using the `MessageBox.Show` method. Here are the subject and caption,

```
string subject = "Service Notification by SybexC6";
string caption = "MessageBox Demo";
```

followed by the buttons, icon, and a parameter designating the default button:

```
MessageBoxButtons mbb = MessageBoxButtons.OK;
MessageBoxIcon mbi = MessageBoxIcon.Exclamation;
MessageBoxDefaultButton mbdb = MessageBoxDefaultButton.Button1;
```

Finally, a `MessageBoxOptions` variable is declared and set:

```
MessageBoxOptions mbo = MessageBoxOptions.ServiceNotification;
```

and the message box can be displayed:

```
MessageBox.Show(subject, caption, mbb, mbi, mbdb, mbo);
```

The full click event code is shown in Listing 3.5. If the project is run and the button is clicked, a message box like this one will be displayed:

Listing 3.5	Using *MessageBox.Show* to Write an Event Log Entry

```
private void btnService_Click(object sender, System.EventArgs e) {
    string subject = "Service Notification by SybexC6";
    string caption = "MessageBox Demo";
    MessageBoxButtons mbb = MessageBoxButtons.OK;
    MessageBoxIcon mbi = MessageBoxIcon.Exclamation;
    MessageBoxDefaultButton mbdb = MessageBoxDefaultButton.Button1;
    MessageBoxOptions mbo = MessageBoxOptions.ServiceNotification;
    MessageBox.Show(subject, caption, mbb, mbi, mbdb, mbo);
}
```

To see the entry that was created, open Server Explorer (View ➤ Server Explorer). Expand it until you see the System Event Logs (Figure 3.10). The message box should have made the most recent addition under the Application Popup category.

FIGURE 3.10:

The new entry can be viewed using Server Explorer (shown here) or using the operating system's administration facilities.

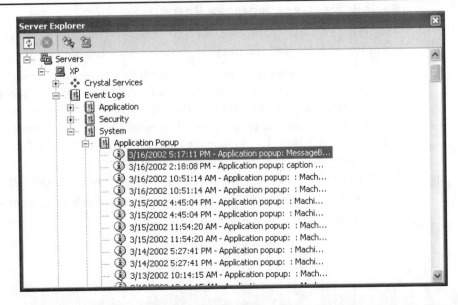

You can right-click the notification and select Properties from the context menu to view the full text of the log entry (Figure 3.11).

FIGURE 3.11:

Expanding the entry in the System log shows the full text of the message box.

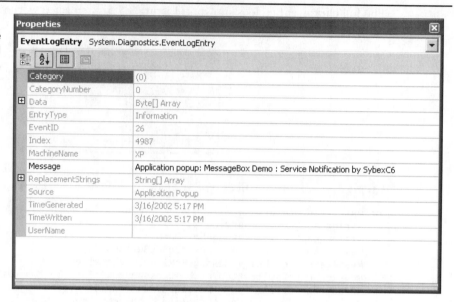

Depending on your operating system, you can also find the log entry by opening the Event Viewer (found in the Administrative Tools Control Panel applet provided by Windows 2000 or Windows XP), and looking for a recent Application Popup entry in the System log. You can expand the entry in the Event Viewer to find the text of the message box.

RadioButtons and Message Boxes

The next application will provide several variations on the theme of allowing the user to decide which text, caption, and buttons should be displayed in a message box.

RadioButton controls are typically used when you want to let a user make one—and only one—choice from multiple options. When you add more than one RadioButton to a container such as a Panel or GroupBox, these RadioButtons form a kind of group in which only one can be "checked," or selected, at a time. We'll use RadioButtons placed on a GroupBox to allow the user to pick the buttons for the message box. (I've hard-coded the value of the MessageBoxIcon parameter to the value MessageBoxIcon.Exclamation, but you could expand this example by allowing the user to pick the message box icon as well as the buttons.)

When the user interface is done, it should look something like the one shown in Figure 3.12.

FIGURE 3.12:

The user interface is shown on the left; on the right, the Tag property is highlighted in the Properties window.

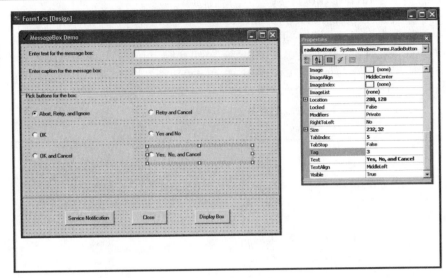

I've left the names of the RadioButton controls with the default, so they are named radioButton1 through radioButton6. In the real world, it might be a good idea to name them after the choice they represent, e.g., rboOK, etc. The Checked property of radioButton1 is set to true, meaning that will be the one checked when the application first starts.

NOTE You can create RadioButtons of uniform size by copying and pasting a RadioButton that has already been positioned on a form. This achieves the same results as dragging the RadioButton control from the Toolbox and can save some time.

It's a good idea to rename any control that you will need to refer to in code with a name that reflects the type of the control and its function in the application. But, in many cases, Label controls are never used in code; they are essentially "decorative" in nature. In these cases, there's no real need to change the default control name, which is Label*n*, as in Label1, Label2, and so on. (This, of course, is a matter of your own taste as a programmer—or the standards that have been established in a team project.)

You can use the Align and Make Same Size options on the Format menu to standardize the appearance of labels and buttons on a form. Alternatively, you can use the control's position coordinates, which can be found in the Location and Size properties in the Properties window, to align controls. For example, to make sure that two controls are aligned vertically, simply set the Location property X coordinate of each control to the same number.

Variation the First

As a programmer, one thing I hate almost more than anything else is typing the same string of text multiple times. Looking at the user interface shown in Figure 3.12, I made the observation that I had already essentially entered the values of the MessageBoxButtons constants (see Table 3.3) in the Text property of each radio button. As things stood, the value of each radio button's Text property was as shown in Table 3.6.

TABLE 3.6: Values for the Buttons Pane

Name	Text	Checked (Initial Value)	Tag Value (For Casting)
radioButton1	Abort, Retry, and Ignore	true	2
radioButton2	OK Only	false	0
radioButton3	OK and Cancel	false	1
radioButton4	Retry and Cancel	false	5
radioButton5	Yes and No	false	4
radioButton6	Yes, No, and Cancel	false	3

Of course, the value of the radio button Text property would be available to me programmatically at run time. Could I use the value of the selected radio button to identify the corresponding MessageBoxButtons enumeration constant? Anything to avoid having to code something along these lines:

```
MessageBoxButtons mbb;
if (radioButton1.Checked) {
    mbb = MessageBoxButtons.AbortRetryIgnore;
}
```

and so on for all the radio buttons.

Actually, this boils down to two problems: identifying the checked radio button, and placing the corresponding enumeration constant in the MessageBoxButtons variable that will be used to display the message box. I'll show you a fairly elegant answer to the first issue in a second.

Regarding the second problem, it occurred to me that maybe I could cast the string in the radio button Text property to an enumeration constant—after all, they appear to be pretty similar, and, if necessary, I could even make them identical. This, it turns out, does not work: you cannot cast a string to an enumeration constant, no matter how close the two are.

You can, however, cast an integer to an enumeration constant, provided you know what integer equates to what enumeration constant value. Short of trial and error, there seems to be no way to find this information, so I used trial and error to come up with the values shown in Table 3.6. I placed the corresponding value in each radio button's Tag property, which is otherwise unused, so that I could access it at run time.

WARNING   Please be careful if you try this "at home." There is no guarantee that the internal values of enumeration constants will stay the same in updated versions of .NET. Furthermore, using a cryptic integer value is bad programming practice because it defeats the purpose of enumeration constants—which is to clearly identify the value represented.

Setting Up the Message Box

Within the click event that will display the message box, here are the preliminary variable declarations and assignments:

```
string subject = txtMsgText.Text;
string caption = txtMsgCaption.Text;
MessageBoxButtons mbb = MessageBoxButtons.OK;
MessageBoxIcon mbi = MessageBoxIcon.Exclamation;
DialogResult answer;
```

Note that I've provided the variable *mbb* with an initial value, even though this will likely change depending upon the user's radio button selection.

Determining the Checked Radio Button

One way to determine which radio button is checked is to use a foreach loop to cycle through the controls on the group box (in other words, the whole bunch of radio buttons). Here's how this works:

```
foreach (object c in this.grpButtons.Controls) {
    if (c is RadioButton) {
        RadioButton rb = (RadioButton) c;
        if (rb.Checked == true) {
        // Is it checked?
        // If so, do the assignment...
        }
    }
}
```

Inside the loop, each control is checked to make sure it is a RadioButton using a variable declared as (lowest common denominator) object, *c*, to do the iteration. If it is, a new variable, *rb*, of type RadioButton is declared. The iterating object variable is then cast to *rb*, and the Checked property of *rb* examined. If rb.Checked evaluates to true, then do the assignment.

NOTE   I could have used a variable of type Control rather than Object to iterate through the group of controls. But I still would have to cast it to type RadioButton—because not all controls have a Checked property.

NOTE   The all-lowercase keyword object is legal shorthand for System.Object, commonly referred to as type Object.

Assigning the Value

The following line of code uses the ToString() method to convert the contents of the Tag property to a string and the ToInt16 method of the Convert object to convert it to integer. The integer value is then cast to the correct constant enumeration constant, which is stored in the variable *mbb*:

```
mbb = (MessageBoxButtons) Convert.ToInt16(rb.Tag.ToString());
```

If this seems a little baroque—or maybe even a little over-the-top rococo—well, maybe it is! But if you followed the example through, you should have learned something about C# objects, casting, and conversion methods.

Displaying the Box and Doing Something Wild with the Result

Now that we have the user's choice, it's easy to display the message box:

```
answer = MessageBox.Show(subject, caption, mbb, mbi);
```

Finally, it would be nice to do something with the result. Here's one way to display it in another message box:

```
MessageBox.Show("You clicked " + answer.ToString(), "Message Box Demo");
```

The complete click event code is shown in Listing 3.6. If the project is run now, the user can enter text and caption and select from a set of buttons (Figure 3.13).

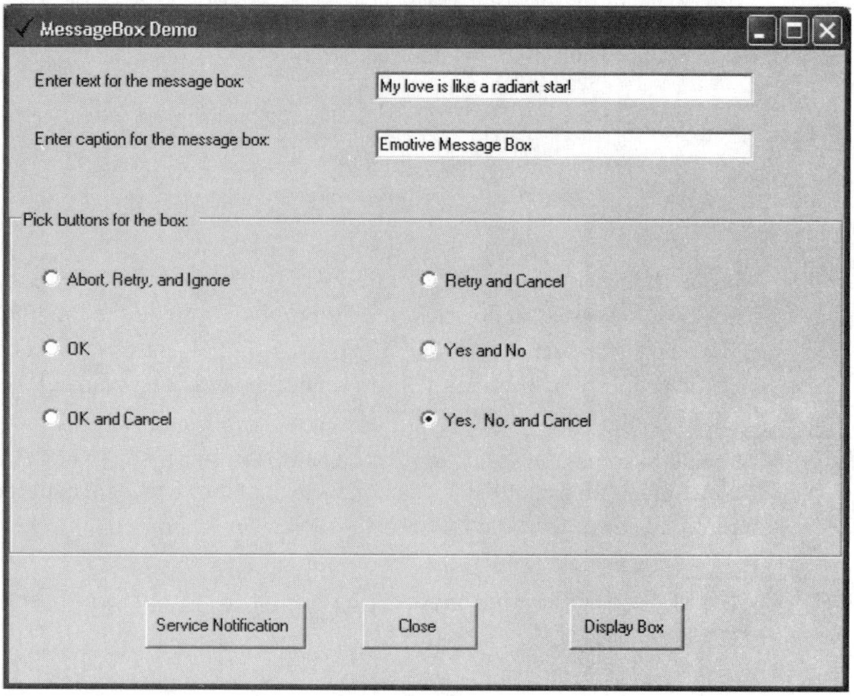

FIGURE 3.13:

The user can enter message box text and caption and can choose the buttons it will display.

Listing 3.6   Displaying a Message Box Based on Which RadioButton Was Checked

```
private void btnDisplay_Click(object sender, System.EventArgs e) {
    string subject = txtMsgText.Text;
    string caption = txtMsgCaption.Text;
    MessageBoxButtons mbb = MessageBoxButtons.OK;
    MessageBoxIcon mbi = MessageBoxIcon.Exclamation;
    DialogResult answer;

    foreach (object c in this.grpButtons.Controls) {
        if (c is RadioButton) {
            RadioButton rb = (RadioButton) c;
            if (rb.Checked == true) {
                mbb = (MessageBoxButtons) Convert.ToInt16(rb.Tag.ToString());
                break;
            }
        }
    }

    answer = MessageBox.Show(subject, caption, mbb, mbi);
    MessageBox.Show("You clicked " + answer.ToString(), "Message Box Demo");
}
```

When the Display Box button is clicked, the designated message box is generated. Next, the button selected in *that* message box is displayed.

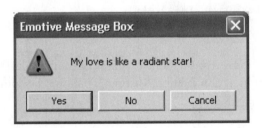

There are a couple of ways to programmatically evaluate the response. Clearly, you could evaluate answer.ToString(), which in the case of the message box shown in Figure 3.13 would contain "Yes", "No", or "Cancel". More rigorously, you could evaluate the DialogResult enumeration constants, shown in Table 3.5, against the value of the variable *answer*.

Second Variation: The *switch* Statement

The code in Listing 3.6 certainly didn't take much work to enter: it is short, which is good. But, for reasons I explained earlier, relying on the integer equivalent of the MessageBoxButtons enumeration constants is not a very good idea. So, let's bite the bullet and try a variation.

We know a good deal programmatically about each RadioButton in the group of controls, including its Text and Name properties. Either of these could be tested when the Checked control is retrieved to determine the right enumeration constant value.

A switch statement is used to branch depending on the value of an expression. Using the Text property, we can use a switch statement to evaluate the value of rb.Text and assign the enumeration constant accordingly.

TIP   Select...Case is the VB equivalent of the C# switch statement.

Here's how the switch statement looks once we know we have the right RadioButton:

```
if (rb.Checked == true) {
    switch (rb.Text) {
        case "Abort, Retry, and Ignore":
            mbb = MessageBoxButtons.AbortRetryIgnore;
            break;
        case "OK":
            mbb = MessageBoxButtons.OK;
            break;
        case "OK and Cancel":
            mbb = MessageBoxButtons.OKCancel;
            break;
    ...
```

OK, so I did have to type in the text strings and all those constants (at least they were supplied by the Code Editor's auto-completion facility). Listing 3.7 shows the complete code for this variation.

Listing 3.7   **Variation on the Message Box Using a *switch***

```
private void btnVar1_Click(object sender, System.EventArgs e) {
    string subject = txtMsgText.Text;
    string caption = txtMsgCaption.Text;
    MessageBoxButtons mbb = MessageBoxButtons.OK;
```

```
    MessageBoxIcon mbi = MessageBoxIcon.Exclamation;
    DialogResult answer;

    foreach (Control c in this.grpButtons.Controls) {
        if (c is RadioButton) {
            RadioButton rb = (RadioButton) c;
            if (rb.Checked == true) {
                switch (rb.Text) {
                    case "Abort, Retry, and Ignore":
                        mbb = MessageBoxButtons.AbortRetryIgnore;
                        break;
                    case "OK":
                        mbb = MessageBoxButtons.OK;
                        break;
                    case "OK and Cancel":
                        mbb = MessageBoxButtons.OKCancel;
                        break;
                    case "Retry and Cancel":
                        mbb = MessageBoxButtons.RetryCancel;
                        break;
                    case "Yes and No":
                        mbb = MessageBoxButtons.YesNo;
                        break;
                    case "Yes, No, and Cancel":
                        mbb = MessageBoxButtons.YesNoCancel;
                        break;
                }
            }
            break;
        }
    }

    answer = MessageBox.Show(subject, caption, mbb, mbi);
    MessageBox.Show("You clicked " + answer.ToString(), "Message Box Demo");
}
```

Third Variation: Conditional on Top

As I was looking at the second variation, it occurred to me that I really haven't gained that much with my fancy loop through the controls contained by the GroupBox. I still had to use a conditional that explicitly assigned each enumeration constant based on a hand-coded value (the control's Text property).

Why not simplify matters by moving the conditionals to the top and forgetting about the loop? Listing 3.8 shows how to do this using if statements—it's the good, old-fashioned way. As you can see in Figure 3.14, it's easy to have lots of fun with the lowly message box.

FIGURE 3.14:

It's easy to have lots of
fun with message boxes.

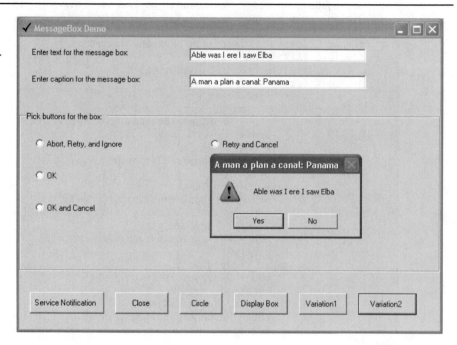

⟳ **Listing 3.8**   **Another Switching Variation**

```csharp
private void btnVar2_Click(object sender, System.EventArgs e) {
    string subject = txtMsgText.Text;
    string caption = txtMsgCaption.Text;
    MessageBoxButtons mbb = MessageBoxButtons.OK;
    MessageBoxIcon mbi = MessageBoxIcon.Exclamation;
    DialogResult answer;

    if (radioButton1.Checked){
        mbb = MessageBoxButtons.AbortRetryIgnore;
    }
    else if (radioButton2.Checked){
        mbb = MessageBoxButtons.OK;
    }
    else if (radioButton3.Checked) {
        mbb = MessageBoxButtons.OKCancel;
    }
    else if (radioButton4.Checked) {
        mbb = MessageBoxButtons.RetryCancel;
    }
    else if (radioButton5.Checked) {
        mbb = MessageBoxButtons.YesNo;
    }
```

```
    else if (radioButton6.Checked) {
        mbb = MessageBoxButtons.YesNoCancel;
    }

    answer = MessageBox.Show(subject, caption, mbb, mbi);
    MessageBox.Show("You clicked " + answer.ToString(), "Message Box Demo");
}
```

Changing the Shape of a Window

Why should windows always be square? One of the great things about .NET is that it is easy to make visual objects, such as Windows forms, any shape that you would like. For example, an oval window might make users think your application is really cool! The trick is to assign a GraphicsPath object to the Form's Region property. The GraphicsPath object can be defined as almost any kind of shape.

Let's do this with the form we've been working with in the message box example. To start, at the top of the form module, import the System.Drawing.Drawing2D namespace to make referring to the Drawing2D library members easier:

```
using System.Drawing.Drawing2D
```

Making a Square Window Round

Next, within the form class code, create a procedure, ApplyInitialRegion. Within ApplyInitialRegion, define a GraphicsPath object using its AddEllipse method, and assign it to the Region property of the Form object.

```
private void ApplyInitialRegion() {
    GraphicsPath myGraphicsPath = new GraphicsPath();
    myGraphicsPath.AddEllipse(new Rectangle(0, 0, 600, 450));
    this.Region = new Region(myGraphicsPath);
}
```

All that remains is to create a way to call the form, which you can do in a button Click event, as shown in Listing 3.9. When the click event is run, the form turns into an oval (Figure 3.15).

Listing 3.9   **Making a Square Form Oval**

```
...
using System.Drawing.Drawing2D;
...
private void ApplyInitialRegion() {
    GraphicsPath myGraphicsPath = new GraphicsPath();
```

```
        myGraphicsPath.AddEllipse(new Rectangle(0, 0, 600, 450));
        this.Region = new Region(myGraphicsPath);
    }
    private void btnCircle_Click(object sender, System.EventArgs e) {
        ApplyInitialRegion();
    }
    ...
```

FIGURE 3.15:

The Region property of the form can be used to make it any shape you'd like.

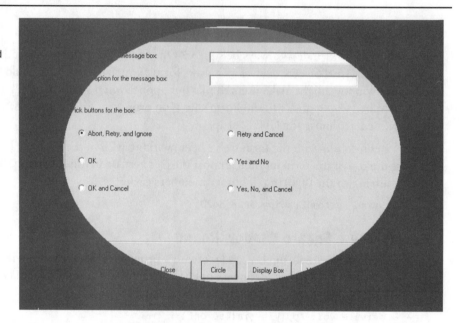

Depending on the shape you choose for your form, it may not have the normal mechanisms for closure, as in the example here, because the top part of form has been eliminated. Make sure that you provide a way to close the form (such as a Close button).

You can open a form with whatever shape you'd like by placing the call to the method that changes the form's shape—in this example, ApplyInitialRegion()—in the form load event or in the form's constructor.

Constructors

A *constructor* is a block of code that is executed when an object that is an instance of a class is created by using the new keyword. In C#, the constructor is a public procedure within the class with the same name as the class; for example, for the Form1 class (see Listing 3.1), you can find the constructor within the class:

Continued on next page

```
            public class Form1 : System.Windows.Forms.Form
            {
                ...
                public Form1()
                {
                    ...
                }
                ...
            }
```
You'll find more about constructors in Chapter 8.

A Polygon Form

By way of variation, let's turn the form into a cute polygon, rather than an oval. To do this, we need to create an array of points:

```
Point[] myArray = {
    new Point(230, 200),
    new Point(400, 100),
    new Point(570, 200),
    new Point(500, 400),
    new Point(300, 400)
};
```

Next, instead of calling the AddEllipse method for the GraphicsPath, we should call the AddPolygon method, with the array of points as the argument:

```
myGraphicsPath.AddPolygon(myArray);
```

Listing 3.10 shows the revised ApplyInitialRegion() procedure; if you run it, the form will be a nice polygon, like the one in Figure 3.16.

Listing 3.10   The Form Is a Nice Polygon

```
private void ApplyInitialRegion() {
    GraphicsPath myGraphicsPath = new GraphicsPath();
    Point[] myArray = {
        new Point(230, 200),
        new Point(400, 100),
        new Point(570, 200),
        new Point(500, 400),
        new Point(300, 400)
    };
    myGraphicsPath.AddPolygon(myArray);
    this.Region = new Region(myGraphicsPath);
}
```

FIGURE 3.16:

Calling the AddPolygon method produces a polygon path from the array of points you provide.

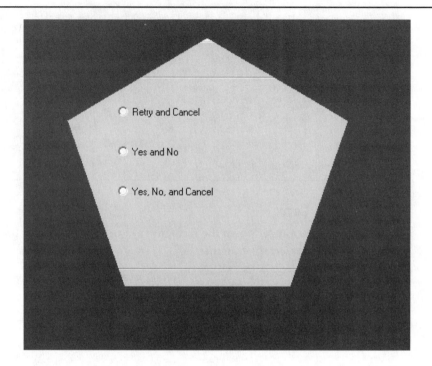

The Asynchronous Pattern

Back in Chapter 2, "Consuming the Service on the Web," I promised you an example that showed how to asynchronously use a web service from a Windows application using the preferred pattern for asynchronous invocations. Before we get there, let's consider briefly what we mean by a "preferred pattern."

Design patterns, which will be explored further in Chapter 5, "Reflecting on Classes," are systematic high-level solutions to a recurring problem in object-oriented programming. As you'll see in Chapter 5, software design patterns are often likened to architectural solutions. A great virtue of patterns is that once you know the best way to do something, you don't have to rethink it each time!

The .NET asynchronous design pattern involves a number of points, including:

- The called object does not know whether it is invoked synchronously or asynchronously.

- The .NET Framework automatically creates `Begin` and `End` asynchronous methods to go along with synchronous methods explicitly exposed by the called object.

- A result object is supplied via a callback mechanism.

NOTE   To find out more about how this design pattern works, look up "Asynchronous Design Pattern Overview" in online help.

Let's have a look at this in the context of a practical example. Although the example shows the asynchronous consumption of the IsPrime web service, the general pattern applies to the asynchronous invocation of anything. (You'll find more material about asynchronous programming in Chapter 10, "Working with Streams and Files.")

Start a new Windows application project with a TextBox for the user to enter a number to check for primality and a Button whose click event will invoke the asynchronous call to the IsPrime web service. You must also add the SybexC2 web service to the project as a web reference, following the process explained in Chapter 2, and rename it theService.

With the user interface in place, and the web reference added, let's start coding.

First, create a new procedure, ServiceCallBack, to hold the result object (note that it takes an IAsyncResult as an argument):

```
public void ServiceCallback(IAsyncResult ar) {

}
```

Moving to the Button's click event, create a variable to hold an instance of the service:

```
private void btnAsync_Click(object sender, System.EventArgs e) {
    theService.SybexC2Service cService = new theService.SybexC2Service();
```

Next, instantiate an AsyncCallback object, passing it the ServiceCallback procedure as an argument so that it knows where to send the results:

```
AsyncCallback cb = new AsyncCallback(ServiceCallback);
```

Invoke the BeginIsPrime method with the two arguments required by IsPrime (the number to check and the delay) followed by the AsyncCallback object and the service object. Assign the return value of BeginIsPrime to the IAsyncResult object that is passed to ServiceCallback:

```
IAsyncResult ar =
    cService.BeginIsPrime(Convert.ToInt64(txtInNum.Text), 10, cb, cService);
```

NOTE   Note that the second parameter sent to the BeginIsPrime method is the delay in seconds. If 10 seconds is too long for you to wait, you can replace it with a smaller integer.

Now you can go ahead and put whatever code you want in for execution while the asynchronous call is completing. In our case, we'll write some text to a label and display a message box:

```
lblResult.Text = "Not blocked, don't have to wait...";
MessageBox.Show("I can do other things!", "AsyncCallback Demo",
    MessageBoxButtons.OK, MessageBoxIcon.Information);
```

Meanwhile, back at the callback ranch, we need to create an instance of the service based on the passed `IAsyncResult` object:

```
theService.SybexC2Service cService = (theService.SybexC2Service) ar.AsyncState;
```

Next, the `EndIsPrime` method can be checked for the return value from the web service:

```
if (cService.EndIsPrime(ar)) {
    lblResult.Text = lblResult.Text + "Is a prime!";
}
else {
    lblResult.Text = lblResult.Text + "Not prime!";
}
```

The project is now ready to run (Listing 3.11 shows the complete click event code, as well as the callback procedure). If you enter a number in the box and click Async, you'll see the message box displayed while the asynchronous call is underway (Figure 3.17).

FIGURE 3.17:

The message box is a demo of the use of a new thread to perform tasks while the asynchronous web call is completing.

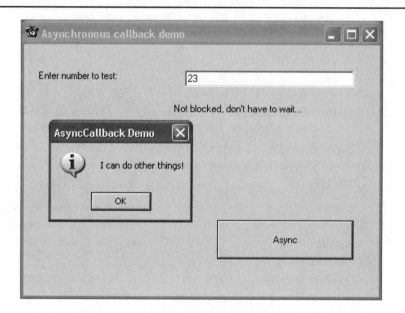

Listing 3.11   Using a Callback to Perform an Asynchronous Call to a Web Method

```
private void btnAsync_Click(object sender, System.EventArgs e) {
    theService.SybexC2Service cService = new theService.SybexC2Service();
    AsyncCallback cb = new AsyncCallback(ServiceCallback);
    IAsyncResult ar =
        cService.BeginIsPrime(Convert.ToInt64(txtInNum.Text), 10, cb, cService);
    lblResult.Text = "Not blocked, don't have to wait...";
```

```
    MessageBox.Show("I can do other things!", "AsyncCallback Demo",
        MessageBoxButtons.OK, MessageBoxIcon.Information);

    // Do more stuff
}
public void ServiceCallback(IAsyncResult ar) {
    theService.SybexC2Service cService =
        (theService.SybexC2Service) ar.AsyncState;
    if (cService.EndIsPrime(ar)) {
        lblResult.Text = lblResult.Text + "Is a prime!";
    }
    else {
        lblResult.Text = lblResult.Text + "Not prime!";
    }
}
```

Clearly, you could place any code you'd like to have executed in place of the message box display. Meanwhile, when the asynchronous call completes, the callback procedure takes care of it and displays the appropriate results in the label.

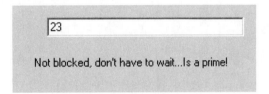

Conclusion

Visual Studio .NET is great for building Windows applications, and this chapter has shown you a lot about building them using C#. Forms were covered in great detail; we spent some time with the lowly message box and playing various variations out in determining which radio button was selected. Along the way, you learned how to create oval- and polygon-shaped windows. Finally, the journey meandered back to something I promised in the last chapter: an asynchronous consumption of the web service developed in Chapter 1 using a callback object for the result.

Chapter 4, "Building a Better Windows Interface," picks up where we left off. You'll find bouncing round controls, ListBoxes, menus, and much more.

CHAPTER 4

Building a Better Windows Interface

- Making round controls

- Animating controls

- Working with CheckedListBoxes

- Building menus

- Taking advantage of the common dialog controls

- Constructing MDI applications

Windows, windows, windows! Here's a truism for you: Most Windows applications have user interfaces built around windows. This chapter picks up where the last chapter left off—there's more information here about building the windowing interface.

One of the examples in Chapter 3, "Windows Uses Web Services, Too!", showed you how to change the shape of a window to a circle (or a polygon). Why just windows? The first project in this chapter will show you how to make ovoid labels, buttons, and other controls—and then use a Timer component to make these controls "dance" across the screen.

In a slightly less frivolous vein, this chapter will show you how to work with ListBoxes, how to create menus using code, how to use the common dialog controls, and how to create an MDI application.

Round Buttons Dancing

In Chapter 3 I used the Region property of a form to set the shape of the form by assigning a GraphicsPath object to the property. (The AddEllipse method was used to make the GraphicsPath oval.)

Region is a member of System.Windows.Forms.Control that sets (or gets) the window region associated with a control. It's therefore a property you can use for all objects that inherit from Control. This includes the Form object, as in the example in Chapter 3, which inherits from Control via ScrollableControl and ContainerControl. It also includes all controls in the Toolbox that have a visual interface: Buttons, TextBoxes, Labels, and so on.

Making a Button Round

Let's write a general method that we can use to make a control round, using the logic explained in Chapter 3 in which the AddEllipse method of a GraphicsPath object is used to make an oval based on the size of the control:

```
public void MakeItRound(Control c) {
    GraphicsPath gp = new GraphicsPath();
    gp.AddEllipse(new Rectangle(0, 0, c.Size.Width - 5, c.Size.Height - 5));
    c.Region = new Region(gp);
}
```

NOTE   I've subtracted five pixels off both the width and the height of the oval to eliminate the line produced by the "raised" bevel when you make a Button round.

Place a button named button1 on the form. (For the sake of aesthetic harmony, use the Properties window to delete the contents of its Text property and the other controls used later in this example—although, of course, this is a matter of your choice. They can have text if you'd like.)

If you call the MakeItRound method with a control, such as button1, as an argument, the control will become round:

```
private void btnRound_Click(object sender, System.EventArgs e) {
    MakeItRound(button1);
}
```

Let's add a Panel, docked along the bottom of a form, to act as the control panel for this application (see Figure 4.1). The panel has three buttons whose click events will be used to:

- Make a single control round, as explained above (this will be expanded in a second to toggle back and forth between "roundness" and "squareness"). This button is named btnRound and has the initial text "Round One".

- Turn all the controls in the client area of the form—that is, the form excluding the panel that I placed on it—round. This button has the text "Round All".

- Animate all controls in the client area, with the text toggling between "Dance" and "Stop".

FIGURE 4.1:

Making round controls dance

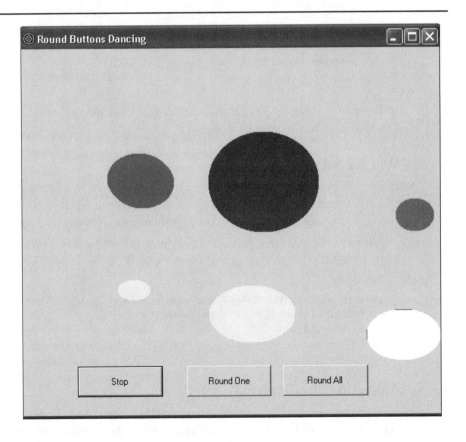

The *client space* of a form is the form background area, exclusive of title bar, toolbars, menus, and border.

Toggling the Round Button

To toggle the single control, we need to store the initial value of its `Region` property in a variable declared outside the click event (so that the value persists). We can do this by declaring a variable named *theRegion* as part of the initial class declaration:

```
public class Form1 : System.Windows.Forms.Form {
    ...
    System.Drawing.Region theRegion;
    ...
```

Next, the click event of `btnRound` can be modified to store the initial control `Region` and restore it when toggled:

```
private void btnRound_Click(object sender, System.EventArgs e) {
    if (btnRound.Text == "Round One") {
        theRegion = button1.Region;
        MakeItRound(button1);
        btnRound.Text = "Square One";
    }
    else {
        button1.Region = theRegion;
        btnRound.Text = "Round One";
    }
}
```

Try it! If you run the project and click Round One, `button1` will become round. If you click again, it is back to its normal shape.

One for All and All for One

It's easy to extend the rounding process to all the controls in a form's control collection. To see this in action, add a gaggle of Buttons, Labels, TextBoxes—and any other control you'd like—to the form, making sure that the `Text` property of each is empty (just to keep the aesthetics neat).

With a bunch of controls added to the client area of the form, code can be added to the click event of the Round All button to cycle through the form's control collection, rounding each one in turn:

```
private void btnRoundAll_Click(object sender, System.EventArgs e) {
    foreach (Control c in this.Controls) {
        MakeItRound(c);
    }
}
```

Animating the Controls

Now that we have all these nice, round controls, let's use a Timer component to animate them. When you drag a Timer component from the Toolbox to a form, it sits on the "tray" beneath the form—which is symbolic of the fact that the Timer has no run-time visual representation.

Essentially, the Timer component is a mechanism for the time-based firing of an event. As you may know, the key Timer members are the properties Enabled and Interval. If Enabled is true, the Timer's sole event—Tick—is repeatedly fired after the Interval (expressed in milliseconds).

The object of animating the controls is to move them in the Tick property in one direction, and to reset things when they reach the edge of a form. If we let the control pass out of the form's coordinates, it won't be visible.

Use the Properties window to set the Timer's Enabled property to false, and its Interval property to 100 (or one-tenth of a second).

In the click event of the button used to start the animation, toggle the Timer's Enabled property:

```
private void btnDance_Click(object sender, System.EventArgs e) {
    if (btnDance.Text == "Dance") {
        timer1.Enabled = true;
        btnDance.Text = "Stop";
    }
    else {
        timer1.Enabled = false;
        btnDance.Text = "Dance";
    }
}
```

Next, in the Timer's Tick event, add the code to move each control in the control's collection, sending each one back to the upper-left of the form as it goes off the lower-right:

```
private void timer1_Tick(object sender, System.EventArgs e) {
    int xIncrement = 5; int yIncrement = 5;
    foreach (Control c in this.Controls) {
        if (c.Location.X > this.Size.Width - 30) {
            xIncrement = -500;
        }
        if (c.Location.Y > this.Size.Height - 50) {
            yIncrement = -500;
        }
        if (c.Location.X <= 0) {
            xIncrement = 5;
        }
        if (c.Location.Y <= 0) {
            yIncrement = 10;
        }
        c.Location = new Point(c.Location.X + xIncrement,
            c.Location.Y + yIncrement);
    }
}
```

In creating this kind of procedure, it's helpful to use the Debug object to track where objects actually are, so that code can be adjusted accordingly, along these lines:

```
using System.Diagnostics;
...
Debug.WriteLine("XLocation: " + c.Location.X.ToString());
Debug.WriteLine("X Increment: " + xIncrement.ToString());
Debug.WriteLine("YLocation: " + c.Location.Y.ToString());
Debug.WriteLine("Y Increment: " + yIncrement.ToString());
```

Save the project (the code is shown in Listing 4.1). If you run it, you'll see that turning controls round and animating them is almost as good as watching a lava lamp!

Listing 4.1   Making Round Controls Dance

```
...
using System.Drawing.Drawing2D;

private void btnRound_Click(object sender, System.EventArgs e) {
    if (btnRound.Text == "Round One") {
        theRegion = button1.Region;
        MakeItRound(button1);
        btnRound.Text = "Square One";
    }
    else {
        button1.Region = theRegion;
        btnRound.Text = "Round One";
    }
}

public void MakeItRound(Control c) {
    GraphicsPath gp = new GraphicsPath();
    gp.AddEllipse(new Rectangle(0, 0, c.Size.Width - 5,c.Size.Height - 5));
    c.Region = new Region (gp);
}

private void btnRoundAll_Click(object sender, System.EventArgs e) {
    foreach (Control c in this.Controls) {
        MakeItRound(c);
    }
}

private void btnDance_Click(object sender, System.EventArgs e) {
    if (btnDance.Text == "Dance") {
        timer1.Enabled = true;
        btnDance.Text = "Stop";
    }
```

```
    else {
       timer1.Enabled = false;
       btnDance.Text = "Dance";
    }
  }

  private void timer1_Tick(object sender, System.EventArgs e) {
     int xIncrement = 5; int yIncrement = 5;
     foreach (Control c in this.Controls) {
        if (c.Location.X > this.Size.Width - 30) {
           xIncrement = -500;
        }
        if (c.Location.Y > this.Size.Height - 50) {
           yIncrement = -500;
        }
        if (c.Location.X <= 0) {
           xIncrement = 5;
        }
        if (c.Location.Y <= 0) {
           yIncrement = 10;
        }
        c.Location = new Point(c.Location.X + xIncrement,
           c.Location.Y + yIncrement);
     }
  }
```

ListBoxes Listing

Moving on, ListBoxes in their various varieties provide a visual mechanism for dealing with collections of items. As such, they are an important part of many user interfaces. (For more information about programming the collections of items that lie underneath the ListBox classes, see Chapter 7, "Array, Indexers, and Collections.")

The three ListBox controls you'll find on the Toolbox—all inheriting from `System` `.Windows.Forms.ListControl`—are ComboBox, ListBox, and CheckedListBox. These controls are all far more alike than they are unalike. The ComboBox combines an editing field with the list of items in a ListBox, which allows the user to select an item from the list or to enter a new item. The CheckedListBox is just like a ListBox, except that it includes a `Checked` property. In addition, CheckedListBoxes do not support multiple selection. (To enable multiple selection with a ListBox, set its `SelectionMode` property to `MultiSimple` or `MultiExtended`.)

The example in this section primarily works with CheckedListBoxes, because those checks are so much fun, but you could substitute ComboBoxes or ListBoxes without changing very much.

Adding an Item

The Add method of the CheckedListBox's Item collection will add an item at the bottom of the CheckedListBox, as shown in Figure 4.2:

```
private void btnAdd_Click(object sender, System.EventArgs e) {
    checkedListBox1.Items.Add(txtAdd.Text);
}
```

FIGURE 4.2:

It's easy to add items to a ListBox.

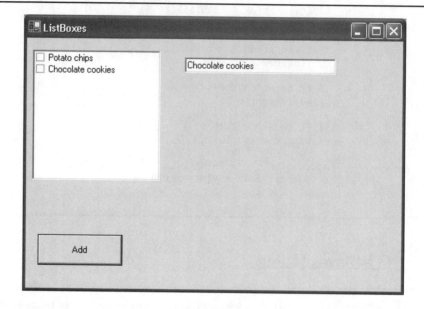

Adding an Array

The Items.AddRange method allows you to add an array of items to the Items collection of a ListBox. Here's code to generate an array of items (Item # 1 ... Item # n) and add them to a ListBox. Both the specific control and the number of items are passed in to the procedure:

```
private void AddToList(ListBox lb, int size) {
    string[] myarray = new string [size];
    for (int i = 0; i < size; i++) {
        myarray[i] = "Item # " + (i+1).ToString();
    }
    lb.Items.AddRange(myarray);
}
```

You can invoke this method with a specific control and the number of elements you want to add, with the results shown in Figure 4.3:

```
private void btnAddArray_Click(object sender, System.EventArgs e) {
    AddToList(checkedListBox1, 10);
}
```

FIGURE 4.3:

You can add an array of items to a ListBox in a single statement.

Positioning by Index

We've already added an item to the bottom of the items collection using `Items.Add`. Alternatively, you can position an item in CheckedListBox's items collection using the `Items.Insert` method.

> **TIP**   Remember that the `Items` collection is zero based, so that the first item in it has an index of zero, and the last item has an index of `Items.Count - 1`.

You could use the `Items.Insert` method to position an item in the specified place as shown in Figure 4.4 (the first argument is the index position, the second is the text to add):

```
checkedListBox1.Items.Insert(Convert.ToInt16(txtIndex.Text), txtAdd.Text);
```

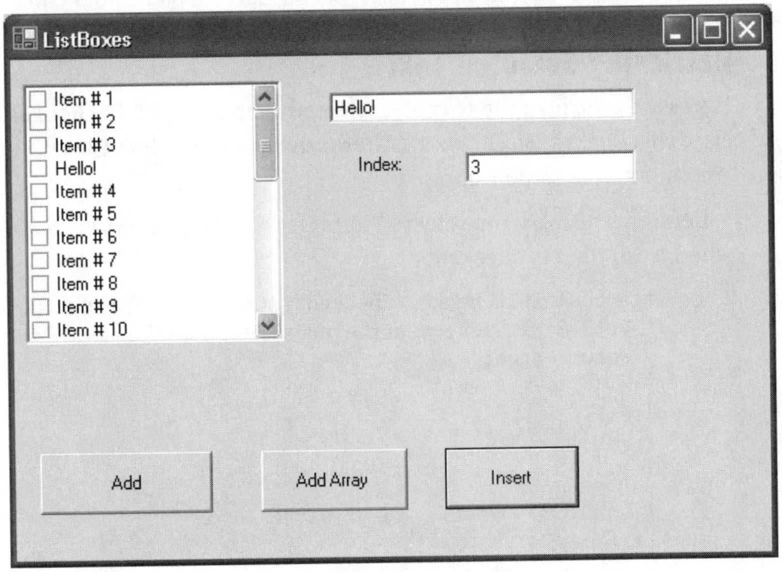

FIGURE 4.4:

You can insert an item anywhere you'd like using an index value.

It's probably a good idea, and easy enough, to check that the insertion is within the range of the items in the collection:

```
private void btnInsert_Click(object sender, System.EventArgs e) {
    if ((Convert.ToInt16(txtIndex.Text) >= 0) &&
        (Convert.ToInt16(txtIndex.Text) <= checkedListBox1.Items.Count)) {
            checkedListBox1.Items.Insert(Convert.ToInt16(txtIndex.Text),
                txtAdd.Text);
    }
    else {
        MessageBox.Show("Out of Range", "Please try again",
            MessageBoxButtons.OK, MessageBoxIcon.Exclamation);
    }
}
```

This way, if the user attempts to enter an index that is out of range, you can display an appropriate message.

Retrieving Selected Text

It's easy to retrieve the text of a selected item from a CheckedListBox by using its Text property, checkedListBox1.Text. (Alternatively, checkedListBox1.SelectedItem.ToString() amounts to the same thing.)

Before we display the selected item, let's write a function that determines, by item index, whether an item is checked:

```
private bool IsItChecked(CheckedListBox clb, int theIndex) {
    if (clb.GetItemChecked(theIndex) == true){
        return true;
    }
    else {
        return false;
    }
}
```

First, we also need to make sure that an item is actually selected by testing the checkedListBox1
.Text property. Assuming that there is an item selected, we can display it (Figure 4.5) and
display whether it is checked:

```
private void btnSelect_Click(object sender, System.EventArgs e) {
    if (checkedListBox1.Text != ""){
        MessageBox.Show("Selected Item Text: " +
            // checkedListBox1.SelectedItem.ToString(),
            checkedListBox1.Text, "Here is your text", MessageBoxButtons.OK,
            MessageBoxIcon.Information);
        if (IsItChecked(checkedListBox1, checkedListBox1.SelectedIndex)) {
            MessageBox.Show("Checked");
        }
        else {
            MessageBox.Show("Unchecked");
        }
    }
    else {
        MessageBox.Show("Nothing selected!","No text today",
            MessageBoxButtons.OK, MessageBoxIcon.Information);
    }
}
```

FIGURE 4.5:

It's easy to retrieve
selected text.

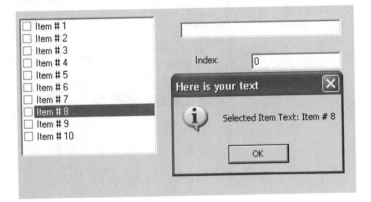

Retrieving by Index

You can also retrieve the text of an item by using its index in the Items collection. For example:

```
private void btnRetrieve_Click(object sender, System.EventArgs e) {
    MessageBox.Show
        (checkedListBox1.Items [Convert.ToInt16(txtIndex.Text)].ToString(),
        "Here is your text", MessageBoxButtons.OK, MessageBoxIcon.Information);
    if (IsItChecked(checkedListBox1, Convert.ToInt16(txtIndex.Text))) {
        MessageBox.Show("Checked");
    }
```

```
        else {
            MessageBox.Show("Unchecked");
        }
    }
```

Retrieving Multiple Checked Items

Sometimes you'd like to get all the checked items in one list (such as a CheckedListBox) and read them into another CheckedListBox. You can do this by iterating through the Items collection of the first CheckedListBox. Each time a checked item is found, the item is added to the new CheckedListBox (and marked checked):

```
private void btnGetChecked_Click(object sender, System.EventArgs e) {
    for (int i = 0; i < checkedListBox1.Items.Count; i++){
        if (IsItChecked(checkedListBox1,i)) {
            clb2.Items.Add(checkedListBox1.Items[i],CheckState.Checked);
        }
    }
}
```

When the iteration is complete, the checked items have been added to the new box (Figure 4.6).

FIGURE 4.6:

You can loop through the
CheckedListBox to retrieve
all checked items.

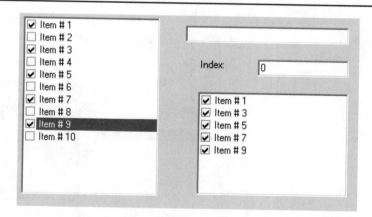

This procedure uses the IsItChecked function, which you'll recall I first showed you in the section on retrieving text. Here it is again:

```
private bool IsItChecked(CheckedListBox clb, int theIndex) {
    if (clb.GetItemChecked(theIndex) == true){
        return true;
    }
    else {
        return false;
    }
}
```

Clearing an Item

It's easy to delete a collection of items using the Clear method. For example, to delete the items in a pair of CheckedListBoxes and a ListBox:

```
private void btnClear_Click(object sender, System.EventArgs e) {
    checkedListBox1.Items.Clear();
    clb2.Items.Clear();
    listBox1.Items.Clear();
}
```

Deleting Items

You can delete an individual item from a CheckedListBox if it is selected using the Remove method of the Items collection:

```
checkedListBox1.Items.Remove(checkedListBox1.SelectedItem);
```

Similarly, if you know the text of the item you want to delete:

```
checkedListBox1.Items.Remove(txtAdd.Text);
```

On the other hand, if you want to delete an item from the items collection by position (index), the RemoveAt method is used. This code checks to see that a given index is within the count of the items collection and, if it is, deletes the corresponding item:

```
if ((Convert.ToInt16(txtIndex.Text) >= 0) &&
    (Convert.ToInt16(txtIndex.Text) <= checkedListBox1.Items.Count)) {
    checkedListBox1.Items.RemoveAt(Convert.ToInt16(txtIndex.Text));
}
```

Retrieving Multiple Selections

Retrieving multiple selections from a ListBox works in the same way as retrieving multiple checked items from a CheckedListBox (see "Retrieving Multiple Checked Items" earlier in this chapter).

First, we'll need to add a ListBox to the project and set its SelectionMode property to MultiSimple. We can populate it, using the same procedure used to populate the CheckedListBox:

```
private void btnPopulateLB_Click(object sender, System.EventArgs e) {
    AddToList(listBox1,30);
}
```

In case you don't remember, here's the AddToList method:

```
private void AddToList(ListBox lb, int size) {
    string[] myarray = new string [size];
    for (int i = 0; i < size; i++) {
        myarray[i] = "Item # " + (i+1).ToString();
    }
    lb.Items.AddRange(myarray);
}
```

Finally, we can iterate through the ListBox, adding items to a "results" CheckedListBox for each selected item in the ListBox:

```
private void btnGetSelect_Click(object sender, System.EventArgs e) {
    for (int i = 0; i < listBox1.SelectedItems.Count; i++){
        clb2.Items.Add(listBox1.SelectedItems[i]);
    }
}
```

If you save the project, run it, populate the ListBox, select some items, and click the Get Selected button, the selected items will be displayed in the new CheckedListBox (Figure 4.7).

FIGURE 4.7:

You can have lots of fun with ListBoxes (retrieving all selected items shown).

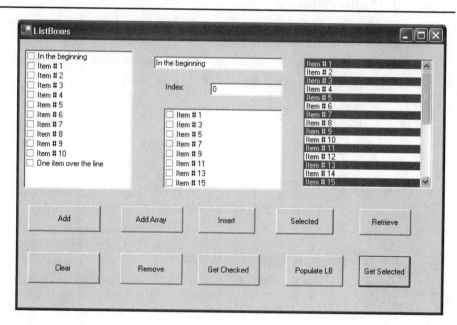

I'm sure you'll agree that ListBoxes, CheckedListBoxes, and their respective Items collections are lots of fun—and very useful. The ListBox operations performed in this section are shown in Listing 4.2.

Listing 4.2   **Fun and Games with CheckedListBoxes (ListBox Operations)**

```
private void btnAdd_Click(object sender, System.EventArgs e) {
    checkedListBox1.Items.Add(txtAdd.Text);
}
private void btnAddArray_Click(object sender, System.EventArgs e) {
    AddToList(checkedListBox1, 10);
}
```

```
private void AddToList(ListBox lb, int size) {
    string[] myarray = new string [size];
    for (int i = 0; i < size; i++) {
        myarray[i] = "Item # " + (i+1).ToString();
    }
    lb.Items.AddRange(myarray);
}
private void btnInsert_Click(object sender, System.EventArgs e) {
    if ((Convert.ToInt16(txtIndex.Text) >= 0) &&
        (Convert.ToInt16(txtIndex.Text) <= checkedListBox1.Items.Count)) {
        checkedListBox1.Items.Insert(Convert.ToInt16(txtIndex.Text),
            txtAdd.Text);
    }
    else {
        MessageBox.Show("Out of Range", "Please try again",
            MessageBoxButtons.OK, MessageBoxIcon.Exclamation);
    }
}
private void btnSelect_Click(object sender, System.EventArgs e) {
    if (checkedListBox1.Text != ""){
        MessageBox.Show("Selected Item Text: " +
            // checkedListBox1.SelectedItem.ToString(),
            checkedListBox1.Text, "Here is your text", MessageBoxButtons.OK,
                MessageBoxIcon.Information);
        if (IsItChecked(checkedListBox1, checkedListBox1.SelectedIndex)) {
            MessageBox.Show("Checked");
        }
        else {
            MessageBox.Show("Unchecked");
        }
    }
    else {
        MessageBox.Show("Nothing selected!", "No text today",
            MessageBoxButtons.OK, MessageBoxIcon.Information);
    }
}
private void btnRetrieve_Click(object sender, System.EventArgs e) {
    MessageBox.Show
        (checkedListBox1.Items[Convert.ToInt16(txtIndex.Text)].ToString(),
        "Here is your text", MessageBoxButtons.OK, MessageBoxIcon.Information);
    if (IsItChecked(checkedListBox1, Convert.ToInt16(txtIndex.Text))) {
        MessageBox.Show("Checked");
    }
    else {
        MessageBox.Show("Unchecked");
    }
}
private bool IsItChecked(CheckedListBox clb, int theIndex) {
    if (clb.GetItemChecked(theIndex) == true){
        return true;
    }
```

```
        else {
            return false;
        }
    }
    private void btnClear_Click(object sender, System.EventArgs e) {
        checkedListBox1.Items.Clear();
        clb2.Items.Clear();
        listBox1.Items.Clear();
    }
    private void btnRemove_Click(object sender, System.EventArgs e) {
    // by index
    //    if ((Convert.ToInt16(txtIndex.Text) >= 0) &&
    //        (Convert.ToInt16(txtIndex.Text) <= checkedListBox1.Items.Count)) {
    //        checkedListBox1.Items.RemoveAt(Convert.ToInt16(txtIndex.Text));
    //    }
    // selected
    //    checkedListBox1.Items.Remove(checkedListBox1.SelectedItem);

    // by text
        checkedListBox1.Items.Remove(txtAdd.Text);
    }
    private void btnGetChecked_Click(object sender, System.EventArgs e) {
        for (int i = 0; i < checkedListBox1.Items.Count; i++){
            if (IsItChecked(checkedListBox1,i)) {
                clb2.Items.Add(checkedListBox1.Items[i],CheckState.Checked);
            }
        }
    }
    private void btnPopulateLB_Click(object sender, System.EventArgs e) {
        AddToList(listBox1,30);
    }
    private void btnGetSelect_Click(object sender, System.EventArgs e) {
        for (int i = 0; i < listBox1.SelectedItems.Count; i++){
            clb2.Items.Add(listBox1.SelectedItems[i]);
        }
    }
}
```

Menus

If ever a user interface cried to heaven, "Give me menus," it is the one shown in Figure 4.7 with its 10 clunky buttons. So let's put this user interface out of its misery, and give it a menu already!

To create a menu visually, using the tools supplied by Visual Studio, drag a MainMenu control to your form. Like the Timer, the instance of the control added to the form appears on the tray beneath the form.

With the MainMenu control sitting on the tray, you can go ahead and add menus—that is, the high-level menu items across the top of the form—and menu items, which are the items beneath each menu, by entering the appropriate information in position (Figure 4.8).

FIGURE 4.8:

When you add a MainMenu control to the tray, you can edit the menu visually (shown here in Edit Names mode).

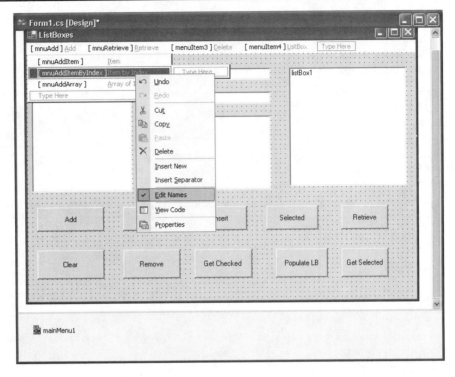

By right-clicking and selecting Edit Names from the context menu, the menu insertion is performed in Edit Names mode, which allows you to edit in place the internal names of the menu items you are adding.

Let's use the visual interface to add some menus and menu items, and then check out the auto-generated menu code that Visual Studio has created on our behalf. The application will have four menus running along the top of the form: Add, Retrieve, Delete, and ListBox.

To keep things simple, I'll just look at the first menu, the Add menu, which as you can see in Figure 4.8 is in the normal place of a File menu. The menu item names and text are as shown in Table 4.1 (with access keys ignored).

TABLE 4.1: Add (*mnuAdd*) Menu Items Names and Text

Menu Item Name	Text
mnuAdd (parent menu)	Add
mnuAddItem	Item
mnuAddItembyIndex	Item by Index
mnuAddArray	Array of Items

In keeping with the RAD "look, Ma, no code" theme of the menu designer, you should note that the Events tab of the Properties window can be used to assign menu item click events to button click event handlers (Figure 4.9). This means that no new code needs to be written to make these menus functional: mnuAdd's click event handler is assigned to the (already existing) handler for btnAdd's click event, and so on.

Menu item events can be assigned an existing handler using the Events tab of the Properties window.

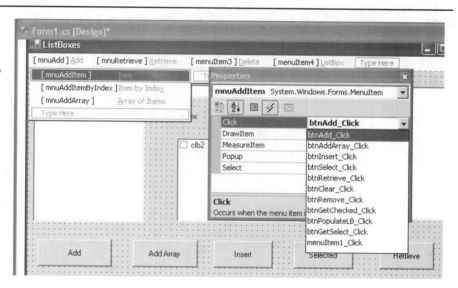

The Auto-Generated Menu Code

What code has been created for us to implement the menus we've visually added? To start with, a variable of type MainMenu has been declared, along with MenuItem variables for each of the menus and menu items:

```
private System.Windows.Forms.MainMenu mainMenu1;
private System.Windows.Forms.MenuItem mnuAdd;
private System.Windows.Forms.MenuItem mnuAddItem;
...
```

NOTE   Most of the action takes place within the "hidden" region of Windows Form Designer–generated code, so you will have to expand the region to view the action.

Next, the MainMenu and each of the MenuItems are instantiated:

```
this.mainMenu1 = new System.Windows.Forms.MainMenu();
this.mnuAdd = new System.Windows.Forms.MenuItem();
this.mnuAddItem = new System.Windows.Forms.MenuItem();
...
```

Next, the main menu collection of menu items is created, using the collection's `AddRange` method to add the four top-level menu items (Add, Delete, Retrieve, and ListBox):

```
this.mainMenu1.MenuItems.AddRange(new System.Windows.Forms.MenuItem[] {
    this.mnuAdd,
    this.mnuRetrieve,
    this.mnuDelete,
    this.mnuListBox});
```

As promised, we'll look at `mnuAdd` only, ignoring the other three menus. Here's the code that positions `mnuAdd` as the first top-level menu and uses the `AddRange` method of *its* menu items collection to add its contents:

```
this.mnuAdd.Index = 0;
this.mnuAdd.MenuItems.AddRange(new System.Windows.Forms.MenuItem[] {
    this.mnuAddItem,
    this.mnuAddItemByIndex,
    this.mnuAddArray});
```

Finally, each menu item *below* `mnuAdd` is given a position by `Index` in `mnuAdd`'s collection, and its properties (e.g., text and event handlers) fleshed out:

```
this.mnuAddItem.Index = 0;
this.mnuAddItem.Text = "&Item";
this.mnuAddItem.Click += new System.EventHandler(this.btnAdd_Click);
```

As a last, but not least, required step, the whole menu construction is then assigned to the Menu property of the form:

```
this.Menu = this.mainMenu1;
```

Listing 4.3 shows the relevant portions of the auto-generated menu code.

Listing 4.3   Auto-Generated Menu Code (Excerpted)

```
public class Form1 : System.Windows.Forms.Form
{
...

    private System.Windows.Forms.MainMenu mainMenu1;
    private System.Windows.Forms.MenuItem mnuAdd;
    private System.Windows.Forms.MenuItem mnuAddItem;
    ...

    // within Initialize Component, called by Form1 constructor
    this.mainMenu1 = new System.Windows.Forms.MainMenu();
    this.mnuAdd = new System.Windows.Forms.MenuItem();
    this.mnuAddItem = new System.Windows.Forms.MenuItem();
    ...
//
```

```
// mainMenu1
//
this.mainMenu1.MenuItems.AddRange(new System.Windows.Forms.MenuItem[] {
    this.mnuAdd,
    this.mnuRetrieve,
    this.mnuDelete,
    this.mnuListBox});
//
// mnuAdd
//
this.mnuAdd.Index = 0;
this.mnuAdd.MenuItems.AddRange(new System.Windows.Forms.MenuItem[] {
    this.mnuAddItem,
    this.mnuAddItemByIndex,
    this.mnuAddArray});
//
// mnuAddItem
//
this.mnuAddItem.Index = 0;
this.mnuAddItem.Text = "&Item";
this.mnuAddItem.Click += new System.EventHandler(this.btnAdd_Click);
...

    this.Menu = this.mainMenu1;

...
}
```

Analyzing what the auto-generation does, the general process is:

- Declare and instantiate a MainMenu and MenuItems for each menu item.

- Use the AddRange method of the MainMenu's menu item collection to add the top-level menus.

- For each top-level menu, position it in the collection using the Index property, and then use its collection's AddRange to add its own menu items.

- For each menu item, use the collection Index property to assign a location on the menu, and assign properties such as text and handlers.

- Assign the whole menu structure to the Menu property of the form.

Based on this, it certainly looks like we could pretty easily construct a menu ourselves in code doing at least as well as the auto-generated one. Ultimately, depending on your preferences, you may find it less work to construct menus in code yourself rather than relying on Visual Studio for auto-generation.

Let's construct a menu in code for a completely new application that will use a RichTextBox control and the common dialog wrappers to build a Notepad-like application. Table 4.2 shows the menus that we need.

TABLE 4.2: "Notepad" Application Menus

File	Edit	Format
Open (mnuFileOpen)	Cut (mnuEditCut)	Font (mnuFormatFont)
Save (mnuFileSave)	Copy (mnuEditCopy)	Color (mnuFormatColor)
- (separator)	Paste (mnuEditPaste)	
Exit (mnuFileExit)		

First, within the form's constructor, instantiate a MainMenu object and assign it to the form's Menu property:

```
Menu = new MainMenu();
```

The above statement is equivalent to this.Menu = new MainMenu();. In other words, the omitted this is implied.

Next, declare and instantiate a File menu item, and add it to the main menu's MenuItems collection:

```
MenuItem mnu = new MenuItem("&File");
Menu.MenuItems.Add(mnu);
```

The File menu will be referred to as Menu.MenuItems[0]. Now, go ahead and add the items to the File menu's menu items collection, starting with the Open menu item:

```
MenuItem mnuFileOpen = new MenuItem("&Open");
mnuFileOpen.Click += new EventHandler(mnuFileOpen_Click);
mnuFileOpen.Shortcut = Shortcut.CtrlO;
Menu.MenuItems[0].MenuItems.Add(mnuFileOpen);
```

In this code, a new menu item, mnuFileOpen, is declared and instantiated. A click handler is assigned to it, so you have to create the framework for the event handler:

```
void mnuFileOpen_Click(object sender, EventArgs e){

}
```

A shortcut key is also assigned to mnuFileOpen. Finally, the Add method for the File menu collection of items is used to add the item (so, effectively, mnuFileOpen is Menu.MenuItems[0] .MenuItems[0]). The key concept is that a MenuItems collection can itself contain a MenuItems collection!

Listing 4.4 shows the completely fleshed-out menu. As you can see in Figure 4.10, this is a fully functional menu, up to all factory specifications. The code shown in Listing 4.4 could, perhaps, be improved by substituting variables for the hard-coded index values. This would create the ability to be easily flexible about menu order in the future.

FIGURE 4.10:
You can easily create fully
functional menus in code.

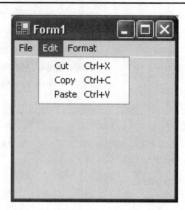

A menu is probably easier to maintain if you create it in code this way than if you auto-generate it. However, the choice is yours; at the least, you should be aware of what the menu designer is doing "under the hood" in case you need to tweak it.

Listing 4.4   **Coding a Menu by Hand**

```
// Form1 constructor
public Form1()
{
    InitializeComponent();

    // Add Menus
    Menu = new MainMenu();

    // File menu
    MenuItem mnu = new MenuItem("&File");
    Menu.MenuItems.Add(mnu);

    // File Open
    MenuItem mnuFileOpen = new MenuItem("&Open");
    mnuFileOpen.Click += new EventHandler(mnuFileOpen_Click);
    mnuFileOpen.Shortcut = Shortcut.CtrlO;
    Menu.MenuItems[0].MenuItems.Add(mnuFileOpen);

    // File Save
    MenuItem mnuFileSave = new MenuItem("&Save");
    mnuFileSave.Click += new EventHandler(mnuFileSave_Click);
    mnuFileSave.Shortcut = Shortcut.CtrlS;
    Menu.MenuItems[0].MenuItems.Add(mnuFileSave);
```

```
    // separator
    mnu = new MenuItem("-");
    Menu.MenuItems[0].MenuItems.Add(mnu);

    // File Exit
    MenuItem mnuFileExit = new MenuItem("E&xit");
    mnuFileExit.Click += new EventHandler(mnuFileExit_Click);
    mnuFileExit.Shortcut = Shortcut.AltF4;
    Menu.MenuItems[0].MenuItems.Add(mnuFileExit);

    // Edit
    mnu = new MenuItem("&Edit");
    Menu.MenuItems.Add(mnu);

    // Edit Cut
    MenuItem mnuEditCut = new MenuItem("Cu&t");
    mnuEditCut.Click += new EventHandler(mnuEditCut_Click);
    mnuEditCut.Shortcut = Shortcut.CtrlX;
    Menu.MenuItems[1].MenuItems.Add(mnuEditCut);

    // Edit Copy
    MenuItem mnuEditCopy = new MenuItem("&Copy");
    mnuEditCopy.Click += new EventHandler(mnuEditCopy_Click);
    mnuEditCopy.Shortcut = Shortcut.CtrlC;
    Menu.MenuItems[1].MenuItems.Add(mnuEditCopy);

    // Edit Paste
    MenuItem mnuEditPaste = new MenuItem("&Paste");
    mnuEditPaste.Click += new EventHandler(mnuEditPaste_Click);
    mnuEditPaste.Shortcut = Shortcut.CtrlV;
    Menu.MenuItems[1].MenuItems.Add(mnuEditPaste);

    // Format
    mnu = new MenuItem("&Format");
    Menu.MenuItems.Add(mnu);

    // Format Font
    MenuItem mnuFormatFont = new MenuItem("&Font");
    mnuFormatFont.Click += new EventHandler(mnuFormatFont_Click);
    mnuFormatFont.Shortcut = Shortcut.CtrlF;
    Menu.MenuItems[2].MenuItems.Add(mnuFormatFont);

    // Format Color
    MenuItem mnuFormatColor = new MenuItem("&Color");
    mnuFormatColor.Click += new EventHandler(mnuFormatColor_Click);
    mnuFormatColor.Shortcut = Shortcut.CtrlShiftC;
    Menu.MenuItems[2].MenuItems.Add(mnuFormatColor);

}
...
void mnuFileOpen_Click(object sender, EventArgs e){
}
```

```
void mnuFileSave_Click(object sender, EventArgs e){
}
void mnuFileExit_Click(object sender, EventArgs e){
}
void mnuEditCut_Click(object sender, EventArgs e){
}
void mnuEditCopy_Click(object sender, EventArgs e){
}
void mnuEditPaste_Click(object sender, EventArgs e){
}
void mnuFormatFont_Click(object sender, EventArgs e){
}
void mnuFormatColor_Click(object sender, EventArgs e){
}
...
```

Doing the Common Dialog Thing

Now that we have a menu, created in code, let's build an application around the menu. This will be a Notepad-like application that allows users to: open and save rich text files; cut, copy, and paste selected text to and from the clipboard; and change the color and font characteristics of selected text. The primary user interface will be provided by a RichTextBox control. Common dialog controls will provide users a way to make choices.

Common dialog controls provide a "wrapper" for dialogs that perform commonly needed tasks, which means that they provide easy access to the functionality of standard Windows dialog boxes. For example, the SaveFileDialog control displays the standard Save As dialog for naming and locating a file to be saved—the same dialog box you see in Microsoft Word and other applications.

By using the .NET common dialog controls to display these dialog boxes, the appearance of your applications becomes standardized. Users see dialog boxes that they recognize and already know how to use.

However, although the common dialog controls show dialog boxes allowing the user to make choices, they don't actually do the work. For example, the SaveFileDialog control doesn't save the contents of a file after the user chooses to save a file. We'll use the methods of the RichTextBox control to do the actual work of changing the characteristics of selected text, working with the Clipboard, and saving and opening files. It's very easy to implement functionality using the methods of the RichTextBox, so that we can concentrate on the common dialogs. But you will need to know how to work directly with files (see Chapter 10, "Working with Streams and Files"). You should also know that the Clipboard can alternatively be programmed using the members of the Clipboard class.

To get the ball rolling, in the same project with the hand-created menu, add a RichTextBox control. Name it rtb and clear its Text property. Set its Dock property to Fill, meaning it will take up the entire client area of the form and change size with the form.

Next, add ColorDialog, FontDialog, OpenFileDialog, and SaveFileDialog controls to the form (these are the common dialog controls the project will implement). Each control appears on the tray beneath the form (Figure 4.11).

FIGURE 4.11:

The form in design mode with common dialog controls in the tray.

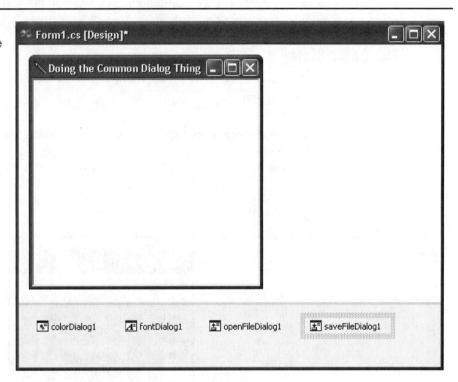

Implementing an Edit Menu

Next, use the methods of the RichTextBox to implement the items on the Edit menu—cut, copy, and paste—as shown in Listing 4.5.

Listing 4.5   An Edit Menu

```
void mnuEditCut_Click(object sender, EventArgs e){
    rtb.Cut();
}
void mnuEditCopy_Click(object sender, EventArgs e){
    rtb.Copy();
}
```

```
void mnuEditPaste_Click(object sender, EventArgs e){
    rtb.Paste();
}
```

These editing methods are inherited by the RichTextBox class from the TextBoxBase class, which implements the core feature set of text-manipulation controls—so, for example, Text-Boxes share most of the same functionality, also via inheritance from TextBoxBase. You'll find that the TextBoxBase class has other useful methods that could be used to extend an Edit menu—for example, Redo and Undo methods.

The Color Dialog

Within the click handler for the Color menu item, configure the Color dialog:

```
colorDialog1.AllowFullOpen = true;
colorDialog1.AnyColor = true;
```

By setting the AllowFullOpen property of the ColorDialog control to true, the user can use the Color dialog to define custom colors. If the AnyColor property is set to true, the dialog displays all available colors; if not, only solid colors—those with 100% opacity—are selectable.

Next, display the dialog (see Figure 4.12):

```
colorDialog1.ShowDialog();
```

FIGURE 4.12:

The Color common dialog is used to set the color of the selected text.

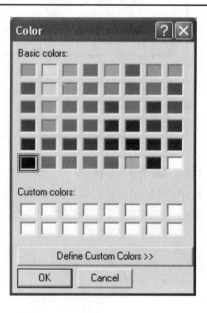

Finally, set the selected text to the color chosen in the dialog:

```
rtb.SelectionColor = colorDialog1.Color;
```

Note that you might want to store the user selection of color, perhaps to reapply it later to some text. To do this, you could use a variable to capture the user's selection, for example:

```
Color theColor = colorDialog1.Color;
```

The Font Dialog

The Font dialog works in much the same way as the Color dialog. If you'd like, you can set its characteristics in advance of invoking it, or you can just use the default, as in the example:

```
void mnuFormatFont_Click(object sender, EventArgs e){
    fontDialog1.ShowDialog();
    rtb.SelectionFont = fontDialog1.Font;
}
```

When the user selects some text and chooses the Font menu item, the Font dialog is displayed (Figure 4.13). Font choices made in the dialog are applied to the selected text, as in Figure 4.14.

FIGURE 4.13:

The Font common dialog is used to set the font and related attributes of the selected text.

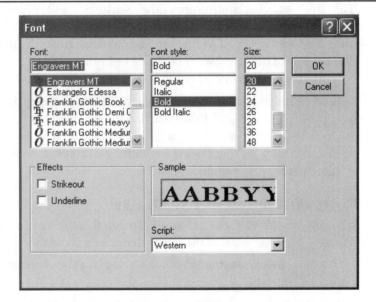

FIGURE 4.14:

Changes to the text formatting are displayed in the RichTextBox.

The Save As and Open Dialogs

The SaveFileDialog control allows the user to pick a file name and location for saving a file via the standard Save As dialog. The OpenFileDialog control lets the user select a file for opening using the Open dialog. To say it once again: designating the file is all these dialogs do; they don't do any of the actual work of saving or loading. We'll let the RichTextBox do the lifting here; for more general information about working with files, see Chapter 10.

As a first order of business, we'll save the contents of the RichTextBox and then retrieve its contents, formatting and all. Note that the functionality for saving the rich text contents is implemented before the functionality for opening it. It's generally easier to do things in this order rather than looking around for an RTF file (and, even when you find one, you can't be absolutely sure what it should look like).

Saving the Contents of a RichTextBox

It's really very easy to use the SaveFileDialog to implement saving the contents of the Rich-TextBox. First, set some of the initial characteristics of the Save As dialog.

```
openFileDialog1.InitialDirectory = Application.ExecutablePath;
```

This sets the initial directory to the application's executable path (in the case of a C# application running in the development environment, this is the \bin\Debug directory that stores the application's EXE file). Next, set the initial file name to Harold.rtf (a name, other than the suffix, that is dear to my heart!).

```
SaveFileDialog1.DefaultExt = "rtf";
SaveFileDialog1.FileName = "Harold";
```

Finally, set a filter to determine the choices that are available to the user in the Save As Type drop-down list.

```
saveFileDialog1.Filter =
    "Rich Text Files (*.rtf) | *.rtf|All files (*.*) | *.*";
```

The `Filter` property is a text string delimited by the pipe character (|). Each item consists of a description, followed by a pipe, followed by the file suffix, usually using wildcard characters. Another pipe is used to start the next item.

In the example above, the following is one item:

```
Rich Text Files (*.rtf) | *.rtf
```

It is the description followed by the specification, namely `*.rtf`.

And here's another item:

```
All Files (*.*) | *.*
```

This has the specification, `*.*`, displaying files of all types.

> **WARNING** Be careful not to include extra spaces between the end of one item and the beginning of the next. Otherwise, the filter may not work properly.

Next, show the dialog:

```
SaveFileDialog1.ShowDialog();
```

The contents of the RichTextBox are saved using its `SaveFile` method, with the file name selected by the user as its argument:

```
rtb.SaveFile(SaveFileDialog1.FileName);
```

To see that this works, run the program and enter some heavily formatted text in the RichTextBox.

Next, choose File ➤ Save. The Save As dialog will open, suggesting a file name, type, and location—`Harold.rtf` in the `\bin\Debug` directory.

> **WARNING** Unless you set the `OverwritePrompt` property of the SaveFileDialog to `true` (either in code or the Properties window), the user can pick an existing file, possibly resulting in overwriting its contents. Setting `OverwritePrompt` to `true` causes a message with a warning to appear but allows the user to proceed if they still want to.

Accept the file name, type, and location suggestions. Click Save. A file with the rich text contents will be created at the indicated location. To verify this, you can locate the file and open it in Microsoft Word.

Retrieving Rich Text from a File

The next step is to create the code that will load rich text into the RichTextBox in the application. To do this, we will display an Open dialog using the OpenFileDialog control.

Initializing the OpenFileDialog works in the same way as initializing the SaveFileDialog:

```
openFileDialog1.InitialDirectory = Application.ExecutablePath;
openFileDialog1.DefaultExt = "rtf";
openFileDialog1.FileName = "Harold";
openFileDialog1.Filter =
    "Rich Text Files (*.rtf) | *.rtf|All files (*.*) | *.*";
```

NOTE   As you probably know, the Filter property works the same way in the OpenFileDialog and the SaveFileDialog.

With the OpenFileDialog's properties set, we then need to show the dialog and use the LoadFile method of the RichTextBox to load the contents of the file selected by the user into the control:

```
OpenFileDialog1.ShowDialog();
rtb.LoadFile(OpenFileDialog1.FileName);
```

When the user selects File ➢ Open from the menu, the Open dialog will allow a choice of a file (Figure 4.15). When a file is selected and the Open button clicked, the file is loaded into the RichTextBox.

FIGURE 4.15:

The contents of the RichTextBox can be saved and then opened.

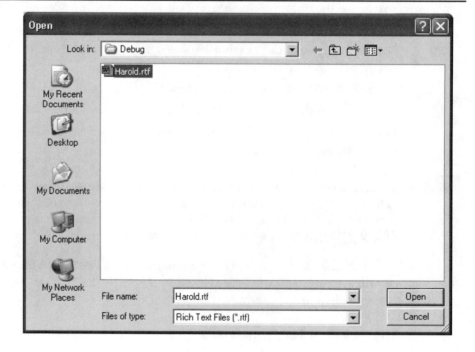

The complete code for opening and saving Rich Text files, and for setting the selected text color and font, is shown in Listing 4.6.

Listing 4.6   **Opening, Saving, and Setting Font and Color with the Common Dialogs**

```
void mnuFileOpen_Click(object sender, EventArgs e){
   openFileDialog1.InitialDirectory = Application.ExecutablePath;
   openFileDialog1.DefaultExt = "rtf";
   openFileDialog1.FileName = "Harold";
   openFileDialog1.Filter =
      "Rich Text Files (*.rtf) | *.rtf|All files (*.*) | *.*";
   openFileDialog1.ShowDialog();
   rtb.LoadFile(openFileDialog1.FileName);
}

void mnuFileSave_Click(object sender, EventArgs e){
   saveFileDialog1.InitialDirectory = Application.ExecutablePath;
   saveFileDialog1.DefaultExt = "rtf";
   saveFileDialog1.FileName = "Harold";
   saveFileDialog1.Filter =
      "Rich Text Files (*.rtf) | *.rtf|All files (*.*) | *.*";
   saveFileDialog1.ShowDialog();
   rtb.SaveFile(saveFileDialog1.FileName);
}

void mnuFormatFont_Click(object sender, EventArgs e){
   fontDialog1.ShowDialog();
   rtb.SelectionFont = fontDialog1.Font;
}

void mnuFormatColor_Click(object sender, EventArgs e){
   colorDialog1.AllowFullOpen = true;
   colorDialog1.AnyColor = true;
   colorDialog1.ShowDialog();
   // Color theColor = colorDialog1.Color;
   rtb.SelectionColor = colorDialog1.Color;
}
```

MDI Applications

In Multiple Document Interface (MDI) applications, there is one MDI form, or *parent form*. There are usually many MDI *child forms*. There can be more than one type of MDI child form, but all children, whatever their type, must fit into the client space of the parent MDI window.

It is perhaps the case that MDI applications are no longer very stylish. The thinking is that it probably makes just as much sense to open multiple copies of a single application as to have one application with multiple client windows. Be that as it may, it's easy to rig MDI applications in .NET—and you should know how.

As an example of how to "wire" an MDI application, let's turn the Notepad applet created in the last section into the child form of an MDI application.

The first step is to add a new form (to serve as the parent) to the project. Choose Project ➤ Add Windows Form to open the Add New Item dialog (Figure 4.16).

FIGURE 4.16:

The Add New Item dialog is used to add a "parent" form to a project.

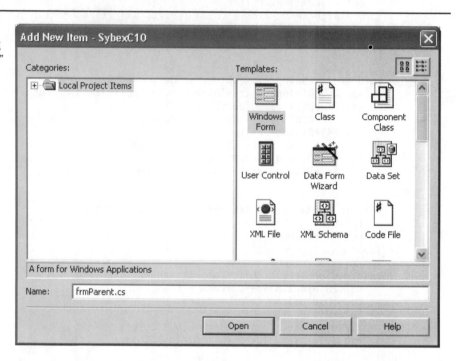

In the Add New Item dialog, make sure Windows Form is selected, name the form frmParent.cs, and click Open. The new parent form will be added to the project.

Open frmParent in its designer. Add a panel to the bottom of the form, and a button, btnShowChild, to the right side of the panel (the bottom-right of the form). Use the Properties window to set the Anchor property of btnShowChild to Bottom, Right.

Next, use the Properties window to set the IsMDIContainer property of frmParent to true (Figure 4.17).

FIGURE 4.17:

Setting the form's
IsMDIContainer to true
means that it can become
a parent.

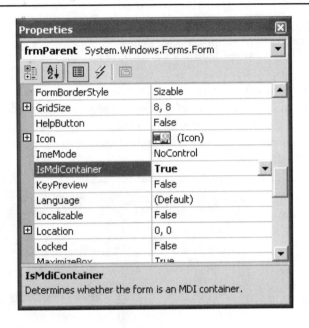

When you set IsMDIContainer to true, you'll note that the client area of frmParent shifts in color, becoming a darker shade of gray.

Setting the Startup Object

The next step in helping frmParent to become a parent is re-jiggering the application to let it start from frmParent. In order for a form to be a Startup Object, it needs a Main method. Because the original form in the project, Form1, the basis for the Notepad applet, had a Main method, Visual Studio didn't automatically give frmParent a main method. You need to give frmParent one now:

```
[STAThread]
static void Main() {
    Application.Run(new frmParent());
}
```

The Run method of the Application object is invoked with the constructor method for the frmParent class.

The [STAThread] attribute tells the Common Language Runtime that a single-threaded apartment model is being used.

Form1 still has its own `Main` method:

```
[STAThread]
static void Main() {
    Application.Run(new Form1());
}
```

You now have a choice: you can delete the `Main` method from Form1—in which case, the application will start by default from frmParent. Or, you can open the project Property Pages dialog—by selecting the project in Solution Explorer, right-clicking, and choosing Properties from the context menu—and explicitly set frmParent as the Startup Object using the General tab (Figure 4.18).

FIGURE 4.18:

If there are multiple modules with entry points—`Main` methods—then the Startup Object is set using the project's properties pages.

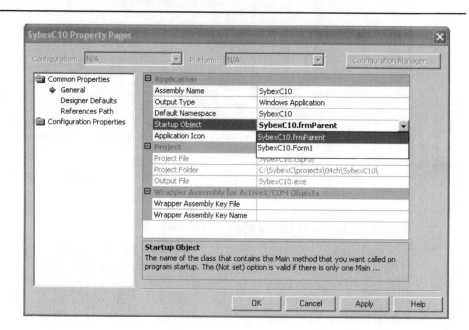

Displaying Children

With the application set to open frmParent first off, the mechanism for displaying the child form needs to be created. This goes in the click event handler for btnShowChild. First, a variable named *frmChild*, of type Form1, is instantiated:

```
Form1 frmChild = new Form1();
```

Next, the MdiParent property of *frmChild* is set to the current form, frmParent:

```
frmChild.MdiParent = this;
```

The child form is given text for its caption bar using a counter variable, *i*, to indicate which child it is:

```
frmChild.Text = "I am child #" + i.ToString();
```

The counter, which was declared at the class level, is iterated:

```
i++;
```

Finally, the new instance of Form1 is shown:

```
frmChild.Show()
```

Listing 4.7 shows the frmParent class declaration, the counter variable, its Main method, and the click event handler for displaying child forms.

Listing 4.7   Adding Child Forms

```
...
public class frmParent : System.Windows.Forms.Form {
    private System.Windows.Forms.Panel panel1;
    private System.Windows.Forms.Button btnShowChild;
    int i = 1;
    ...
    [STAThread]
    static void Main() {
        Application.Run(new frmParent());
    }
    ...
    private void btnShowChild_Click(object sender, System.EventArgs e) {
        Form1 frmChild = new Form1();
        frmChild.MdiParent = this;
        frmChild.Text = "I am child #" + i.ToString();
        i++;
        frmChild.Show();
    }
}
...
```

The MDI Window Menu

A crucial part of the look and feel of an MDI application is a special MDI Window menu. This menu displays a list of all open MDI children and places a check mark next to the currently active child window. It allows the user to navigate between child windows, by selecting one from the list on the MDI Window menu. In addition, it's also conventional and convenient to include the ability to arrange the children forms (in several ways) on the MDI Window menu.

The MDI Window is constructed in the MDI container—frmParent, in our example. You can create it by adding a MainMenu control to the form and using the visual menu designer—or by constructing it entirely in code, as shown in Listing 4.8. Note that setting a top-level menu's MdiList property to true:

```
mnu.MdiList = true;
```

sets up the MDI list of child windows. It's also worth observing that the menu shown in Listing 4.8 *merges* with the menu belonging to a child form when the child is displayed. Aesthetically, the child menu should come before the Window menu. This is controlled by the MergeOrder property:

```
mnu.MergeOrder = 3;
```

Listing 4.8   **An MDI Window Menu**

```
Menu = new MainMenu();

// MDI Window menu
MenuItem mnu = new MenuItem("&Window");
mnu.MdiList = true;
mnu.MergeOrder = 3;
Menu.MenuItems.Add(mnu);

// Cascade
MenuItem mnuCascade = new MenuItem("&Cascade");
mnuCascade.Click += new EventHandler(MDImenu_Click);
Menu.MenuItems[0].MenuItems.Add(mnuCascade);

// Tile Horizontal
MenuItem mnuTileH = new MenuItem("&Tile Horizontal");
mnuTileH.Click += new EventHandler(MDImenu_Click);
Menu.MenuItems[0].MenuItems.Add(mnuTileH);

// Tile Vertical
MenuItem mnuTileV = new MenuItem("Tile &Vertical");
mnuTileV.Click += new EventHandler(MDImenu_Click);
Menu.MenuItems[0].MenuItems.Add(mnuTileV);

// Arrange Icons
MenuItem mnuArrange = new MenuItem("&Arrange Icons");
mnuArrange.Click += new EventHandler(MDImenu_Click);
Menu.MenuItems[0].MenuItems.Add(mnuArrange);
```

Note that the menu shown in Listing 4.8 does not implement functionality in child window arrangements; for each choice, it merely invokes a common event, MDImenu_Click. The MDIMenu_Click event handler, shown in Listing 4.9, has the job of determining which menu item invoked it by casting the *sender* parameter to a MenuItem and then checking its Text property:

```
MenuItem mnu = (MenuItem) sender;
switch (mnu.Text) {
    ...
```

The LayoutMdi method of the parent form is then used with the appropriate argument to arrange the child windows as shown in Listing 4.9.

Listing 4.9   **Implementing MDI Window Functionality**

```
void MDImenu_Click(object sender, EventArgs e) {
    MenuItem mnu = (MenuItem) sender;
    switch (mnu.Text) {
        case "&Cascade":
            this.LayoutMdi(MdiLayout.Cascade);
            break;
        case "&Tile Horizontal":
            this.LayoutMdi(MdiLayout.TileHorizontal);
            break;
        case "Tile &Vertical":
            this.LayoutMdi(MdiLayout.TileVertical);
            break;
        case "&Arrange Icons":
            this.LayoutMdi(MdiLayout.ArrangeIcons);
            break;
    }
}
```

If you run the application, you'll see that it is fully functional within normal parameters for an MDI application (Figure 4.19).

FIGURE 4.19:

It's easy to create MDI applications.

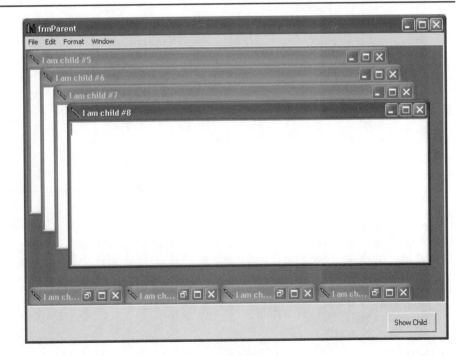

Conclusion

This chapter—and the previous one—has explored using Visual C#, Visual Studio, and the .NET Framework to create functional and exciting user interfaces.

In Chapter 5, "Reflecting on Classes," we'll move on to have a look at the organization of the classes within the .NET Framework. Using this organization as a model of clarity leads to an interesting and fruitful field of speculation: what are the best ways to organize classes? And, more generally, are there patterns of practice that are useful in constructing class-based applications? What is the vocabulary used to notate these patterns and how are they recognized?

CHAPTER 5

Reflecting on Classes

- Assemblies and namespaces

- Using .NET namespaces

- Reflection

- Working with the Class View window and the Object Browser

- Creating a class library

"No man is an island," wrote seventeenth century poet John Donne. This famous epigram equally applies to program code—it runs in a context, after compilation, on an operating system, and quite likely invoking run-time libraries of code. Certainly, this is true of C# .NET code, which uses the class libraries of the .NET Framework for functionality and can only run through the grace of the Common Language Runtime (CLR).

So far in this book, C# code has been presented basically as separate and apart—as an island, as it were. It's time to have a look at the connectedness of C# programs that you write to the class libraries that make up the .NET Framework.

This chapter explores the organization of programs, internally and for deployment. I also explain reflection, which is used to glean information about the types that make up a compiled program; this information can be used dynamically while the program in question is running.

How are the classes in the .NET Framework organized? I explain how to use the Object Browser, the best discovery tool for exploring the .NET Framework. When it comes time to deploy your own class libraries, following the design guidelines for .NET classes will help you organize for maximum usability.

Assemblies and Namespaces

Assemblies are the fundamental unit for deployment, version control, security, and more for a .NET application. In other words, assemblies are deployable units of code that correspond to stand-alone executable files or DLL libraries. Each compiled C# .NET program has at least one related assembly. Every time you build an executable (EXE) or a library (DLL) file in .NET, you are creating an assembly.

Namespaces are used to organize the classes within assemblies. Assemblies can contain many namespaces, which, in turn, can contain other namespaces. Namespaces are used to make it easier to refer to items, to avoid ambiguity, and to simplify references when large groups of classes are involved.

The Assembly Manifest

When you start a new C# project, it is the basis of an assembly. Within each built assembly is a *manifest*, as part of the executable or library. In C#, some of the general manifest information is contained in a file that is part of the project, named `AssemblyInfo.cs`. Figure 5.1 shows a small project in the Visual Studio Solution Explorer and shows the contents of a sample `AssemblyInfo.cs` file when opened with the Visual Studio editor.

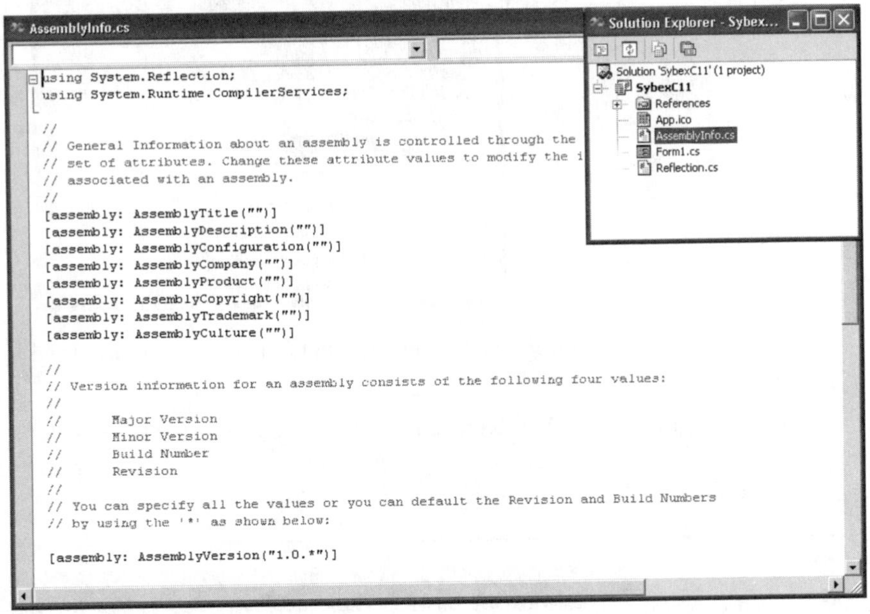

FIGURE 5.1:

Each C# .NET project includes a file that forms the basis of the assembly manifest. The manifest carries information about content, version, and dependencies so that C# .NET applications don't depend on Registry values.

The assembly manifest can be thought of as a "table of contents" for an application. It includes the following information:

- The assembly's name and version number
- A file table, listing and describing the files that make up the assembly
- An assembly reference list, which is a catalog of external dependencies

The external dependencies in the assembly reference list may be library files created by someone else, and it's likely that some of them are part of the .NET Framework.

Assembly References

To use an assembly, or a class within an assembly, the assembly must be referenced in your project. Depending on the type of project, you'll find that many of the assemblies that are part of the .NET Framework are referenced by default.

Different project types have different default references. The references that come "out of the box" for a Windows forms project are not the same as those for a web forms project, although both do reference certain important .NET assemblies such as System.dll.

You can see which assemblies are already referenced in a project by expanding the References node in the Solution Explorer.

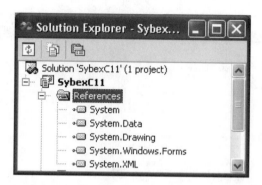

If you need to reference an assembly that is not already included in your project, follow these steps:

1. Select Project ➢ Add Reference. (Alternatively, select the References node in Solution Explorer. Right-click, and select Add Reference from the context menu.) The Add Reference dialog will open, as shown in Figure 5.2.

FIGURE 5.2:

The Add Reference dialog is used to add a reference to a project.

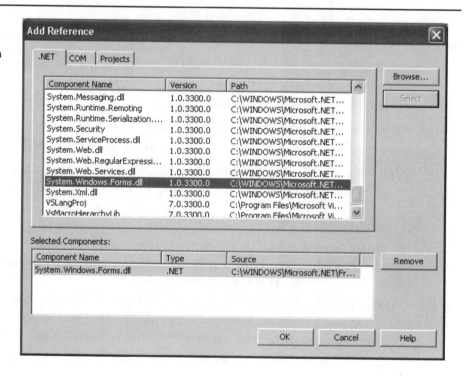

2. Select a .NET assembly to add (listed in the Component Name column of the .NET tab).

3. Click the Select button to add the assembly to the Selected Components list (shown at the bottom of Figure 5.2).

4. Click OK to add the reference to the .NET component.

Alternatively, if the assembly you want to add a reference to does not appear on the .NET tab, click the Browse button in the upper-right corner of the Add Reference dialog. The Select Component dialog will open. Locate the assembly to be added and click Open. The assembly will be added to the Selected Components panel of the Add Reference dialog. Click OK to add the reference to your project.

Namespaces

If you drill down one step below the assembly level, you'll find that the members of a given assembly are namespaces. Another way of putting this is that namespaces are the internal organization of the classes defined in an assembly. For example, Microsoft.CSharp is a namespace that is part of the System assembly. It contains classes that support compilation and code generation using the C# language. (What can get a little confusing is that sometimes a namespace and an assembly can have the same name.)

By default, every executable file you create in C# .NET contains a namespace with the same name as your project, although you can change this default name.

You should also know that namespaces can span multiple assemblies. In other words, if two assemblies both define classes within a namespace myNameSpace, then myNameSpace is treated as a single set of names.

The .NET Framework uses a dot operator (.) syntax to designate hierarchies. Related types are grouped into namespaces, so that they can be more easily found. Reading left to right, the first part of a type, up to the first dot, is the namespace name. The last part of the name, to the right of the final period, is the type name. For example System.Boolean designates a Boolean value-type in the System namespace. System.Windows.Forms.MessageBox designates the MessageBox class within the Forms namespace, that is part of the Windows namespace, that is part of System.

As these examples suggest, the System namespace is the root namespace for all types within the .NET Framework. All base data types used by all applications are included in the System namespace or the Microsoft namespace.

One of the most important types within the System namespace is System.Object, also called the Object class. This class is the root of the .NET type hierarchy and the ultimate parent (or *superclass*) of all classes in the .NET Framework. This implies that the members of the Object class—such as GetType() and ToString()—are contained in all .NET classes.

Namespace Directives

You have several ways of referring to an object based on a class within a namespace once the assembly containing the class you are interested in has been referenced.

The *using* Directive

You can use the *fully qualified* name of the item, as in this variable declaration for *btnClear*:

```
private System.Windows.Forms.Button btnClear;
```

Alternatively, you can place a using *namespace* directive at the beginning of a code module, as shown here:

```
using System.Windows.Forms;
```

After you add a using directive, all of the names in the imported namespace can be used (provided they are unique to your project), like this:

```
private Button btnClear;
```

NOTE   The using System directive will automatically be included in most C# modules. This means that you don't have to explicitly invoke System: Windows.Forms.Button btnClear will mean the same thing as System.Windows.Forms.Button btnClear.

The Alias Directive

An alias namespace directive allows a program to use its own, internally assigned, shorthand name for a namespace (or a namespace plus a type belonging to the namespace). This can save you a great deal of typing of long, qualified namespaces, possibly followed by types—and it can help make your code clearer.

Here's how it works. If you add an identifier and an assignment to the using directive, then the identifier can be used in place of the assigned namespace (and type). For example:

```
using swfb = System.Windows.Forms.Button;
```

Given this directive, a corresponding variable declaration for a variable named *btnClear* of type Button could look like this:

```
private swfb btnClear;
```

Creating Namespaces

It's truly easy to create a namespace. The keyword namespace is followed by an identifier that is the name of the namespace. Curly braces enclose the contents of the namespace—meaning, the members of the namespace (see the following section). Namespaces can be nested within each other.

Listing 5.1 shows an example of namespaces nested three levels deep containing a single class. The class contains a single static method that displays a message box (because the method is static, there's no need to instantiate an object based on the class to use it).

Listing 5.1   **Nested Namespaces**

```
// Namespaces.cs
using System;
using swf = System.Windows.Forms;
namespace noman {
   namespace isan {
      namespace island {
         public class theClass {
            public theClass() {
            // No constructor code
            }
            public static void bellTolls (string inStr){
               swf.MessageBox.Show("The bell tolls for " + inStr + "!",
                  "For thee...", swf.MessageBoxButtons.OK,
                  swf.MessageBoxIcon.Exclamation);
            }
         }
      }
   }
}
```

The static method shown in Listing 5.1 can easily be invoked. For example, from within a form module button's click event, in the same project as the nested namespaces code module, the following will do the trick:

```
private void btnGreeting_Click(object sender, System.EventArgs e) {
   noman.isan.island.theClass.bellTolls("Dolly");
}
```

NOTE   If the namespace code is compiled in an assembly external to the code trying to invoke the method, then a reference to the assembly must be added to the calling project.

Namespace Members

Namespaces are at the pinnacle of the tree of C# language elements. Namespaces can encapsulate other namespaces (as shown in Listing 5.1), but no other language element can encapsulate a namespace. So one way of answering the question of what can go in a namespace is, everything. Somewhat more formally, namespace blocks may contain:

- Other namespaces
- Classes
- Delegates
- Enumerations
- Interfaces
- Structs
- `using` and alias directives

NOTE   If you don't know what these things are, don't worry. You'll find out more in this chapter and in Chapters 6, "Zen and Now: The C# Language," and 8, "The Life of the Object in C#."

.NET Namespaces

Some of the built-in namespaces that are likely to be most important to C# .NET programmers are described in Table 5.1.

TABLE 5.1: Important .NET Namespaces

Namespace	Description
`Microsoft.CSharp`	Supports compilation and code generation using the C# language.
`System`	Contains fundamental classes that define types, arrays, strings, events, event handlers, exceptions, interfaces, data-type conversion, mathematics, application environment management, and much more.
`System.Collections`	Includes a set of classes that lets you manage collections of objects, such as lists, queues, arrays, hash tables, and dictionaries.
`System.Data`	Consists mainly of the classes that comprise the ADO.NET architecture.
`System.Diagnostics`	Provides classes used for debugging, tracing, and interacting with system processes, event logs, and performance counters.
`System.Drawing`	Contains classes that provide access to GDI+ basic graphics functionality (namespaces that are hierarchically beneath `System.Drawing`—including `System.Drawing.Drawing2D` and `System.Drawing.Text`—provide more advanced and specific GDI+ graphics functionality).

Continued on next page

TABLE 5.1 CONTINUED: Important .NET Namespaces

Namespace	Description
System.IO	Contains types and classes used for reading and writing to data streams and files, and general input/output (I/O) functionality.
System.Reflection	Contains classes and interfaces that provide type inspection and the ability to dynamically bind objects.
System.Reflection.Emit	Generates assemblies on the fly.
System.Text	Contains classes used for character encoding, converting blocks of characters to and from blocks of bytes, and more.
System.Text.RegularExpressions	Contains classes that provide access to the .NET Framework regular expression engine.
System.Timer	Provides the Timer component (see the section "Round Buttons Dancing" in Chapter 4, "Building a Better Windows Interface," for an example using the Timer).
System.Web	Contains the classes that are used to facilitate browser-server communication and other web-related functionality.
System.Web.Services	Contains the classes used to build and consume web services.
System.Web.UI	Provides classes and interfaces used in the creation of the user interface of web pages and controls.
System.Windows.Forms	Contains the classes for creating a Windows-based user interface.
System.XML	Provides classes that support processing XML.

Reflection

Reflection is the ability to use the metadata provided by a program to gather information about its types. The example in this section will show you how to use reflection to gather type and member information about compiled .NET assemblies. The information you can gather is not as extensive or as convenient to use as that provided by the Object Browser tool that ships with Visual Studio, explained later in this chapter. However, with the ability to gather information about the internal program elements of compiled code on the fly, a great deal of advanced functionality becomes possible, including automated and dynamic code and assembly generation, dynamic "late bound" run-time determination of what code needs to be executed, and automated code documenters.

To see how reflection works, let's create a Windows forms application that will open and "inspect" any .NET assembly (.exe or .dll file). The application will provide an Open button. When the user clicks this button, the OpenFileDialog will allow the choice of a file for reflection.

Clicking Open in the common dialog displays the selected file in a TextBox. When the Perform Reflection button is clicked, the types in the selected file are displayed in a Types ListBox. When a type, or class, is selected, and the user clicks the Get Type Info button, the constructors, fields, methods, properties, and events for the type are displayed in respective ListBoxes. This user interface is shown in design mode in Figure 5.3.

FIGURE 5.3:

The form has a ListBox for types in an assembly and separate ListBoxes for each kind of member of a type.

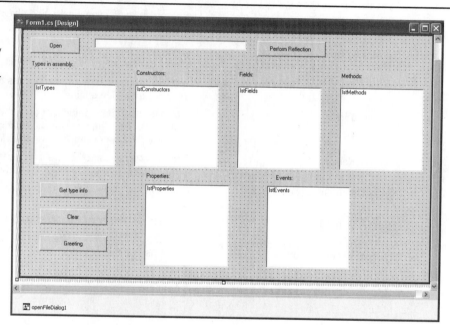

NOTE   Working with ListBoxes and the common dialog controls was explained in Chapter 4.

Here's the code that displays the Open dialog and loads the user's choice into the TextBox:

```
private void btnOpen_Click(object sender, System.EventArgs e) {
    openFileDialog1.InitialDirectory = Application.ExecutablePath;
    openFileDialog1.DefaultExt = "exe";
    openFileDialog1.Filter = "Executable (*.exe)|*.exe|DLL (*.dll)|*.dll";
    openFileDialog1.ShowDialog();
    txtFileToOpen.Text =openFileDialog1.FileName;
}
```

The user can now select any .NET assembly to examine—including the running file, as shown in the Open dialog depicted in Figure 5.4.

FIGURE 5.4:

You can use
reflection to examine
the metadata of the
program that is
running.

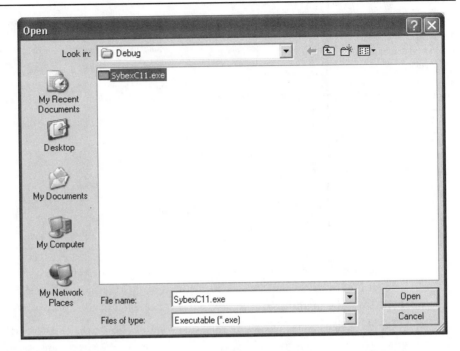

To use reflection to pull the types out of the assembly, first add a directive to use the
System.Reflection namespace:

```
using System.Reflection;
```

Next, within the form class, declare an array (named *typeArray*) to hold the type information
and a variable, *theAssembly*, of type System.Reflection.Assembly:

```
Type[] typeArray;
Assembly theAssembly;
```

When the user clicks Perform Reflection, *theAssembly* is set to the file selected by the user
using the Assembly.LoadFrom method, and the Assembly.GetTypes method is used to load the
types in the assembly into *typeArray*. The elements of the array are then added to the Type
ListBox (see Figure 5.5):

```
private void btnReflect_Click(object sender, System.EventArgs e) {
    theAssembly = Assembly.LoadFrom(txtFileToOpen.Text);
    GetTypeInfo(theAssembly);
}
private void GetTypeInfo(Assembly theAssembly){
    typeArray = theAssembly.GetTypes();
    foreach (Type type in typeArray) {
        lstTypes.Items.Add(type.FullName);
    }
}
```

FIGURE 5.5:

The types, or classes, within the assembly are displayed.

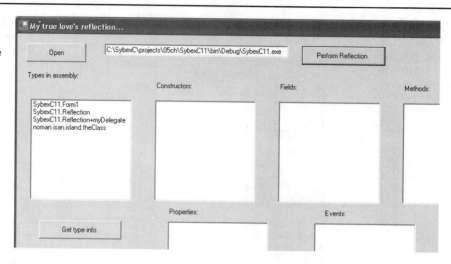

So far, this is great! We've used reflection to display the types in an assembly. The next step is to let the user choose a type, by selecting it in the Types ListBox. When the user clicks Get Type Info, the members of the type will be displayed in the appropriate ListBox.

But, before we get started with this, we probably should make sure that the ListBoxes we are going to use are empty—so that the type information for only one assembly is displayed. To do this, I've used the code explained in Chapter 3, "Windows Uses Web Services, Too!" to loop through all the ListBoxes on the form (rather than clearing them by name):

```
private void btnGetTypeInfo_Click(object sender, System.EventArgs e) {
    // Clear the ListBoxes except lstTypes
    foreach (object o in this.Controls) {
        if (o is ListBox) {
            ListBox lb = (ListBox) o;
            if (!(lb.Name == "lstTypes"))
                lb.Items.Clear();
        }
    }
    ...
```

Continuing with the reflection, here's the code that checks to see whether a type is selected, uses the `System.Reflection.Type[].GetMethods` method to retrieve the methods for the type, then displays them by adding them to the Methods ListBox (I'm showing method reflection here, but if you look below at the complete code for the Get Type Info procedure, you'll see that the other kinds of members are reflected as well):

```
if (lstTypes.Text != ""){
    ...
```

```
    MethodInfo[] theMethods =
        typeArray[lstTypes.SelectedIndex].GetMethods();
        foreach (MethodInfo method in theMethods) {
            lstMethods.Items.Add(method.ToString());
        }
    ...
}
else {
    MessageBox.Show("Please select a type for further info!",
        "Nothing Selected!", MessageBoxButtons.OK, MessageBoxIcon.Information);
}
```

Listing 5.2 shows the complete code for generating member information—that is, information about constructors, fields, properties, methods, and events—about types in an assembly using reflection. Listing 5.3 shows a class module, SybexC11.Reflection, that I added to the reflection project to simply show a variety of type members. You'll see these members "reflected" in Figure 5.6.

FIGURE 5.6:

Member information for a type is displayed.

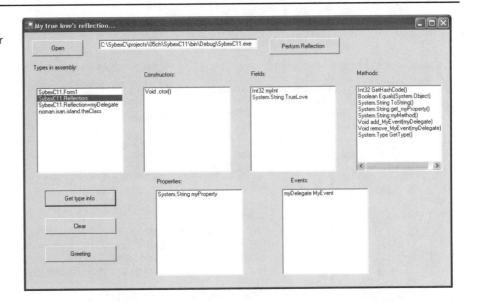

Listing 5.2   **Displaying Types and Members Using Reflection**

```
// Form1.cs
...
using System.Reflection;
...
```

```
public class Form1 : System.Windows.Forms.Form
{
...
Type[] typeArray;
Assembly theAssembly;
...
    private void btnOpen_Click(object sender, System.EventArgs e) {
        openFileDialog1.InitialDirectory = Application.ExecutablePath;
        openFileDialog1.DefaultExt = "exe";
        openFileDialog1.Filter = "Executable (*.exe)|*.exe|DLL (*.dll)|*.dll";
        openFileDialog1.ShowDialog();
        txtFileToOpen.Text =openFileDialog1.FileName;
    }

    private void btnReflect_Click(object sender, System.EventArgs e) {
        theAssembly = Assembly.LoadFrom(txtFileToOpen.Text);
        GetTypeInfo(theAssembly);

    }
    private void GetTypeInfo(Assembly theAssembly){
        typeArray = theAssembly.GetTypes();
        foreach (Type type in typeArray) {
            lstTypes.Items.Add(type.FullName);
        }
    }

    private void btnGetTypeInfo_Click(object sender, System.EventArgs e) {
        // Clear the ListBoxes except lstTypes
        foreach (object o in this.Controls) {
            if (o is ListBox) {
                ListBox lb = (ListBox) o;
                if (!(lb.Name == "lstTypes"))
                    lb.Items.Clear();
            }
        }

        if (lstTypes.Text != ""){
        ConstructorInfo[] theConstructors =
            typeArray[lstTypes.SelectedIndex].GetConstructors();
        foreach (ConstructorInfo constructor in theConstructors){
            lstConstructors.Items.Add(constructor.ToString());
        }
        FieldInfo[] theFields = typeArray[lstTypes.SelectedIndex].GetFields();
        foreach (FieldInfo field in theFields) {
            lstFields.Items.Add(field.ToString());
        }
        MethodInfo[] theMethods =
             typeArray[lstTypes.SelectedIndex].GetMethods();
        foreach (MethodInfo method in theMethods) {
            lstMethods.Items.Add(method.ToString());
        }
```

```
            PropertyInfo[] theProps =
                typeArray[lstTypes.SelectedIndex].GetProperties();
            foreach (PropertyInfo prop in theProps) {
                lstProperties.Items.Add(prop.ToString());
            }
            EventInfo[] theEvents = typeArray[lstTypes.SelectedIndex].GetEvents();
            foreach (EventInfo anEvent in theEvents) {
                lstEvents.Items.Add(anEvent.ToString());
            }

        }
        else {
            MessageBox.Show("Please select a type for further info!",
                "Nothing Selected!", MessageBoxButtons.OK,
                MessageBoxIcon.Information);
        }
    }
    ...
}
```

Listing 5.3   A Class with Members to Demonstrate Reflection

```
// Reflection.cs
using System;
namespace SybexC11
{
    public class Reflection
    {
        public int myInt;
        public string TrueLove;
        public Reflection()
        {

        }
        public string myProperty {
            get {
                return "reflection";
            }
        }
        public static string myMethod() {
            return "True love";
        }
        public delegate string myDelegate();

        public event myDelegate MyEvent = new myDelegate(myMethod);
    }
}
```

NOTE The code in Listing 5.3 uses the `ToString()` method to simply display information about each member. You'll find quite a bit of additional programmatic capabilities in the `System.Reflection` namespace.

Of course, you can also turn the reflection spotlight on the form module itself in the project. Before we do, let's add some class-level variable declarations and assignments (these will show up as Fields):

```
...
public class Form1 : System.Windows.Forms.Form
{
    ...
    public string myTrueLove = "Phyllis";
    public bool isTheFairest = true;
```

When you run the application now, reflecting on itself and getting type information about the class that represents the form module, you'll see these fields as well as the standard form methods, properties, and events (Figure 5.7).

FIGURE 5.7:

Variables declared at the form's class level appear as Fields; all form methods, properties, and events are displayed in the appropriate ListBoxes.

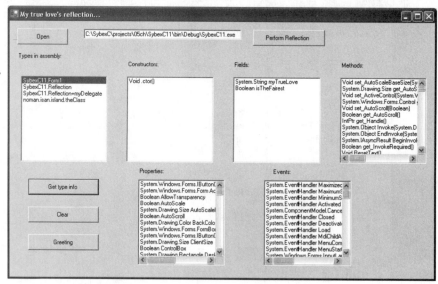

The reflection application can be used to inspect the assemblies that are part of the .NET Framework, as shown in Figure 5.8.

FIGURE 5.8:

Select System.dll, a
key class of the .NET
Framework (top), and
click Open. All the types
in the assembly will be
displayed (bottom).

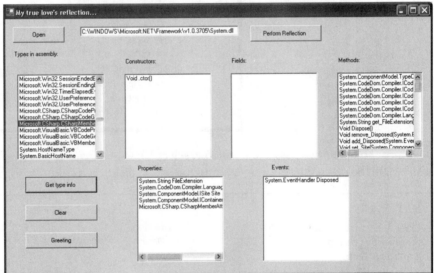

Tracking Members with the Class View Window

Visual Studio's Class View window (Figure 5.9) is an excellent way to keep track of namespaces, classes, and class members within a project.

FIGURE 5.9:

You can use the Class View
window to understand how
namespaces, classes, and
their members are
structured in a project.

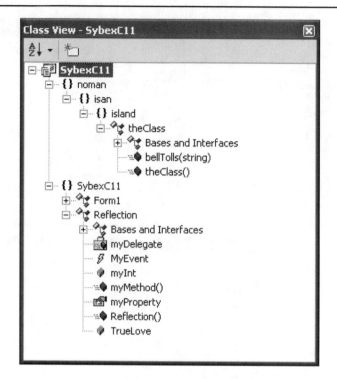

To open the Class View window, select View ≻ Class View. The Class View window can
also be opened by clicking a button on the Visual Studio toolbar (Figure 5.10).

FIGURE 5.10:

The Class View window can
be conveniently opened
using a toolbar icon.

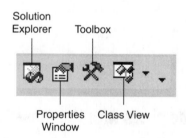

With a member of a class selected in the Class View window, if you right-click, a context
menu appears. From this context menu, Go To Definition takes you to the code that declares
the member (opening the Code Editor if necessary). Go To Reference takes you to the first use
of the member. And Browse Definition opens the Object Browser with the member loaded
(Figure 5.11).

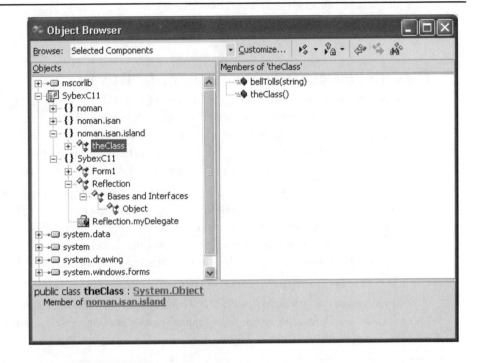

Navigating with the Object Browser

The Object Browser lets you determine the members of .NET objects, or classes, and the relationships of objects to each other. You can easily use the Object Browser to learn about the objects available for use in your programs.

The Object Browser also teaches about the structure of the .NET Framework. You can use it to discern the hierarchy of classes, members of classes, as well as the properties, events, and methods of each object.

Thus, the Object Browser is a tool of discovery, rather than a tool you use to actually do anything. But it's probably the single most important discovery tool included in the Visual Studio .NET development environment.

Opening the Object Browser

To open the Object Browser, use one of the following methods:

- Select View ➢ Other Windows ➢ Object Browser from the Visual Studio menus.

- Highlight a member in the Class View window, right-click, and choose Browse Definition.

- Press the keyboard shortcut, Ctrl+Alt+J.
- In the Code Editor, place the cursor on a .NET object, right-click, and choose Go To Definition.

Opening the Object Browser Using Go To Definition

When you open the Object Browser from the Code Editor (by choosing Go To Definition from a .NET object's context menu), the Object Browser will open with the highlighted object defined. Note that this does not work if the cursor is hovering over a variable or keyword. In the case of a keyword, Go To Definition does nothing. In the case of a variable, method, or procedure or functional call, Go To Definition takes you to the declaration for the object.

For example, suppose you have a component in your project named *openFileDialog1* of type System.Windows.Forms.OpenFileDialog. With the cursor over the statement using *openFileDialog1*, right-click and select Go To Definition. You will be taken to the declaration for *openFileDialog1* at the beginning of the module. Likely, this declaration was generated for you when you added the OpenFileDialog control to your form. It's probably along these lines:

```
private System.Windows.Forms.OpenFileDialog openFileDialog1;
```

If you move the cursor to OpenFileDialog at the end of this declaration statement, and then select Go To Definition again, the Object Browser will open to the definition of the Open-FileDialog class, as shown in Figure 5.12.

FIGURE 5.12:

The class definition of an object is shown in the Object Browser.

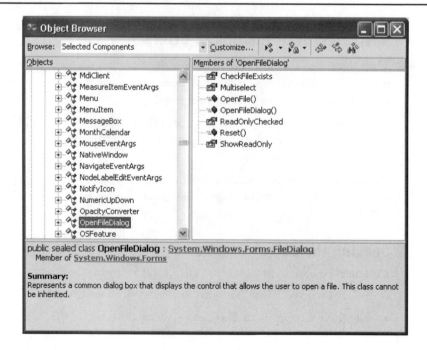

Using the Object Browser Interface

The Object Browser interface consists of a toolbar and three panes: the Objects pane, the Members pane, and the Description pane. Figure 5.13 shows the full Object Browser interface, with information for the MessageBox class.

FIGURE 5.13:

The Members pane shows the members of an object selected in the Objects pane, and the Description pane provides information about the selected object.

Objects pane   Toolbar

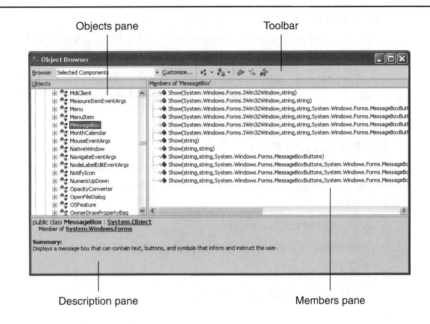

Description pane   Members pane

The Objects Pane

The Objects pane provides a hierarchical view of the objects (or classes) contained in the namespaces that are within the scope of the Object Browser. Here is an example of the Objects pane with System.Drawing.Color selected and some of the members of Color visible in the Members pane.

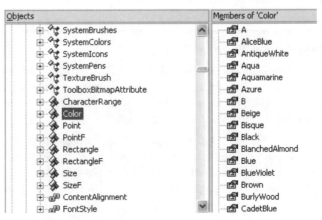

Clicking the + or − icons in the Objects pane expands or contracts the tree view of objects. (Color is a member of System.Drawing, so expanding System.Drawing shows the Color class.)

If you fully expand an object in the Objects pane, a great deal about the object—such as the classes that it is based on—will be displayed in the Objects pane.

The Members Pane

The Members pane shows the members of an object selected in the Objects pane. *Members* mean properties, methods, events, variables, constants, and enumeration values.

A different icon indicates each different kind of member. In addition, one other icon, a key, means the member is protected, or only accessible from within its own class (or a derived class). (For more on this topic, see Chapter 8.)

The Description Pane

The Description pane provides a great deal of information about the object currently selected in the Objects pane. This information isn't the same for all objects, but it usually includes the following:

- A description of the object
- The name of the object and its parent object
- The object syntax
- Links to related objects and members

NOTE   The links in the Description pane take you to objects that are related to the selected object. They are immensely valuable for quickly gathering information about an object.

The Toolbar

The Object Browser toolbar is used to customize the Object Browser scope, arrange the contents of the Object Browser, navigate, and find identifiers (such as object names, but called *symbols* here).

Setting the Object Browser Scope

When the Object Browser opens, you have a choice regarding the *scope* of the browser (or which objects it will see). The two scope options are available in the Browse drop-down list in the upper-left corner of the Object Browser. Selected Components is the default initial selection. You can customize the objects included in this scope.

The other scope option is Active Project, which includes the active project and its references (for example, System, and, in the case of a form-based application, System.Windows.Forms). The Active Project setting does not allow any customization of the objects that can be browsed. (But you could go back to the project and add or remove a reference in the Solution Explorer.)

Continued on next page

> To customize the objects included within the Selected Components scope of the Object Browser, click the Customize button to the right of the Browse drop-down list.
>
> Click the Add button in the Selected Components dialog to open the Component Selector dialog. You can use the Component Selector to choose .NET and COM components to add. To add other projects, executables, and other types of files (such as OLB or TLB type libraries or dynamic link libraries), click the Browse button. Components added to the Selected Components box at the bottom of the Component Selector will appear in the Selected Components dialog and, if checked, will be available to browse in the Object Browser.

It's likely that the most useful toolbar button is Find Symbol (the button with the binoculars icon). When you click the Find Symbol button, the dialog shown in Figure 5.14 opens.

FIGURE 5.14:

The Find Symbol dialog lets you search for objects using the object's name.

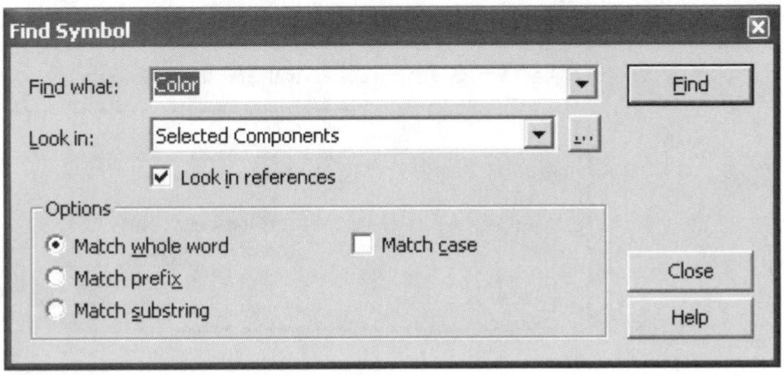

The Find Symbol dialog allows you to search for objects including namespaces, classes, and structures—and the members of these objects—using the object's name.

NOTE   Obviously, the Object Browser tools such as the Find Symbol dialog are the easiest way to locate specific objects within the Object Browser. But pure recreational browsing can teach you a great deal about the way .NET is structured, how to work with it, and even the best way to construct your own object hierarchies (for more on this, see the next section).

Creating a Class Library

Now that you've seen how to inspect the class libraries that are part of the .NET Framework, let's walk through the process of creating your own class library. The class library will contain a single class, which will in turn contain a field, a property, a method, and an event. The point of this is to be very bare-bones. These class members will not be fancy.

After I've shown you how to create each of these members, I'll show you how to use them from a Windows forms project.

To start with, use the New Project dialog to create a Class Library project by selecting Visual C# Projects in the Project Types pane and Class Library in the Templates pane, and giving the project a name (Figure 5.15).

FIGURE 5.15:

A new project can be opened to serve as the basis for a class library.

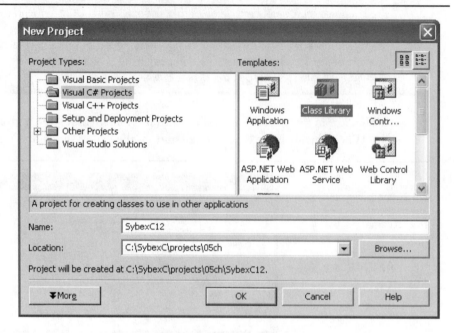

When the project opens, it will have a class code module containing (by default) the project name as the namespace and a class named Class1. Our class will be the template representing a baby, and the objects based on the class will be specific babies.

If we keep the namespace, change the class name to Baby to reflect the kinds of objects that will be created based on the class, and remove the class constructor—since we're not going to be using it—we'll now have a code module that looks like this:

```
using System;

namespace SybexC12
{
   public class Baby
   {

   }
}
```

NOTE   It probably goes without saying, but let's say it anyhow: the order of members within a class does not matter.

Adding a Field

A field is simply a variable declared at the class level using the `public` keyword. Since each baby object has a name, let's reflect that fact by giving the Baby class a Name field:

```
...
public class Baby
{
    public string Name = "";
    ...
```

Adding a Property

Properties differ from fields, since *accessor* `get` and `set` methods serve as a kind of "gatekeeper" for access to the value contained in the property.

Let's add an Age property to the Baby class. The first step is to declare a private variable to hold the property value internally (in the example, it is initialized to 0):

```
private int m_Age = 0;
```

Next, a property procedure is used to provide read—using the `get` accessor—and write—using the `set` accessor—access to the property:

```
public int Age {
    get {
        return m_Age;
    }
```

```
    set {
      m_Age = value;
    }
  }
```

The property is set using the special keyword `value`. If you want to, you can make the property read-only or write-only by only including a `get` or `set` accessor function, respectively. You can also include validation code within the property procedures—or, as you'll see in a moment, raise (meaning "fire" or "trigger") an event when a property value is changed.

Adding a Method

A method is simply a public function belonging to the class. Here's one that returns a sound often made by baby objects:

```
public string GetSound() {
    return "Waaah!";
}
```

Adding an Event

To raise an event in the `Baby` class, we must first declare a *delegate*, which is a type that defines a method signature—meaning a method's arguments, their types, and the method return type. A delegate instance can hold and invoke a method (or methods) that matches its signature. In turn, the class declares the event by applying the event keyword to a delegate.

Here are the delegate and event declarations for an `OnBirthDay` event:

```
public delegate void BirthDayEventHandler (object sender, System.EventArgs e);
public event BirthDayEventHandler OnBirthDay;
```

It remains to raise the event, which is done by calling the `OnBirthDay` method with the arguments indicated in the related delegate's signature.

In our `Baby` class, let's raise the `OnBirthDay` method when the `Age` property changes so that it is greater than it was (since it is an integer field, this presumably means that the baby object is a year older). We can do this from within the `Age` property set method, as follows:

```
...
set {
    if (value > m_Age) {
        // Raise the event
        if (OnBirthDay != null) {
            System.EventArgs e = new System.EventArgs();
            OnBirthDay(this, e);
        }
    }
```

```
        m_Age = value;
    }
    ...
```

The conditional OnBirthDay != null checks to see that something is using, or, in the lingo, *subscribing to* the event—otherwise there is no point in firing it. Assuming that the event has subscribers, it is then raised. By the way, the two lines of code

```
System.EventArgs e = new System.EventArgs();
OnBirthDay(this, e);
```

could be rewritten for compactness (although not for clarity):

```
OnBirthDay(this, new System.EvenetArgs());
```

OK. Let's go ahead and build the class library (Build ➤ Build Solution). The next step will be to open a new Windows forms project with the purpose of instantiating a baby object based on the Baby class and invoking the class methods. In the meantime, Listing 5.4 shows the complete code in the Baby class, with a few comments added for clarity.

Listing 5.4   **The *Baby* Class**

```
using System;

namespace SybexC12
{
    public class Baby
    {
        // Field
        public string Name = "";

        // Private variable for property
        private int m_Age = 0;

        // Property
        public int Age {
            get {
                return m_Age;
            }
            set {
                if (value > m_Age) {
                    // Raise the event
                    if (OnBirthDay != null) {
                        System.EventArgs e = new System.EventArgs();
                        OnBirthDay(this, e);
                    }
                }
                m_Age = value;
            }
        }
    }
```

```
// Method
public string GetSound(){
   return "Waaah!";
}

// Event declarations
public delegate void BirthDayEventHandler(object sender,
   System.EventArgs e);
public event BirthDayEventHandler OnBirthDay;
   }
}
```

Invoking the Class Members

Open a new Windows forms project. The first step is to add a reference to the SybexC12 assembly so that we can instantiate an object based on the Baby class contained in that assembly. To do so, as explained earlier in this chapter, open the Add Reference dialog (Project ➤ Add Reference), and click the Browse button in its upper-right corner. In the Select Component dialog, shown in Figure 5.16, locate SybexC12 and click Open.

FIGURE 5.16:

The Select Component dialog, opened from the Add Reference dialog, is used to locate the assembly containing the class library.

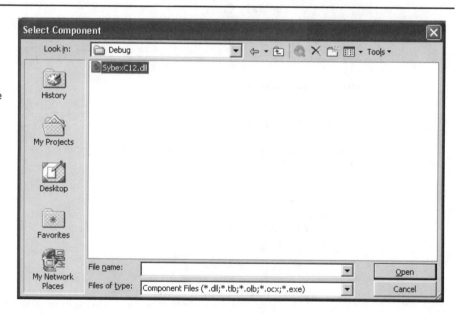

The SybexC12.dll assembly, which contains the Baby class library, now appears in the Selected Components pane of the Add Reference dialog (Figure 5.17). Click OK to add the reference.

FIGURE 5.17:

The assembly
containing the class
library now appears
in the Selected
Components pane.

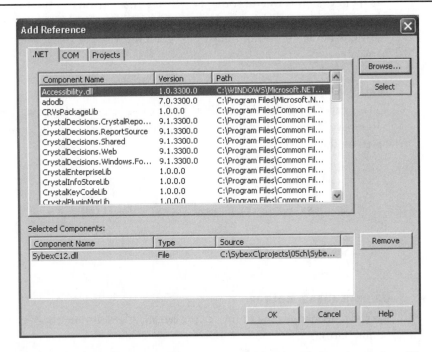

The reference to the SybexC12.Baby class library has now been added to the project. If you
open the Object Browser, you'll easily be able to find the Baby class members (Figure 5.18).

FIGURE 5.18:

Once the reference has
been added, the class
members appear in the
Object Browser.

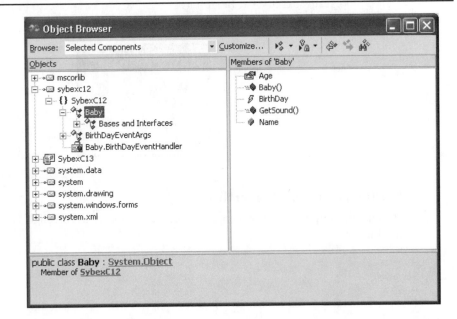

The next step is to add some TextBoxes and Buttons to the form to use to invoke the members of the class library. Let's add TextBoxes for the baby name and age, a Button to set them, and a Get Sound button to get a representation of the noise often made by the baby object.

Instantiating an Object Based on the Class

Turning to the form code, the first step is to add a using directive that refers to the SybexC12 namespace. Next, we'll instantiate an object, in this case stored in a variable named *myBaby*, based on the Baby class:

```
...
using SybexC12;
...
public class Form1 : System.Windows.Forms.Form
{
    ...
    Baby myBaby = new Baby();
    ...
```

Using a Class Method

It's a simple matter now to invoke the myBaby.GetSound method in the click event of the Get Sound button:

```
private void btnGetSound_Click(object sender, System.EventArgs e) {
    string msg = myBaby.GetSound();
    MessageBox.Show(msg, "Hi from my Baby!", MessageBoxButtons.OK,
        MessageBoxIcon.Exclamation);
}
```

Setting Fields and Properties

It's equally simple to set the Name field and Age property in the click event handler of the Set button:

```
private void btnSet_Click(object sender, System.EventArgs e) {
    myBaby.Age = Convert.ToInt16(txtAge.Text);
    myBaby.Name = txtName.Text;
}
```

Wiring the Event

To wire the event, we first need to create a method in the form class with the same signature as the event delegate. This method will be executed whe
n the event is raised. For example, we can simply display a message box in a method named Baby_OnBirthDay whose signature matches the event delegate:

```
private void Baby_OnBirthDay(object sender, System.EventArgs e) {
    MessageBox.Show("The Baby.OnBirthDay event was raised!",
        "Happy, Happy Birthday to my baby!", MessageBoxButtons.OK,
        MessageBoxIcon.Exclamation);
}
```

Next, in the form's constructor, the myBaby.OnBirthDay event is wired via the event delegate to the Baby_OnBirthDay method.

```
myBaby.OnBirthDay += new Baby.BirthDayEventHandler(this.Baby_OnBirthDay);
```

If you run the project and enter an age for the baby object that will trigger the event (for example, 1, since the initial value for the age is 0), you will see that the OnBirthDay event will be triggered, as shown in Figure 5.19.

FIGURE 5.19:

The OnBirthDay event is raised when the age is changed.

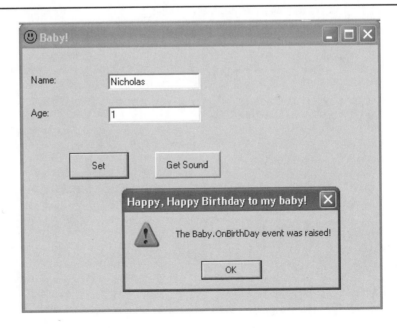

Conclusion

Programming with C# and the .NET Framework means programming with classes. This chapter has covered a lot of ground and started you down the path of programming well with classes. But it is not an island! You'll find a great deal more about object-oriented programming in Chapter 8. In the meantime, it is back to basics: Chapter 6 explains the basic building blocks of the C# language.

PART III

Courante: The Dance of the Language

CHAPTER 6

Zen and Now: The C# Language

- C# vocabulary: Identifiers and keywords

- Manipulating values: Variables and constants

- Types and type conversion

- Commenting C# code

- C# syntax: Operators and flow control

- Structs

- Exceptions

"O, wonder!" exclaims Miranda in Shakespeare's play *The Tempest.* "How many goodly creatures are there here! How beauteous mankind is! O brave new world that has such people in't!"

Our brave new world is, in fact, a brave new language: C#.

It has no "creatures" in it. Nor, for that matter, does it have the pharmacopoeia of Aldous Huxley's famous dystopia, *Brave New World.*

C# does have things like types, operators, variables, and expressions, glued together using a distinctive syntax. O brave new language! The introduction of a new language is a rare event. While C# borrows from Java, C++, C, and even Visual Basic and Pascal, it is a truly new language—and, in the opinion of this author, quite wondrous.

Since C# is new, and since language and syntax are the blocks on which programs are built, it's especially important to pay attention to the rules of the language. This chapter reviews the nuts and bolts of the C# language.

Identifiers

Identifiers are names used to denote variables, constants, types, methods, objects, and so on. An identifier begins with a letter or an underscore and ends with the character just before the next white space.

C# identifiers are case sensitive. For example, the three variables *deeFlat*, *DeeFlat*, and *DEEFLAT* are all different, as running this click procedure will show:

```
private void btnClickMe_Click(object sender, System.EventArgs e) {
    string deeFlat = "deeFlat";
    string DeeFlat = "DeeFlat";
    string DEEFLAT = "DEEFLAT";
    MessageBox.Show(deeFlat + " " + DeeFlat + " " + DEEFLAT,
        "Hello, Variables!", MessageBoxButtons.OK);
}
```

Microsoft suggests using "camel notation" for identifiers used as names of variables. Camel notation means an initial lowercase letter followed by uppercase letters ("internal caps") for initial letters of subsequent words in the identifier—for example, deeFlat.

Pascal notation—an initial uppercase letter, with internal caps as needed—is supposed to be used for identifiers that represent method names and most other non-variable objects. In addition, an identifier used for a method should use a verb-noun combination to describe the purpose of the method—for example, GetColorValues.

For more on Microsoft's suggested identifier naming conventions, look up "Naming Guidelines" using the Search feature in online help.

NOTE   It's always good programming practice to use identifiers that clearly communicate the contents and/or nature of the variable or other object identified. Code that uses clear identifiers may be almost self-documenting. For more suggestions of this kind, see the "Self-Documenting Code" section later in this chapter.

It is not legal to use an identifier that is also a C# keyword. (You'll find a list of C# reserved keywords in the next section.) If, for some really perverse reason, you must use a keyword as an identifier, you can preface the keyword with the @ symbol. For example, if cannot be used as an identifier (because it is a keyword), but @if can; this code snippet shows it employed as a string variable:

```
string @if = "@if";
MessageBox.Show(@if, "Hello, Variables!", MessageBoxButtons.OK);
```

For that matter, if you were really bound and determined to create an identifier like a keyword, you could simply vary the case. So If is a perfectly legal identifier—albeit an idiotic choice because it is similar to a keyword and so potentially confusing—because the keyword if is all lowercase.

TIP   Visual Basic programmers, who are used to case insensitivity, may find that C#'s case sensitivity regarding identifiers leads to the introduction of bugs. Fortunately, these kinds of bugs are found pretty easily once you are on the watch for them, and paying attention to the case of identifiers will become second nature shortly.

Keywords

Another way to think of a keyword is as a predefined reserved identifier. Table 6.1 shows the complete list of C# keywords.

TABLE 6.1: C# Keywords (Reserved Identifiers)

abstract	do	in	protected	true
as	double	int	public	try
base	else	interface	readonly	typeof
bool	enum	internal	ref	uint
break	event	is	return	ulong
byte	explicit	lock	sbyte	unchecked
case	extern	long	sealed	unsafe
catch	false	namespace	short	ushort
char	finally	new	sizeof	using
checked	fixed	null	stackalloc	virtual
class	float	object	static	void
const	for	operator	string	volatile
continue	foreach	out	struct	while
decimal	goto	override	switch	
default	if	params	this	
delegate	implicit	private	throw	

You can find this list of C# keywords by looking up "keyword, C#" using the online help's Index facility. The online help topic is then hyperlinked to the definition of each keyword.

Variables

A *variable* combines a type with a way to store a value of the specified type. (I discuss types later in this chapter, but you are certainly already familiar with some of the C# types, such as int [integer] and string.) The value of a variable can be assigned, and that value can also be changed programmatically at any point.

A variable is created in C# by declaring its type and then giving it an identifier. For example:

```
int theInt;
string deeFlat;
```

The variable can be initialized, meaning given an initial value, at the time it is declared—although this is not required. Here are the same variables declared *and* initialized:

```
int theInt = 42;
string deeFlat = "This is a string!";
```

Alternatively, of course, with the same effect, you could declare the variables and later assign them values:

```
int theInt;
string deeFlat;
```

```
...
theInt = 42;
deeFlat = "This is a string!";
```

To digress for a second here: you may not know that even simple value types such as int inherit from object. This implies that you could declare an int (or other value type) variable using the new constructor. So

```
int i = new int();
```

is the equivalent to the standard int declaration:

```
int i;
```

Definite Assignment

One thing you should know is that C# requires that variables be assigned a value—either through initialization or programmatic assignment—before they are used. This is known as *definite assignment* and codifies what is good practice in any case. As they say, an uninitialized variable is like an unmade bed—you never know what you'll find in it.

For example,

```
string unMadeBed;
MessageBox.Show(unMadeBed, "Hello, Variables!", MessageBoxButtons.OK);
```

produces a syntax error and will not compile because of the attempted use of an unassigned variable.

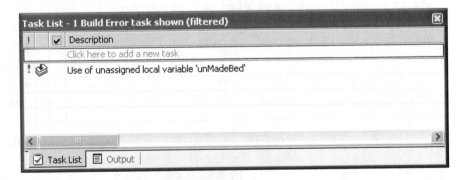

Constants

A *constant* is an identifier used in place of a value. (You can think of a constant as a variable whose value cannot be changed.) Constants should be used for fixed values that occur many places in your code. They should also be used in place of a value whose purpose is not immediately clear from the value.

Constants used in this way—also called *symbolic constants*—are declared in C# using the `const` keyword followed by the constant's type, an identifier, and the assignment of value. A constant must be initialized when it is declared, and once it has been initialized the value cannot be changed.

For example, here are the declarations for three notional constants:

```
const int maxSearchRecords = 41928;
const decimal interestRate = 6.75M;
const string companyMotto = "Best of the Best of the Best!";
```

The first of these, `maxSearchRecords`, might represent the maximum number of records in a search routine. Even if you use this value only once, using an identifier in this manner makes it much clearer what it represents than would be the case if the value itself was used.

NOTE   For constants that you may need to change, it is also a good idea to put them in a place where you can find them—at the top of a procedure, or in their own class module, as appropriate.

The second constant, `interestRate`, might be used in a financial application. The `M` following the value tells the compiler that the value is of type `decimal` rather than `double`. Assigning 6.75, which alone would be a literal of type `double`, to a `decimal`-type constant would produce a conversion error. (The trailing letter here can be upper- or lowercase: `m` or `M`.)

If the `interestRate` value is used repeatedly in the program, it's certainly easier—and a better practice—to only change it once, when the constant value is assigned, rather than throughout the application. (Of course, in the real world you'd probably want to do this technique one better and provide a way to change the interest rate used without having to edit—and recompile—code.)

The final constant example, `companyMotto`, is included primarily to show that constants can contain string values, as well as other data types. Here's `companyMotto` used with a `MessageBox.Show` method:

```
MessageBox.Show(companyMotto, "Sir!", MessageBoxButtons.OK);
```

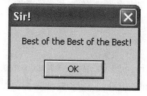

The same reasons for using constants rather than literal values apply to string types, and perhaps companyMotto is an example of this: You don't have to retype the string in numerous places in your application, and if the company changes its motto, you only have to change it in one place.

NOTE Dynamic properties, found at the top of the Properties window, allow you to load properties from an external configuration file. These values, which can easily be changed without the need for recompiling a project, can be used in the place of constants in an application. For more information, look up "Introduction to Dynamic Properties" in online help.

Enumeration Constants

Enumerations are lists of named constants—called *enumeration constants*—of the same type. (The list of constants within an enumeration is also called the *enumerator list*.)

Built-In Enumerations

You've almost certainly used the enumeration constants that are part of the .NET Framework's pre-built types. For example, use of the MessageBox.Show method was explained in Chapter 3, "Windows Uses Web Services, Too!".

The fourth MessageBox.Show method argument represents the icon that will be displayed in the message box. This icon is selected by choosing from a list of enumeration constants, each a member of the MessageBoxIcon enumeration. You'll see the list of constants for the enumeration supplied by the auto-completion feature of the Code Editor when you type in a MessageBox.Show (Figure 6.1).

FIGURE 6.1:

The auto-completion feature of the Code Editor supplies the members of an enumerator list.

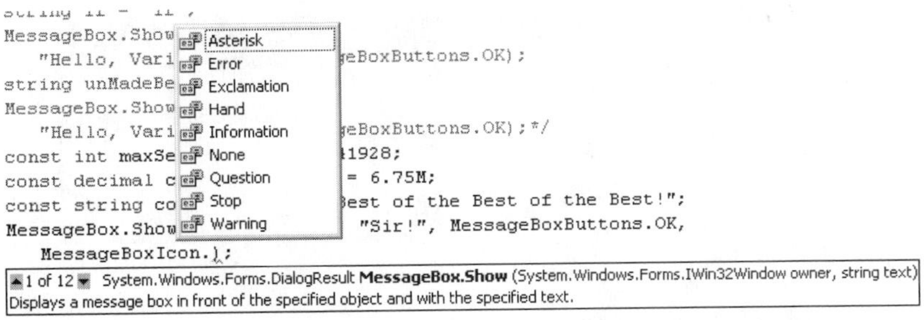

You can also find member information for an enumerator list in the Object Browser, as shown in Figure 6.2.

FIGURE 6.2:

The members of an
enumeration constant
list are shown in the
Object Browser.

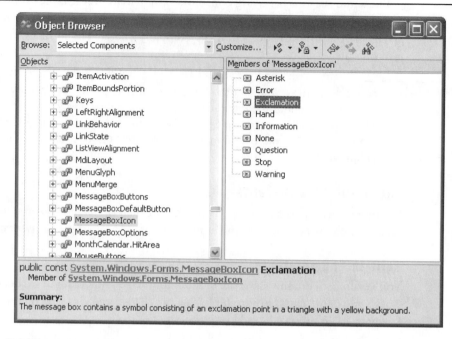

The icon that represents the choice made by the selection of the enumeration constant from the list of MessageBoxIcon members will be displayed when the message box is displayed:

```csharp
const string companyMotto = "Best of the Best of the Best!";
MessageBox.Show(companyMotto, "Sir!", MessageBoxButtons.OK,
    MessageBoxIcon.Exclamation);
```

Custom Enumerations

Enumerations are too good to just use with types provided by .NET—you'll want to use your own enumerations, using the enum keyword, in situations where related items form a natural list of possibilities.

An enumeration has a *base* type, which is the underlying C# intrinsic type for items in the enumeration. If the base type of an enumeration is not specified, it defaults to `int`. In addition, you needn't assign a value to each enumeration constant (but you can if you wish). In the default case, the first item in the enumerator list has a value of zero, and each successive enumerator is increased by one. For example, if you created an enumeration named *toys* with three items:

```
enum toys {train, dinosaur, truck};
```

the items would have values as follows:

Enumerator	Value
toys.train	0
toys.dinosaur	1
toys.truck	2

Now, when you attempt to use this enumeration, the members appear alphabetically in the Code Editor's auto-completion list, just like a built-in enumeration.

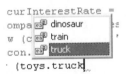

The members of the *toys* enumeration will also appear in the Object Browser.

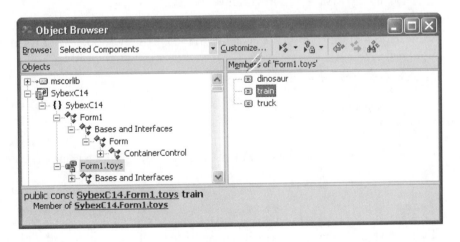

By the way, if you attempted to display the value of `toys.truck` using a statement along the lines of

```
MessageBox.Show(toys.truck.ToString());
```

you'd get the string "truck" rather than the underlying value.

To access the underlying value of the enumeration constant, you would have to cast it to integer type. For example, under this scenario,

```
int x = (int) toys.truck;
```

the variable *x* now has a value of 2. For more about casting, see "Type Conversion" later in this chapter.

NOTE   The enum declaration should appear as part of a class definition, rather than inside a method, as placing one inside a method causes compilation errors.

If you wish to explicitly assign values to the enumeration items, you can do so in the enum declaration. For example:

```
enum toys {train = 12, dinosaur = 35, truck = 42};
```

You can also start an enumeration list at whatever value you'd like, and only assign values to some items—in which case, the default is to increment by 1. So, if the *toys* enumeration were modified as follows:

```
enum toys {train = 12,
    dinosaur,
    excavator = 41,
    truck
};
```

then `toys.dinosaur` would have a value of 13 and `toys.truck` a value of 42.

Types

Everything in C# is a type—which is why the topic of types has already come up numerous times in this discussion of basic C# syntax. So we had better get C# and types under our belt right away to put an end to the continuing possibility of circular definitions.

So far in this chapter I've used a few types—int, string, and decimal—to provide examples of constants, variables, and enumerations. Table 6.2 shows the complete list of C# predefined, or intrinsic, types (also sometimes called *primitive* types). These predefined types are declared using a keyword that functions as an alias or shorthand for the type provided by the system. For example, the keyword int refers to the System.Int32 type, and the keyword string refers to the System.String type. (Stylistically, you should use the keyword rather than the fully-qualified name of the underlying type to refer to the type.)

TABLE 6.2: Predefined C# Types

Keyword	.NET Type	Bytes Reserved in Memory	Description
byte	System.Byte	1	Unsigned 8-bit integer value (0 to 255).
char	System.Char	1	Unicode character.
bool	System.Boolean	1	Boolean type: either true or false. Visual Basic users should note that the bool type can contain only true or false, and not an integer value of 0, 1, or –1 as in some versions of VB.
sbyte	System.Sbyte	1	Signed 8-bit integer value (–128 to 127).
short	System.Int16	2	Signed 16-bit integer value (–32,768 to 32,767).
ushort	System.Uint16	2	Unsigned 16-bit integer value (0 to 65,535).
int	System.Int32	4	Signed 32-bit integer value (–2,147,483,647 to 2,147,483,647).
uint	System.Uint32	4	Unsigned 32-bit integer value (0 to 4,294,967,295).
float	System.Single	4	Single-precision floating point number.
double	System.Double	8	Double-precision floating point number.
decimal	System.Decimal	8	Fixed-precision number up to 28 digits and the position of the decimal place. Used in financial calculations. Requires an m or M appended (see example in the "Constants" section earlier in this chapter).
long	System.Int64	8	Signed 64-bit integer.
ulong	System.Uint64	8	Unsigned 64-bit integer.
object	System.Object	N/A	All data types, predefined and user-defined, inherit from the System.Object class, aliased as object.
string	System.String	N/A	A sequence of Unicode characters. See the next section and Chapter 9, "Everything Is String Manipulation."

In Table 6.2, `object` and `string` are *reference* types, meaning that a pointer to the data is stored rather than the data itself, while the other types in the table are *value* types (meaning that the actual value of the type is stored in memory).

In addition to the predefined types, you can use C# to create custom reference types. As you've probably gathered in the previous chapters of this book, the heart of programming in C# is creating your own types by designing classes (which are reference types) that serve as a blueprint for objects. Besides classes, other important reference types include arrays, delegates, and interface types.

In Chapter 5, "Reflecting on Classes," I showed you how to create your own classes and a class library and provided a delegate example. You'll find more material about creating your own types using classes and interfaces in Chapter 8, "The Life of the Object in C#."

String Variables

As you probably know, you can't build much of a program without using strings. (Strings are so important that I've devoted a whole chapter—Chapter 9—to some of C#'s sophisticated ways to work with them.)

Placing double quotes around a string of alphanumeric characters creates a string literal. For example,

```
"I am a string!"
```

NOTE   Obviously, within string literals, white space does have a meaning—as opposed to everywhere else in C# where it does not. So the string literal `"I am a string!"` is not the equivalent of `"Iamastring!"`.

String variables are declared using the keyword `string`. You've already seen many examples of string variables in this book, and here's another that declares a string variable and assigns a literal string value to it:

```
string sloganOfTheDay = "Today is the first day of the rest of your life.";
```

As usual, you can declare an uninitialized variable of type `string`, and later assign a value to it programmatically. However, definite assignment requires that you never actually use an unassigned variable, string or otherwise.

Unicode Character Encoding System

As I noted in Table 6.2, strings in .NET are made up of Unicode characters—actually, characters encoded using UTF-16 (Unicode transformation format, 16-bit encoding).

The Unicode formats provide a unique number for every character, no matter what the platform, no matter what the program, and no matter what the language.

You can find out more information about Unicode at www.unicode.org.

As I mentioned before, the keyword `string` is actually a kind of alias to the `System.String` class, so by declaring a variable of type `string` you are creating an instance of a `System.String` object. You'll find out more about working with `System.String` objects in Chapter 9, but for now, you might want to have a look at the members of the `System.String` class using the Object Browser (Figure 6.3).

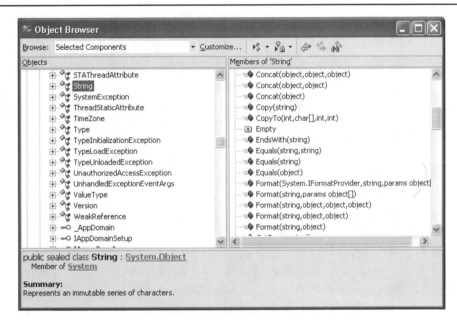

To view the `System.String` type—and the other predefined C# types—in the Object Browser, first expand the `mscorlib` assembly node, and then expand the System namespace node. Alternatively, you can use the Find Symbol dialog, as explained in Chapter 5.

C# Is a Strongly Typed Language

You've probably already heard the phrase "C# is a strongly typed language"—and may, indeed, already know what it means (in which case, you can skip this section with "type safety"). However, this whole area of strong typing and type conversions is one of the most frustrating things for programmers coming to C# from a weakly typed environment such as Visual Basic—so this and the next section are especially for those of you in that boat.

In a strongly typed language, all variables have a type that must be declared. In addition, the compiler verifies the type consistency of expressions (and expressions are always of a type defined by the C# language, or are user-defined types).

TIP To make VB .NET strongly typed in much the way that C# .NET is, you'd run VB .NET with the compiler option `Strict` set to On, accomplished either in the IDE Options dialog, or by adding the statement `Option Strict On` at the beginning of each code module. Note that VB6 and earlier versions of Visual Basic had no way to enforce strong typing—and were, by definition, weak type environments.

As a practical matter, working in a strongly typed language means that you need to be very clear about the type of information that will be stored in a variable. Strong typing enforces programming discipline and clarity about the contents of variables. It also prevents possible program errors that can occur in weakly typed environments when the compiler finds the wrong kind of value in a type. Another way of thinking of this is that weak typing allows a programmer to be lazy—in a possibly dubious type conversion, the compiler "guesses" what the programmer most likely meant (which can occasionally introduce errors).

The trade-off for the benefits of strong typing is more work up front. For one thing, you must explicitly declare the type of all variables (which is good programming practice even in weakly typed environments, where it may not be required). For another, you must pay close attention in your code every time a value of one type is converted to another. Much of the time, you must provide explicit guidance to the compiler using casting or a conversion method about the type conversion you'd like (see the "Explicit Conversion" section later for information about how to do this).

Type conversion can get pretty convoluted, and can involve multiple conversions within a single statement. For example, the statement

```
mbb = (MessageBoxButtons) Convert.ToInt16(rb.Tag.ToString());
```

in the "RadioButtons and Message Boxes" section of Chapter 3 involves three conversions that had to be specified by the programmer:

- A cast to type `MessageBoxButtons`
- A conversion to type `short` using the `ToInt16` method of the `System.Convert` object
- A conversion to type `string` using the `ToString` method inherited by all objects from `System.Object`

A simple example is probably the best way for getting a feel for the difference between working in a weakly and strongly typed environment.

If you run the following code in VB .NET (with `Option Strict` disengaged),

```
Dim theFloat As Double = 3.5
Dim X As Integer = 2
X = X + theFloat
MessageBox.Show(X)
```

the program will run without syntax errors. The value of *theFloat* will be rounded up and off to 4 when it is added and assigned to the integer *X*.

Next, in the message box statement, the integer argument *X* is automatically converted to a string type, and the value 6 is displayed.

TIP   This is convenient if it is what you want to have happen, but it is also the possible source of the introduction of errors in more complex programs if you are not counting on the round-up. Adding 3.5 and 2 and getting 6 as the integer result is not unreasonable. However, adding 2.5, 3.5, and 2 and getting 9—which is what would happen in VB—is pretty weird (8 would be a better result).

The comparable code in C#,

```
double theFloat = 3.5;
int X = 2;
X = X + theFloat;
MessageBox.Show(X);
```

simply will not compile due to several conversion-related syntax errors.

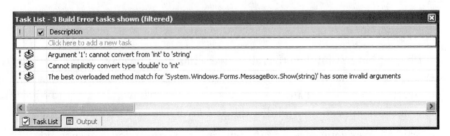

You can correct the C# code snippet by casting the double-type variable *theFloat* to int and using the ToString method to display the contents of the variable *X* in the message box:

```
double theFloat = 3.5;
int X = 2;
X = X + (int) theFloat;
MessageBox.Show(X.ToString());
```

This code compiles and runs just fine without any syntax errors, but—interestingly—it produces different results than the VB code, truncating *theFloat* to 3 and displaying 5 as the result. The (int) cast has simply taken the whole-number portion of *theFloat* variable. To perform the round-off operation that you'd normally expect when converting 3.5 to an integer value (e.g., 4), you need to use the explicit Convert.ToInt16 method:

```
double theFloat = 3.5;
int X = 2;
X = X + Convert.ToInt16(theFloat);
MessageBox.Show(X.ToString());
```

Type Conversion

All this leads us to the topic of type conversion. It isn't rocket science, and if you pay attention to it in the beginning, you will save yourself a great deal of grief. It's your job as a programmer in C# to stage-manage conversions from one type to another. As the example at the end of the previous section shows, there can be subtle differences between various ways of converting. (The example showed that casting a double to integer produced a different round-off result than using an explicit conversion function on the double.)

There are three general ways to convert from one type to another:

- Implicit conversion
- Explicit conversion via casting
- Use of a conversion method

NOTE   You can define implicit and explicit conversions for types you create yourself. For more information, look up "User-Defined Conversions Tutorial" in online help.

I hope I haven't implied that all conversions must be explicit in C#—because that's not the case. Provided that there is no way that the conversion will lose information, C# will implicitly convert for you without any special syntax. Implicit conversions must be guaranteed to succeed and not lose information, while explicit conversions are needed if either:

- run-time exigencies determine whether the conversion will succeed;
- or, some data might be lost during conversion.

In other words, if you explicitly convert using casting, you are responsible for making sure that the results are what you anticipate and don't lead to any unexpected run-time errors.

Implicit Conversion

Table 6.3 shows the implicit conversions that are available for simple types.

TABLE 6.3: Implicit Conversions for Simple C# Types

Type (Conversion From)	Legal Implicit Conversion To
sbyte	short, int, long, float, double, or decimal
byte	short, ushort, int, uint, long, ulong, float, double, or decimal
short	int, long, float, double, or decimal
ushort	int, uint, long, ulong, float, double, or decimal
int	long, float, double, or decimal
uint	long, ulong, float, double, or decimal
long	float, double, or decimal
char	ushort, int, uint, long, ulong, float, double, or decimal
float	double
ulong	float, double, or decimal

In addition:

- There are no allowable implicit conversions from the bool, double, or decimal types.

- There are no implicit conversions allowed *to* the char type.

- There are no implicit conversions allowed between the floating-point types and the decimal type.

As its name implies, no special syntax is required to perform implicit conversion, which can take place in several situations, including assignment statements and method invocations. For example,

```
double F;
int X = 2;
F = X; // implicit conversion
```

implicitly (and successfully) converts an int value to type double.

Here's another example that implicitly converts an int to a long in a method invocation (the method takes a long as its argument):

```
long doubleIt(long inNum) {
   return inNum * 2;
}
...
int X = 2;
MessageBox.Show(doubleIt(X).ToString()); // displays 4
```

NOTE   For a discussion of the ToString method, which converts the integral return value of the doubleIt method to a string so that it can be displayed by the MessageBox.Show method, see the "Conversion Functions" section.

Implicit conversions are also possible for more complex reference types. Generally, when you eyeball two reference types to see whether you can do an implicit conversion, you should be asking the same question as with simple type conversions: Can I guarantee the success of the operation without data loss?

In addition, some rules do apply to reference-type implicit conversions. For example, any reference type can be implicitly converted to `object`. And, any derived class can be implicitly converted to the class it was derived from.

For more information about implicit reference conversions, search for the topic "Implicit Reference Conversions" in online help.

Explicit Conversion

In the previous example, I showed you that an `int` value could be implicitly converted to a `long` value implicitly without any additional C# syntax. As you'd probably suppose, and you can see in Table 6.3, the reverse is not true: a `long` value cannot be implicitly converted to type `int`. It is easy to see why this should be the case. `long`s have a much larger range of possible values than `int`s, and there is no way the compiler can know that a `long`-to-`int` conversion won't occur when the `long` stores a bigger value than the `int` can store, causing a run-time error. In other words, the conversion isn't guaranteed safe.

If you change the code in the example around, to attempt to cause an implicit conversion,

```
int doubleIt(int inNum) {
    return inNum * 2;
}
...
long X = 2;
MessageBox.Show(doubleIt(X).ToString());
```

it won't compile, and you'll get a syntax error.

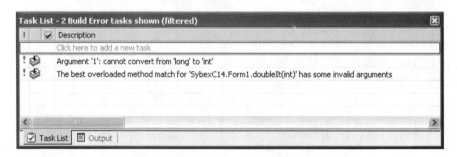

However, it might be perfectly reasonable on the part of you, the all-knowing programmer, to want to convert the `long` value to an `int`. You might know perfectly well that the variable holding the `long` value in the program will never hold a big enough number at the point it is converted to `int` to cause a problem.

In this case, you'd use an explicit conversion by placing a cast operator in front of the expression to be converted. A cast operator is the name of the type being converted to inside parentheses. For example, to convert the `long` variable *X* to an integer variable *Y*:

```
int Y = (int) X;
```

Using this cast in the example that gave us a syntax error, it will compile and run fine now:

```
int doubleIt(int inNum) {
    return inNum * 2;
}
...
long X = 2;
int Y = (int) X; // cast the long value to an int
MessageBox.Show(doubleIt(Y).ToString()); // now it displays 4
```

Note that you don't really need a separate statement for the performance of the cast; it can be done at the same time as the method invocation. The `doubleIt` method, which expects an `int` argument, receives it in the form of a cast from `long` to `int`:

```
...
long X = 2;
MessageBox.Show(doubleIt((int)X).ToString());
```

Table 6.4 shows the explicit numeric conversions that you can do using casting.

TABLE 6.4: Permissible Explicit Numeric Conversions

Type (Conversion From)	Legal Explicit Conversion To
sbyte	byte, ushort, uint, ulong, or char
byte	sbyte or char
short	sbyte, byte, ushort, uint, ulong, or char
ushort	sbyte, byte, short, or char
int	sbyte, byte, short, ushort, uint, ulong, or char
uint	sbyte, byte, short, ushort, int, or char
long	sbyte, byte, short, ushort, int, uint, ulong, or char
ulong	sbyte, byte, short, ushort, int, uint, long, or char
char	sbyte, byte, or short
float	sbyte, byte, short, ushort, int, uint, long, ulong, char, or decimal
double	sbyte, byte, short, ushort, int, uint, long, ulong, char, float, or decimal
decimal	sbyte, byte, short, ushort, int, uint, long, ulong, char, float, or double

NOTE   You can explicitly cast one type to another even if the conversion could be handled by implicit conversion (for example, `int` to `long`).

Casts can be done between more complex reference types as well as simple numeric types, of course. Some rules do apply. For example, `object` can be cast to any reference type, and a base class can be explicitly converted to a derived class.

For example, in Chapter 3, in the section "Determining Which Object Fired an Event," I cast the *sender* parameter of an event procedure to the type `Control`:

```
Control ctrl = (Control) sender;
```

I knew that this cast would not fail, because each object stored in the *sender* parameter had to be a control and derived from the `Control` class.

In actual practice, you may have to test these conversions on a case-by-case basis. If an explicit reference conversion fails, a `System.InvalidCastException` is thrown. (For more information about exceptions, see the "Exceptions" section toward the end of this chapter.)

The *as* Operator

Operators aren't really discussed until later in this chapter. However, I've already used many of them in this book—for example, the simple assignment operator (=). Casts, which we've just discussed, are operators. You probably have a pretty good notion of what most of the operators in C# are likely to be (for more information, see the "Operators" section later in this chapter).

So it seems appropriate to discuss the `as` operator here. The `as` operator works like a cast, except that if it can't perform the indicated conversion, it returns `null` rather than throwing an exception.

> **NOTE**   The `null` keyword represents a null reference, one that does not refer to any object.

For example, the following code snippet will store a `null` reference in the variable *str* (with the resulting display that "i is not a string"):

```
object i = 42;
string str = i as string;
if (str == null){
    MessageBox.Show("i is not a string");
}
else {
    MessageBox.Show(str);
}
```

Had the variable *i* contained string data, such as

```
object i = "hello";
```

then the string data "hello" would have been displayed in the message box after the object type *i* was converted to the string type *str*.

Conversion Methods

The shared public members of the System.Convert class can be used to convert a base data type to another base data type. For example, somewhat trivially, the Convert.ToBoolean method converts the string "False" to the bool value false:

```
if (Convert.ToBoolean("False") == false){
    MessageBox.Show("False");
}
else {
    MessageBox.Show("True");
}
```

If you run this code snippet, you can use it to display yet another "False" string!

In theory, a Convert class method exists to convert every base type to every other base type, and you'll probably find yourself using these methods quite a bit. For example, in Chapter 4, "Building a Better Windows Interface," I showed you how to retrieve an item's text from a ListBox by index. As part of that demonstration, the user entered the index to be retrieved as a text string. That string, for example "4", needed to be converted to an integral value so that the item's text could be displayed:

```
MessageBox.Show
    (checkedListBox1.Items [Convert.ToInt16(txtIndex.Text)].ToString(),
    "Here is your text", MessageBoxButtons.OK, MessageBoxIcon.Information);
```

If you look up the System.Convert class in the Object Browser, as shown in Figure 6.4, you'll see that there are really a huge number of these conversion methods.

FIGURE 6.4:

If you look in the Object Browser, you'll see that the Convert class has a great many conversion methods.

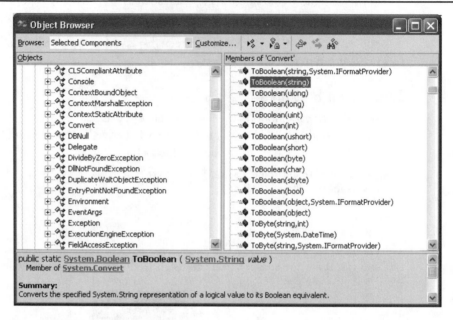

You should know that the Convert methods throw an exception (and don't do any conversion) when meaningful results cannot be obtained. For example, calling any of the methods that convert the reference type System.DateTime to or from anything other than string always produces an exception (and no conversion takes place).

NOTE   If a method always throws an exception when invoked, this is noted in the summary in the Descriptions pane of the Object Browser. Why include these methods, such as ToDateTime(long), which throw an exception whenever invoked and *never* convert anything? Beats the heck out of me...

In addition, an overflow exception is thrown (and no conversion takes place) if you try to stuff too large a value into a type that cannot store it.

The *ToString* Method

Another very useful conversion method is System.Object.ToString. I've already used this method quite a bit in this book (including several times in this chapter). For example, in the demonstration of reflection in Chapter 5, I used the ToString method to display method information about objects that were being reflected:

```
foreach (MethodInfo method in theMethods){
    lstMethods.Items.Add(method.ToString());
```

The good news about the ToString method is that since it is a member of the object type, all other types inherit it. Whatever your object is, it has a ToString method that delivers a string.

One thing that ToString is always good for is converting numbers to their string representation—a common task in displaying numbers, among other things. For example, you can use the ToString method to display the first four places of the expansion of Π:

```
double theNumber = 3.1415;
MessageBox.Show(theNumber.ToString());
```

A moment ago, I told you that the good news is that the ToString of any object will always deliver a string. The bad news is that it may not always be the string you want or need. By definition, the ToString method of an object returns a string that represents the object. The problem is that it is up to the implementer of a class to decide what is returned by objects based on the class. Most of the time, ToString is implemented so that it returns something reasonably useful, but you won't know until you try.

For example, if you invoke a Form's ToString method, you'll get the fully qualified form name, followed by the literal ", Text:", followed by the contents of the form's Text property (its caption), as shown in Figure 6.5.

FIGURE 6.5:

The ToString method of a Form provides quite a bit of information.

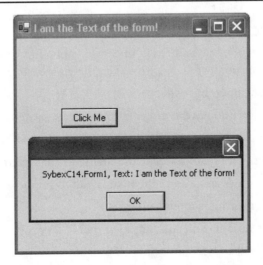

Now, most likely what you really wanted was the unqualified name of the form—and it is true that you could parse this out of the string returned by the ToString method—but the point stands that with complex objects you need to be careful about exactly what ToString returns.

> **NOTE** When it comes time to create your own classes, you should understand that you are responsible for implementing the ToString method in a way that returns a useful value. See Chapter 9 for information about adding ToString methods to your own classes.

Commenting Code

I described the mechanisms for commenting, or annotating, C# code early in this book, in Chapter 1, "Creating a Web Service"—but commenting is such an important part of producing good code that it is worth reminding you about them.

Two forward slash marks (//) designate a comment in the so-called C++ style. Everything on the line following the two forward slash marks is considered a comment and is ignored by the compiler. Here are two examples:

```
// I am a comment!
double theNumber = 3.1415; // This is another comment...
```

C# also supports comments that begin with /* and end with */. (This is called C-style commenting.) Everything within these delimiters is a comment, which can span multiple lines. For example:

```
/* I am a comment! */
/* I
    am
    another
    comment! */
```

Self-Documenting Code

The content of a comment is, of course, more important than its form. Comments should be used in the context of code that is crafted for clarity. Clear code is largely self-documenting.

Self-documenting code:

- Pays attention to the structural and conceptual design of a program and the objects used in it.
- Uses expressions and statements that are written for clarity of purpose.
- Makes sure that flow control statements clearly express what they are doing.
- Uses white space and statement layout to promote clarity of intention.
- Uses identifiers intelligently.
- Uses variable and constant identifiers that express the nature of the variable or value being stored.

- Makes sure that method identifiers express what the method does.
- Uses method parameters that clearly convey expected inputs and outputs.
- Uses class identifiers to convey the nature of objects that can be instantiated based on the class.
- Doesn't try to make objects (or methods) serve multiple purposes.

So, What About Comments?

So if the code is clearly written and it's so gosh darn self-documenting, when should comments be used?

Comments should be used to clarify anything that is not otherwise obvious—for example, the expected value range of a method argument. In another example, if you have a complicated double or triple cast and conversion, you might want to add a comment to the code explaining what it is doing (so that you don't have to figure it out again next time you look at the code).

It is also a good general practice to add a comment at the beginning of each type—such as a class—indicating the author, date, revision history, and purpose of the type, with notes about anything unusual or not likely to be clear on casual inspection.

XML Documentation

As I explained in Chapter 1, C# lines beginning with three slashes (///) are XML documentation, a special form of commenting. XML documentation is information contained between tags that can be used to automatically create a set of documentation for a program. This documentation can be used online in a special viewer provided by Visual Studio or to create a separate documentation file.

The great advantage of using XML documentation is that it is easy to document projects while you work—but harder if someone has to come back later and do it. (The upshot most of the time is that if you don't document it while you do it, a project most likely never gets documented.)

For more information, see "XML Comments" in Chapter 1. For a complete list of the XML tags that can be used with the documentation facility, see the "Tags for Documentation Comments" topic in online help.

Operators

As you'd expect, C# has a full complement of operators in various categories, most of which are shown in Table 6.5. You should also know that many operators can be *overloaded* in user-defined types—in other words, the meaning of the operators can be customized when user-defined types, such as classes, are involved in operations (for more on overloading, see Chapter 8).

TABLE 6.5: C# Operators

Operator	Meaning
Arithmetic	
+	Addition.
–	Subtraction.
*	Multiplication.
/	Division.
%	Modulus.
Logical (Boolean and Bitwise)	
&	AND.
|	OR.
^	Exclusive OR.
!	NOT.
~	Bitwise complement.
&&	Conditional AND—only evaluates its second operand if necessary.
||	Conditional OR—only evaluates its second operand if necessary.
String Concatenation	
+	Concatenates two strings.
Increment, Decrement	
++	Increments operand by 1 (see following text).
– –	Decrements operand by 1 (see following text).
Comparison	
==	Equality. Note that this operator, which compares two operands, should not be confused with the assignment operator (=).
!=	Inequality.
<	Less than.
>	Greater than.
<=	Less than or equal.
>=	Greater than or equal.
Assignment	
=	Assigns the value of the right operand to the left operand. Not to be confused with the equality comparison operator (==).
+=	Addition assignment.
–=	Subtraction assignment.
*=	Multiplication assignment.
/=	Division assignment.

Continued on next page

TABLE 6.5 CONTINUED: C# Operators

Operator	Meaning
%=	Modulus assignment.
&=	AND assignment.
|=	OR assignment.
^=	Exclusive OR assignment.
Member Access	
.	The member access operator, also called the dot operator; used to access members of a type. For example, Form1.Text can be used to get or set the Text property of Form1.
Indexing	
[ ]	Array indexing (square brackets are also used to specify attributes). For more about indexing, see Chapter 7, "Arrays, Indexers, and Collections."
Casting	
( )	See "Explicit Conversion" earlier in this chapter.
as	See "The *as* Operator" earlier in this chapter.
Conditional	
?:	Conditional operator (see following text).
Delegate Addition and Removal	
+	Adds a delegate. (Delegates are pointers to methods such as events. See "Adding an Event" in Chapter 5 for an example of how to use a delegate.)
−	Removes a delegate.
Object Creation	
new	Creates an instance of an object.
Type Information	
is	Type comparison (see following text).
sizeof	Returns the size, in bytes, of a value type.
typeof	Returns the type of an object as a System.Type object.

When the increment operator is placed before the operand (a prefix increment operator), the result of the operation is the value of the operand after it has been incremented. When placed after the operand (a postfix increment operator), the result of the operation is the value of the operand before it has been incremented. The decrement operator works in similar fashion.

The conditional operator (?:), also called the ternary operator, returns one of two values depending on the value of a conditional expression. For example, the variable *whichOne* in the expression

```
string whichOne = (1 == 0) ? "Condition True" : "Condition False";
```

is assigned the value "Condition False" because the expression 1 == 0 always evaluates to false, thus causing the second choice to be selected.

The is operator checks to see whether the run-time type of an object is of a given type. A little more precisely, it evaluates true if the test expression, which must be a reference type, can be cast to the specified type without throwing an exception. For an example that uses the is operator, see "RadioButtons and Message Boxes" in Chapter 3.

TIP   VB programmers are used to one operator symbol (=) performing both assignment and comparison. In contrast, C# uses different symbols for the two different operators: == for comparison, and = for assignment. This can be a little confusing until you get used to it, but probably is a better way of doing things in the long run because using a single operator for a single purpose has less potential for confusion.

Short-Circuit Evaluation

The conditional AND and OR operators (&& and ||) perform what is sometimes called *short-circuit evaluation*. This means that they do not evaluate the second part of an expression if there is no need to. For example, if you have the expression a && b, and a has evaluated to false, b will not be evaluated. Obviously, there is some performance benefit to not having to look at the second operand.

However, this contains the seeds of a hidden pitfall if the evaluation of an expression contained in b is required for successful execution. (In the classic example, b is a function that performs other tasks before returning its Boolean result.) Since b never gets evaluated, the program will fail. So have some caution using short-circuit evaluation to make sure that you aren't introducing an unexpected side effect by not evaluating an operand.

As a matter of good programming practice, I'd hate to see you writing code that uses evaluations performed in a logical operation to perform some other action needed for program success. This kind of tricky code can be fun to write, but it violates the precepts of writing clear code and keeping objects and methods from doing more than one thing. If you don't try to get too fancy for your own good, you shouldn't have problems with short-circuit evaluations.

NOTE   The indirection and address operators (*, ->, [ ], and &) are used to declare, reference, and deference pointers, and obtain memory addresses, all within "unsafe" code—that is, code within a context, such as a method, that has been marked with the unsafe keyword. Although you should know that they exist, it is unlikely that you will want to use them. Code using them cannot be run as "safe" by the .NET Common Language Runtime (CLR), and it's obvious why they are unsafe. If you have direct access to memory, and can control pointers to memory, corruption can always occur. Generally, you should not have any use for these operators—except in certain specialized situations, such as interoperating with COM objects.

Table 6.6 shows operator *precedence*, or the order in which a series of operators are evaluated, in C#. When an operand occurs between two operators of equal precedence, operations are performed from left to right (except in the case of the assignment and conditional operators, which are evaluated right to left).

TABLE 6.6: Operator Precedence (in Descending Order of Category Precedence)

Category	Operators
Primary	Member access operator (.), order indicated by parentheses, indexing, x++, x--, new, typeof
Unary	Cast operator, +, -, !, ~, ++x, --x
Multiplicative	*, /, %
Additive	+, -
Relational and type testing	< , > , <= , >=, is, as
Equality	==, !=
Logical AND	&
Logical exclusive OR	^
Logical OR	|
Conditional AND	&&
Conditional OR	||
Conditional	?:
Assignment	=, *=, /=, %=, +=, -=, <<=, >>=, &=, ^=, |=

As a matter of good programming practice and to make code clearer to read, you should not rely on the order of operator precedence if this might be confusing—instead, use parentheses to make the evaluation order explicit and clear. Order indicated by parentheses takes precedence over operator-driven order, except that of the member access operator.

Flow Control Statements

In Chapters 3 and 4, I showed you how to work with break, if...else, for, foreach, and switch statements. Heaven forbid I should repeat myself! I'll assume that you know how to work with the flow control statements that have already been demonstrated—and which are fairly straightforward in any case—and use this section to explain some other C# flow control statements.

Flow to with *goto*

The lowly goto statement is alive and well in C#. goto statements are easy to use and direct; however, as is well known, over-reliance on them leads to unmanageable "spaghetti" code. In C#, goto statements are useful in a special situation—with switch statements. So it's worth having a look at the ancient, decrepit granddaddy of all flow control statements, one that surely gets no respect, the goto.

A goto statement causes an immediate, unconditional jump to a label, which is an identifier followed by a colon. For example:

```
IamAlabel:
```

To put this in the context of a short program, suppose the user gets to input a favorite member of the Beatles musical group in a TextBox named *txtBeatle*. The following code in a Button click event procedure uses goto statements and labels to display an appropriate message box if the user enters "John" or "Ringo," as shown in Figure 6.6, and otherwise displays no message:

```
private void btnClickMe_Click(object sender, System.EventArgs e) {
    string msg = "";
    if (txtBeatle.Text == "John")
        goto john;
    if (txtBeatle.Text == "Ringo")
        goto ringo;
    goto done;
    john:
        msg = "I like John best, too!";
        goto done;
    ringo:
        msg = "Are you a drummer?";
        goto done;
    done:
        if (msg != "")
            MessageBox.Show(msg, "Beatle choice", MessageBoxButtons.OK);
}
```

FIGURE 6.6:

Flow control can be achieved using goto statements and labels.

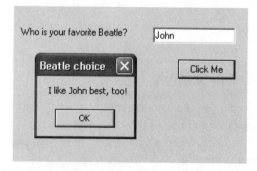

A couple of things are worth noting about the code snippet shown above. First, even in this simple example, one can see why using goto statements produces fragmented, confusing code.

Second, the if statements in this example are the simplest form possible, namely the expression to be evaluated followed by a single statement. Previously in this book, I've used curly braces following the evaluation expression in the if statement, which allows you to include a *statement block*—as many statements as you'd like—even when this wasn't strictly necessary because I only had one statement to execute.

Using *goto* in a *switch*

Of course, you can easily simplify this code by using a switch statement rather than goto statements and labels:

```
string msg = "";
switch (txtBeatle.Text) {
    case "John":
        msg = "I like John best, too!";
        break;
    case "Ringo":
        msg = "Are you a drummer?";
        break;
}
if (msg != "")
    MessageBox.Show(msg,"Beatle choice", MessageBoxButtons.OK);
```

Let's say you want to add another possibility to this switch statement, for people who enter "Mick" but really mean they like John. For this situation, a goto case statement—to the "John" case—can be added at the end of the "Mick" case. Users who enter "Mick" will be told they really like John and then redirected so they also get the "John" message:

```
switch (txtBeatle.Text) {
    case "John":
        msg = "I like John best, too!";
        break;
    case "Mick":
        MessageBox.Show("People who like Mick really like John.",
            "Beatle choice", MessageBoxButtons.OK);
        goto case "John";
    case "Ringo":
        msg = "Are you a drummer?";
        break;
}
```

while Statements

Looping is an important flow control element of most programs. I've shown you examples of looping using for and foreach, but I haven't yet demonstrated while and do...while statements—so let's take a quick look.

As in most other languages that have a while statement, the code within a while statement block is executed as long as the Boolean test at the beginning of the statement evaluates to true. As soon as the test evaluates to false, execution jumps to the statement immediately following the while statement block.

For example, the following while loop displays the integers from 1 to 9 in the title bar of a Form:

```
int i = 1;
string caption = "While";
while (i < 10){
    caption = caption + " + " + i.ToString();
    i++;
}
this.Text = caption;
```

do...while Statements

The do...while statement works like the while statement, except that the evaluation takes place at the end of the loop. Statements in a do...while loop will get executed at least once—even if the condition evaluates to false at the end. In contrast, if the condition is false, the statements in a while loop never get executed at all because the condition is evaluated at the start. Most of the time, the same results can be accomplished using either loop syntax, but there are some times when one works better than the other.

NOTE For example, if you are reading and operating on data, and don't know whether there is any data, you might want use a while statement to test for the existence of the data—perhaps testing for an end of file marker—so that if the data doesn't exist, no statements get executed. For more on reading files, see Chapter 10, "Working with Streams and Files."

Here's a do...while statement that displays the first 9 numbers in the Fibonacci series in the title bar of a form:

```
int A = 1; int B = 1; int C;
string caption = "Fibonacci: ";
do {
    caption = caption + A.ToString() + " ";
```

```
      C = A + B;
      A = B;
      B = C;
} while (A < 50);
this.Text = caption;
```

NOTE   If the condition in this loop were impossible, e.g., A < 0, it would still print the first number in the series, which would not be the case in a while loop with the condition at the top.

Structs

A struct is a simple user-defined type, a poor person's lightweight alternative to a class. Like classes, structs can contain properties, methods, and fields. Unlike classes, structs do not support inheritance. More precisely, structs derive from System.Object, like all types in C#, but they cannot inherit from any other class (or struct), and no class or struct can derive from a struct.

NOTE   A class can also be marked so that it cannot be inherited from, by using the sealed keyword, as I'll explain in Chapter 8.

Structs are value types, not reference types, and—like simple value types—they can be used without the new keyword.

Memory, Value-Type Variables, and Reference-Type Variables

Value-type variables hold their values, or data, within their own memory allocation. Technically, these values are stored in memory allocated for the value-type variable within a structure known as the program's *stack*, and can be accessed from within the program as long as they are within scope.

In contrast, reference-type variables—such as classes and strings—are implemented using a global memory structure called the *run-time heap*. Reference-type variables contain instances of classes, which are "pointers" to objects stored in memory on the heap.

Here's a simple example of a struct that might be used to store information about an employee:

```
public struct Employee {
    public string fullName, rank;
```

```
public long SSN;
public Employee (string fullName, string rank, long SSN){
   this.fullName = fullName;
   this.rank = rank;
   this.SSN = SSN;
}
}
```

You can create properties, using get and set accessors, within structs.

Here's one way the Employee struct might be declared, initialized, and used:

```
// Declare an instance
Employee HopperK;

// Initialize
HopperK.fullName = "Ken Hopper";
HopperK.rank = "Master Sergeant";
HopperK.SSN = 000112222;

// Display it
string str = HopperK.fullName + " has the rank of " + HopperK.rank + "!";
MessageBox.Show(str, "Structs Forever!",MessageBoxButtons.OK,
   MessageBoxIcon.Information);
```

Alternatively, you could create the instance of the struct by invoking its constructor, and initialize it in one fell swoop:

```
Employee DavisJ = new Employee("Julian Davis", "City Hall", 123456789);
```

Exceptions

An *exception* is an unexpected condition in a program. For example, an exception may occur if you attempt to connect to the database but can't, because it's down. The C# Exception object is used to store information about errors and abnormal events.

In real-world practice, industrial-strength programs must anticipate run-time errors. For example, a network resource might not be available because the network is down. Or a file can't be written to disk because the disk drive is full. With the best code in the world, these things happen. In the release version of a program, these and other errors must be handled, which in C# is done with exceptions.

What does it mean to "handle" an exception (or error)? These are the basics:

- Your program should not crash under any circumstances.

- If the situation can be recovered from, and the program can continue execution, it should.

- If execution cannot continue, a reasonably comprehensible message should explain that the program is terminating, and if appropriate, explain why.

- Data should not be lost due to an unplanned failure.

- The program should shut down gently.

- In any case, information necessary for debugging the problem should be saved, either to a file or the system event log. (It's easy to simultaneously send the user a message and write to the system log with MessageBox.Show, as I demonstrated in Chapter 3.)

Understanding Structured Exception Handling

Structured exception handling is recognized as the best way for a programming language to deal with common errors.

Using *try...catch...finally* Statements

When an exception does occur, you can use try...catch...finally statements to handle it.

The program statements in the try block are the body of the program that is being monitored for errors. Statements in a catch block are executed in response to a particular exception being thrown, as indicated in the catch statement's argument—or, if without an argument, the statement will catch any kind of exception, in which case it is referred to as a *general catch clause*.

As you would expect, code in the optional finally block is executed, whether an error has been caught or not.

NOTE   Not only is finally optional, so is catch. In other words, you can have a try without a finally and also a try...finally construction with no catch block, as I'll show you in a moment.

For example, if you have a form with a TextBox control and a Button control, you could add the following code in the button's Click event to catch different kinds of problems:

```
private void btnExceptions_Click(object sender, System.EventArgs e) {
    int i; double d;
    try {
        i = Convert.ToInt16(txtIn.Text);
        d = 42 / i;
    }
    catch (DivideByZeroException){
        MessageBox.Show("You are naughty to even think of dividing by zero!",
            "Exceptions", MessageBoxButtons.OK, MessageBoxIcon.Error);
    }
    catch (FormatException){
        MessageBox.Show("Please enter a number!", "Exceptions",
            MessageBoxButtons.OK, MessageBoxIcon.Error);
    }
}
```

In the example, catch deals with the situation if the user enters zero—which would cause a division by zero—as shown in Figure 6.7.

FIGURE 6.7:

The DivideByZero-Exception (left) and FormatException (right) are caught.

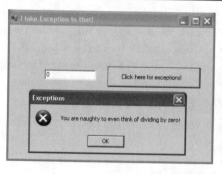
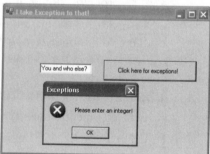

As you can also see in the figure, a FormatException catch block can be used to handle the exception that occurs when the user enters something that can't be converted to integer by Convert.ToInt16.

It's possible to have the first catch filter without any conditions:

```
catch
    statement block
```

You could also just catch the general Exception type:

```
catch (Exception excep)
```

In these cases, the catch filter will catch all errors. In some situations, you can use this as a centralized error-processing mechanism along the lines of "if any error happens, go here and take care of it." Often, however, it is a better idea to use specific catch clauses to handle certain types of exceptions. A final, generic catch clause could deal with all exceptions that don't need special handling—or that you didn't think of when you wrote the code.

Listing 6.1 shows the exception example with an added, general catch clause at the end.

Listing 6.1   **Handling Exceptions with *try...catch***

```
private void btnExceptions_Click(object sender, System.EventArgs e) {
    int i; double d;
    try {
        i = Convert.ToInt16 (txtIn.Text);
        d = 42 / i;
    }
    catch (DivideByZeroException){
        MessageBox.Show("You are naughty to even think of dividing by zero!",
            "Exceptions", MessageBoxButtons.OK, MessageBoxIcon.Error);
    }
    catch (FormatException){
        MessageBox.Show("Please enter a number!", "Exceptions",
            MessageBoxButtons.OK, MessageBoxIcon.Error);
    }
    catch (Exception excep) {
        MessageBox.Show(excep.Message);
    }
}
```

WARNING   If you reverse the order shown in Listing 6.1, and put the general catch clause before the specific catch exceptions, then the specific exception blocks are never processed.

If you run the code shown in Listing 6.1, you can trigger an error that is not handled by one of the specific catch handlers—for example, an overflow exception if the user enters a number larger than will fit in the data type, as shown in Figure 6.8.

FIGURE 6.8:

Since the OverflowException is not handled by a specific catch clause, it is handled by the general catch clause at the end of the catch blocks.

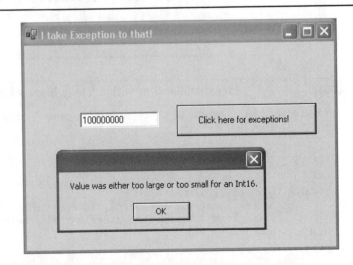

By the way, instead of displaying the Message property of the Exception object, you could make use of its ToString method, which contains a great deal of information, including the procedure, method, and line number that threw the exception. If you changed the final catch clause in Listing 6.1 to show the information returned by the ToString method:

```
catch (Exception excep) {
    MessageBox.Show(excep.ToString());
}
```

it would appear as shown in Figure 6.9.

FIGURE 6.9:

The ToString method of the Exception object contains a great deal of information about a thrown exception.

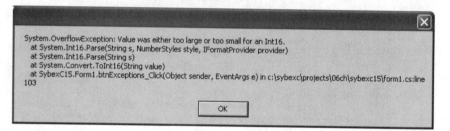

Boy, is that finally clause out of its mind, or what? You can't stop it from being executed, regardless of whether exceptions are thrown or, if thrown, handled or unhandled. This makes the finally clause the place to put clean-up code that you want executed no matter what happens.

Listing 6.2 shows the exception handling demonstration with a finally clause added. When you run the program, you'll see that the message box invoked in the finally clause is always displayed whether or not the exceptions are handled.

Listing 6.2   Exception Handling with a *finally* Block Added

```
private void btnExceptions_Click(object sender, System.EventArgs e) {
    int i; double d;
    try {
        i = Convert.ToInt16(txtIn.Text);
        d = 42 / i;
    }
    catch (DivideByZeroException){
        MessageBox.Show("You are naughty to even think of dividing by zero!",
            "Exceptions", MessageBoxButtons.OK, MessageBoxIcon.Error);
    }
```

```
catch (FormatException){
   MessageBox.Show("Please enter an integer!", "Exceptions",
      MessageBoxButtons.OK, MessageBoxIcon.Error);
}
catch (Exception excep) {
   MessageBox.Show(excep.Message);
   MessageBox.Show(excep.ToString());
}
finally {
   MessageBox.Show("You can't stop me from being executed!", "Exceptions",
      MessageBoxButtons.OK, MessageBoxIcon.Information);
}
}
```

NOTE In the real world, you'll want to use finally blocks to close open files and database connections, and generally to make sure that all resources used by a program are released.

What happens if you leave off the catch blocks—resulting in a try...finally statement? We can find out by modifying the code shown in Listing 6.2 to remove the catch blocks:

```
private void btnExceptions_Click(object sender, System.EventArgs e) {
   int i; double d;
   try {
      i = Convert.ToInt16(txtIn.Text);
      d = 42 / i;
   }
   finally {
      MessageBox.Show("You can't stop me from being executed!", "Exceptions",
         MessageBoxButtons.OK, MessageBoxIcon.Information);
   }
}
```

If the click event procedure runs without generating exceptions, the code in the finally block executes as you'd expect and the message box displays.

What happens next depends on whether you are running in debug mode in the development environment or whether the compiled executable was launched. Within the development environment, a Visual Studio exception message is displayed.

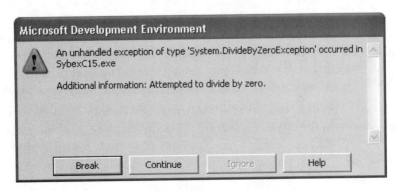

If Break is clicked, the program terminates. If Continue is clicked, the code in the `finally` clause is executed and the message box displayed, and then the application shuts down.

Of somewhat more interest is the behavior of the stand-alone executable (because exception handling is meant to deal with problems that occur in the run-time environment, not at design time).

If you run the stand-alone executable, the `finally` block code executes. Then, if an exception had been thrown, the .NET Framework dialog shown in Figure 6.10 is displayed.

FIGURE 6.10:

When run outside the development environment, if an exception is thrown, the `finally` block executes, and then this dialog is displayed.

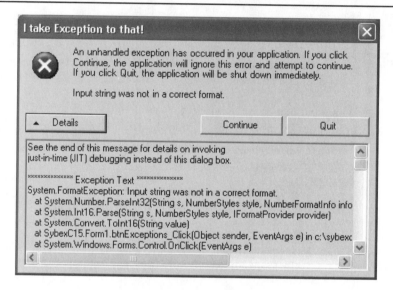

Not bad, really, as a user interface for all unhandled exceptions—and the `finally` code did execute before it was displayed, so in the real world you could have saved data, closed open files, and so forth!

If the user clicks Continue in the dialog shown in Figure 6.10, the application reopens.

Throwing Exceptions

Throwing an exception means creating your own exception under certain conditions. Throwing custom exceptions should not be done to facilitate normal program communication, but it may make sense as part of a scheme for dealing with *logical errors*, which occur when a program works properly but produces wrong results. Throwing an exception is what your application should do in many circumstances if it asked to do something impossible.

To throw an exception, use the `throw` keyword with a new instantiation of the `Exception` class, or one of the classes derived from `Exception` (the `Exception` object and classes are described in the next section). `ApplicationException` is the subclass of `Exception` used for exceptions thrown by an application, so it's a good one to throw.

NOTE   As a good programming practice, your application should throw only `ApplicationException` objects, or those that inherit `ApplicationException`. It's not good practice to throw instances of `System.Exception`.

In the real world, you may want to subclass `ApplicationException` to add functionality to the exception thrown.

A string representing the `Exception.Message` property is used to instantiate the new exception, which can then be used to catch it, as in this example:

```
throw(new ApplicationException("AttilaTheHun"));
```

This exception would probably be caught within a `catch (Exception excep)` block using a conditional:

```
catch (Exception excep) {
    if (excep.Message == "AttilaTheHun"){
...
```

Let's look at an example of throwing and catching an exception in practice.

There is something in business—and software development—known as the "cockroach" theory: if one problem becomes apparent, there are probably more problems lurking (like roaches).

Suppose, in the example I've used so far to show you exceptions, that the user types the phrase "cockroaches" in the TextBox. We take it this means there are more roaches in the system and decide to throw an exception. Here's how to throw a "roaches" exception:

```
if (txtIn.Text == "cockroaches"){
    throw(new ApplicationException("roaches"));
}
```

The next step is to catch the exception to handle the situation and make sure the roaches check in but don't check out:

```
catch (Exception excep) {
    if (excep.Message == "roaches"){
        MessageBox.Show("You have roaches in your program!", "Exceptions",
            MessageBoxButtons.OK, MessageBoxIcon.Error);
    }
    else {
    ...
```

Listing 6.3 shows the complete code for the example, including throwing and catching the exception related to cockroaches.

Listing 6.3   Throwing and Catching an Exception

```
private void btnExceptions_Click(object sender, System.EventArgs e) {
    int i; double d;
    try {
```

```
      if (txtIn.Text == "cockroaches") {
         throw(new ApplicationException("roaches"));
      }
      i = Convert.ToInt16(txtIn.Text);
      d = 42 / i;
   }
   catch (DivideByZeroException) {
      MessageBox.Show("You are naughty to even think of dividing by zero!",
         "Exceptions", MessageBoxButtons.OK, MessageBoxIcon.Error);
   }
   catch (FormatException) {
      MessageBox.Show("Please enter an integer!", "Exceptions",
         MessageBoxButtons.OK, MessageBoxIcon.Error);
   }
   catch (Exception excep) {
      if (excep.Message == "roaches") {
         MessageBox.Show("You have roaches in your program!", "Exceptions",
            MessageBoxButtons.OK, MessageBoxIcon.Error);
      }
      else {
         MessageBox.Show(excep.Message);
         MessageBox.Show(excep.ToString());
      }
   }
   finally {
      MessageBox.Show("You can't stop me from being executed!", "Exceptions",
         MessageBoxButtons.OK, MessageBoxIcon.Information);
   }
}
```

When the program is run, "cockroaches" entered in the TextBox, and the button clicked, the exception is thrown, and the bad news is out (Figure 6.11)!

FIGURE 6.11:

This "cockroach" exception illustrates that you can throw and catch custom exceptions.

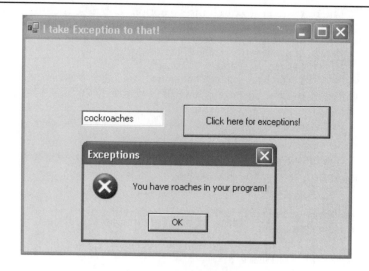

Exception Objects

So far in this discussion, exceptions have been used only as *sentinels*—the presence of the exception signals the error like a canary falling ill in a mine. It's worth thinking a little about the nature of an exception object, because they can be used for more than this.

The first thing you should know about the Exception object and the classes that inherit from it is that (for the most part) the subclasses do not vary from Exception by implementing additional members or functionality. This means that—by and large—the only difference between the parent and child classes is the name of the class. (An important exception to this is SqlException, which is thrown when SQL Server returns a rather specific warning or error.) The implication is that if you have a compelling reason to add additional information to the exception class, you certainly can, but it should still make sense to deal with your exception as a generic exception (meaning, no matter how much information you add, you should still implement a meaningful "message" property so that programmers can throw and catch it in the normal fashion).

Table 6.7 shows some of the commonly used properties and methods of the Exception object.

TABLE 6.7: Commonly Used Properties and Methods of the Exception Object

Property or Method	Purpose
HelpLink	A link to the help file associated with the exception.
Message	Gets a message that describes the current exception.
StackTrace	A string that contains the stack trace immediately before the exception was thrown.
TargetSite	The method that threw the current exception.
ToString	A string that contains the name of the exception and a great deal of other information, such as the error message and the stack trace.

In general, the Exception class has two subclasses: ApplicationException and SystemException. In theory, ApplicationExceptions are created by your application, and SystemExceptions are created by the run-time (CLR) and operating environment.

As you would expect, there are a great many subclasses of SystemExceptions, some of which you've seen in the examples earlier in this section (for example, FormatException). Most of these exception classes are the members of the System namespace, but others are located further down the namespace tree (for example, IOException is a member of System.IO rather than System directly).

The best place to learn about individual exceptions and their class relationships is the Object Browser (details of which were explained in Chapter 5).

Conclusion

This chapter has covered a great deal of ground and explained a great deal of the syntax that you need to successfully program in C#. Great flights of fancy and soundly engineered heroic structures cannot be created without good foundations; with this material under your belt, you can build wonderful things!

I started this chapter with Miranda's wonder at the "goodly creatures" in her "brave new world." Of course, the joke in *The Tempest* is that she had seen few people of any kind. One wonders whether they soon became commonplace to her. Perhaps she picked up the magic book belonging to Prospero and began to create new worlds and visions… which is my hope for what you will do with the rudiments of C# syntax presented in this chapter.

CHAPTER 7

Arrays, Indexers, and Collections

- Creating an array

- Arrays of structs

- Multidimensional and jagged arrays

- Changing the lower bound of a C# array

- Creating a class with an indexer

- Working with collection classes

- Pushing and popping stacks

- Queues

- Dynamic resizing with ArrayList

- Implementing a key/value lookup

In the real world, programming usually involves groups of objects. Arrays are specifically designed to store groups of objects, with the object being retrieved using an index value. Collections—and the structures based on collections in C#, such as queues, ArrayLists, and much more—are an alternative mechanism for grouping and coping with multiple objects.

In Chapter 4, "Building a Better Windows Interface," you learned about working with the Items collection that is used with ListBoxes. It's worth recalling the material in Chapter 4, because I assume in this chapter that you know how to work with ListBoxes and the ListBox items collection. Also, the techniques for working with this collection is basically similar to the techniques explained in this chapter. (In fact, as you may have already suspected, the items in a ListBox are an instance of a collection class.)

If you don't know how to deal with multiple items in arrays (and other classes designed for use with multiples, such as those based on the System.Collection classes), then your programs will never scale—or be of much use when dealing in an automated fashion with the large amount of data presented by the real world.

It's important to pick the right underlying structure for dealing with groups of objects, and you also need to know how to work with the structure you've selected. This chapter covers both aspects of dealing with arrays, collections, and related classes.

Arrays

In C#, an *array* is an object that is used to store objects of the same type and provides access to the objects using an index. You should know that—just as the string keyword is used to create an object of type System.String—the syntax and expressions used to create arrays actually create an object based on the System.Array class. This means that you can use the members—methods and properties—provided by the Array class when you work with arrays. Most Array methods are shown in Table 7.1, and Array properties are shown in Table 7.2.

TABLE 7.1: Array Methods

Method	Meaning
BinarySearch	Searches a one-dimensional sorted array.
Clear	Sets a range of elements in an array to 0, to false, or to a null reference, depending on the type of the array elements.
Copy	Copies a range of elements from one array to another.
CopyTo	Copies all the elements of a one-dimensional array to another one-dimensional array, starting at the specified destination array index in the new array.

Continued on next page

TABLE 7.1 CONTINUED: Array Methods

Method	Meaning
CreateInstance	A static method that explicitly instantiates and initializes a new array instance. Note that this method allows you to specify a lower bound for the array that is non-zero (see example later in this chapter).
GetLength	Gets the number of elements in a specified dimension of the array.
GetLowerBound	Gets the lower bound of the specified dimension in the array. Note that if the array has been created using normal syntax—e.g., not using CreateInstance— the lower bound of each dimension will be 0.
GetUpperBound	Gets the upper bound of the specified dimension in the array.
GetValue	Gets the value of the specified element in the array.
IndexOf	Returns the index of the first occurrence of a value in a one-dimensional array (or in a portion of the array).
Initialize	Initializes every element of a value-type array by calling the default constructor of the value type.
LastIndexOf	Returns the index of the last occurrence of a value in a one-dimensional array (or in a portion of the array).
Reverse	Reverses the order of the elements in a one-dimensional array (or in a portion of the array).
SetValue	Sets the specified element in the current array to the specified value.
Sort	Sorts the elements in a one-dimensional array.

TABLE 7.2: Array Properties

Property	Returns
IsFixedSize	A Boolean value indicating whether the array has a fixed size.
IsReadOnly	A Boolean value indicating whether the array is read-only.
IsSynchronized	A Boolean value indicating whether the array is thread-safe.
Length	The total number of elements in all the dimensions of an array.
Rank	The number of dimensions of an array.
SyncRoot	An object that can be used to synchronize access to the array.

Arrays in C# are, for the most part, zero-indexed—meaning that the array indices start at 0 (but see the example later in this chapter that shows how to start an array at another index).

One-dimensional arrays can be thought of as a table with one column that can be accessed using an index. Multidimensional arrays use multiple indices to access their values, so a two-dimensional array can be pictured as a table with rows and columns. In a *jagged* array—also called an array of arrays—each "row" in the array is itself an array, with a potentially different size than the arrays making up the other rows.

Boxing and Unboxing

You may have observed that types of a class that are derived from a class can be assigned to an array of that class, even though, as I mentioned above, an array is used to store objects of "the same type." Specifically, objects of any type can be stored in an array of *objects* (since all types are derived from the object type).

For example, the following is legal code, and creates an array of objects that are assigned three different types:

```
int theInt; string theString; Button1 button1;
object [] stuff = new object [3];
stuff [0] = theInt;
stuff [1] = theString;
stuff [2] = button1;
```

What has actually happened is that the various types have been implicitly converted to type object. (If you look at the members of each element of the stuff [] array, you'll find the members of an object type.) However, the extended information relating to the derived type has been preserved. This is called "boxing."

To reverse the process, and "unbox" the types stored as objects, you need to explicitly cast the element of the object array to the original type. For example:

```
int newInt = (int) stuff [0];
string newString = (string) stuff [1];
Button button2 = (Button) stuff [2];
```

Creating an Array

Let's start with one-dimensional arrays. The process of creating an array is a three-step dance (although these steps can be combined, as we'll see in a moment):

- The array must be declared.
- Next, it is instantiated.
- Finally, it is initialized with values.

To declare an array, follow a type with square brackets and continue with the array's identifier. For example, you could declare an integer array *numbers* and a string array *names* as follows:

```
int [] numbers; // declares integer array
string [] names; // declares string array
```

To instantiate the array, as you'd expect, the new keyword is used. The statement

```
numbers = new int [3];
```

instantiates a new three-element, zero-based array with the previously declared variable *numbers*. (The elements are *numbers[0]*, *numbers[1]*, and *numbers[2]*.)

The two statements can be combined into one, so that you can instantiate while you declare:

```
int [] numbers = new int[3];
```

At this point, you should know that the three elements of the integer array *numbers* have been initialized to 0. (Arrays of reference-type elements are initialized to a null reference.)

NOTE   You can use a constant or variable rather than a literal to size the dimensions of an array.

As it turns out, you can initialize the array at the same time as you declare and instantiate it, by placing the initial values within curly braces. Here are one-step examples that declare, instantiate, and initialize an integer array and a string array:

```
int [] numbers = new int[3] {3,1,4};
string [] names = new string[3] {"Tom", "Dick", "Harry"};
```

There are a couple of shorthand ways to say the same thing. If you are initializing an array, you can leave off the dimension, in which case it is created with the number of elements specified by the initialization. So these statements create three-element arrays just like the preceding ones:

```
int [] numbers = new int[] {3,1,4};
string [] names = new string[] {"Tom", "Dick", "Harry"};
```

If you really prefer to be terse, you can also leave off the new part of the statement (once again, assuming you've provided initial values). The compiler is smart enough to know that it is implied. So here's the shortest way to declare, instantiate, and initialize these two arrays:

```
int [] numbers = {3,1,4};
string [] names = {"Tom", "Dick", "Harry"}
```

Moving on, let's try a little example of creating and using an array. Let's suppose we want an array to store the first seven numbers in the Fibonacci series, which comes up in art, nature, mathematics, and mysticism. Here's the shorthand way to create that array and stuff the right values into it:

```
int [] fibArray = new int[7] {1,1,2,3,5,8,13};
```

Let's say, instead, that we are fond of iteration. As you probably know, the first two elements of the Fibonacci series are 1; after that, the element n in the series is equal to the sum of the elements $(n-1)$ and $(n-2)$.

First, we can declare and instantiate the array with seven zero-based elements:

```
int [] fibArray = new int[7];
```

Next, we can assign the first two values in the series.

```
fibArray[0] = fibArray[1] = 1;
```

Finally, we can use iteration to assign the rest of the values in the array:

```
for (int i = 2; i < 7; ++i)
    fibArray[i] = fibArray[i - 1] + fibArray[i - 2];
```

You can use a message box to display an element of the array to make sure that this has all worked correctly, as shown in Listing 7.1.

Listing 7.1   Creating an Integer Array and Displaying an Element

```
private void btnCreate_Click(object sender, System.EventArgs e) {
    // int [] fibArray = new int[7] {1,1,2,3,5,8,13};
    int [] fibArray = new int[7];
    fibArray[0] = fibArray[1] = 1;
    for (int i = 2; i < 7; ++i)
        fibArray[i] = fibArray[i - 1] + fibArray[i - 2];
    string fifthFib = fibArray[4].ToString();
    MessageBox.Show("The fifth number in the Fibonacci series is " + fifthFib,
        "Arrays", MessageBoxButtons.OK, MessageBoxIcon.Information);
}
```

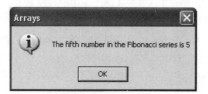

foreach Statement

The foreach statement is a simple way to iterate through the elements of an array. If we continue with our array of Fibonacci numbers, it's easy to use a foreach statement

```
foreach (int fib in fibArray) {
    lstFib.Items.Add(fib.ToString()); }
```

to cycle through the Fibonacci array and, one by one, add the string representation of each element to a ListBox (named *lstFib*).

The complete revised click event procedure that creates the array and then uses foreach to cycle through it, adding the elements to the ListBox, is shown in Listing 7.2. If you run the code and then click the button, the Fibonacci numbers will appear in the ListBox as shown in Figure 7.1.

FIGURE 7.1:

The foreach statement can be used to display array elements in a ListBox.

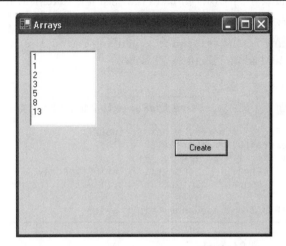

Listing 7.2   Adding the Integer Array to a ListBox

```
private void btnCreate_Click(object sender, System.EventArgs e) {
    int [] fibArray = new int[7];
    fibArray[0] = fibArray[1] = 1;
    for (int i = 2; i < 7; ++i)
        fibArray[i] = fibArray[i - 1] + fibArray[i - 2];
    string fifthFib = fibArray[4].ToString();
    foreach (int fib in fibArray) {
        lstFib.Items.Add(fib.ToString());
    }
}
```

By the way, if you'd stored the Fibonacci numbers as elements in a string array in the first place (rather than as integers), you could add the elements in the array to the ListBox with a single AddRange method call. Here's the declaration and instantiation of the Fibonacci array as string:

```
string [] fibArray = new string[7];
```

followed by the assignment of the first two numbers, as strings, of course, in the series:

```
fibArray[0] = fibArray[1] = "1";
```

To pull off the iteration, we have to get a little tricky in our conversions. First, the n - 1 and n - 2 elements are each converted to integer. The integers are added together, and the result converted back to string:

```
for (int i = 2; i < 7; ++i) {
    fibArray[i] = (Convert.ToInt16(fibArray[i - 1]) +
        Convert.ToInt16(fibArray[i - 2])).ToString(); }
```

Finally, the payoff—it takes only a single statement to fill the ListBox:

```
lstFib.Items.AddRange (fibArray);
```

Listing 7.3 shows the process of filling a string array with strings representing the Fibonacci series and adding them to a ListBox.

Listing 7.3   Using AddRange to Add a String Array to a ListBox

```
string [] fibArray = new string[7];
fibArray[0] = fibArray[1] = "1";
for (int i = 2; i < 7; ++i) {
    fibArray[i] = (Convert.ToInt16(fibArray[i - 1]) +
        Convert.ToInt16(fibArray[i - 2])).ToString();
}
lstFib.Items.AddRange (fibArray);
```

Arrays of Structs

Who says the elements of your array have to be simple value types? Often, it makes sense to define classes or structs that are used as the template for each element of an array.

As an example, let's go back to the *Employee* struct defined in Chapter 6, "Zen and Now: The C# Language":

```
public struct Employee {
    public string fullName, rank;
    public long SSN;
    public Employee(string fullName, string rank, long SSN) {
        this.fullName = fullName;
        this.rank = rank;
        this.SSN = SSN;
    }
}
```

It's easy to create instances based on this struct. For example:

```
Employee DavisN = new Employee("Nicholas Davis", "Opera Singer", 12345678);
```

Next, we can declare, instantiate, and initialize a three-element array with *Employee* structs for elements (assuming all three struct elements are defined):

```
Employee [] theRoster = {HopperK, DavisN, DavisJ};
```

As I explained earlier in this chapter, this statement is shorthand for the more formal

```
Employee [] theRoster = new Employee [3] {HopperK, DavisN, DavisJ};
```

Next, if you'd like, you can display some of the information stored in a struct element:

```
MessageBox.Show(theRoster[1].fullName + " is an " + theRoster[1].rank +  ".",
    "Arrays", MessageBoxButtons.OK, MessageBoxIcon.Information);
```

Finally, it's easy to use a foreach statement to iterate through the array of structs and add specific field information to a ListBox:

```
foreach (Employee emp in theRoster) {
    lstRoster.Items.Add(emp.fullName);
}
```

If you run the code shown in Listing 7.4, the contents of the *fullname* field of each struct in the array will be added to a ListBox (Figure 7.2).

FIGURE 7.2:

You can create arrays of structs, and display struct elements.

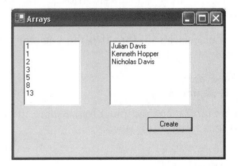

Listing 7.4   **Creating and Displaying an Array of Structs**

```
public struct Employee {
    public string fullName, rank;
    public long SSN;
    public Employee (string fullName, string rank, long SSN) {
        this.fullName = fullName;
        this.rank = rank;
        this.SSN = SSN;
    }
}

private void btnCreate_Click(object sender, System.EventArgs e) {
    Employee DavisJ = new Employee("Julian Davis", "City Hall", 12345678);
    Employee DavisN = new Employee("Nicholas Davis", "Opera Singer", 12345678);
    Employee HopperK = new Employee("Kenneth Hopper", "Proprietor", 12345678);

    Employee [] theRoster = {HopperK, DavisN, DavisJ};
```

```
MessageBox.Show(theRoster[1].fullName + " is an " + theRoster[1].rank + ".",
    "Arrays", MessageBoxButtons.OK, MessageBoxIcon.Information);

foreach (Employee emp in theRoster) {
    lstRoster.Items.Add(emp.fullName);
}
}
```

n-Dimensional Arrays

n-dimensional, or multidimensional, arrays are easy to declare and use. They work just like one-dimensional arrays, except that a comma is placed within the square brackets between the array dimensions.

It's easy to see why you might want to use a two-dimensional array to represent the "board" of a game like checkers or chess. *n*-dimensional arrays become handy when more information is needed to adequately model a situation. For example, a three-dimensional array might be used to store stock prices and volume over time.

Here are the declarations for a two-dimensional integer array and a three-dimensional string array:

```
int [,] numbers;
string [,,] words;
```

Let's have a look at an example. First, declare and instantiate a two-dimensional integer array *the2d*, with five "rows" and three "columns":

```
const int rows = 5;
const int cols = 3;
int [,] the2d = new int [rows, cols];
```

Next, populate the array by assigning as a value to each element its row times its column:

```
for (int i = 0; i < rows; i++) {
    for (int j = 0; j < cols; j++) {
        the2d[i,j] = i * j;
    }
}
```

Next, iterate through both dimensions of the array. For each element, create a string consisting of its coordinates in the array followed by its value, and add it to a ListBox:

```
for (int i = 0; i < rows; i++) {
    for (int j = 0; j < cols; j++) {
        string theItem = "the2d [" + i.ToString() + "," + j.ToString() + "] is "
            + the2d[i,j].ToString() + ".";
        lstMulti.Items.Add(theItem);
    }
}
```

If you run the code (see Listing 7.5), you'll see that the contents of the array are displayed in the ListBox (Figure 7.3).

FIGURE 7.3:

It's easy to declare and initialize multidimensional arrays.

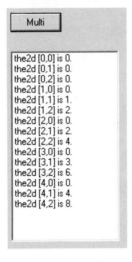

```
Multi
```

```
the2d [0,0] is 0.
the2d [0,1] is 0.
the2d [0,2] is 0.
the2d [1,0] is 0.
the2d [1,1] is 1.
the2d [1,2] is 2.
the2d [2,0] is 0.
the2d [2,1] is 2.
the2d [2,2] is 4.
the2d [3,0] is 0.
the2d [3,1] is 3.
the2d [3,2] is 6.
the2d [4,0] is 0.
the2d [4,1] is 4.
the2d [4,2] is 8.
```

Listing 7.5   **Creating and Displaying a Two-Dimensional Array**

```csharp
private void btnMulti_Click(object sender, System.EventArgs e) {
    const int rows = 5;
    const int cols = 3;

    // declare 5X3 array
    int [,] the2d = new int [rows, cols];

    // populate the array
    for (int i = 0; i < rows; i++) {
        for (int j = 0; j < cols; j++) {
            the2d[i,j] = i*j;
        }
    }

    // display it
    for (int i = 0; i < rows; i++) {
        for (int j = 0; j < cols; j++) {
            string theItem = "the2d [" + i.ToString() + "," + j.ToString() +
                "] is " + the2d[i,j].ToString() + ".";
            lstMulti.Items.Add(theItem);
        }
    }
}
```

Arrays of Arrays

An array of arrays (also called a *jagged* array because of its "unevenness" compared to a standard *n*-dimensional array) is an array where each row is a one-dimensional array. Jagged arrays can be declared and instantiated in a single statement—using side-by-side square braces—but there is no way to initialize the elements of the jagged array in the same statement.

For example, here's how you might declare a two-dimensional jagged string array, with the first dimension having seven rows and the second dimension varying—considerably—in the number of elements:

```
const int rows = 7;
string [] [] jaggedA = new string [rows] [];

jaggedA[0] = new string [2];
jaggedA[1] = new string [3];
jaggedA[2] = new string [1];
jaggedA[3] = new string [4];
jaggedA[4] = new string [40];
jaggedA[5] = new string [2];
jaggedA[6] = new string [86];
```

Next, individual elements could be assigned values. For example:

```
jaggedA [1] [2] = "jagged";
```

Some of the jagged one-dimensional arrays within arrays are filled using iteration:

```
for (int dash = 0; dash < 86; dash++)
    jaggedA [6] [dash] = "-";
```

Next, each "column" can be displayed as a single concatenated item in a ListBox:

```
string column = "";
for (int i = 0; i < 2; i++) {
    column = column + " " + jaggedA [0] [i] + " ";
}
lstMulti.Items.Add(column);
```

Listing 7.6 shows the rather messy code that does this for the entire seven rows (messy because with each "column" array a different size, nested iteration is not easy). If you run the code, a graph depiction of "jaggedness" will appear in the ListBox (Figure 7.4).

FIGURE 7.4:

When the column elements of a jagged string array are displayed in a ListBox, rows of unequal length are created.

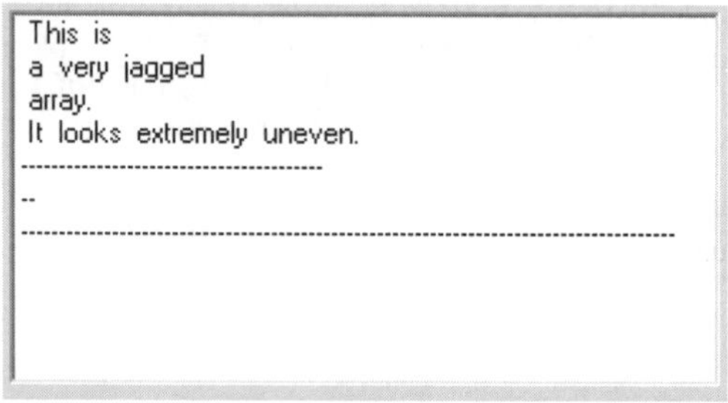

Listing 7.6   **Declaring, Populating, and Displaying a Jagged String Array**

```
private void btnJagged_Click(object sender, System.EventArgs e) {
    // declare a jagged array with 7 rows
    const int rows = 7;
    string [] [] jaggedA = new string [rows] [];

    // give it some column arrays
    jaggedA[0] = new string [2];
    jaggedA[1] = new string [3];
    jaggedA[2] = new string [1];
    jaggedA[3] = new string [4];
    jaggedA[4] = new string [40];
    jaggedA[5] = new string [2];
    jaggedA[6] = new string [86];

    // populate it
    jaggedA [0] [0] = "This";
    jaggedA [0] [1] = "is";

    jaggedA [1] [0] = "a";
    jaggedA [1] [1] = "very";
    jaggedA [1] [2] = "jagged";

    jaggedA [2] [0] = "array.";

    jaggedA [3] [0] = "It";
    jaggedA [3] [1] = "looks";
    jaggedA [3] [2] = "extremely";
    jaggedA [3] [3] = "uneven.";

    // fill the final three columns with dashes (-)
    for (int dash = 0; dash < 40; dash++)
        jaggedA [4] [dash] = "-";
    for (int dash = 0; dash < 2; dash++)
        jaggedA [5] [dash] = "-";
    for (int dash = 0; dash < 86; dash++)
        jaggedA [6] [dash] = "-";

    // display it
    string column = "";
    for (int i = 0; i < 2; i++) {
        column = column + " " + jaggedA [0] [i] + " ";
    }
    lstMulti.Items.Add(column);
    column = "";
    for (int i = 0; i < 3; i++) {
        column = column + " " + jaggedA [1] [i] + " ";
    }
    lstMulti.Items.Add(column);
    column = "";
```

```
    for (int i = 0; i < 1; i++) {
        column = column + " " + jaggedA [2] [i] + " ";
    }
    lstMulti.Items.Add(column);
    column = "";
    for (int i = 0; i < 4; i++) {
        column = column + " " + jaggedA [3] [i] + " ";
    }
    lstMulti.Items.Add(column);
    column = "";
    for (int i = 0; i < 40; i++) {
        column = column + jaggedA [4] [i];
    }
    lstMulti.Items.Add(column);
    column = "";
    for (int i = 0; i < 2; i++) {
        column = column + jaggedA [5] [i];
    }
    lstMulti.Items.Add(column);
    column = "";
    for (int i = 0; i < 86; i++) {
        column = column + jaggedA [6] [i];
    }
    lstMulti.Items.Add(column);
}
```

Creating a Non-zero Lower Bound

I teased you towards the beginning of the chapter by saying I would show you how to create an array with a non-zero lower bound. Here goes!

WARNING   You probably won't want to use non-zero lower bounds very often in C#, because arrays created in the way shown in this example do not have many of the conveniences—such as square bracket notation—that we've come to expect when working with arrays.

First, you need to create two integer arrays. The first array is used to store in its elements the size of each dimension you wish to create (the number of elements indicates the number of dimensions). The second array stores the lower bound for each dimension.

In this example, I've used one-dimensional arrays to create an array with six elements where the index of the first element is five—but you could use multidimensional arrays to create an array with different numbers of elements and different lower bounds for different dimensions.

Here are statements that create the two arrays:

```
int [] theLengths = new int [1] {6};
int [] theBounds = new int [1] {5};
```

Next, the CreateInstance method of the System.Array class is used to create a non-zero-lower-bound array in the variable *theArray*. The CreateInstance method is static, indicating that an object of the Array class is not instantiated to use it—as the name of the method implies, it does its own creating of instances.

The first argument of the method is the System.Type of the array to be created, which is derived using the typeof operator—for example, for an integer array, typeof(int). The second and third arguments are the arrays we previously created, which represent the size and lower bound of each dimension:

```
Array theArray = Array.CreateInstance(typeof(int), theLengths, theBounds);
```

To test this, let's assign values to each of the putative elements of the array:

```
for (int i = 5; i < 11; i++) {
    theArray.SetValue(i,i);
}
```

We can then use the GetValue method to retrieve and display a value by its index:

```
MessageBox.Show(theArray.GetValue(7).ToString());
```

The GetLowerBound method, used with an argument of 0 to retrieve the first—and, in this case, only—dimension of the array, shows that the lower bound is what it is supposed to be, 5:

```
MessageBox.Show(theArray.GetLowerBound(0).ToString());
```

Finally, if you try to invoke an element using an index that would normally be in-bounds for a six-element array,

```
MessageBox.Show(theArray.GetValue(2).ToString());
```

an out-of-bounds exception is fired.

The code for generating and testing the non-zero-lower-bound array is shown in Listing 7.7.

Listing 7.7   **Creating, Populating, and Testing an Array with a Specified (Non-zero) Lower Bound**

```
private void btnNonZero_Click(object sender, System.EventArgs e) {
    int [] theLengths = new int [1] {6};
    int [] theBounds = new int [1] {5};
    Array theArray = Array.CreateInstance(typeof(int), theLengths, theBounds);

    for (int i = 5; i < 11; i++) {
        theArray.SetValue(i,i);
    }

    MessageBox.Show(theArray.GetValue(7).ToString());
    MessageBox.Show(theArray.GetLowerBound(0).ToString());
    MessageBox.Show(theArray.GetValue(2).ToString());
}
```

Indexers

An indexer is a class member that allows an object to be referenced in the same way as an array using square brackets ([]). Since indexers use the square bracket array notation, they neither need nor have a name.

Listing 7.8 shows a class that contains an indexer. The class encapsulates a 42-element integer array, which is private to the class, and the indexer simply provides a means of saving or retrieving array values, providing that the index passed to the indexer is within range of the array.

Listing 7.8   **Creating a Class with an Indexer**

```
class IAmAnIndexerClass {
    private int [] theArray = new int[42];

    //declare the indexer
    public int this [int ndx] {
        get {
            if (ndx < 0 || ndx >= 42)
                return 0;
            else
                return theArray [ndx];
        }
        set {
            if (!(ndx < 0 || ndx >= 42))
                theArray [ndx] = value;
        }
    }
}
```

Here's the indexer declaration:

```
public int this [int ndx] {
  ...
}
```

If you look at Listing 7.8, you'll see get and set accessors within the indexer—just like in a property statement.

To use the IAmAnIndexerClass class, an object of the type of the class must be instantiated:

```
IAmAnIndexerClass iaaio = new IAmAnIndexerClass();
```

As a demonstration, I'll use the IAmAnIndexerClass indexer to access *iaaio*—short for "I am an indexer object"—using array syntax. Each "element" in *iaaio* will be examined using the IsPrime web service developed in the beginning of this book. If the index of the element is a prime, then that prime is saved to the element; otherwise, the value of the element is left at the default, which is 0.

As a first step, you'll need to add a web reference to the SybexC2 service as explained in Chapter 2, "Consuming the Service on the Web."

Before invoking the web service, you might want to turn the mouse pointer to an hourglass so that the user knows to expect a delay:

```
this.Cursor = Cursors.WaitCursors;
```

The service needs to be named and instantiated as *theService*:

```
theService.SybexC2Service theService = new theService.SybexC2Service();
```

Next, we can easily check whether a given integer is prime, and if it is, use the *iaaio* indexer to store the value:

```
for (int i = 0; i < 42 ; i++) {
    if (theService.IsPrime(i,0))
        iaaio [i] = i;
}
```

NOTE   As you may remember from Chapter 2, the second argument sent to the IsPrime method represents a delay in seconds; this is irrelevant to the current task.

Once the calls to the web service have completed, the mouse pointer should be returned to the normal default:

```
this.Cursor = Cursors.Default;
```

Finally, we can do a bit of displaying to make sure this came out right. Since 23 is a prime and 24 is not, the value of iaaio[23] should be 23 and the value of iaaio[24] should be 0, as shown here.

The code for instantiating an object based on the class and accessing its members using the indexer is shown in Listing 7.9.

Listing 7.9   **Instantiating an Object Based on the *Indexer* Class and Accessing Its Members Using Index Syntax**

```
private void btnIndexer_Click(object sender, System.EventArgs e) {
    IAmAnIndexerClass iaaio = new IAmAnIndexerClass();
    this.Cursor = Cursors.WaitCursors;
```

```
theService.SybexC2Service theService = new
    theService.SybexC2Service();
for (int i = 0; i < 42 ; i++) {
    if (theService.IsPrime(i,0))
        iaaio [i] = i;
}
this.Cursor = Cursors.Default;
MessageBox.Show("iaaio [23] is " + iaaio [23].ToString() +
    " and iaaio [24] is " + iaaio [24].ToString(), "Indexers",
    MessageBoxButtons.OK, MessageBoxIcon.Information);
}
```

Collection Classes

In quite a few cases, structures that are based on classes other than System.Array will work better to organize groups of items for specific purposes. We'll have a look at working with objects based on some of these classes—ArrayList, Queue, Stack, and SortedList—in the remainder of this chapter. In the meantime, you should know that these classes appear for the most part in the System.Collections namespace (some of the classes that are based on Dictionary structures are located in the System.Collections.Specialized namespace).

As you can see in Figure 7.5, you can find out a great deal about these classes by pointing the Object Browser at System.Collections.

FIGURE 7.5:

You can use the Object Browser to inspect the collection classes that are the members of System.Collections.

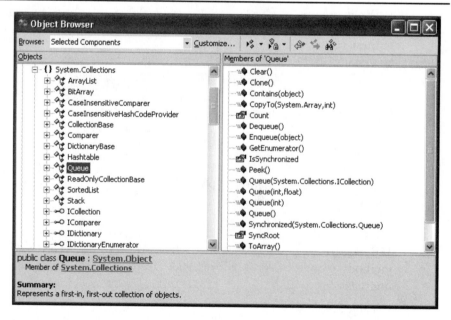

Table 7.3 describes some of the most useful collection classes. You should know that each one of these classes has quite a few members (properties and methods) that you will need to

know about to successfully use the class. (Most of these classes have members comparable in extent and utility to the Array members shown in Tables 7.1 and 7.2.)

TABLE 7.3: Useful Collection Classes

Class	Description
ArrayList	Used to create an array-like structure whose size is dynamically altered as items are added and removed (see example later in this chapter).
CollectionBase	Provides the abstract base class—meaning the class cannot be instantiated, only inherited, and can contain abstract (or nonimplemented) members—for a collection.
DictionaryBase	Provides the abstract base class for a dictionary-style collection of key/value pairs.
Hashtable	Used to create a collection of key/value pairs that are organized based on the hash code of the key.
Queue	Used to create a first in, first out collection of objects (see example later in this chapter).
SortedList	Used to create a collection of key/value pairs that are sorted by the keys and are accessible by key and by index—so it combines the features of an array with those of a dictionary (see example later in this chapter).
Stack	Used to create a last in, first out collection of objects (see example later in this chapter).

You can find out a lot about collection classes and class members using the Object Browser (and auto-completion in the Code Editor), but if you are programming an object based on one of these classes, you really should review the full list of the (copious) properties and methods by looking up the class name followed by the word *Members* in online help (for example, "ArrayList Members" or "Queue Members").

Collection Interfaces

An interface provides a binding contract with any class that uses the members specified in the interface. In other words, when a class implements an interface, it tells any object that uses the class that it will support the methods, properties, events, and indexers of the named interface.

This means that objects based on classes that implement the interface all work in the same, comfortable, familiar way.

Interfaces in the .NET Framework, by convention, start with a capital I—for example, IEnumerator. Internally, the syntax of an interface looks like the signatures for a bunch of methods, properties, etc.—without the implementation specifics for these members. I discuss interfaces further in Chapter 9, "Everything Is String Manipulation."

Table 7.4 shows some of the interfaces implemented by the collection classes. In addition, if you need to implement a custom data structure, you should plan to implement at least some of these interfaces.

TABLE 7.4: Selected Collection Interfaces

Interface	Description
ICollection	Defines size, enumerators, and synchronization methods for all collections.
IComparer	Exposes a method that compares two objects.
IDictionary	Represents a collection of key/value pairs.
IDictionaryEnumerator	Enumerates the elements of a dictionary.
IEnumerable	Exposes the enumerator, which supports a simple iteration over a collection.
IEnumerator	Supports a simple iteration over a collection.
IHashCodeProvider	Supplies a hash code for an object, using a custom hash function.
IList	Represents a collection of objects that can be individually accessed by index.

Stacks

A stack is a last in, first out (LIFO) collection of items. The most recent thing to go on the stack (in stack terminology, "pushed") is also the first to come off the stack (called "popped").

NOTE In addition to pushing and popping, stacks (and queues) support "peeking," which returns the object on top of the stack (or queue) without removing it from the stack. I'll show you how this works in the Queue demonstration.

An array can fairly easily be used to simulate a stack (or a queue), but why go to the trouble of doing this if the functionality you need is already built into the Stack class? The essential difference between stacks and queues on the one hand, and arrays and lists on the other, is that when you pop an item off the stack or queue, it goes away. Arrays don't normally work this way.

To demonstrate the System.Collections.Stack class, let's write an application that puts the current form of the mouse pointer (or cursor) on a stack. Here's how it will work: the user will be able to change the mouse pointer to a random pointer (referred to as the "current" mouse pointer). The current mouse pointer can always be pushed on the stack. When the stack is popped, the last pointer placed on it becomes the current mouse pointer.

Before we get started, you should know that the mouse pointer is set using a form's Cursor property, the default mouse pointer being indicated, naturally enough, by the Cursors enumeration value Default (for example, Form1.Cursor = Cursors.Default).

Our application will need:

- A mechanism for choosing a new mouse pointer. This will be accomplished by randomly choosing a new enumeration value from the Cursors enumeration list.

- A way to push the stack to store the current mouse pointer.

- A way to pop the stack to make the mouse pointer on the top of the stack the current cursor.

Figure 7.6 shows the interface that will be used to accomplish this, with one button for each task.

FIGURE 7.6:

The current cursor can be changed, placed on a stack, and popped off the stack.

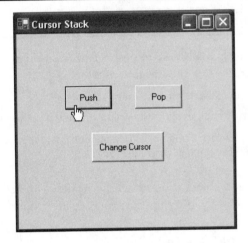

First let's look at Listing 7.10, which shows the click event that randomly selects a new cursor and assigns it to the form. This code declares an array of type Cursor named *acursor*, and loads it with all possible values of the Cursors enumeration. Next, a new Random object is created using a default seed value.

> **WARNING** The System.Random class generates pseudo-random numbers and should not be relied on to return truly random numbers in applications that involve things like cryptography.

With a Random object in place, its Next method is used to generate a random integer between 0 and 27 that is used to select an element (there are 28 members of the Cursors enumeration, so the *acursor* array index goes between 0 and 27). The selected element, which is of type Cursor, is then assigned to the form's current cursor.

Listing 7.10 **Changing the Cursor to a Random Cursor**

```
private void btnChange_Click(object sender, System.EventArgs e) {
    Cursor [] acursor = {
        Cursors.AppStarting, Cursors.Arrow,      Cursors.Cross,
        Cursors.Default,     Cursors.Hand,       Cursors.Help,
        Cursors.HSplit,      Cursors.IBeam,      Cursors.No,
        Cursors.NoMove2D,    Cursors.NoMoveHoriz, Cursors.NoMoveVert,
        Cursors.PanEast,     Cursors.PanNE,      Cursors.PanNorth,
        Cursors.PanNW,       Cursors.PanSE,      Cursors.PanSouth,
        Cursors.PanSW,       Cursors.PanWest,    Cursors.SizeAll,
        Cursors.SizeNESW,    Cursors.SizeNS,     Cursors.SizeNWSE,
        Cursors.SizeWE,      Cursors.UpArrow,    Cursors.VSplit,
```

```
    Cursors.WaitCursor
    };
    Random rnd = new Random();
    Cursor cur = acursor[rnd.Next(27)];
    this.Cursor = cur;
}
```

It's actually really easy to push a cursor on the stack. First, a new `Stack` object needs to be instantiated, using the variable *curStack*:

```
Stack curStack = new Stack();
```

Next, this click event code pushes the current form mouse pointer onto the stack:

```
private void btnPush_Click(object sender, System.EventArgs e) {
    curStack.Push(this.Cursor);
}
```

Popping the stack is only slightly trickier. You need to make sure that something is actually on the stack—by using the `curStack.Count` property—before you try to pop:

```
private void btnPop_Click(object sender, System.EventArgs e) {
    if (curStack.Count > 0)
        this.Cursor = (Cursor) curStack.Pop();
    else
        MessageBox.Show("Nothing on the stack to pop!", "Too tired to pop!",
            MessageBoxButtons.OK, MessageBoxIcon.Exclamation);
}
```

The code for pushing and popping the stack is shown in Listing 7.11. If you run the demonstration application, you'll see that you can change the mouse pointer for a random new selection, place the current mouse pointer on the stack, and assign the mouse pointer on the top of the stack to the form. If you've popped everything off the stack—or there isn't anything on it to begin with—an error message will be displayed.

Listing 7.11   Pushing and Popping a Cursor on a Stack

```
...
Stack curStack = new Stack();

private void btnPush_Click(object sender, System.EventArgs e) {
    curStack.Push(this.Cursor);
}
```

```
private void btnPop_Click(object sender, System.EventArgs e) {
   if (curStack.Count > 0)
      this.Cursor = (Cursor) curStack.Pop();
   else
      MessageBox.Show("Nothing on the stack to pop!", "Too tired to pop!",
         MessageBoxButtons.OK, MessageBoxIcon.Exclamation);
}
   ...
```

Queues

Queues are just like stacks, except that the objects collected by them are first in, first out (FIFO). The metaphor is waiting in line or, as the British say, "on queue." The idea is that if you are the first one waiting for the ticket booth to open, you should be the first one able to buy tickets.

The Enqueue method puts an item on the queue; the Dequeue method returns (and removes) the item that is at the front of the queue; and the Peek method looks at the item at the front of the queue (without removing it from the queue).

As an example, let's set up a queue of strings. The user can use TextBoxes and Buttons to put a string on the queue (Enqueue), take the front string off the queue (Dequeue), or just have a quiet look at the front string (Peek).

To make this application a little clearer to follow, I've added a ListBox named lstQ and set its Enabled property to False in the Properties window. The contents of the queue are shown in this ListBox, which is updated every time an item is put on or taken off of the queue.

First, a Queue object needs to be declared and instantiated:

```
Queue theQueue = new Queue();
```

Here's the code to enqueue a string:

```
private void btnEnqueue_Click(object sender, System.EventArgs e) {
   theQueue.Enqueue(txtIn.Text);
   txtIn.Text = "";
   lstQ.Items.Clear();
   foreach (string s in theQueue) {
      lstQ.Items.Add(s);
   }
}
```

Dequeuing is pretty much the same thing, although (as you'd suspect) a check needs to be added to see that there is actually something on the queue:

```
private void btnDequeue_Click(object sender, System.EventArgs e) {
   if (theQueue.Count > 0) {
      txtOut.Text = (string) theQueue.Dequeue();
      lstQ.Items.Clear();
      foreach (string s in theQueue) {
         lstQ.Items.Add(s);
      }
```

```
      }
    else
        MessageBox.Show("Nothing on the queue to dequeue!",
            "No more waiting in line!", MessageBoxButtons.OK,
            MessageBoxIcon.Exclamation);
    }
```

You should also note that the string value could be enqueued directly, but when it is dequeued, it needs to be cast to `string`, since items on the queue are maintained as type `object`.

TIP   You can implicitly cast from `string` to `object`, but not from `object` to `string`.

Peeking works like dequeuing:

```
private void btnPeek_Click(object sender, System.EventArgs e) {
    if (theQueue.Count > 0) {
        string str = (string) theQueue.Peek();
        MessageBox.Show("'" + str + "' is at the head of the queue!",
            "You peeked!", MessageBoxButtons.OK, MessageBoxIcon.Exclamation);
    }
    else
        MessageBox.Show("Nothing on the queue to peek at!", "You peeked!",
            MessageBoxButtons.OK, MessageBoxIcon.Exclamation);
}
```

It's time to compile and run the project. Next, enter a text string word by word in the Text In box—for example, "Able" "Was" "I" "Ere" "I" "Saw" "Elba". After you've entered the last word in your string, you can peek to make sure the first word is at the head of the queue (Figure 7.7).

FIGURE 7.7:

Peeking retrieves the object at the front of the queue without removing it from the queue.

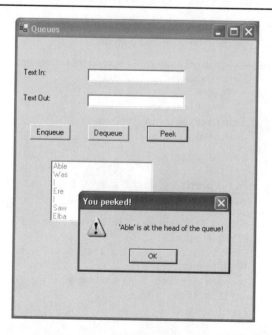

Next, dequeue the first item ("Able"). If you peek now, you'll see that "Was" is now at the front of the queue (Figure 7.8).

FIGURE 7.8:

With "Able" dequeued, peeking discloses that "Was" is at the front of the queue.

Of course, if you keep dequeuing, pretty soon there will be nothing left "in line" to dequeue (Figure 7.9)—all the words must have bought their tickets!

FIGURE 7.9:

It's important to check that something is on the queue before attempting to dequeue (or peek).

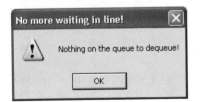

We'll be discussing queues further in Chapter 11 in the context of messaging. For now, the code for queuing, enqueuing, and peeking is shown in Listing 7.12.

Listing 7.12   **Queuing, Dequeuing, and Peeking**

```
...
Queue theQueue = new Queue();

private void btnEnqueue_Click(object sender, System.EventArgs e) {
    theQueue.Enqueue(txtIn.Text);
    txtIn.Text = "";
    lstQ.Items.Clear();
    foreach (string s in theQueue) {
        lstQ.Items.Add(s);
    }
}

private void btnDequeue_Click(object sender, System.EventArgs e) {
    if (theQueue.Count > 0)
        txtOut.Text = (string) theQueue.Dequeue();
    else
        MessageBox.Show("Nothing on the queue to dequeue!",
            "No more waiting in line!", MessageBoxButtons.OK,
            MessageBoxIcon.Exclamation);
}

private void btnPeek_Click(object sender, System.EventArgs e) {
    if (theQueue.Count > 0) {
        string str = (string) theQueue.Peek();
        MessageBox.Show("'" + str + "' is at the head of the queue!",
            "You peeked!", MessageBoxButtons.OK, MessageBoxIcon.Exclamation);
    }
    else
        MessageBox.Show("Nothing on the queue to peek at!", "You peeked!",
            MessageBoxButtons.OK, MessageBoxIcon.Exclamation);
}
...
```

ArrayList

The ArrayList works like an array, except that it's dynamically resized depending on how many elements are actually stored in it.

TIP   VB6 programmers will welcome this functionality as comparable to the ReDim statement.

The demonstration application in this section shows you how to add and remove objects from an ArrayList, and—more or less for purposes of verifying that the structure is working—how to display a single element by index and how to display all ArrayList elements.

Figure 7.10 shows the user interface (in design mode) that we'll use for this purpose.

FIGURE 7.10:

In design mode, the
ErrorProvider sits on the
"tray" at the bottom of
a form.

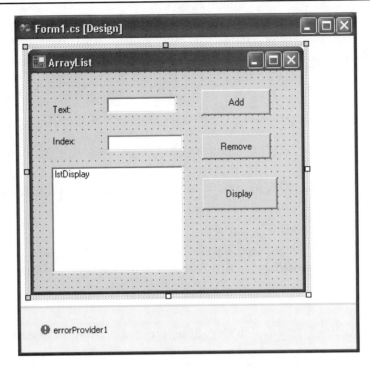

Note that an ErrorProvider component has been added from the Toolbox to the "tray" at the bottom of the form. This ErrorProvider—in a (hopefully) profitable detour from the main topic of this section—will be used to check that user input in the Index TextBox really is a number.

To set this up, add the code shown in Listing 7.13 to the Validating event of the TextBox to check.

Listing 7.13   Using an ErrorProvider to Validate Numeric Input

```csharp
private void txtIndex_Validating(object sender,
   System.ComponentModel.CancelEventArgs e) {
   try {
      int x = Int32.Parse(txtIndex.Text);
      errorProvider1.SetError(txtIndex, "");
   }
   catch {
      errorProvider1.SetError(txtIndex, "Requires an integer value!");
      txtIndex.Text = "0";
   }
}
```

If the user tries to enter nonnumeric data in this TextBox and then navigates away from the field, a red warning icon appears, and the error message specified in Listing 7.13 is displayed (see Figure 7.11). Next, the TextBox Text property is set in code to 0, presumably an innocuous value.

FIGURE 7.11:

If the user input in the TextBox fails the validation—because it is a noninteger value—an error message is displayed.

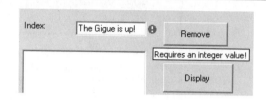

The routine for working with the ArrayList should seem pretty familiar by now. First, an ArrayList object is instantiated:

```
ArrayList al = new ArrayList();
```

You'll find the code for adding a text element to the ArrayList, removing an element by index, displaying an element by index, and displaying all elements along with an ArrayList count, in Listing 7.14.

Listing 7.14   Adding, Removing, and Displaying the Items in an ArrayList

```
...
ArrayList al = new ArrayList();

private void btnAdd_Click(object sender, System.EventArgs e) {
    al.Add(txtIn.Text);
    txtIn.Clear();
}

private void btnRemove_Click(object sender, System.EventArgs e) {
    int i;
    if (txtIndex.Text == "")
        i = 0;
    else
        i = Convert.ToInt32(txtIndex.Text);
    if (i >= 0 && i < al.Count) {
        al.RemoveAt(i);
        txtIndex.Clear();
    }
    else
        MessageBox.Show("Please try to keep within range!", "ArrayList Demo",
            MessageBoxButtons.OK, MessageBoxIcon.Information);
}

private void btnDisplay_Click(object sender, System.EventArgs e) {
    int i;
    if (txtIndex.Text == "")
        i = 0;
```

```
    else
        i = Convert.ToInt32(txtIndex.Text);
    if (i >= 0 && i < al.Count) {
        MessageBox.Show("Element " + txtIndex.Text + " of the ArrayList is " +
            al[i].ToString() + ".", "ArrayList Demo",
            MessageBoxButtons.OK, MessageBoxIcon.Information);
        txtIndex.Clear();
    }
    else
        MessageBox.Show("Please try to keep within range!", "ArrayList Demo",
            MessageBoxButtons.OK, MessageBoxIcon.Information);
}

private void btnDisAll_Click(object sender, System.EventArgs e) {
    for (int i = 0; i < al.Count; i++)
        lstDisplay.Items.Add(al[i]);
    lstDisplay.Items.Add("ARRAY COUNT IS: " + al.Count.ToString());
}
...
```

Run the application and play with it to verify that the ArrayList is resizing dynamically (Figure 7.12).

FIGURE 7.12:

It's easy to dynamically resize ArrayLists.

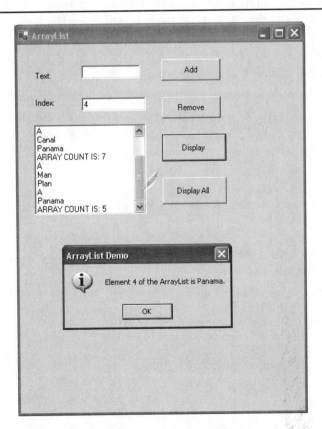

Dictionaries

Dictionaries are structures that implement the IDictionary interface providing for a collection of keys and values—the key is used to access the value. There are several dictionary classes that can be used, such as HashTable and SortedList in the System.Collections namespace and HybridDictionary, ListDictionary, and StringDictionary in the System.Collections .Specialized namespace.

The *SortedList* Class

One of the more useful classes that implements IDictionary is SortedList. SortedList is actually kind of a cross-breed because it implements both dictionary key/value access and also array-style access by index.

The demonstration example will show you how to save a text string and a color to a SortedList using key/value pairing. The text and color will then be retrieved from the SortedList and used to populate the Text and BackColor properties, respectively, of a form. I'll show you how to retrieve these values using indices as well as key/value pairs.

The user interface consists of a TextBox for the user to enter the text, a button that opens the Color common dialog—explained in Chapter 4—for the user to select a color, another button to save the choices to the SortedList, and a third button to retrieve the values and use them to populate the properties of a new form (this user interface is shown in Figures 7.13 and 7.14 at the end of this section).

As a preliminary, add a new Form to the project by selecting Project > Add Windows Form, selecting Windows Form in the Add New Item dialog, and clicking Open.

Next, in the original form and at the form class level, declare a Form variable, then instantiate the new Form, a ColorDialog variable, a Color variable initialized to the quaintly named Color.AliceBlue—which happens to be the first value in the Color enumeration—and the SortedList:

```
Form2 Form2 = new Form2();
private System.Windows.Forms.ColorDialog colorDialog1;
Color theColor = Color.AliceBlue;
SortedList sl = new SortedList();
```

Implement the Color common dialog—which also sets the background color of the button that invokes it—as follows:

```
private void btnColor_Click(object sender, System.EventArgs e) {
    colorDialog1.AllowFullOpen = true;
    colorDialog1.AnyColor = true;
    colorDialog1.ShowDialog();
    theColor = colorDialog1.Color;
    btnColor.BackColor = theColor;
}
```

Save the keys and values to the SortedList:

```
private void btnSave_Click(object sender, System.EventArgs e) {
    sl.Add("Text",txtText.Text);
    sl.Add("BackColor", theColor);
}
```

The only thing remaining is to show the new form, retrieve the values, and use them to set the *Form2* properties. Here's how this would look if one were using the index features of the SortedList:

```
private void btnGet_Click(object sender, System.EventArgs e) {
    Form2.Show();
    Form2.BackColor = (Color) sl.GetByIndex(0);
    Form2.Text = sl.GetByIndex(1).ToString();
}
```

Note that the BackColor has to be cast to (Color) since—once again—it has been stored as simply an object. Similarly, the text value that has been saved as an object must be reconverted to a string.

Actually, I think it's much more fun to use keys and values than an index, and, anyhow, if you wanted to use an index, you'd have used an array in the first place. Here's how the procedure looks using the dictionary functionality of the SortedList:

```
private void btnGet_Click(object sender, System.EventArgs e) {
    Form2.Show();
    Form2.Text = sl["Text"].ToString();
    Form2.BackColor = (Color) sl["BackColor"];
}
```

Note once again that conversion and casting from object to string and Color is required.

It is time to run the project. Enter a text string in the TextBox, and click the Choose Color button to open the Color dialog (Figure 7.13).

FIGURE 7.13:

The user enters text and a color via the common dialog; these choices are then saved with appropriate keys to a SortedList.

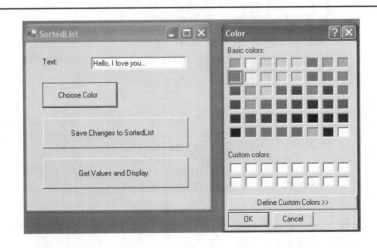

Next, save the changes to the SortedList. Finally, click the third button to display the new form with the properties retrieved from the SortedList (Figure 7.14).

FIGURE 7.14:

User selections are retrieved by key from the SortedList and applied to a new form.

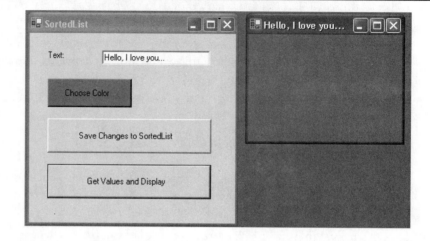

Listing 7.15   **Using a SortedList to Store and Retrieve Text and a Color by Key**

```
...
Form2 Form2 = new Form2();
private System.Windows.Forms.ColorDialog colorDialog1;
Color theColor = Color.AliceBlue;
SortedList sl = new SortedList();

private void btnColor_Click(object sender, System.EventArgs e) {
    colorDialog1.AllowFullOpen = true;
    colorDialog1.AnyColor = true;
    colorDialog1.ShowDialog();
    theColor = colorDialog1.Color;
    btnColor.BackColor = theColor;
}

private void btnSave_Click(object sender, System.EventArgs e) {
    sl.Add("Text", txtText.Text);
    sl.Add("BackColor", theColor);
}

private void btnGet_Click(object sender, System.EventArgs e) {
    Form2.Show();
    // Form2.Text = sl.GetByIndex(1).ToString();
    Form2.Text = sl["Text"].ToString();
    // Form2.BackColor = (Color) sl.GetByIndex(0);
    Form2.BackColor = (Color) sl["BackColor"];
}
...
```

Conclusion

This chapter explained how to work with arrays and other structures, such as collections, stacks, and queues, for storing groups of objects. This is not the most exciting topic in the universe, but it has great utility. Almost all programs use these structures. Choosing the proper structure for manipulation of your data, and implementing it correctly, will go a long way towards assuring the soundness of your projects.

Let's move to something that is truly exciting, and the heart of programming in C#: object-oriented programming.

CHAPTER 8

The Life of the Object in C#

- Guns, Germs, and Steel

- The Facade pattern

- Working with classes, class members, and access modifiers

- Instance vs. static members

- Constructors

- Working with instances of forms

- Working with methods, including overriding virtual methods

- Five steps to creating an event

- Overloading methods and operators

- Polymorphism

- Creating a custom collection

Is object-oriented programming "much ado about nothing"? (Please don't hate me because I dare to ask the unthinkable.)

In the words of Bertrand Meyer, a distinguished OOP evangelist and creator of the Eiffel language, "Object technology is at its core the combination of four ideas: a structuring method, a reliability discipline, an epistemological principle, and a classification technique." In my opinion, these four ideas boil down as follows:

- The "structuring method" is the concept of classes used as the blueprint for objects.
- The "reliability discipline" is the concept of a contract between objects.
- The "epistemological principle" is the idea of describing classes by their interfaces and members.
- The "classification technique" creates a taxonomy for a given domain by following the chain of class inheritance within the domain.

I believe that object-oriented programming is much, much more than a fad and is here to stay as an important part of the way software developers work. But it's also not suitable as the solution to every problem. (Remember the saying that, to a hammer, everything looks like a nail.)

In non-OOP procedural languages—such as FORTRAN and early versions of Visual Basic—one can create structures that simulate an object-oriented programming environment. Oddly enough, in a completely object-oriented environment such as C#, sometimes one wants to do the reverse: create procedural code and ignore (as much as possible) C#'s classes.

Object-oriented programming in C# has two faces: inward and outward. The inward face is the C# language and the .NET class libraries: no matter what you do, you are writing code that is placed in the context of an OOP system, so you may as well make good use of it as much as you can.

The outward face is projects that you create, in which you can use the taxonomy, structures, and mechanisms of C# as models for how your classes should be structured and what your code should look like (that is, if you are not creating a single procedural piece of code with a click event).

The chapter details the mechanics of creating OOP applications in C#.

Guns, Germs, and Steel

Jared Diamond's Pulitzer Prize–winning book *Guns, Germs, and Steel* (W.W. Norton, 1996) is an attempt to answer the broad question of why some human societies achieve material success and others do not. Diamond's answer—in short—is that the fate of human societies depends on the availability of various kinds of resources far more than on any cultural or racial differences between peoples. He summarizes his own book as follows:

History followed different courses for different peoples because of differences among peoples' environments, not because of biological differences among peoples themselves.

In his book, Diamond has created a wonderfully deterministic model for predicting the success of human populations. As I explain in more detail below, according to this model, the extent that certain environmental resources are present determine whether a given society will succeed and expand—if they are not, the society will never achieve the critical mass required for success and will be easy prey for assimilation by a more successful society.

At this point, you, dear reader, may well be wondering what a section on the historical causes of the fate of human societies is doing in a programming book. The answer is that I have adopted—and greatly simplified—the model proposed in *Guns, Germs, and Steel* to create the running example of object-oriented programming used in this chapter. In this example, "tribes" are created with an initial population and resource characteristics. We can then see whether over time these tribes succeed (turning first into city-states and then large civilizations), become static (reaching an equilibrium situation in which the population neither expands nor contracts), or wither (and become extinct). We can also see what happens when two tribes clash. For example, our model should be able to predict the outcome of the one-sided sixteenth-century conflict between the Spaniards and the Incas, which is used as a case study in *Guns, Germs, and Steel*.

In Diamond's book, numerous factors (including population density, raw materials, climate, topography, and the presence of certain kinds of plants and animals) are said to determine whether a tribe will graduate from the hunter-gatherer stage. In my "back of the envelope" model, I've used just two of Diamond's factors as a proxy for all of them: the number of species of large-seeded grasses and of animal species suitable for domestication.

The next step in the book's model is to observe that if a society does not become large and dense, it will never develop the germs (and resistance to those germs) that kill off less dense, less resistant populations that the society comes into contact with. In my simplified model, complications such as density and proximity to disease-carrying animals are ignored; once a tribe hits 100,000 people, it starts producing germs (and resistance) in proportion to its growth. An index of bacteria density represents this in my application—even though, in the real world, much of the harm to indigenous peoples was done via viral disease (rather than bacterial) and via single diseases such as smallpox rather than a high overall count.

Finally, successful tribes must develop technology and commerce. For this to happen, there must be a leisure class—people who don't have to spend all their time hunting, gathering, or farming for food. (This implies that the number of calories expended in getting and preparing the food is less than the calories obtained in eating the food.) In my simplified model, once a tribe hits 1,000,000 people, and provided it has a growth rate of greater than 50% every twenty years, we assume it is creating technology and commerce (in proportion to its rate of growth).

NOTE   Not all the code for the Guns, Germs, and Steel model can fit in the text of this chapter. You can download the complete code for the project from the Sybex website.

The User Interface

The primary user interface for the Guns, Germs, and Steel application is based on a single MDI form, shown in Figure 8.1. Each culture created by the user is shown in a child window in the client area of the form. (MDI applications are explained in Chapter 4, "Building a Better Windows Interface.")

FIGURE 8.1:

Statistics on cultures created by the user are displayed within the client area of the primary MDI form.

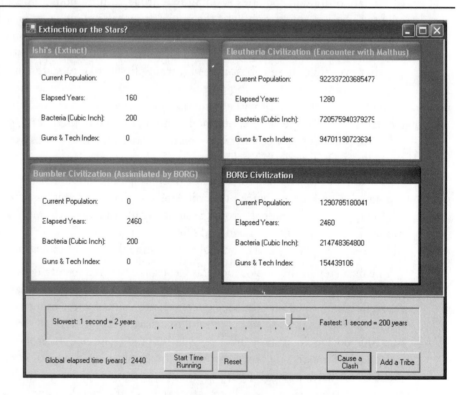

The mechanism for simulating advancing time is provided by a Timer component (which was explained in Chapter 4.)

The panel along the bottom of the form shown in Figure 8.1 allows the user to "slow time down" or "speed time up" using a TrackBar control. To achieve the effect I wanted, I set the TrackBar Minimum property to 1, its Maximum to 100, and its Value to 90. I then added code to the TrackBar `ValueChanged` event to change the value of the Timer `Interval` property:

```
private void trackBar1_ValueChanged(object sender, System.EventArgs e){
    timer1.Interval = Math.Abs(trackBar1.Value - 101) * 100;
}
```

NOTE   The little formula in the TrackBar `ValueChanged` event produces a range of values between 1,000 and 10,000 (one to ten seconds) for the Timer `Interval` property.

The buttons beneath the TrackBar allow the user to

- Start and stop the global timer
- Reset the application by closing all child forms and de-referencing the items in the collection they are based upon
- Cause a clash between two cultures
- Add a tribe

Tribes are the first stage of cultures in this model—they may, with luck and perseverance, grow up to be city-states or civilizations. Figure 8.2 shows the interface used to initialize a tribe by assigning it a name, an initial population, and colors for screen display, and indicating the resources available to it.

FIGURE 8.2:

Tribes are started with an initial population and access to the specified plant and animal resources.

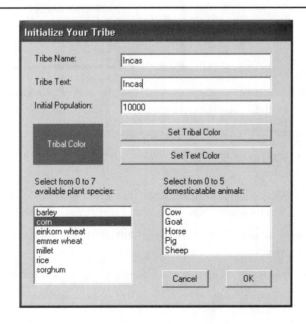

The Application Architecture

Successful tribes grow to become city-states, and city-states that are lucky and play their cards right become civilizations (think classical Rome). This progression is modeled in the application with a base `Tribe` class. The `CityState` class inherits from the `Tribe` class, and the `Civilization` class inherits from the `CityState` class because each inherited class adds to the functionality of its base. This relationship is shown in the Class View window in Figure 8.3.

FIGURE 8.3:

The Class View window shows that `Civilization` inherits from `CityState`, which inherits from `Tribe`, adding new (or overridden) members as it inherits.

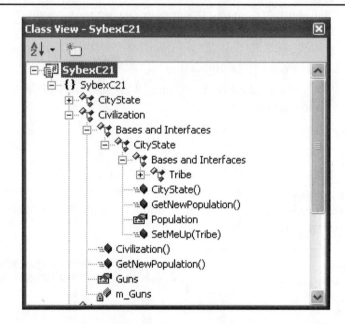

An encapsulating class, `GroupOfPeople`, serves as a kind of traffic director among the three classes in the `Tribe` inheritance chain. The `GroupOfPeople` class

- Instantiates objects of the classes it encapsulates
- Directs to the appropriate class in the inheritance chain based on the current characteristics of a people
- Fires events as appropriate, such as when a tribe has become extinct, or when a civilization reaches its Malthusian limits (and must reach for the stars)
- Implements "clashes" between different peoples through the use of overloaded comparison
- Manages the display of a peoples' current characteristics

By the way, GroupOfPeople, as an encapsulating class, is an example of the "Facade" design pattern—a *design pattern* being an abstraction that identifies the key aspects of a common design structure that is useful for creating a reusable object-oriented design. According to Gamma, Helm, Johnson, and Vlissides, sometimes affectionately referred to as the "Gang of Four" and authors of the well-known *Design Patterns: Elements of Reusable Object-Oriented Software* (Addison-Wesley, 1994):

> *The intent of the Facade pattern is to provide a unified interface to a set of interfaces in a subsystem. Facade defines a higher-level interface that makes the subsystem easier to use.*

In other words, the programmer—or the MDI parent form, which contains the bulk of the user-driven program logic—does not have to worry about Tribe, CityState, or Civilization objects, or managing the display based on these objects. GroupOfPeople objects—which are items of a collection named PeoplesCollection—handle it all.

This general architecture is shown in Figure 8.4.

FIGURE 8.4:

A collection is formed of GroupOfPeople objects, which, in turn, manage subsystem functionality.

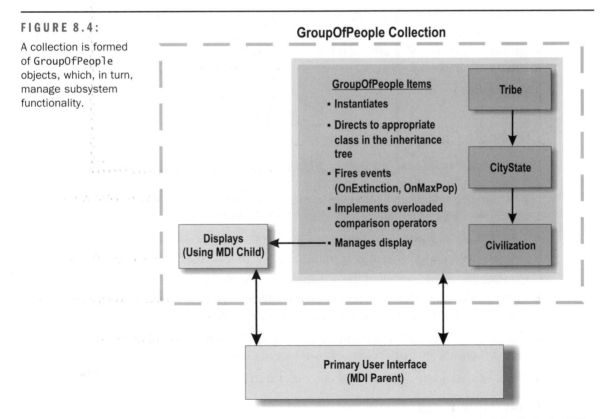

© Phyllis Davis 2002

Within the primary application form (the MDI form), the user can start and stop the Timer, and speed up or slow down how fast time appears to go by. In addition, code that uses the members of instantiated GroupOfPeople objects accomplishes the following tasks:

- Add a new GroupOfPeople (which starts as a tribe).

- Respond to the Timer's Elapsed event (which signifies that a generation, defined as twenty years, has gone by).

- Respond to the events fired by objects in the PeoplesCollection collection of GroupOfPeople.

- Determine the results of a clash between two GroupOfPeople objects—using the overloaded comparison operators provided by the object—and publish the results.

This application was built using several OOP design features, but, of course, not all OOP facilities found their way into it. It's self-evident that trade-offs are involved in constructing a chapter like this one around a large single example; on the whole, I think the pluses outweigh the minuses.

I found that the bulk of the work was creating a single instance that worked the way I wanted it to. After that, thanks to C#'s object-oriented context, I was able to quickly generalize my single instance into as many objects as I'd like, and easily engineer interactions between different instances. Readers should be able to interpolate these techniques and use them in their own applications.

Creating a Class

The class is the basic unit, or blueprint, for object construction in C# .NET. All objects in C#—and everything is an object, including variables, types, forms, and so on—are based on classes and their members. The members of an object correspond to the members of the class upon which it is based.

Inheritance is an important mechanism for extending the usefulness of a class. A *derived* class is one that has inherited from a *base* class.

Creating and invoking a simple class with a field, a property, a method, and an event as members was explained in the "Creating a Class Library" section of Chapter 5, "Reflecting on Classes." You'll find the material in Chapter 5 a good introduction to the information presented here.

A class is created by first declaring it—using the class keyword—and then defining its members.

Declaring a Class

The basic form of a class declaration is to provide an access level (as described later in this section), followed by the keyword class, followed by an identifier (the class name). By convention, class names start with an initial capital. Members of the class follow the declaration, between curly braces. For example:

```
public class Tribe {
    // Class body goes here
}
```

NOTE You can also include attributes in the class declaration. An *attribute* is metadata associated with an element of a program. For more information about attributes, search for the topic "Attributes Tutorial" in online help.

To create a class that inherits from another base class, at the end of the class declaration place the colon operator (:), followed by the base class name. For example, the CityState class inherits from the Tribe class, so it is declared as follows:

```
public class CityState : Tribe {
    // Class body goes here
}
```

TIP The Visual Basic .NET equivalent of the : operator is the Inherits keyword.

Class Modifiers

The public keyword in the class declaration is an *access modifier*. Access modifiers are used to control access to classes and class members (see "Member Access" later in this chapter). The access modifiers allowed for a class are listed in Table 8.1, and general modifiers are shown in Table 8.2.

TABLE 8.1: Class Access Modifiers

Modifier	Description
internal	Only accessible to classes within the same assembly (this is the default access level).
public	Accessible to classes outside the assembly. Most classes are declared with public access.

NOTE Nested classes—classes within classes—are actually class members, and can be marked with the full set of class member (rather than class) access keywords, including protected and private. Those modifiers are discussed later in this chapter.

Classes can be marked internal, in which case they are only visible within an assembly, or public—meaning they can be accessed externally to the assembly that they are in. If you leave the access modifier off, the class will default to internal. However, in practice most classes are declared public.

TABLE 8.2: Class General Modifiers

Modifier	Description
abstract	Contains no implementation and is unusable as is; derived classes implement the members of an abstract class.
new	Explicitly hides a member inherited from a base class. Infrequently used in a class declaration, since it must be used with a nested class.
sealed	Cannot be inherited.

Classes can also be marked using the abstract modifier, which means that the class can only be used as the base class for other classes (put another way, an abstract class *must* be inherited from), or sealed, meaning that the class cannot be used as a base class (put another way, a sealed class *cannot* be inherited from).

It is perfectly reasonable to combine an access modifier with general modifiers in a class declaration. For example, the Dinosaur class declaration used in an example later in this chapter is

```
public abstract class Dinosaur
```

Using the Class Template

If you open the Add New Item dialog (shown in Figure 8.5), select the Class template, give the class a name, and click Open, Visual Studio will create for you the default class module shown in Listing 8.1.

FIGURE 8.5:

Adding a class module with the Add New Item dialog

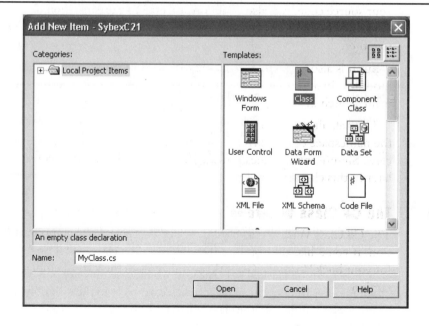

Listing 8.1   **Default Class Module**

```
using System;

namespace SybexC21
{
    /// <summary>
    /// Summary description for myClass.
    /// </summary>
    public class MyClass
    {
        public MyClass()
        {
            //
            // TODO: Add constructor logic here
            //
        }
    }
}
```

What, exactly, does the default class produced by this class template buy you? I'll answer this question in a moment, but the overall answer is, not much. Class modules are good places to start class libraries. And, as a matter of style, it can aid the clarity of the overall program architecture to put each substantive class in a module by itself. If you put each class in its own module file (.cs file) and name each file with the class name, it makes it very easy to find classes in your source code. It is also common and effective organization to group related classes in one module—for example, a business object class along with the collection class that groups them together.

But it is also perfectly reasonable to add short classes to existing modules—such as form modules. In addition, obviously it is not much work to create your own declaration from scratch in an empty Code File module (also available via the Add New Item dialog).

The default class code gives you some comments, a using System directive, and inclusion in the namespace of the current assembly. It does not provide a base class for the newly created class. Significantly, it does provide the framework for a class constructor (see "Constructors" later in this chapter).

The C# Class Wizard

The C# Class Wizard is a visual interface that gives you a jump start in creating a class definition. If you'd like aid from the IDE in creating a class, you'll find you get much more "bang for your buck" from the Class Wizard than from the Class Template described in the previous section.

To start the Class Wizard, you must have the Class View window open. In Class View, right-click a namespace and select Add ➤ Add Class from the context menu. The first panel of the wizard, shown in Figure 8.6, will open.

FIGURE 8.6:

The C# Class Wizard provides a flexible and thorough mechanism for the creation of a class module.

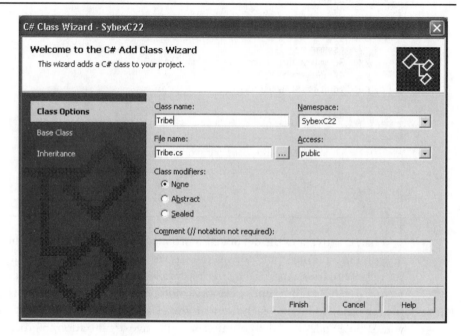

The first panel lets you set general class elements, such as its name and accessibility level. The Base Class panel, opened by clicking the link in the left pane, lets you select a namespace and the base class from which the new class will be derived. Finally, the Inheritance panel, also opened via a link, lets you select multiple interfaces that the new class inherits (interfaces are discussed in Chapter 9, "Everything Is String Manipulation").

Class Members

C# classes can contain the following ten kinds of members (in alphabetic order):

- Classes (in other words, classes can be nested within classes)
- Constructors
- Delegates
- Destructors
- Enumerations
- Events

- Fields
- Indexers
- Methods
- Properties

Member Access

Table 8.3 shows the access modifiers that can be used in a class member declaration. The access modifier controls the *scope* of the member—in other words, where it is "visible" and can be used.

TABLE 8.3: Class Member Access Modifiers

Modifier	Description
internal	Accessible to class methods within the same assembly
private	Only available to members of the same class (this is the default access level)
protected	Accessible to members of the same class and of classes derived from the current class
protected internal	Accessible to both assembly class methods and derived class members
public	Accessible to the methods of any class

If you leave the access modifier off a class member, it defaults to private access. However, as a matter of good programming style, you should explicitly mark the access level of your class members: if they are local in scope to the class, declare them using the private access modifier.

At the risk of getting a little bit ahead of ourselves, let's make the concept of protected access a little more concrete. Suppose you have a class named Surprise, with a single member, the protected string hiddenValley:

```
namespace SybexC22 {
   public class Surprise {
      public Surprise() {

      }
      protected string hiddenValley = "How green was it?";
   }
}
```

You might then attempt to instantiate an object based on Surprise and access hiddenValley, perhaps in a click event like so:

```
private void btnGet_Click(object sender, System.EventArgs e) {
   Surprise surprise = new Surprise();
   MessageBox.Show (surprise.hiddenValley);
}
```

If you attempt to run this, you will get a compile-time syntax error, due to the inaccessibility of the hiddenValley member.

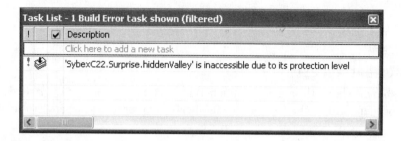

However, you can use Surprise as the base class for a new class, UnWrap:

```
namespace SybexC22 {
    public class UnWrap : Surprise {
        public UnWrap() {

        }
        public string GetSurprise(){
            return hiddenValley;
        }
    }
}
```

UnWrap has access to the protected members of its base class (Surprise). Using this access, UnWrap can make hiddenValley available in a public method, in the example named Get-Surprise. UnWrap can then be instantiated, and hiddenValley returned via the GetString method:

```
private void btnGet_Click(object sender, System.EventArgs e) {
    UnWrap unWrap = new UnWrap();
    MessageBox.Show (unWrap.GetSurprise(), "Got it",
        MessageBoxButtons.OK, MessageBoxIcon.Exclamation);
}
```

Running this code shows that the value of the protected field can be displayed via a method of a derived class (Figure 8.7). The two classes and the click event are shown in Listing 8.2.

FIGURE 8.7:

A protected member can be accessed via public methods of a derived class.

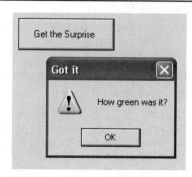

Listing 8.2   **A Derived Class to Access a Protected Member of Its Base Class**

```
namespace SybexC22 {
    public class Surprise {
        public Surprise() {

        }
        protected string hiddenValley = "How green was it?";
    }
}
namespace SybexC22 {
    public class UnWrap : Surprise {
        public UnWrap() {

        }
        public string GetSurprise(){
            return hiddenValley;
        }
    }
}

// in class Form1
private void btnGet_Click(object sender, System.EventArgs e) {
    UnWrap unWrap = new UnWrap();
    MessageBox.Show (unWrap.GetSurprise(), "Got it",
        MessageBoxButtons.OK, MessageBoxIcon.Exclamation);
}
```

Member Modifiers

In addition to the access modifiers, class member declarations can be modified with other keywords, which are shown in Table 8.4.

TABLE 8.4: Class Member Modifiers

Modifier	Meaning
const	The field or variable cannot be modified. See the section "Constants" in Chapter 6, "Zen and Now: The C# Language."
extern	The marked method is implemented outside the C# code, probably in an imported library. For more information, look up "extern" in online help.
override	The member provides a new implementation of a virtual member inherited from a base class. See "Polymorphism and Overriding" later in this chapter.
readonly	The field can be assigned a value only in its declaration or in its class constructor.
static	The member belongs to a type itself rather than an instance of the type. See "Instance vs. Static Members" later in this chapter.

Continued on next page

TABLE 8.4 CONTINUED: Class Member Modifiers

Modifier	Meaning
unsafe	The member is operating in an unsafe context (as is required for explicit pointer operations). For more information, look up "unsafe" in online help.
virtual	The implementation of the member (or property accessor) can be changed by an overriding member in a derived class. See "Polymorphism and Overriding" later in this chapter.
volatile	The field is modifiable by something external to the current program (such as the operating system, hardware, or a program operating on another thread). For more information, look up "volatile" in online help.

Using the Member Wizards

A little earlier in this chapter, I showed you how to use the C# Class Wizard to add a class definition. Member wizards, also accessible from the Class View window, provide an interface that helps you to add fields, methods, properties, and indexers to a class.

To open a member wizard, select a class in Class View. Right-click the class, then select Add. A submenu will open, as shown in Figure 8.8.

FIGURE 8.8:

Member wizards help you add methods, properties, fields, and indexers to a class.

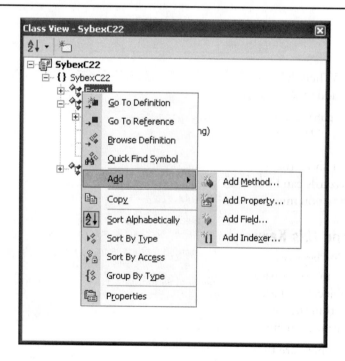

From the submenu, select the kind of member you would like to add. Figure 8.9 shows the Add Method Wizard being used to create the declaration for a method.

When the method shown in the wizard interface in Figure 8.9 is created, the following code is added to the class:

```
public bool GetAddresses(int lbound, int ubound, string flag) {
    return true;
}
```

I show the generated code here essentially to make the point that running the member wizards can be helpful, particularly when you are getting started with C#, but will not really save you much work as opposed to creating members by hand.

The *this* Keyword

The keyword this means the current instance of an object. (I almost said "current instance of an object based on a class," but in C# the "based on a class" clause is redundant—since all objects are based on classes.) In other words, this references each instance of a class from within the instance (see the next section of this chapter for an explanation of static versus instance members of a class).

There are three ways you might use this:

- To refer to instance members that would otherwise be hidden by parameters of a method or property (for an example, see "Class Variables, Fields, and Properties" later in this chapter)

- To pass as a parameter a reference to the current object (for some examples, see "Whose Form Is It?" later in this chapter)

- With indexers (for an example, see "Indexers" in Chapter 7, "Arrays, Indexers, and Collections")

It's also good practice to use this.*member* syntax when referring to object instance members—because the syntax makes it clear exactly what you are referring to even when the member is not hidden by a local variable or parameter.

> **TIP**   The Visual Basic equivalent of the this keyword is the me keyword.

Instance vs. Static Members

Class members are either *instance* or *static*. Instance members require that a reference to an object based on the class be created in memory before the member can be used. This process is called *instantiation*.

In contrast, static members of a class are associated with the class itself rather than an instance of a type based on the class. You access a static member by simply qualifying it with the name of the class it belongs to. In C#, static members cannot be accessed through an instance—so you cannot use the this keyword to invoke a static method.

By default, members of a class are instance members. To make a member static, it must be marked with the static keyword as a modifier following the access modifier. For example, many members of the String class, such as String.Format, are static, meaning you do not have to create an instance of System.String to use the System.String.Format method. (The String class is discussed in detail in Chapter 9.)

> **TIP**   The VB .NET equivalent to static is the Shared keyword.

Instance Member Example

Let's take an example of using an instance member from the Guns, Germs, and Steel project. As you'll recall, the GroupOfPeople class is used as the "facade"—or combination of traffic cop and gateway—for managing the growth and display of cultures added by the user. One of the instance members of GroupOfPeople is the method CreateNewTribe. Here's the declaration for CreateNewTribe:

```
public void CreateNewTribe(frmSettings dlg) {
    ...
}
```

Now let's take a look at instantiating a GroupOfPeople object and invoking the CreateNewTribe method. This is done, as you probably are aware, with the new keyword.

In the application, the instantiation takes place after the user clicks the Add a Tribe button on the program's main form, within the Button's click event method. However, *gop*, the variable that holds the instance of GroupOfPeople, is declared at the form class level, not within the Button's click method. This is done so that the variable holding the instance will be available to other members of the form class. Here's the excerpted code:

```
...
GroupOfPeople gop;
private void btnAddaTribe_Click(object sender, System.EventArgs e) {
    frmSettings dlg = new frmSettings();
    ...
    gop = new GroupOfPeople();
    ...
    gop.CreateNewTribe (dlg);
    ...
}
```

Had I not needed to keep the declaration of the GroupOfPeople variable at the form class level—so that it would be accessible to all members of the form class—I could, of course, have declared and instantiated it in one statement:

```
GroupOfPeople gop = new GroupOfPeople();
```

rather than the two actually used:

```
GroupOfPeople gop;
...
gop = new GroupOfPeople();
```

NOTE   It is conventional to name classes starting with an uppercase letter and to name the variables that hold instances of the class starting with a lowercase letter—for example, GroupOfPeople (the class) and *gop* (the instance variable).

Static Members Example

In C#, all code is within classes that are declared as explained earlier in this chapter. There is no such thing as a global module of code. This leads to the question of where to put declarations for variables and constants that you will need in multiple class instances.

NOTE   Constants are considered static members. Therefore, they do not need to be—for that matter, they cannot be—marked with the static keyword.

A good answer is to mark global variables public as well as static, mark constants you will need globally as public, and place them all in one class devoted just for that purpose. Listing 8.3 shows the class used for that purpose in the Guns, Germs, and Steel application.

Listing 8.3   A Class Used for Global Variables and Constants

```
namespace SybexC21
{
   public class Globals
   {
      // Global Constants and Variables
      public static long globalTime = 0000;
      public const int totalAnimals = 5;
      public const int totalPlants = 7;
      public const int generation = 20;
   }
}
```

Here's how I used the *globalTime* variable and the *generation* constant with the main form class of the program to increment the time by a generation:

```
Globals.globalTime += Globals.generation;
```

The Main Method Is Static

As you may have noticed, every C# application requires a Main method as an *entry point*—the place where the program starts execution. The Main method is always static. Here's the Main method added by default to Form1 when you open a new C# Windows application:

```
static void Main() {
   Application.Run(new Form1());
}
```

Unlike in C++, static members cannot directly access instance members of a class—hence the need to instantiate Form1 using the new keyword.

Constructors

A *constructor* is a method that is used to initialize a class instance. A constructor is invoked when a class is instantiated. Every C# class must have one or more constructors—or rely on the default constructor provided by the Common Language Runtime (CLR) environment.

To define a class constructor in C#, declare a method within the class whose name is the same as the class that it constructs.

Earlier in this chapter I reproduced the default code generated by the Class template (back in Listing 8.1). If the class were named MyClass, the important parts looked like this:

```
public class MyClass
{
```

```
   public MyClass()
   {

   }
}
```

The method with the same name as the class, within the MyClass class declaration,

```
   public MyClass()
```

is the framework for a class constructor.

TIP   Constructors are defined using a rather different syntax in VB .NET (by declaring a New subroutine within the VB class).

If you don't declare a class constructor, or don't add implementation code within the constructor declaration, the CLR provides a default constructor for you. This default constructor creates an object and initializes members innocuously—numeric members to 0, strings to the empty string, and so on—but takes no other action.

Most of the time, you'll want to define your own constructors so that instances of the class are initialized to appropriate values. But don't worry! You don't have to actually take care of creating an object by allocating a reference in memory—the compiler and the CLR take care of that for you. All you have to do is assign appropriate values for members in the constructor.

As a matter of fact, you can have more than one constructor for a given class, provided that the *signature*—meaning method type and the types of its arguments—of each constructor method is different. (Having multiple methods with the same name and different signatures is called *overloading*, discussed later in this chapter.) The point of having multiple constructors for a class is that you can use whichever constructor is right, depending on circumstances.

Listing 8.4 shows three constructors for the Guns, Germs, and Steel Tribe class.

Listing 8.4   **Three *Tribe* Class Constructors**

```
public class Tribe
{
   public Tribe()
   {

   }

   public Tribe(string theName, string theText) {
      this.Name = theName;
      this.Text = theText;
   }
```

```
public Tribe(string theName, string theText, long theStartYear,
    Color theTrCol, Color theTextCol, int numAnimals, int numPlants,
    long numGenerations) {
    this.Name = theName;
    this.Text = theText;
    this.StartYear = theStartYear
    this.TribalColor = theTrCol;
    this.TextColor = theTextCol;
    this.SpeciesAnimals = numAnimals;
    this.SpeciesPlants = numPlants;
    this.numGenerations = numGenerations;
    }
    ...
}
```

The first empty (default) constructor shown in Listing 8.4 is what is invoked if you instantiate with a statement like

```
Tribe tr = new Tribe();
```

The other two constructors are invoked if the instantiation matches their signature. For example, to invoke the third constructor shown, you could instantiate a Tribe object like this:

```
Tribe tr = new Tribe("Gondor", "Numenorians", 1064, System.Drawing.Color.Green,
    System.Drawing.Color.Gold, 5, 7, 1020);
```

It's really neat that, as one types in the code that instantiates a class in the Code Editor, dropdown arrows display the signature of each possible constructor.

```
public void CreateNewTribe(frmSettings dlg) {
    tr = new Tribe(;
    this.[▲2 of 3▼  Tribe.Tribe (string theName, string theText)]
    this.Text = tr.Text = dlg.tribeText;
```

Class Variables, Fields, and Properties

Class fields are simply public variables belonging to a class—also referred to as *member* variables—meaning that they are declared at the class level. (A variable declared inside a method is always private to the method and cannot be declared using the public keyword.)

Like other instance class members, fields can be declared with access modifiers. A variable declared using private can only be accessed within an instance and is intended to be used internally, while a public member variable (a field) can be accessed outside the instance.

For example, in the GroupOfPeople class, the lines

```
private Tribe tr;
private CityState cs;
private Civilization civil;
```

declare private instance variables, while the lines

```
public bool isAlive = false;
public string Name;
public frmTribe frmTribe;
```

all declare public instance variables—also known as class fields.

Properties are more elegant versions of class variables. As you've previously seen, properties can be accessed externally to a class in the same way as a class field. However, internally, classes are implemented using the special methods known as get and set *accessors*. Here's a simple example from the GroupOfPeople class:

```
private long m_Population = 0;
public long Population {
    get {
        return m_Population;
    }
    set {
        m_Population = value;
    }
}
```

The get accessor of the property uses the return keyword to return a value when the property is accessed. The set accessor uses the value keyword to assign a value when the property is set. An internal class variable, *m_Population*, is used to keep track of the property's value between use of the accessors.

NOTE   By convention, the private variables that track property values are named with an m_ prefix.

The property mechanism can be used to validate values, calculate changes to values, and access internal object state information. Properties can be made read-only (by omitting the set accessor) or write-only (by omitting the get accessor). In this way, they serve as an effective object-oriented programming mechanism, by encapsulating the implementation details.

For example, in the Tribe class in the Guns, Germs, and Steel application, the SpeciesAnimals property validates a value passed to it to make sure that it does not exceed the allowable value set in a global constant field before updating the property value by setting the private member variable:

```
private int m_SpeciesAnimals = 0;
...
public int SpeciesAnimals {
    get {
        return m_SpeciesAnimals;
    }
```

```
set {
    if (value <= Globals.totalAnimals)
        m_SpeciesAnimals = value;
}
}
```

Whose Form Is It?

And, in whose instance am I, anyway? These turn out to be not entirely rhetorical questions. As we've seen in this chapter, all code in C# is within classes. Furthermore, applications start running by invoking an object instance of a class, e.g.:

```
Application.Run(new Form1());
```

These facts lead to the natural question of how to communicate references and values between class instances. Since Windows forms are wholly encapsulated as individual classes, communicating between instances of different form class objects is something that must be done in any multiform Windows application.

NOTE   This issue was essentially papered over in VB6 (and earlier versions of VB). In VB6, you can invoke a form member as though the form were a static class without formally creating a class instance—so inter-form communication is a non-issue. VB6 programmers who are new to .NET should pay special attention to this section.

One way of dealing with this is to use public static variables to pass references and values back and forth—since these variables can be accessed without instantiation from any class. Creating a class module for static public variables and constants was explained earlier in this chapter in the "Static Members Example."

However, for several reasons, this is probably not the best way to communicate between class instances. (Extensive use of static public variables in this way is unnecessarily consumptive of resources. It also violates the encapsulation features of good OOP design.)

In particular, there are better options for managing Windows forms applications intra-communication. Let's look at a couple of possibilities.

Using a Property to Pass a Form Instance

Properties are ideal for holding a reference to a class instance in a second form class. To see how this works, use the Add New Item dialog to add a new form to a Windows application project. If you didn't change their default names, you now have two forms—and classes—in the project named Form1 and Form2.

Before we get started, use the Properties window to change the value of the Text property of Form1 to something like "The first form is very happy!". We'll be accessing this value from the Form2 instance in our demonstration.

Next, add a property named OtherForm of type Form to the Form2 class:

```
private Form m_OtherForm = null;
public Form OtherForm {
    get {
        return m_OtherForm;
    }
    set {
        m_OtherForm = value;
    }
}
```

NOTE   The OtherForm property is actually of type System.Windows.Forms.Form, but since the System.Windows.Forms namespace is included by default in the Form2 class in a using directive, we don't have to fully qualify the Form type. Form1 (and Form2) inherit from the general Form class, so Form, as the base type, will do to store a reference to either derived class—or to any class derived from Form.

Next, back in Form1, add code to a Button click event that declares and instantiates an instance of the Form2 class named *form2*:

```
Form2 form2 = new Form2();
```

Use the this keyword to store a reference to the current instance of Form1 in Form2's OtherForm property:

```
form2.OtherForm = this;
```

Finally, use the Show method *form2* instance of the Form2 class to display the second form:

```
form2.Show();
```

Back in *form2*, we can add a click procedure that demonstrates that we can access the instance members of the object based on Form1, by changing the Text in the caption bar of the Form2 instance to include the Text value in the Form1 instance:

```
private void btnWho_Click(object sender, System.EventArgs e) {
    this.Text = "Form1 was called and said, \" " + OtherForm.Text + "\"";
}
```

If you run this code, display the second form, and click the button on it, you'll see that methods belonging to the second form instance can, indeed, access the instance members of the first form (Figure 8.10). The complete code in this example is shown in Listing 8.5.

FIGURE 8.10:

A reference to the instance of the Form1 class can be stored in a Form2 class instance property.

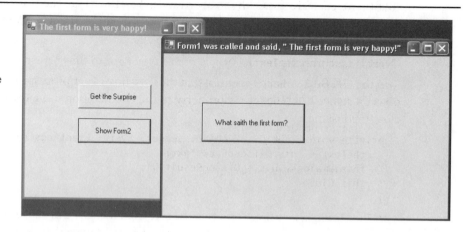

Listing 8.5   **Using a Property to Pass a Reference to a Form Instance**

```
// Form1
...
private void btnShow_Click(object sender, System.EventArgs e) {
   Form2 form2 = new Form2();
   form2.OtherForm = this;
   form2.Show();
}
...
// Form2
...
private Form m_OtherForm = null;

public Form OtherForm {
   get {
      return m_OtherForm;
   }
   set {
      m_OtherForm = value;
   }
}
private void btnWho_Click(object sender, System.EventArgs e) {
   this.Text = "Form1 was called and said, \" " + OtherForm.Text + "\"";
}
...
```

Using a Reference to a Form Instance

A different approach is to use a reference to another form class instance in the current instance. Here's how this might work.

Go back to the example shown in the previous section, and use the Add New Item dialog to add a new form class to the project (by default, it will be called Form3).

In Form3, add OK and Cancel buttons and a TextBox. The TextBox will be used for text that will be retrieved in a TextBox on Form1 when the user presses OK. Add a declaration for a public field to hold the string at the class level:

```
public string theText;
```

In the OK Button's click event, assign the TextBox's Text property to the field. Next, set the object instance's DialogResult property to the enumeration value DialogResult.OK. Finally, close the instance:

```
private void btnOK_Click(object sender, System.EventArgs e) {
    theText = this.txtSendBack.Text;
    this.DialogResult = DialogResult.OK;
    this.Close();
}
```

In Form1, add a TextBox to receive the text from the Form3 instance, add a Button to display the instance, and wire the logic. Here's the click event code that declares and instantiates an instance of Form3 and retrieves the text when the user clicks OK:

```
private void btnShow3_Click(object sender, System.EventArgs e) {
    Form3 form3 = new Form3();
    if (form3.ShowDialog(this) == DialogResult.OK){
        this.txtGiveHere.Text = form3.theText;
    }
    form3.Dispose();
}
```

The *ShowDialog* Method

The ShowDialog method of a form instance displays the form modally, meaning that when the form is open, a user cannot switch to another form in the application and that the code below the ShowDialog statement doesn't get executed until the form is closed. (With a regular Show method, the code below the statement runs immediately.)

By including the current form instance as a parameter (with the this keyword) in the ShowDialog method call, the current instance becomes the *owner* of the Form3 instance. When one form is an owner of a second form, it means that the second form always appears "on top" of the first form, and that when the first form is minimized, so is the second form.

WARNING It's a good idea to include a call to the Dispose method of the modal form instance. This is the rare case in the .NET Framework where you need to be somewhat concerned about explicit de-allocation of resources. When a modal form is closed via the button with the X at the top-right of the form window, it is actually hidden, not disposed of (marked as garbage)—so you need to call its Dispose method to mark it for collection. In production code, it probably makes sense to include the Dispose method in a Finally block, as explained in Chapter 6, to make sure that it gets run.

Run the project and click Show Form3. Next, enter some text in the TextBox in Form3 and click OK (Figure 8.11). The text that you entered in the TextBox in Form3 is now displayed in the original form.

FIGURE 8.11:

If you enter text in the TextBox in the instance of Form3 (left) and click OK, the text will appear in the TextBox of the original form (right).

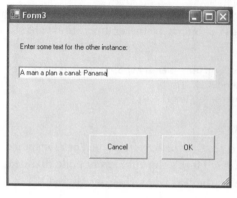
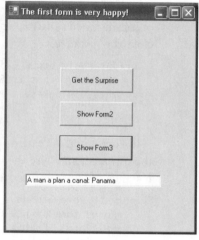

Listing 8.6 shows the code for this example.

Listing 8.6   Using a Reference to a Form Instance

```csharp
// Form1
...
private void btnShow3_Click(object sender, System.EventArgs e) {
    Form3 form3 = new Form3();
    if (form3.ShowDialog(this) == DialogResult.OK){
        this.txtGiveHere.Text = form3.theText;
    }
    form3.Dispose();
}
...
// Form3
...
public string theText;
private void btnOK_Click(object sender, System.EventArgs e) {
    theText = this.txtSendBack.Text;
    this.DialogResult = DialogResult.OK;
    this.Close();
}
private void btnCancel_Click(object sender, System.EventArgs e) {
    this.Close();
}
...
```

Passing a Form Instance to a Method

It's also easy—and very useful—to pass form instances to instance methods. In this section, I'll show you two examples from the Guns, Germs, and Steel application.

In the first example, a modal dialog is opened from a click event in the application's primary form, using the technique just explained:

```
private void btnAddaTribe_Click(object sender, System.EventArgs e) {
    frmSettings dlg = new frmSettings();
    if (dlg.ShowDialog(this) == DialogResult.OK){
        ...
```

Within the modal dialog, in the OK button's click event before the DialogResult property is set, the user's choices are stored in member fields and properties, as explained earlier in this chapter:

```
private void btnOK_Click(object sender, System.EventArgs e) {
    m_Name = txtName.Text;
    m_Text = txtText.Text;
    ...
    this.DialogResult = DialogResult.OK;
    this.Close();
}
```

Back in the Form1 code, the instance of frmSettings is passed to the CreateNewTribe instance method of the GroupOfPeople class:

```
gop.CreateNewTribe (dlg);
```

Within the CreateNewTribe method, the instance of frmSettings is used to populate member values:

```
public void CreateNewTribe(frmSettings dlg) {
    tr = new Tribe();
    this.Name = tr.Name = dlg.tribeName;
    this.Text = tr.Text = dlg.tribeText;
    ...
}
```

The second example centers around the fact that I used MDI child forms to display the changing values of population and so forth for each culture. (MDI applications are explained in Chapter 4.)

For this to work, I needed to be able to assign the reference to the instance of the MDI parent form (Form1) to the MdiParent property of each child form. But this couldn't be done from Form1 itself because of the facade functionality of the GroupOfPeople class (in fact, it had to be done from an instance method within that class).

So I passed the current instance to the instance method:

```
gop.CreateForm (this);
```

The CreateForm method was declared with a Form as its argument in a parameter named *parentForm*:

```
public void CreateForm (System.Windows.Forms.Form parentForm)
```

Within the method, I created a new instance of frmTribe, the MDI child form:

```
frmTribe = new frmTribe();
```

The newly instantiated frmTribe's MdiParent property was assigned to the instance value of the main form passed into the method:

```
frmTribe.MdiParent = parentForm;
```

And then I could go merrily about populating the form:

```
frmTribe.BackColor = tr.TribalColor;
frmTribe.ForeColor = tr.TextColor;
...
```

Listing 8.7 shows these two examples of passing form instances to methods.

Listing 8.7   Passing Form Instances to Methods

```
// Form1
...
GroupOfPeople gop;
private void btnAddaTribe_Click(object sender, System.EventArgs e) {
    frmSettings dlg = new frmSettings();
    if (dlg.ShowDialog(this) == DialogResult.OK){
        gop = new GroupOfPeople();
        gop.CreateNewTribe (dlg);
        gop.CreateForm (this);
        ...
    }
    dlg.Dispose();
}
...
// frmSettings
...
private void btnOK_Click(object sender, System.EventArgs e) {
    m_Name = txtName.Text;
    m_Text = txtText.Text;
    ...
    this.DialogResult = DialogResult.OK;
    this.Close();
}
...
// GroupOfPeople
...
public void CreateNewTribe(frmSettings dlg) {
    tr = new Tribe();
    this.Name = tr.Name = dlg.tribeName;
    this.Text = tr.Text = dlg.tribeText;
    ...
```

```
    }
    public void CreateForm (System.Windows.Forms.Form parentForm){
        frmTribe = new frmTribe();
        frmTribe.MdiParent = parentForm;
        frmTribe.BackColor = tr.TribalColor;
        frmTribe.ForeColor = tr.TextColor;
        ...
    }
    ...
```

Methods

A method is, of course, the class member that used to be called a function (if it returned a value) or a procedure (if it did not). In fact, in today's world, a method is sometimes referred to as a *member function*.

As you've already seen numerous times in this book, a method declaration specifies the return type of the method, followed by the method's identifier, followed by the method's typed parameter list within parentheses (the parentheses are required whether or not there are any parameters). If the method does not return a value, it is said to return `void`. Using the `void` keyword rather than a return type specifies this. For example, the declaration of the `CreateNewTribe` method shown in Listing 8.7

```
    public void CreateNewTribe(frmSettings dlg)
```

makes it clear that no return value is expected from the method.

Methods are usually declared using one of the member access modifiers described earlier, in Table 8.3, and can also be marked with one of the modifiers described in Table 8.4.

out, *ref*, and Arrays as Parameters

If a method parameter is marked with the `out` or `ref` keyword, the method refers to the same variable that was passed into the method. Any changes made to the parameter within the method will be reflected in that variable when control returns to the calling method. By default, method parameters do not behave this way. Changes made inside a method to a parameter declared without these keywords are not made to the variable when control is passed back to the calling method. (Of course, you can use an object reference passed to a method within the method to change the members of the referenced object. Since the object reference is already a reference, it doesn't need to be marked with `out` or `ref` as a value type would.)

The difference between `out` and `ref` is that an argument passed to a `ref` parameter must be definitely assigned, while that is not the case for `out` parameters.

NOTE   If one version of a method has an `out` or `ref` parameter and another does not, that is sufficient for the method to be considered overloaded.

Arrays can be used as method parameters, and passed as arguments to methods, like any other type. When the array parameter is marked with out or ref, this is a useful way to encapsulate actions taken on arrays.

For example, the following method fills a string array marked with out:

```
private void FillArray (out string [] theArray){
    theArray = new string[3] {"Madam ", "I'm", " Adam"};
}
```

Since out rather than ref was used, the array need not be initialized when the method is called:

```
string [] theArray;
FillArray (out theArray);
```

The contents of the array can then be displayed in a TextBox, as shown in Figure 8.12:

```
for (int i=0; i <theArray.Length; i++){
    txtGiveHere.Text += theArray[i];
}
```

FIGURE 8.12:

Arrays passed to a method using out or ref retain value changes to the array elements in the calling method.

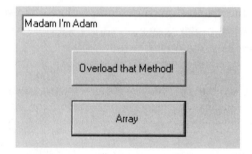

Listing 8.8 shows the method with the array parameter marked with out, and the method that calls it.

Listing 8.8   Passing an Array to a Method Using an *out* Parameter

```
private void FillArray (out string [] theArray){
    theArray = new string[3] {"Madam ", "I'm", " Adam"};
}
private void btnArray_Click(object sender, System.EventArgs e) {
    string [] theArray; // Initialization not needed
    FillArray (out theArray);
    for (int i = 0; i < theArray.Length; i++){
        txtGiveHere.Text += theArray[i];
    }
}
```

Overloading Methods

Within a class, you can have more than one declaration for a given method name, provided that the method return type, and the types of the parameters of each same-named method, are different. (The same idea was discussed earlier in this chapter relating to class constructors, in the "Constructors" section.)

The point of having multiple overloads for a method is that the programmer using the method (who may be the same programmer who wrote the overloads) can use whichever version is right for a particular circumstance. It's often the case that the most basic version of a method doesn't require much in the way of arguments—and leads to a default, prefabricated version of the action that the method takes. More complex overloaded versions of the method take more arguments and give the method invoker more control over what the method does. In other words, the more parameters that an overloaded method specifies, the more detail a developer using the overloaded method can specify.

To take a rather trivial example, let's create two overloaded versions of a method that builds a message box. In the prefabricated, "fast-food" version, the calling code need only pass the text of the message box as an argument. In the more complex version, the calling code gets to specify not only the text but also the title, buttons, and icon:

```
public void DisplayBox (string inText){
    MessageBox.Show (inText, "Hello!",
    MessageBoxButtons.OK, MessageBoxIcon.Exclamation);
}
public void DisplayBox (string inText, string capText,
    MessageBoxButtons mbb, MessageBoxIcon mbi){
    MessageBox.Show (inText, capText, mbb, mbi);
}
```

When the programmer starts typing in the code to invoke the DisplayBox method from another class, both overloaded signatures are provided by the Code Editor's auto-completion feature, as indicated by the "1 of 2" markings in the Code Editor and the arrows that allow you to toggle between the overloaded versions of the method.

```
private void btnOverload_Click(object sender, System.EventArgs e) {
    Overload overload = new Overload();
    overload.DisplayBox(
```
⌐ ▲1 of 2▼ void Overload.DisplayBox (**string inText**)

Invoking the two overloaded versions of the method

```
overload.DisplayBox("Prefab dialog box.");
overload.DisplayBox("Not the prefab version...", "A rose is a rose is a rose",
    MessageBoxButtons.YesNoCancel, MessageBoxIcon.Question);
```

shows both a prefab version of the message box and one that can be custom designed (Figure 8.13).

In some cases, the simplest version of an overloaded method serves as a kind of prefab version (left), while a more complex version of the overloaded method allows the programmer to set more options (right).

 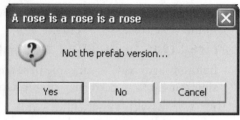

Listing 8.9 shows the overloaded versions of the method and how to invoke them from a click event.

Listing 8.9   Invoking Overloading Methods

```
// Invoking the two method overloads
private void btnOverload_Click(object sender, System.EventArgs e) {
   Overload overload = new Overload();
   overload.DisplayBox("Prefab dialog box.");
   overload.DisplayBox("Not the prefab version...",
      "A rose is a rose is a rose", MessageBoxButtons.YesNoCancel,
      MessageBoxIcon.Question);
}
// The class containing the overloaded method
using System.Windows.Forms;

namespace SybexC22 {
   public class Overload {
      public Overload() {

      }
      public void DisplayBox (string inText){
         MessageBox.Show (inText, "Hello!",
            MessageBoxButtons.OK, MessageBoxIcon.Exclamation);
      }
      public void DisplayBox (string inText, string capText,
         MessageBoxButtons mbb, MessageBoxIcon mbi){
         MessageBox.Show (inText, capText, mbb, mbi);
      }
   }
}
```

Delegates and Events

In the "Creating a Class Library" section of Chapter 5, I showed you how to add a delegate—a kind of pointer to an event method—and an event to a class. Let's go over a couple of other examples here as well as the general process for creating an event.

Five Steps to Creating an Event

Before we get to the examples, here are the five steps involved in creating, firing, and wiring an event:

1. A delegate is a type whose name and parameters constitute a method signature. A delegate instance references a method that matches the signature in its name and parameters. The first step is to create a delegate that has the right signature in its parameters.

2. An event is declared in the firing class by applying the event keyword to a delegate that modifies an instance member method name that is invoked with the same parameter types as the delegate. The second step is to use the event keyword to associate the delegate with an event method.

3. The event is actually fired, or "raised," in a class instance by calling the method. The third step is to write the code that invokes the event method.

4. Another class is "wired" to receive the event by adding a method to the class that matches the parameter types contained in the delegate's parameters. This will be the *event handler*. The fourth step is to write a method in the class that will receive the event—a method that has parameters that match in type the delegate's.

5. Finally, the firing class instance must be told that the event handler method in the receiving class should be notified when the event is fired. This is accomplished using the += operator. The class instance member that raises the event is assigned (using +=) a new instance of the delegate with the instance event handler as an argument. The fifth, and final, step is to let the instance firing the event know that the instance event handler should be notified when the event is fired.

NOTE   The final step—wiring the event to the event handler method—can alternatively be accomplished using the Events interface in the Properties window, as I explained in Chapter 3, "Windows Uses Web Services, Too!".

The *OnExtinction* and *OnMaxPop* Events

Instances of the GroupOfPeople class of the Guns, Germs, and Steel application fire two events. These are the OnExtinction event, fired when a GroupOfPeople instance approaches zero population, and the OnMaxPop event, fired when the population of an instance approaches the maximum value that can be stored in the C# long value type.

I'll show you how these two events are implemented, using the five steps outlined in the previous section.

Step One: Creating the Delegates

In the GroupOfPeople class, the two delegates are declared:

```
public delegate void ExtinctionEventHandler (object sender, System.EventArgs e);
...
public delegate void MaxPopEventHandler (object sender, System.EventArgs e);
```

Note that the parameters of an event method should always include an object representing the instance firing the event (object sender), and a parameter of type System.EventArgs (you can include other parameters if you need to).

NOTE   There's no real need to declare both delegates in this example, since their signature is the same—in fact, there's no real need to declare delegates at all, because the signatures already match the built-in EventHandler delegate. However, in the interest of clarity, it is good practice to declare a delegate for each custom event.

Step Two: Associating the Delegates with Events

The delegates are associated with event methods (OnExtinction and OnMaxPop):

```
public event ExtinctionEventHandler OnExtinction;
...
public event MaxPopEventHandler OnMaxPop;
```

Step Three: Firing the Events

Still in GroupOfPeople, when appropriate conditions are met, the events are fired by calling OnExtinction and OnMaxPop.

OnExtinction is called when the population (represented by the internal variable *m_population*) gets below 100. The this keyword is used to call OnExtinction with the current instance of the class, along with the new instance of the type System.EventArgs stored in the variable e:

```
if (m_Population >= 0 && m_Population < 100 ) {
   // fire the extinction event
   m_Population = 0;
   this.isAlive = false;
   System.EventArgs e = new System.EventArgs();
   OnExtinction (this, e);
}
```

OnMaxPop is called, with the same arguments as OnExtinction, when the population becomes bigger than the maximum value that can be stored in the long type divided by two.

```
const long veryBig = long.MaxValue / 2;
...
if (m_Population >= veryBig) {
    m_Population = long.MaxValue - 1;
    this.isAlive = false;
    System.EventArgs e = new System.EventArgs();
    OnMaxPop (this, e);
}
```

NOTE   The MaxValue field of a numeric type represents the largest value that can be stored in that type.

Step Four: Adding Event Handlers

Event handlers with the same parameter types as the parameters of the delegate (and the event method) are added to the receiving class (Form1).

```
private void GroupOfPeople_OnExtinction (object sender, System.EventArgs e) {
}
private void GroupOfPeople_OnMaxPop (object sender,
    System.EventArgs e) {
}
```

By convention, the event handlers are usually named with the firing class name, followed by an underscore, followed by the name of the event method (e.g., GroupOfPeople_OnExtinction)—but, in fact, any valid identifier could be used, such as Fred, and the event would still work.

Step Five: Arranging for Event Notification

The last step is to add notifications to the instances of the event methods so that the code placed in the receiving event handlers (whether they are named GroupOfPeople_OnExtinction or Fred) is processed when the instance event method is called:

```
gop = new GroupOfPeople();
gop.OnExtinction += new
    GroupOfPeople.ExtinctionEventHandler (this.GroupOfPeople_OnExtinction);
gop.OnMaxPop += new
    GroupOfPeople.MaxPopEventHandler (this.GroupOfPeople_OnMaxPop);
```

Adding Code to the Event Handlers

If you don't place any code within the receiving event handlers, then there's no real point in going to all this trouble.

The code in the OnExtinction handler casts the *sender* parameter to a GroupOfPeople:

```
GroupOfPeople aGoP = (GroupOfPeople) sender;
```

Using the `GroupOfPeople` instance thus obtained, a message box is displayed and the instance's screen representation is updated (Figure 8.14):

```
MessageBox.Show ("Sorry, " + aGoP.Name + " tribe is extinct!",
    "Guns, Germs, and Steel", MessageBoxButtons.OK, MessageBoxIcon.Information);
aGoP.frmTribe.Text += " (Extinct)";
```

FIGURE 8.14:

When the `OnExtinction` event is fired, a message is displayed and the culture's screen display is marked.

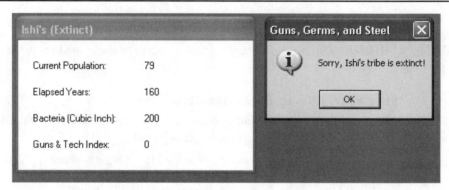

Similarly, the code in the `OnMaxPop` handler displays a message box, and marks the form representing the culture (Figure 8.15):

```
private void GroupOfPeople_OnMaxPop (object sender,
    System.EventArgs e) {
    GroupOfPeople aGoP = (GroupOfPeople) sender;
    MessageBox.Show ("Time to populate the stars!",
        "GO " + aGoP.Name + " Civilization" , MessageBoxButtons.OK,
        MessageBoxIcon.Information);
    aGoP.frmTribe.Text += " (Encounter with Malthus)";
}
```

FIGURE 8.15:

When the `OnMaxPop` event is fired for an instance, the instance culture is marked ("Encounter with Malthus") and a message is displayed.

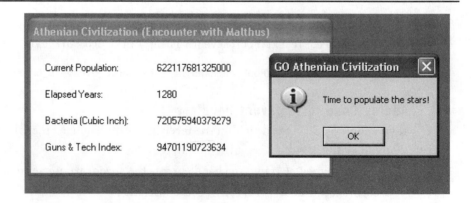

Listing 8.10 shows the implementation of the `OnExtinction` and `OnMaxPop` events with some of the implementation context.

Listing 8.10   **Implementing the *OnExtinction* and *OnMaxPop* Events**

```
// In GroupOfPeople (firing class)
// Delegate and Event Declarations
public delegate void ExtinctionEventHandler(object sender, System.EventArgs e);
public event ExtinctionEventHandler OnExtinction;
public delegate void MaxPopEventHandler(object sender, System.EventArgs e);
public event MaxPopEventHandler OnMaxPop;

// Fire the events
public void ProgressTheTribe() {
   const long veryBig = long.MaxValue / 2;
   if (m_Population <= 100000){
      if (m_Population >= 0 && m_Population < 100 ) {
         // fire the extinction event
         m_Population = 0;
         this.isAlive = false;
         System.EventArgs e = new System.EventArgs();
         OnExtinction (this, e);
      }
   ...
   else {
      ...
      // fire the maximum population event
      if (m_Population >= veryBig) {
         m_Population = long.MaxValue - 1;
         this.isAlive = false;
         System.EventArgs e = new System.EventArgs();
         OnMaxPop (this, e);
      }
      ...
   }
}
// In Form1 (the "receiving" class)
// Arranging for event notification
private void btnAddaTribe_Click(object sender, System.EventArgs e) {
   frmSettings dlg = new frmSettings();
   if (dlg.ShowDialog(this) == DialogResult.OK){
    gop = new GroupOfPeople();
    gop.OnExtinction += new
       GroupOfPeople.ExtinctionEventHandler (this.GroupOfPeople_OnExtinction);
    gop.OnMaxPop += new
       GroupOfPeople.MaxPopEventHandler (this.GroupOfPeople_OnMaxPop);
    ...
   }
 ...
}
```

```
// The Event Handlers
private void GroupOfPeople_OnExtinction (object sender, System.EventArgs e) {
    GroupOfPeople aGoP = (GroupOfPeople) sender;
    MessageBox.Show ("Sorry, " + aGoP.Name + " tribe is extinct!",
        "Guns, Germs, and Steel", MessageBoxButtons.OK,
        MessageBoxIcon.Information);
    aGoP.frmTribe.Text += " (Extinct)";
}
private void GroupOfPeople_OnMaxPop (object sender,
    System.EventArgs e) {
    GroupOfPeople aGoP = (GroupOfPeople) sender;
    MessageBox.Show ("Time to populate the stars!",
        "GO " + aGoP.Name + " Civilization", MessageBoxButtons.OK,
        MessageBoxIcon.Information);
    aGoP.frmTribe.Text += " (Encounter with Malthus)";
}
```

Overloading Operators

Operator overloading means creating custom implementations for standard operators in the context of the instances of a class.

In the context of the Guns, Germs, and Steel application, the user can initiate clashes between cultures (remember that cultures are instances of the GroupOfPeople class). A clash between cultures A and B has three possible outcomes: A assimilates B, B assimilates A, or the confrontation is a draw and things remain at the status quo.

The user interface for creating a clash between two cultures is shown in Figure 8.16.

FIGURE 8.16:

The user can initiate clashes between cultures.

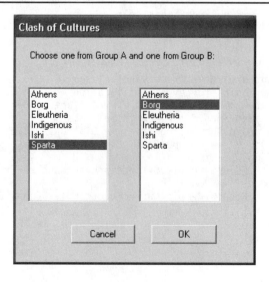

When I started to consider how best to implement the clash between cultures, I realized that the conditions for determining the outcome of a given confrontation were fairly complex and involved three measures: population, bacteria, and technology. In addition, relatively equivalent cultures produce no winner when they clash—there has to be a big quantitative difference between two cultures to result in the assimilation of one by the other.

I could have written a method that would have evaluated all these things based on two passed objects of type GroupOfPeople, but it seemed more elegant to overload the less than (<) and greater than (>) comparison operators within the GroupOfPeople class. That way I could easily determine whether A should assimilate B, because the expression A > B would be true. Conversely, if B should assimilate A, B > A would be true. Since I did not implement an overload of the equality comparison operator, a stand-off would be reached when neither A > B nor B > A, e.g.,

```
(!(A > B) && !(B > A))
```

NOTE   The careful reader will observe that the expressions used in the last three sentences to determine the outcome of a clash use only the > operator. The C# compiler requires that if you overload one comparison operator in a class, you also overload the opposite one. (If > is overloaded, < must also be. If = is overloaded, you must also overload !=.) Since I also implemented the < operator as required, as a matter of taste the expressions could be rewritten to use it.

Here are the declarations that tell the compiler that the < and > operators are being overloaded for instances of the class:

```
public static bool operator > (GroupOfPeople a, GroupOfPeople b){
}
public static bool operator < (GroupOfPeople a, GroupOfPeople b){
}
```

Listing 8.11 shows the complete static method within the GroupOfPeople class that overloads the operators.

Listing 8.11   **Overloading the < and > Operators in the *GroupOfPeople* Class**

```
public static bool operator > (GroupOfPeople a, GroupOfPeople b){
    if (a.Guns > b.Guns + 10000){
        return true;
    }
    else if (a.Bacteria > b.Bacteria + 100000){
        return true;
    }
    else if (a.Population > b.Population + 1000000){
        return true;
    }
```

```
      else {
         return false;
      }
   }
   public static bool operator < (GroupOfPeople a, GroupOfPeople b){
      if (!(a.Guns > b.Guns + 10000)){
         return true;
      }
      else if (!(a.Bacteria > b.Bacteria + 100000)){
         return true;
      }
      else if (!(a.Population > b.Population + 1000000)){
         return true;
      }
      else {
         return false;
      }
   }
}
```

The code in Listing 8.12 populates the form used to originate culture clashes. Next, it determines which cultures were selected for a clash based on the user choices from the form shown in Figure 8.16. Finally, it determines whether there is a stand-off, or a winner and a loser, using the overloaded > operator. (I've excerpted the message boxes that are displayed under the various conditions.) If there is a winner and a loser, the private Assimilate method performs the actual assimilation.

Listing 8.12   **Using the Overloaded > Operator**

```
private void btnClash_Click(object sender, System.EventArgs e) {
   GroupOfPeople a = gop;
   GroupOfPeople b = gop;
   frmClash frmClash = new frmClash();
   foreach (GroupOfPeople aGoP in peoples) {
      if (aGoP.isAlive){
         frmClash.lstA.Items.Add(aGoP.Name);
         frmClash.lstB.Items.Add(aGoP.Name);
      }
   }
   if (frmClash.ShowDialog(this) == DialogResult.OK){
      foreach (GroupOfPeople aGoP in peoples) {
         if (aGoP.Name == frmClash.lstA.SelectedItem.ToString())
            a = aGoP;
         if (aGoP.Name == frmClash.lstB.SelectedItem.ToString())
            b = aGoP;
      }
   }
   if (!(a > b) && ! (b > a)) {
     // no winner or loser
     // display appropriate message
```

```
    }
    else if (a > b){
        // a is the winner
        Assimilate (a, b);
    }
    else {
        // b > a
        // b is the winner
        Assimilate (b, a);
    }
}
private void Assimilate (GroupOfPeople winner, GroupOfPeople loser){
    winner.Population += loser.Population;
    winner.ProgressTheTribe();
    loser.Population = 00;
    loser.Guns = 0;
    loser.Bacteria = 200;
    loser.frmTribe.Text += " (Assimilated by " + winner.Name + ")";
    loser.DrawForm();
    loser.isAlive = false;
}
```

Figure 8.17 shows the results of one culture being assimilated by another.

FIGURE 8.17:

The Borg has assimilated the Bumblers.

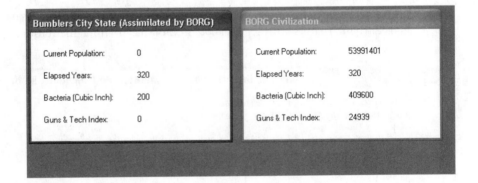

Polymorphism and Overriding

Polymorphism means the ability to make different objects perform the same task, with each object potentially implementing the task in its own way. Another way of putting this is that polymorphism is the ability of a program to perform dynamic operations by implementing methods of multiple derived classes through a common base class reference.

In C#, polymorphism is primarily implemented when members—commonly methods—in a derived class are marked with the override keyword. The override keyword means that a derived-class method can be invoked at run time and supersedes the base-class method with the same name. The base-class method must be marked as either virtual or abstract. By the way, in order to mark a member as abstract, the class it is in must also be abstract.

WARNING   If you attempt to override a base-class member that has not been marked as virtual or abstract, you will get a compile-time syntax error.

The difference between virtual and abstract base-class members is that virtual methods are implemented and can optionally be overridden. In contrast, abstract methods *must* be overridden and are not implemented (in the abstract base class, they consist solely of the declaration).

Polymorphism Demonstration

Let's have a simple polymorphism dino—oops, I mean demo—in the context of dinosaurs. Jared Diamond, in *Guns, Germs, and Steel*, quotes the famous first sentence of Tolstoy's *Anna Karenina*: "Happy families are all alike; every unhappy family is unhappy in its own way." Well, let's also assume that all dinosaurs are pretty much alike, that they all have something called the GetFood method—which happens to return a string—and that each species of dinosaur implements its GetFood method differently depending on the kind of food it likes to eat.

To start with, in Listing 8.13, you'll see that the base Dinosaur class has been declared abstract, and that its abstract GetFood method has no implementation.

Listing 8.13   *Dinosaur GetFood Abstract Method and Overridden Methods in Derived Classes*

```
public abstract class Dinosaur {
   public abstract string GetFood();
}
class Lessemsaurus : Dinosaur {
   public override string GetFood (){
      return "Lessemsaurus bites branches from treetops.";
   }
}
class Apatosaurus : Dinosaur {
   public override string GetFood (){
      return "Apatosaurus eats plants.";
   }
}
class Allosaurus : Dinosaur {
   public override string GetFood (){
      return "My name is Allosaurus and I eat Apatosaurus.";
   }
}
```

```
class TRex : Dinosaur {
    public override string GetFood (){
        return "I am Tyrannosaurus Rex. I eat everything. I am always hungry.";
    }
}
```

Each of the four classes derived from Dinosaur in Listing 8.13 implement their overridden GetFood method in their own way—that is, each returns a different string. (After all, the method—like dinosaurs—is pretty simpleminded!)

The objects in the *jPark* array shown in Listing 8.14 are of type Dinosaur. However, when the foreach statement is used to loop through the array, because of the override modifier marking the GetFood method in each of the derived classes, those versions of the method are invoked, as shown in Figure 8.18.

Listing 8.14   **Invoking the *GetFood* Methods of the Classes Derived from *Dinosaur***

```
private void btnPoly_Click(object sender, System.EventArgs e) {
    Dinosaur [] jPark = new Dinosaur [4];
    jPark[0] = new Lessemsaurus();
    jPark[1] = new Apatosaurus();
    jPark[2] = new Allosaurus();
    jPark[3] = new TRex();
    foreach (Dinosaur dino in jPark){
        lstDino.Items.Add(dino.GetFood());
    }
}
```

FIGURE 8.18:

The same-but-different polymorphic behavior of the classes derived from Dinosaur can be seen in the text each one adds to the ListBox Items collection.

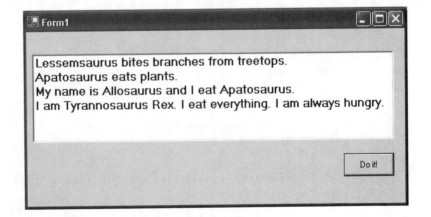

Overriding Virtual Methods

You may recall that in the Guns, Germs, and Steel application, the Civilization class is derived from the CityState class, which in turns derives from Tribe. (Put the other way round, Tribe is the base class for CityState, which is the base class for Civilization.)

Instances of the GroupOfPeople class act as the facade for the Tribe, CityState, and Civilization class. Specifically, the ProgressTheTribe method of GroupOfPeople, shown excerpted in Listing 8.15, determines which kind of object is currently instantiated.

Listing 8.15	Portions of the *ProgressTheTribe* Method

```
private Tribe tr;
// tr is instantiated in GetNewTribe

public void ProgressTheTribe() {
   const long veryBig = long.MaxValue / 2;
   if (m_Population <= 100000){
      if (m_Population >= 0 && m_Population < 100 ) {
         // fire the extinction event
         ...
      }
   else
      m_Population = tr.GetNewPopulation();
      this.DrawForm();
      tr.IncrementGenerations();
   }
   else if (m_Population <= 1000000) {
      // initialize city state
      if (cs == null){
         cs = new CityState();
         cs.SetMeUp(tr);
         frmTribe.Text = cs.Text + " City State";
      }
      m_Population = cs.GetNewPopulation();
      this.Bacteria = cs.Bacteria;
      this.DrawForm();
      cs.IncrementGenerations();
   }
   else {
      // initialize city state
      if (civil == null) {
         civil = new Civilization();
         civil.SetMeUp(cs);
         frmTribe.Text = civil.Text + " Civilization";
      }
      if (m_Population >= veryBig) {
         // fire max pop event
         ...
      }
```

```
        else
            m_Population = civil.GetNewPopulation();
        this.Bacteria = civil.Bacteria;
        this.Guns = civil.Guns;
        this.DrawForm();
        civil.IncrementGenerations();
    }
}
```

If you look at Listing 8.15, you'll see a recurring theme: at each pass, whether the instance is a Tribe, a CityState, or a Civilization, a version of GetNewPopulation is called.

As you would likely expect, the GetNewPopulation method as originally declared in the Tribe class is virtual (Listing 8.16)—so that it can be overridden in its derived classes.

Listing 8.16 The Virtual *GetNewPopulation* Method

```
public virtual long GetNewPopulation () {
    long increment = (long) (GetGrowthRatePerGeneration() * m_Population);
    m_Population += increment;
    if (m_Population >= 0 && m_Population < 10) {
        m_Population = 0;
    }
    return m_Population;
}
```

The pace picks up in the CityState class (Listing 8.17), where the population incremental increase is subject to a multiplier, and the bacteria measure of disease production and resistance is introduced for the first time.

Listing 8.17 The *GetNewPopulation* Override Method in the *CityState* Class

```
public override long GetNewPopulation () {
    const long veryBig = long.MaxValue / 2;
    long increment = (long) (GetGrowthRatePerGeneration() * m_Population);
    if (m_Bacteria < veryBig - 1) {
        m_Bacteria += m_Bacteria;
    }
    m_Population += (long) (increment * 1.2);
    return m_Population;
}
```

As the culture starts to really race for the stars in the Civilization class, things pick up still more, with the introduction of the guns and technology index if the population growth rate is sufficiently high (Listing 8.18).

Listing 8.18   The *GetNewPopulation* Method in the *Civilization* Class

```
public override long GetNewPopulation () {
   const long veryBig = long.MaxValue / 2;
   float growthRate = GetGrowthRatePerGeneration();
   long increment = (long) (growthRate * m_Population);
   if (m_Population >= veryBig) {
      m_Population = long.MaxValue - 1;
      return m_Population;
   }
   if (m_Bacteria < veryBig - 1) {
      m_Bacteria += m_Bacteria;
   }
   if ((growthRate * 2) >= 0.5){
      if (m_Guns < veryBig - 1) {
         m_Guns = m_Guns + Convert.ToInt64(m_Guns * growthRate);
      }
   }
   m_Population += (long) (increment * 1.2);
   return m_Population;
}
```

As these overrides of the GetNewPopulation method show, you can add features to a derived class that were not present in the original class by using the mechanism of overriding methods marked virtual.

Creating a Custom Collection

All along in the Guns, Germs, and Steel application, I've had the issue of how to deal with all the instances of GroupOfPeople. These instances need to be easily available for programmatic reference in several circumstances.

The obvious answer is create a custom collection for them, derived from one of the collection classes explained in Chapter 7. Listing 8.19 shows a simple—but powerful—collection class derived from ArrayList with two member methods: AddAPeople and RemoveAPeople.

Listing 8.19   A Custom Collection Class Derived from *ArrayList*

```
using System;
using System.Collections;

namespace SybexC21
{
   public class PeoplesCollection : ArrayList
```

```
    {
        public PeoplesCollection() {

        }
        public void AddAPeople (GroupOfPeople aGoP) {
            this.Add(aGoP);
        }
        public void RemoveAPeople (GroupOfPeople aGoP) {
            this.Remove(aGoP);
        }
    }
}
```

In the main form of the application, it's now easy to instantiate a collection based on this class:

```
PeoplesCollection peoples = new PeoplesCollection();
```

We can now use the power of the *peoples* collection—which includes the derived members from the ArrayList class—to access all the instances of GroupOfPeople, making for some fairly compact code. For example, Listing 8.20 shows the entire code of the Timer's Elapsed event—which uses the *peoples* collection to advance each GroupOfPeople instance through time.

Listing 8.20   Using the Collection to Progress Each Instance through Time

```
private void timer1_Elapsed(object sender,
    System.Timers.ElapsedEventArgs e) {
    this.lblYears.Text = Globals.globalTime.ToString();
    foreach (GroupOfPeople aGoP in peoples) {
        if (aGoP.isAlive)
            aGoP.ProgressTheTribe();
    }
    Globals.globalTime += Globals.generation;
}
```

Conclusion

Objects, classes, and object-oriented programming in C# are fun and heady stuff! In a fully OOP language and environment, the concepts explained in this chapter are extremely important. Object and classes are the notes and score that keep the C# music playing!

I'm glad I've had the chance to share some of this material with you. Although in some respects, this chapter has touched only the surface of this topic, important material has been explained. I also hope that I've given you some sense of how OOP concepts might be used in real-world projects.

CHAPTER 9

Everything Is String Manipulation

- The immutability of the string type

- The char type and static char methods

- Control characters

- Creating strings, string methods, and verbatim strings

- The *StringBuilder* class

- Implementing the *ToString* method

- String class interfaces, implementing *IComparable*, and creating your own interface

- Regular expression classes and syntax

Why is string manipulation so important? Because, as programmers, we do so much of it. In fact, on some days, it seems—like the title of this chapter—that everything is string manipulation.

Fortunately, C# provides great and powerful facilities for working with and manipulating strings. This chapter explains the types and methods related to strings, so that you can make short work of most common string-manipulation tasks in your projects.

The String class implements several interfaces, including IComparable and IEnumerable. In this chapter, I'll explain what it means to implement an interface and show you what String's implementation of these interfaces means to you. We'll also take a—hopefully profitable—detour to explore how you can implement an interface such as IComparable in your own classes, using the Dinosaur classes developed at the end of Chapter 8 as an example. Continuing with the interface detour, I'll show you how to create a custom interface of your own—ICarnivore—that can be implemented by the Dinosaur classes.

The last part of this chapter explains the basics of working with regular expressions in C#.

C# String Basics

As I explained in Chapter 6, "Zen and Now: The C# Language," a text string is stored in a data type named string, which is an alias to the System.String type. In other words, when you create a string, you instantiate a System.String object.

In addition to its instance members, the System.String class has quite a few important static methods. These methods don't require a string instance to work and are discussed later in this chapter in "The *String* Class."

It's important to understand that the string type is *immutable*. This means that once it has been created, a string cannot be changed. No characters can be added or removed from it, nor can its length be changed.

But wait, you say; my strings change all the time when I do things like:

```
string str = "I am going to have a lot of fun";
str += " with Dudley this summer. ... ";
str += " The End";
```

Well, my friend, what this set of statements actually does is create a new instance of the variable *str* each time a value is assigned to *str*. In other words, in this example, an instance of *str* has been created—and a literal string value assigned to it—three times. The statement that the type is immutable means that an instance cannot be edited—but it can be assigned.

Using an instance method without an assignment is syntactically legal, but it doesn't do anything (has no effect). For example

```
string str = "hello";
str.Replace ("l", "L"); // Doesn't do anything
```

does not change the contents of the variable *str*, although combining it with an assignment would work:

```
string str = "hello";
str = str.Replace ("l", "L");
```

The value of the "new," assigned *str* is, of course, "heLLo".

Is there any real problem with this? Well, no, it's easy enough to use assignments when you need to change the value of a string. But instantiating and destroying strings every time you need to change or edit one has negative performance consequences. If performance is an issue, you should consider working with instances of the `System.Text.StringBuilder` class, which are mutable (can be changed). The `StringBuilder` class is discussed later in this chapter in more detail.

Once created, a string has a specific length—which, of course, is fixed (since the type is immutable). A C# string is not a terminated array of characters (unlike in the C language, in which a string is simply an array of characters terminated with a zero byte). So, how does one determine the length of a C# string? As you probably know, you can query the read-only `Length` property of the string instance to find its length.

The Char Type

Char is a value type that contains a single Unicode character. While chars have a numeric value from hexadecimal 0x0000 through 0xFFFF, they are not directly numerically usable without explicit casting.

Literal values are assigned to char variables using single quotes. The literal can be a simple, single letter, or an escape sequence (for more on escape sequences, see the next section). Here are two examples:

```
char chr = 'P';     // contains capital P
char pi = '\u03A0'; // contains capital Pi
```

The char data type is related to the string data type: A string can be constructed from and converted into an array of characters—but string and char are two distinct types.

Suppose you have a string defined like this:

```
string str = "rotfl";
```

You can retrieve a character of the string using the string's indexer. For example, the following statement

```
char chr = str[1];
```

stores the character 'o' in the variable *chr*. But you cannot set a character in the string with a statement like

```
str[1] = 'a';
```

because the indexer property of the String class is read-only. (Actually, one would expect this in any case, because the string instance is immutable.)

If you use the Object Browser to have a look at the String class, you'll see that its indexer property, declared as this[int], has a get accessor, but no set accessor.

Control Characters

The backslash (\) is a special control character, also called the *escape* character. The character after the backslash has a special meaning, as shown in Table 9.1.

TABLE 9.1: Common C# Escaped Characters

Character	Meaning
\0	Null
\b	Backspace
\t	Tab
\r	Carriage return
\n	New line
\v	Vertical tab
\f	Form feed
\u, \x	A single Unicode character when followed by a four-digit hexadecimal number
\"	Double quote
\'	Single quote
\\	Backslash

The escape sequences \u or \x are used (interchangeably) to specify a single Unicode character. For example, \x03A9 and \u03A9 both mean the Greek letter capital omega (Ω). The escape sequences \x03A3 and \u03A3 will appear as the Greek letter capital sigma (Σ), as in this example, in which a button displays a capital sigma as its text when it is clicked:

```
private void btnDoIt_Click(object sender, System.EventArgs e) {
    char chr = '\u03A3';
    btnDoIt.Text = chr.ToString();
}
```

NOTE You can find a complete list of the Unicode character sets and their four-digit hexadecimal representations at www.unicode.org/charts/.

Char Static Methods

The methods of the Char class are, for the most part, static. These static methods allow you to determine whether a character is a letter, number, white space, etc. Figure 9.1 shows some of these static methods in the Object Browser.

FIGURE 9.1:

The static methods of the Char class—shown here in the Object Browser— allow discovery of the nature of individual characters.

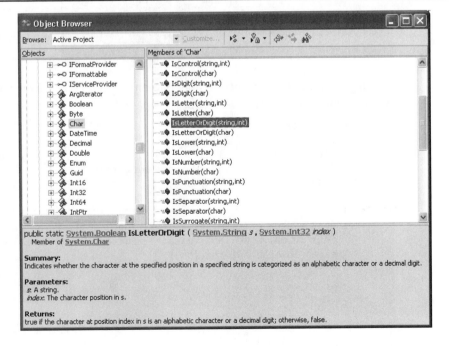

These methods return Boolean values, and each comes in two styles. One style takes a char as an argument. The other takes two arguments: a string, and an index representing the position of the character to be tested in the string. For example, here are the signatures of the static Char methods that test to see whether a character is a number:

```
bool IsNumber (char chr)
bool IsNumber (string str, int iIndex)
```

As an example, the following click event tests to see whether Unicode (hex) 0x0041 is a letter.

```
private void btnChar_Click(object sender, System.EventArgs e) {
    char chr = '\u0041'; // capital Latin A
    if (Char.IsLetter(chr)){
        MessageBox.Show ("\'" + chr.ToString() + "\' is a letter.",
            "Char re me fa so la", MessageBoxButtons.OK,
            MessageBoxIcon.Information);
    }
}
```

Since 0x0041 is a Unicode capital *A*, the IsLetter method returns true, and the message box is displayed.

Using the other form of the method, one can check to see whether the third character that the user enters in a TextBox is a letter:

```
string str = txtDoIt.Text;
if (Char.IsLetter (str, 2)) {
    MessageBox.Show ("\'" + str[2].ToString() + "\' is a letter.",
        "Char re me fa so la", MessageBoxButtons.OK,
        MessageBoxIcon.Information);
}
else {
    MessageBox.Show ("\'" + str[2].ToString() + "\' is NOT a letter.",
        "Char re me fa so la", MessageBoxButtons.OK,
        MessageBoxIcon.Information);
}
```

Running this code determines whether the third character entered by the user is a letter, and displays an appropriate message.

> **WARNING** There is no user input validation or exception handling in this code. If there is no third character—because the user has not entered one—this code will cause a run-time exception.

> **NOTE** The static method invocation Char.IsLetter (str, 2) is equivalent to Char.IsLetter (str[2]).

> **NOTE** You may have noticed the rather oddly named static Char IsSurrogate methods. If you are curious about the name, you may like to know that they test a character to see whether it has a Unicode value that is reserved for future expansion of the Unicode system (with values between 0xD800 and 0xDFFF).

Creating Strings

String, how shall I make thee: let me count the ways. There are many ways to create string variables, and no doubt you've used most of them. But let's go over this familiar ground one more time.

String Assignment

First, and most obviously, you can create a string by assigning a literal to a string variable:

```
string str = "I am a string!";
```

By the way, you can—of course—declare a string variable without initializing it:

```
string str;
```

As I showed you in Chapter 6, attempting to use this uninitialized variable causes a compiler error. What you may not know is that a string variable, since it is a reference type, can be initialized to `null`:

```
string str = null;
```

Initializing a string to `null` is not the same as initializing it to an empty string:

```
string str = "";
```

In the case of the `null` assignment, no memory has been allocated for the string. An attempt to determine the length of a null string—by using its `Length` property—causes an exception to be thrown. In contrast, the `Length` property of an empty string is 0.

NOTE   An alternate way to initialize an empty string is to use the static `Empty` field of the `String` class: `string str = string.Empty;`.

Methods

When you pass a method a string literal, you are also creating a string. This is the case for pre-built methods, such as the `Show` method of the `MessageBox` class:

```
MessageBox.Show ("Thanks for making me a string!");
```

This is also the case when you send a string literal argument to a user-defined method with a string parameter:

```
MakeAStr ("'Tis noble to be a string!");
...
private void MakeAStr (string str) {
    // Do something with str
    txtDoIt.Text = str;
}
```

It's also the case that many methods create strings as their return value. This is famously so for the `System.Object` class's `ToString` method. All classes derive from `Object`, so all types provide a `ToString` method, which is intended to return a string that represents the current object. For example, the expression

```
42.ToString();
```

returns the string "42".

NOTE   In your own classes, it is your responsibility to provide a `ToString` method that returns a string that represents the objects based on your classes. The "Implementing the *ToString* Method" section later in this chapter provides an example.

Many other .NET Framework class methods besides `ToString` return strings. As one good example, have a look at the `System.Convert` class, which sports 36 different static (overloaded) `Convert.ToString` methods, each of which returns a string. Some of these are shown in the Object Browser in Figure 9.2.

FIGURE 9.2:

Each of the 36 overloaded `Convert.ToString` methods returns a string.

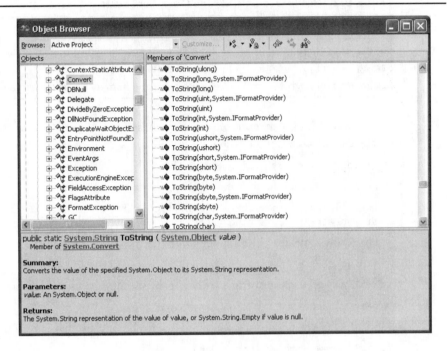

String Constructors

The `String` class itself has eight constructors. If you look in the Object Browser, you'll find that five of these use pointers and are not safe under the Common Language Specification (CLS).

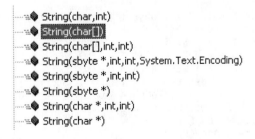

The unsafe constructors are not discussed here (to find out more about them, look up "String Constructor" in online help). The remaining three safe `String` overloaded constructor methods are shown in Table 9.2.

TABLE 9.2: Overloaded Safe String Class Constructors

Method	Meaning
String (char, int)	Creates a string consisting of a char repeating *int* times.
String (char[])	Creates a string from a char array.
String (char[], int, int)	Create a string from a char array with a start position and length.

Let's have a look at an example that uses these constructors. It's easy to use the first form and create a string consisting of the lowercase letter *a* 23 times:

```
string str1 = new String ('a', 23);
```

To use the second form, we must first create a char array:

```
char [] achra = new char[6] {'H', 'e', 'l', 'l' ,'o', '!'};
string str2 = new String (achra);
```

Third time pays for all! First, let's initialize a string:

```
string str3 = "Beasts of England";
```

Next, we can use the string's ToCharArray method to turn it into a char array:

```
char [] achra2 = str3.ToCharArray();
```

Finally, it's a hop, skip, and a jump to assign the first six elements of the char array to a string:

```
str3 = new String (achra2,0,6);
```

Listing 9.1 shows the code that uses the three constructors and displays the results in a ListBox.

Listing 9.1   The Safe String Constructors

```
private void btnStr_Click(object sender, System.EventArgs e) {
    lstStr.Items.Clear();
    string str1 = new String ('a', 23);
    char [] achra = new char[6] {'H', 'e', 'l', 'l' ,'o', '!'};
    string str2 = new String (achra);
    string str3 = "Beasts of England";
    char [] achra2 = str3.ToCharArray();
    str3 = new String (achra2,0,6);
    lstStr.Items.Add (str1);
    lstStr.Items.Add (str2);
    lstStr.Items.Add (str3);
}
```

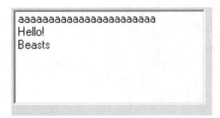

Verbatim Strings

In Chapter 6, I mentioned that you could use the @ symbol to use a keyword as an identifier—if you were so inclined, you could create variables named, for example, *@if*, *@string*, and *@true*. (To repeat what I said back in Chapter 6, just because one can do something, doesn't mean it is a good idea.)

In the context of strings, the @ symbol is used to create *verbatim* string literals. The @ symbol tells the string constructor to use the string literal that follows it "literally"—even if it includes escape characters or spans multiple lines.

This comes in handy when working with directory paths (without the @, you would have to double each backslash). For example, the following two strings are equivalent:

```
string noat = "\\\\BIGSERVER\\C";
string withat = @"\\BIGSERVER\C";
```

Here's how you could use the @ symbol to take the place of the \r\n escape sequence of control characters, which means "carriage return, new line":

```
private void btnVer_Click(object sender, System.EventArgs e) {
    string str =
        @"It's fun
    to be
            split into a number
                    of lines!";
    txtDoIt.Text = str;
}
```

If you assign the verbatim string to a TextBox that has its Multiline property set to True, you'll see that the line breaks (and white spaces) are preserved exactly as entered in the verbatim string.

If you are curious, here's how you'd create the same string as a non-verbatim string, using the control characters and string concatenation:

```
string str = "It's fun\r\n            to be\r\n"+
    "            split into a number\r\n" +
    "            of lines!";
txtDoIt.Text = str;
```

String Methods

The String class provides many powerful instance and static methods. These methods are described in this section. Most of these methods are overloaded, so there are multiple ways that each can be used.

Instance Methods

Table 9.3 describes many of the instance methods of the String class.

TABLE 9.3: Instance Methods of the *String* Class

Method	What It Does
Clone	Returns a reference to the instance of the string.
CompareTo	Compares this string with another.
CopyTo	Copies the specified number of characters from the string instance to a char array.
EndsWith	Returns true if the specified string matches the end of the instance string.
Equals	Determines whether the instance string and a specified string have the same value.
GetEnumerator	Method required to support the IEnumerator interface (see "Interfaces" later in this chapter).
IndexOf	Reports the index of the first occurrence of a specified character or string within the instance.
Insert	Returns a new string with the specified string inserted at the specified position in the current string.
LastIndexOf	Reports the index of the last occurrence of a specified character or string within the instance.
PadLeft	Returns a new string with the characters in this instance right-aligned by padding on the left with spaces or a specified character for a specified total length.
PadRight	Returns a new string with the characters in this instance left-aligned by padding on the right with spaces or a specified character for a specified total length.
Remove	Returns a new string that deletes a specified number of characters from the current instance beginning at a specified position.

Continued on next page

TABLE 9.3 CONTINUED: Instance Methods of the *String* Class

Method	What It Does
Replace	Returns a new string that replaces all occurrences of a specified character or string in the current instance, with another character or string.
Split	Identifies the substrings in this instance that are delimited by one or more characters specified in an array, then places the substrings into a string array.
StartsWith	Returns true if the specified string matches the beginning of the instance string.
Substring	Returns a substring from the instance.
ToCharArray	Copies the characters in the instance to a character array.
ToLower	Returns a copy of the instance in lowercase.
ToUpper	Returns a copy of the instance in uppercase.
Trim	Returns a copy of the instance with all occurrences of a set of specified characters from the beginning and end removed.
TrimEnd	Returns a copy of the instance with all occurrences of a set of specified characters at the end removed.
TrimStart	Returns a copy of the instance with all occurrences of a set of specified characters from the beginning removed.

Static Methods

Table 9.4 describes many of the static methods of the String class.

TABLE 9.4: Static Methods of the *String* Class

Method	What It Does
Compare	Compares two string objects.
CompareOrdinal	Compares two string objects without considering the local national language or culture.
Concat	Creates a new string by concatenating one or more strings.
Copy	Creates a new instance of a string by copying an existing instance.
Format	Formats a string using a format specification. See "Formatting Overview" in online help for more information about format specifications.
Join	Concatenates a specified string between each element in a string to yield a single concatenated string.

The *StringBuilder* Class

As I mentioned earlier in this chapter, instances of the StringBuilder class—as opposed to the String class—are mutable, or dynamically changeable. StringBuilder is located in the System .Text namespace. As you can see in Table 9.5, it does not have nearly as many members as the

String class—but it does have enough to get most jobs done. If you have a situation in which you need to perform many string operations—for example, within a large loop—from a performance viewpoint it probably makes sense to use StringBuilder instances instead of String instances.

TABLE 9.5: Key Instance Members of the *StringBuilder* Class

Member	What It Does
Append	Method adds string information to the end of the current StringBuilder instance. Overloads make for some flexibility regarding the kinds of objects that can be appended (if not already string, then the method converts the object to be appended to a string representation).
AppendFormat	Method appends a formatted string to the current instance (see "Formatting Overview" in online help for more information about format specifications).
Capacity	Property sets or retrieves the maximum number of characters that can be stored in the memory allocated for the StringBuilder instance.
Insert	Method inserts a string, or string representation of an object, into the current StringBuilder instance at the specified position.
Length	Property gets or sets the length of the instance. Setting this to a value that is less than the length of the current instance truncates the instance.
Remove	Method removes a specified number of characters from the current StringBuilder instance.
Replace	Method replaces all occurrences of a specified character in the current instance (or part of the current instance) with a specified string.

There are six different overloads of the StringBuilder constructor, designed so that you can create an instance already containing text and—if desired—set the Length and Capacity properties. As you'd suspect, the shortest StringBuilder constructor simply creates an instance without storing any text in it. Listing 9.2 demonstrates creating a StringBuilder instance on the fly. Next, the Append method is used to store the contents of a TextBox in the StringBuilder. The Length property is used to truncate the StringBuilder to four characters. Finally, the String-Builder is converted to a just plain vanilla string and displayed in a message box.

Listing 9.2   **Creating and Truncating a StringBuilder on the Fly**

```
private void btnSB_Click(object sender, System.EventArgs e) {
    System.Text.StringBuilder theSB = new System.Text.StringBuilder();
    theSB.Append (txtSB1.Text);
    theSB.Length = 4;
    MessageBox.Show (theSB.ToString(), "StringBuilder",
        MessageBoxButtons.OK, MessageBoxIcon.Information);
}
```

If you run the code shown in Listing 9.2, first adding some text to the TextBox, you'll see that the text has been appended to the StringBuilder, which is truncated at four characters (Figure 9.3).

Text added to the TextBox is appended in the StringBuilder instance.

Let's do another StringBuilder example. Listing 9.3 appends the contents of three TextBoxes into one StringBuilder. The user then enters two characters in a fourth TextBox. All instances of the first character are replaced in the StringBuilder with the second character, and the StringBuilder is then displayed in a multiline TextBox.

Listing 9.3   Appending and Replacing in a StringBuilder

```
private void btnSB_Click(object sender, System.EventArgs e) {
    System.Text.StringBuilder theSB = new System.Text.StringBuilder();
    theSB.Append (txtSB1.Text);
    theSB.Append (txtSB2.Text);
    theSB.Append (txtSB3.Text);
    txtDoIt.Text = "";
    string str = txtReplace.Text;
    theSB.Replace (str[0],str[1]);
    txtDoIt.Text = theSB.ToString();
}
```

The result of running this code, entering the strings "A nose ", "is a nose ", and "is a nose" in the TextBoxes, and replacing the character "n" with "r", is shown in Figure 9.4.

FIGURE 9.4:

The StringBuilder
Replace method can be
used to replace all
instances of a character
in a StringBuilder with
another character.

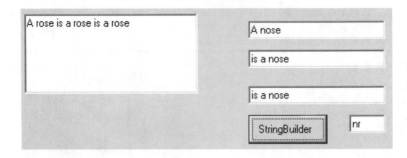

Implementing the *ToString* Method

I can't even start to think how many times in this book so far that I've used an object's ToString method. It's very handy-dandy, and you always know you'll get a string returned with the method—although it's sometimes not entirely clear, until you try, what the string will consist of. (For example, the ToString method of a Form instance returns the value of the Form's Text property as well as the instance name.) Since Object has a ToString method, and all classes are ultimately derived from Object, you can be sure that any instance in fact has some kind of ToString method.

I've repeated the mantra many times that it's up to you to implement a meaningful ToString method in your own classes. Before we proceed to an implementation example, let's think for a second about what "meaningful" means. Clearly, we'd like a number to be converted to a string representation of the number, so 423.ToString() returns the string "423". It's also reasonable to expect a Boolean value to return a string representation of the value it represents. The expression false.ToString() returns the string "False". With a capital *F*, it differs from the keyword false used to evaluate a C# Boolean expression, but it is still acceptable.

Simple value types are easy, but more complex objects don't always have a clear string representation. What should ToString return for a Button control? One thing seems fairly consistent—that when there is a Text or Name property for the class, the instance ToString method returns it as part or all of the return value.

To construct a ToString implementation example, let's return for a moment to the abstract Dinosaur class that was used in Chapter 8, "The Life of the Object in C#," to demonstrate polymorphism in its derived classes. Here's the entire class definition from Chapter 8:

```
public abstract class Dinosaur {
    public abstract string GetFood();
}
```

I'll be using the Dinosaur class in the next section to demonstrate implementing an interface, and interface inheritance, so let's redo the base Dinosaur class so that it is no longer abstract, and, while we're at it, let's add a few members, as shown in Listing 9.4.

Listing 9.4   The Base *Dinosaur* Class

```
public class Dinosaur
{
    private string m_Name;
    private bool m_EatMeat;
    public int Length = 0;
    public virtual string GetFood(){
        return "You are what you eat!";
    }
    public string Name {
        get {
            return m_Name;
        }
        set {
            m_Name = value;
        }
    }
    public bool EatMeat {
        get {
            return m_EatMeat;
        }
        set {
            m_EatMeat = value;
        }
    }
}
```

The base Dinosaur class shown in Listing 9.4 is no longer abstract; instead, it has a virtual GetFood method that can be overridden. In addition, a field, Length, and two properties, Name and EatMeat, have been implemented. The EatMeat property is a Boolean used to get or set the fact that the instance is a carnivore. Also, note that the class has no constructor.

It's easy to add a GetString method to the Dinosaur class using the override keyword. This GetString method combines the members of the class to return a string, and will be invoked in instances of Dinosaur and its derived classes:

```
public override string ToString() {
    string retval = "Dino Name: " + this.Name;
    retval += ", GetFood: " + this.GetFood();
    retval += ", Length: " + this.Length.ToString() + " meters";
    retval += ", Carnivore: " + this.EatMeat.ToString();
    return retval;
}
```

Listing 9.5 shows the `Dinosaur` class with the `ToString` method added.

Listing 9.5   ***Dinosaur* Class with *ToString* Method**

```
public class Dinosaur
{
    private string m_Name;
    private bool m_EatMeat;
    public int Length = 0;
    public virtual string GetFood(){
        return "You are what you eat!";
    }
    public string Name {
        get {
            return m_Name;
        }
        set {
            m_Name = value;
        }
    }
    public bool EatMeat {
        get {
            return m_EatMeat;
        }
        set {
            m_EatMeat = value;
        }
    }
    public override string ToString() {
        string retval = "Dino Name: " + this.Name;
        retval += ", GetFood: " + this.GetFood();
        retval += ", Length: " + this.Length.ToString() + " meters";
        retval += ", Carnivore: " + this.EatMeat.ToString();
        return retval;
    }
}
```

Before we can actually take our `ToString` method out for a spin, we need to derive some classes from `Dinosaur` and instantiate some objects based on the derived classes. Listing 9.6 shows five classes derived from `Dinosaur`. Each class has a constructor that requires values for the instance `Length` field, and `Name` property, when an instance is created. Note that the `EatMeat` property is set in the constructor for each class, meaning that it cannot be set as part of instantiation. In addition, each derived class overrides the virtual `Dinosaur` `GetFood` method.

Listing 9.6   Classes Derived from *Dinosaur*

```
class Lessemsaurus : Dinosaur {
    public Lessemsaurus (string theName, int length){
        this.Name = theName;
        this.Length = length;
        this.EatMeat = false;
    }
    public override string GetFood (){
        return "Lessemsaurus bites branches from treetops.";
    }
}
class Apatosaurus : Dinosaur {
    public Apatosaurus (string theName, int length){
        this.Name = theName;
        this.Length = length;
        this.EatMeat = false;
    }
    public override string GetFood (){
        return "Apatosaurus eats plants.";
    }
}
class Diplodocus : Dinosaur {
    public Diplodocus (string theName, int length){
        this.Name = theName;
        this.Length = length;
        this.EatMeat = false;
    }
    public override string GetFood (){
        return "Diplodocus likes his greens.";
    }
}
class Allosaurus : Dinosaur {
    public Allosaurus (string theName, int length){
        this.Name = theName;
        this.Length = length;
        this.EatMeat = true;
    }
    public override string GetFood (){
        return "My name is Allosaurus and I eat Apatosaurus.";
    }
}
class TRex : Dinosaur {
    public TRex (string theName, int length){
        this.Name = theName;
        this.Length = length;
        this.EatMeat = true;
    }
    public override string GetFood (){
        return "I am Tyrannosaurus Rex. I eat everything. I am always hungry.";
    }
}
```

Next, in a Form class, declare an array of type Dinosaur named *jPark[ ]*, and in a Button click event instantiate five new objects based on the classes derived from Dinosaur. As shown in Listing 9.7, add a concatenated string containing each object's GetFood method and name to a ListBox's Items collection.

Listing 9.7   **Instantiating Objects Based on Classes Derived from *Dinosaur***

```
Dinosaur [] jPark;
private void btnPoly_Click(object sender, System.EventArgs e) {
    lstDino.Items.Clear();
    jPark = new Dinosaur [5];
    jPark[0] = new Lessemsaurus("lessaemsaurus", 7);
    jPark[1] = new Apatosaurus("apatosaurus", 34);
    jPark[2] = new Allosaurus("allosaurus", 12);
    jPark[3] = new TRex("tRex", 14);
    jPark[4] = new Diplodocus("doc", 9);
    foreach (Dinosaur dino in jPark){
        lstDino.Items.Add(dino.GetFood() + " -- " + dino.Name);
    }
}
```

Finally—and it's about time, before all those dinosaurs go extinct—implement a click event that places the ToString return value from a dinosaur selected in the ListBox into a multiline TextBox (Listing 9.8).

Listing 9.8   **Displaying the *ToString* Return Value for the Selected *Dinosaur* Object**

```
private void btnToStr_Click(object sender, System.EventArgs e) {
    if (lstDino.Items.Count > 0) {
        if (lstDino.SelectedItems.Count > 0){
            txtToStr.Text = "";
            txtToStr.Text = jPark [lstDino.SelectedIndex].ToString();
        }
    }
}
```

If you run this project and select an item representing an instantiation of a class derived from Dinosaur in the ListBox, the return value of its ToString method—based on the ToString method placed in the base Dinosaur class—will be shown. Figure 9.5 shows the ToString value for the instantiation of the TRex class.

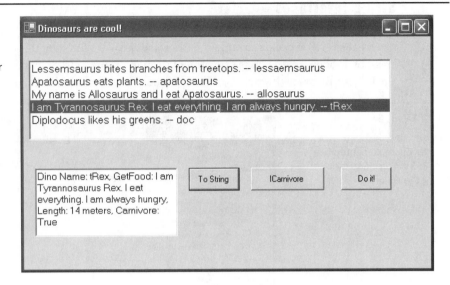

FIGURE 9.5:

It's up to you to implement a meaningful ToString method for your classes (the ToString return value for a TRex instance is shown).

Interfaces

An interface is like an abstract base class: both do not spell out implementation details and are used by derived classes. However, a class can derive from a base class and can also implement an interface—or, in fact, implement multiple interfaces. (In contrast, C# classes can only inherit from one base class.) In this respect, interfaces are more general—and more useful—than class inheritance.

What it boils down to is that an interface is a kind of contract. If a class implements an interface, it means that it—and its derived classes—must have implementations for the members whose signatures are included in the implementation specification. This means that if you know that a class implements an interface, you know that it implements certain members, and you know what to expect about how those members work.

Interface implementations help to ensure consistency. Studies have shown that software written with class libraries that implement interfaces tends to have fewer defects.

Interfaces work well in situations in which one set of programmers has created a class library (for example, the creators of the .NET Framework) and another set will be using the classes (you and me). Interface implementation also provides a good way for a team leader to deliver project specifications: the project lead writes the interfaces, and specifies mandatory implementation within classes.

By convention, an interface identifier always starts with a capital I, followed by another capital letter.

String Interfaces

The String class implements four interfaces: ICloneable, IComparable, IConvertible, and IEnumerable. You can determine the interfaces implemented by this class (or any other .NET class) by looking up the class's documentation in online help or by having a look at the class in the Object Browser (Figure 9.6). Each of these interfaces is documented in online help.

FIGURE 9.6:

You can find the interfaces implemented by the String class by using the Object Browser.

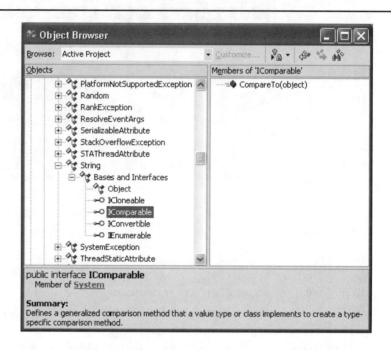

The Object Browser will also tell you the members that the interface "contract" requires to be implemented, and define those members for you.

Of the String class interface implementations, IComparable and IEnumerable are the most important.

The fact that String implements IEnumerable implies that you can use the foreach syntax to enumerate the characters in a string, using a statement like this:

```
foreach (char chr in str) {
    ...
}
```

Implementing the IComparable interface means that the class must contain a CompareTo method that compares the current instance with another object of the same type. Once this method is implemented, objects of the class work with the BinarySearch and Sort methods of the Array class.

Implementing *IComparable* in Your Own Class

Let's go ahead and implement IComparable in the Dinosaur class (it will then be implemented in all the classes derived from Dinosaur). The first step is to add the interface name following the inheritance operator in the Dinosaur class declaration:

```
public class Dinosaur : IComparable
```

NOTE   If you don't actually add the members specified in an interface to a class (or derived class) that implements the interface, you will get a compile-time error.

Next, we need to add a CompareTo method to the Dinosaur class. CompareTo has a fairly complex int return type that must be less than zero if the current instance is less than its comparison instance, zero if the two instances are the same, and greater than zero if the current instance is greater that its comparison instance. You can read more about the implementation details by looking up "IComparable.CompareTo Method" in online help. In the meantime, I'm going to take a shortcut: the Dinosaur class CompareTo will be implemented as a string CompareTo on the Name property of each dinosaur instance created from Dinosaur and its derived classes. You can see the code for this method in Listing 9.9. The long and the short of it is that Dinosaur instances will be sorted in arrays based on their Name property.

Listing 9.9   Implementing *IComparable* in the *Dinosaur* Class

```
public class Dinosaur : IComparable
{
   ...
   public int CompareTo (object obj) {
      Dinosaur dino = (Dinosaur) obj;
      return this.Name.CompareTo (dino.Name);
   }
}
```

To try this out, we can add a call to the static method Array.Sort after the Dinosaur objects have been instantiated in the *jPark* array:

```
Array.Sort (jPark);
```

The code that uses the IComparable implementation to sort the objects created from classes derived from Dinosaur is shown in Listing 9.10.

Listing 9.10   Sorting the Dinosaurs

```
private void btnPoly_Click(object sender, System.EventArgs e) {
   lstDino.Items.Clear();
   jPark = new Dinosaur [5];
   jPark[0] = new Lessemsaurus("lessaemsaurus", 7);
```

```
    jPark[1] = new Apatosaurus("apatosaurus", 34);
    jPark[2] = new Allosaurus("allosaurus", 12);
    jPark[3] = new TRex("tRex", 14);
    jPark[4] = new Diplodocus("doc", 9);
    Array.Sort (jPark);
    foreach (Dinosaur dino in jPark){
        lstDino.Items.Add(dino.GetFood() + " -- " + dino.Name);
    }
}
```

When you run this code, you'll see that the Dinosaur instances have been added to the ListBox alphabetically by name (Figure 9.7), because that's the way they were sorted in the *jPark* Array.

FIGURE 9.7:

You can tell that the classes derived from Dinosaur have implemented IComparable because they are ordered by dinosaur name.

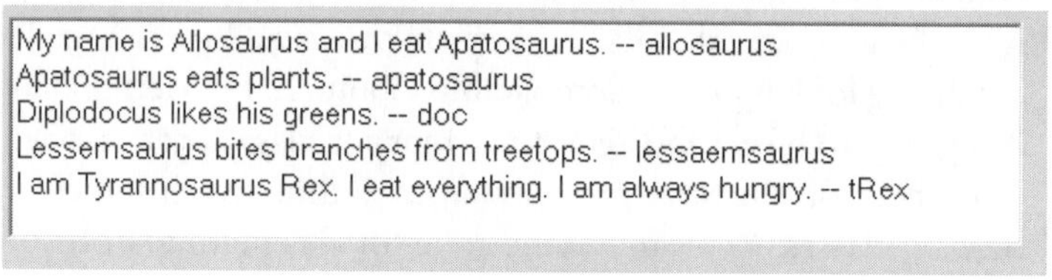

```
My name is Allosaurus and I eat Apatosaurus. -- allosaurus
Apatosaurus eats plants. -- apatosaurus
Diplodocus likes his greens. -- doc
Lessemsaurus bites branches from treetops. -- lessaemsaurus
I am Tyrannosaurus Rex. I eat everything. I am always hungry. -- tRex
```

NOTE   If the ListBox Sorted property were set to True, then the ListBox would be sorted by the text strings in the Items collection, not the Dinosaurs' Name properties. ("Apatosaurus" in Figure 9.7 would be first, and "My name" would be last.)

Implementing the *ICarnivore* Interface

Kicking this all up a notch, let's implement our own interface. Since it is ours, we get to name it and to define its members. Let's make an ICarnivore interface that consists of the Boolean property EatMeat (already implemented in the Dinosaur class) and a Boolean method CanIEatU, which determines whether one dinosaur instance can eat another. Listing 9.11 shows the interface definition.

NOTE   It's worth saying explicitly that the interface definition only defines the members required for the interface. There is no implementation code in the interface definition.

Listing 9.11   **The *ICarnivore* Interface**

```
interface ICarnivore {
    bool EatMeat {get; set;}
    bool CanIEatU (object obj);
}
```

To implement the interface, we need to add ICarnivore to the inheritance clause of the Dinosaur class declaration:

```
public class Dinosaur : IComparable, ICarnivore
```

Next, we need to create an implementation of CanIEatU for the Dinosaur base class. The logic of this method is that I can eat you if I am a carnivore and you are not, or if we both are carnivores and I am bigger than you:

```
public bool CanIEatU (object obj){
    Dinosaur dino = (Dinosaur) obj;
    if (this.EatMeat == false)
        return false;
    else if (this.EatMeat == true && dino.EatMeat == false)
        return true;
    else  // this.EatMeat == true && dino.EatMeat == true
    {
        if (this.Length > dino.Length)
            return true;
        else
            return false;
    }
}
```

Listing 9.12 shows the complete Dinosaur class with the ToString method, the CompareTo method, and the CanIEatU implementation of ICarnivore. (You'll find the CanIEatU method towards the bottom of the listing.)

Listing 9.12   **The Complete *Dinosaur* Class (*CanIEatU* Method at the End)**

```
public class Dinosaur : IComparable, ICarnivore
{
    private string m_Name;
    private bool m_EatMeat;
    public int Length = 0;
    public virtual string GetFood(){
        return "You are what you eat!";
    }
    public string Name {
        get {
            return m_Name;
        }
        set {
            m_Name = value;
        }
    }
    public bool EatMeat {
        get {
```

```
            return m_EatMeat;
         }
         set {
            m_EatMeat = value;
         }
      }
      public override string ToString() {
         string retval = "Dino Name: " + this.Name;
         retval += ", GetFood: " + this.GetFood();
         retval += ", Length: " + this.Length.ToString() + " meters";
         retval += ", Carnivore: " + this.EatMeat.ToString();
         return retval;
      }
      public int CompareTo (object obj) {
         Dinosaur dino = (Dinosaur) obj;
         return this.Name.CompareTo (dino.Name);
      }
      public bool CanIEatU (object obj){
         Dinosaur dino = (Dinosaur) obj;
         if (this.EatMeat == true && dino.EatMeat == false)
            return true;
         else if (this.EatMeat == false && dino.EatMeat == true)
            return false;
         else if (this.EatMeat == false && dino.EatMeat == false)
            return false;
         else  // this.EatMeat == true && dino.EatMeat == true
         {
            if (this.Length > dino.Length)
               return true;
            else
               return false;
         }
      }
   }
}
```

You can now alter the project to add a click event that instantiates two dinosaur objects, uses the CanIEatU method to determine who is lunch (and who is not), and then uses the members of the instances to display an appropriate message:

```
private void btnICarnivore_Click(object sender, System.EventArgs e) {
   lstDino.Items.Clear();
   TRex chomper = new TRex ("Chomper", 14);
   Diplodocus doc = new Diplodocus ("Doc", 9);
   if (chomper.CanIEatU (doc)){
      lstDino.Items.Add(chomper.Name + " the " + chomper.GetType().ToString());
      lstDino.Items.Add("has eaten");
      lstDino.Items.Add(doc.Name + " the " + doc.GetType().ToString());
      lstDino.Items.Add("for lunch.");
   }
}
```

Figure 9.8 shows the results of running this code displayed in the ListBox at the top of the form.

FIGURE 9.8:

The ICarnivore interface determines who has eaten whom.

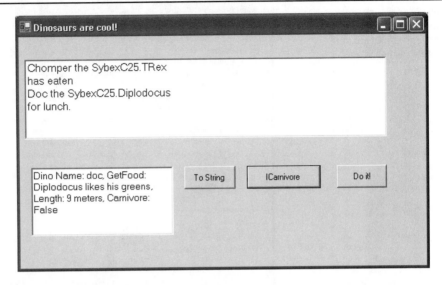

You should also note that the ICarnivore interface and implementation members appear in the Class View window when you examine one of the classes derived from Dinosaur (Figure 9.9) and also in the Object Browser (Figure 9.10).

FIGURE 9.9:

The ICarnivore interface (and the members of the TRex class) are shown in Class View.

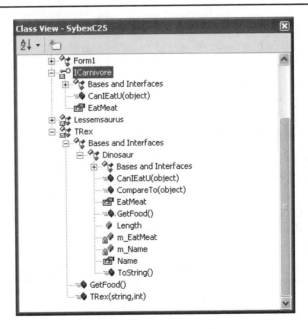

The `ICarnivore` interface and the classes derived from `Dinosaur` appear in the Object Browser.

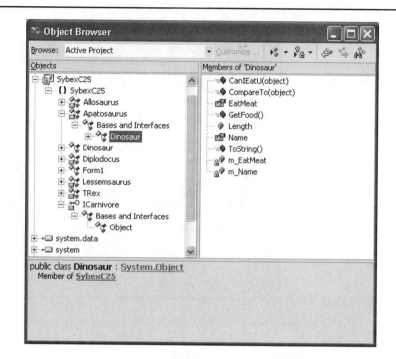

This discussion of interfaces and interface implementation has necessarily been somewhat superficial. For one thing, you are unlikely to need to implement `Dinosaur` and derived classes—and an `ICarnivore` interface—unless the dinosaurs come back. But the principles are the same when they are used in more substantive ways—as an important mechanism requiring adherence to standards—and you should know about interfaces and interface inheritance; arguably, it is as important as class inheritance for creating industrial-strength software.

Regular Expressions

One of the most powerful tools in the string manipulator's arsenal is the *regular expression*. A regular expression is used to define a pattern of characters. These patterns can be used for many purposes, including string manipulation, user input validation, and searching and replacing. Typically, the pattern represented by the regular expression is matched against a string. In the simplest example, the regular expression is a literal string of characters—for example, "saur". This simple regular expression pattern matches against a string that contains it—for example, "Allosaurus". The regular expression fails to match a string that does not contain it, such as "Montezuma".

While this example seems simple enough, you should not underestimate the importance of regular expressions, which provide access to powerful algorithms that are the natural and easy answer to many programming problems. The simplest solution to many programming problems—particularly those involving strings—often involves regular expressions.

> **NOTE**   The .NET Framework's powerful regular expression syntax is based on the `regexp` syntax used in Perl5.

In this section, I'll

- Tell you about the .NET regular expression classes.

- Show you how to set up a regular expression test bed.

- Explain the language of regular expression patterns.

- Provide an example using regular expressions that shows how the .NET regular expression classes interrelate.

This is an ambitious agenda—using regular expressions in C# is a subject that would easily fill an entire book—which implies that in the remainder of this chapter I can only scratch the surface of the topic. I invite you to use this material as a jumping off place, so that you can experiment with C# and regular expressions, and become a "regex" master in your own right.

The Regular Expression Classes

The regular expression classes are located in the `System.Text.RegularExpressions` namespace, which means that you should add a `using` directive to the beginning of any module that involves regular expressions, like so:

```
using System.Text.RegularExpressions;
```

Figure 9.11 shows the regular expression classes in this namespace in the Object Browser.

Here are brief descriptions of the regular expression classes (you may need to view online documentation or browse through the later parts of this chapter to understand some of the terminology):

Regex   This class can be used to instantiate an immutable regular expression object. It also provides a few static methods (for example, `Escape` and `Unescape`) that can be used with other classes.

Match   The results of a regular expression matching operation. The `Match` method of the `Regex` class returns a `Match` object.

MatchCollection   A sequence of nonoverlapping successful matches. The `Matches` method of the `Regex` class returns a `MatchCollection` object.

Capture   A single subexpression match.

Group   The results of a single capturing group, which contains a collection of `Capture` objects. Instances of `Group` are returned by the `Match.Groups` property.

CaptureCollection   A sequence of captured substrings. The `Captures` property of the `Match` and `Group` classes returns a `CaptureCollection` object.

GroupCollection   A collection of captured `Group` objects. The `Groups` property of the `Match` object returns a `GroupCollection` object.

FIGURE 9.11:

The Regular Expression classes, shown in the Object Browser.

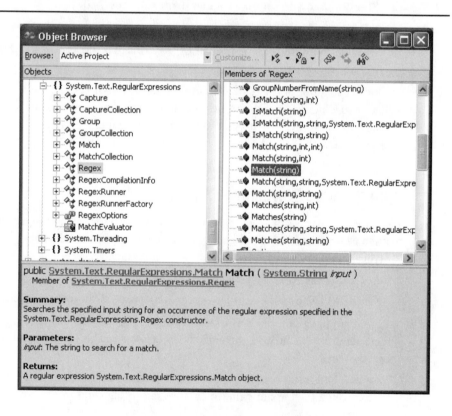

NOTE   The best way to find online documentation about regular expression classes and language is to set the Help Search filter to ".NET Framework SDK." Next, search for "Regular Expressions." (You'll find details on using and configuring online help in the Appendix, "Using C# .NET's Help System.")

A Regular Expression Test Bed

At a very basic level, you don't have to do much to use regular expressions. The general form is to create a `Regex` object that is a pattern. For example, the following regular expression will match any integer with between one and three digits:

```
Regex regex = new Regex (@"\d{1,3}");
```

The string verbatim symbol (@) is required before the regular expression pattern—otherwise the compiler will throw an exception because of an unrecognized escape character.

The \d{1,3} regular expression will be explained later in this section.

Next, provide a string to test against as an argument, and assign the results of the `Regex` instance's `Match` method to a `Match` object:

```
Match match = regex.Match ("42");
```

The properties of the `Match` object will then contain information about the first match: whether it was successful, the substring matched, the location of the match, and so on.

Figure 9.12 shows the user interface for a general regular expression test bed using this construction. Three multiline TextBoxes are intended for user entry of a test string and a pattern and to display the results.

FIGURE 9.12:

It's easy to set up a program that can be used to test regular expressions.

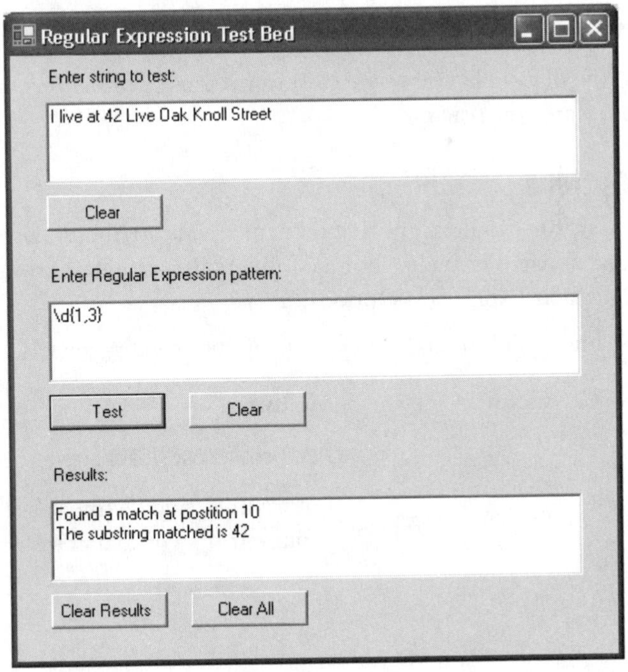

Listing 9.13 shows the click event code used to test for a regular expression match when the user enters a test string and pattern.

Listing 9.13   Testing Regular Expressions

```
private void btnTest_Click(object sender, System.EventArgs e) {
    Regex regex = new Regex (txtPattern.Text);
    Match match = regex.Match(txtStrTest.Text);
    if (match.Success) {
        string str = "Found a match at postition " + match.Index;
        str += "The substring matched is " + match.Value;
        txtResults.Text = str;
    }
    else {
        txtResults.Text = "Sorry, no regular expression pattern match!";
    }
}
```

WARNING   It perhaps doesn't need to be said this late into this book, but—in the real world—you'd want to include exception handling in this code. It's fairly easy to throw exceptions in the Regex class by entering strings that are not recognized as well-formed patterns. For example, entering a backslash (\) by itself as a pattern will cause an exception to be thrown when the compiler attempts to instantiate a Regex object based upon it.

The Syntax of Regular Expressions

Now that we have a way to test our regular expressions, we can start looking generally at how they are constructed.

Options

First, you should know that there are some attributes, also called *options*, which impact the way that a match is made. (For a complete list of these options, search online help for the topic "Regular Expression Options.")

These options are specified using inline characters. The most commonly used are:

Character	Meaning
i	Perform a case-insensitive match.
x	Ignore unescaped white space within a pattern, and enable commenting within a pattern following a pound sign (#).

To enable an attribute inline, prefix the pattern with a question mark followed by the attribute character followed by a colon, and enclose the whole thing within parentheses. For example, the pattern:

```
(?i:saur)
```

matches the string "ApatoSaUrus". Of course, if you had tried to match the pattern "saur" against the string, it would have behaved in a case-sensitive way, and there would have been no match.

Attributes can also be passed as an argument to an overloaded Regex constructor. For example,

```
Regex regex = new Regex ("saur", RegexOptions.IgnoreCase);
```

would create the same, case-insensitive pattern.

Literal Characters

You've already seen that an alphanumeric character within a regular expression matches itself. In addition, you can match many non-alphabetic characters using escape sequences.

Regular expression literal character matches are shown in Table 9.6.

TABLE 9.6: Regular Expression Characters and Character Sequences, and Their Matches

Character or Sequence	Matches
Alphabetic (a–z and A–Z) or numeric (0–9)	Itself (all characters other than . $ ^ { [(	) * + ? \ match themselves)
\b	Backspace (see note following table)
\f	Form feed
\n	New line
\r	Carriage return
\t	Tab
\/	Slash ("forward slash," literal /)
\\	Backslash (literal \)
\.	.
*	*
\+	+
\?	?
|		
\(	(
\)	)
\[	[

Continued on next page

TABLE 9.6 CONTINUED: Regular Expression Characters and Character Sequences, and Their Matches

Character or Sequence	Matches
\]	]
\{	{
\}	}
\xxx	The ASCII character specified by the octal number xxx
\uxxxx	The Unicode character specified by the hexadecimal number xxxx

> **NOTE**   The escaped character \b is a special case. Within a regular expression, \b means a word boundary, except within a [] character class, where it means a backspace. (Character classes are explained in the next section.)

It's not a bad idea to see that these escape sequences really do match as specified. Let's use the test environment developed earlier in this chapter to make sure that \r matches a carriage return. In the first box, as the string to test, just hit the Enter key. For a regular expression, use \r. When you click the Test button, you'll see that there is, indeed, a match.

Character Classes

Individual literal characters can be combined into *character classes* in regular expressions. Character classes are contained within square brackets. A match occurs when one or more of the characters contained in the class produces a match with the comparison string.

For example, the regular expression

```
[csharp]
```

matches against any string that contains at least one of the letters (such as "abc"). If you run the pattern in the test environment against "abc", you'll find that the first match is the letter 'a'.

The characters within a class can be specified using ranges, rather than by specific enumeration. A hyphen is used to indicate a range. Here are some examples:

Sequence	Meaning
[a-z]	All lowercase characters from *a* to *z*
[a-zA-L]	All lowercase characters from *a* to *z* and all uppercase characters from *A* to *L*
[a-zA-Z0-9]	All lower- and uppercase letters and all numerals

Using this notation, [a-zA-L] does not produce a match with the string "XYZ" but does match the string "xyz". By the way, you may have noticed that you could use the case attribute instead of separately listing uppercase and lowercase ranges. (?i:[a-z]) is the equivalent to [a-zA-Z].

Negating a Character Class

A character class can be negated. A negated class matches any character *except* those defined within brackets. To negate a character class, place a caret (^) as the first character inside the left bracket of the class. For example, the regular expression [^a-zA-Z] will match if and only if the comparison string contains at least one nonalphabetic character. "abcABC123" contains a match, but "abcABC" does not.

Common Character Class Representations

Because some character classes are frequently used, the syntax of regular expressions provides special sequences that are shorthand representations of these classes. Square brackets are not used with most of these special character "abbreviations." The sequences that can be used for character classes are shown in Table 9.7.

TABLE 9.7: Character Class Sequences and Their Meanings

Character Sequence	Matches
[...]	Any one character between the square brackets.
[^...]	Any one character not between the brackets.
.	Any one character other than new line; equivalent to [^\n].
\w	Any one letter, number, or underscore; equivalent to [a-zA-Z0-9_].
\W	Any one character other than a letter, number, or underscore; equivalent to [^a-zA-Z0-9_].
\s	Any one space character or other white-space character; equivalent to [\t\n\r\f\v].
\S	Any one character other than a space or other white-space character; equivalent to [^ \t\n\r\f\v].
\d	Any one digit; equivalent to [0-9].
\D	Any one character that is not a digit; equivalent to [^0-9].

For example, the pattern \W matches a string containing a hyphen (-) but fails against a string containing only letters (such as "abc").

In another example, \s matches a string containing a space, such as "lions and tigers, and bears". But \s fails against strings that do not contain white-space characters, such as "ineedsomespace".

Repeating Elements

So far, if you wanted to match a multiple number of characters, the only way to achieve this using a regular expression would be to enumerate each character. For example, \d\d would match any two-digit number. And \w\w\w\w\w would match any five-letter alphanumeric string, such as "string" or "94707".

This isn't good enough. In addition to being cumbersome, it doesn't allow complex pattern matches involving varied numbers of characters. For example, you might want to match a number between two and six digits in length, or a pair of letters followed by a number of any length.

This kind of "wildcard" pattern is specified in regular expressions using curly braces ({}). The curly braces follow the pattern element that is to be repeated and specify the number of times it repeats. In addition, some special characters are used to specify common types of repetition. Both the curly-brace syntax and the special repetition characters are shown in Table 9.8.

TABLE 9.8: Syntax for Repeating Pattern Elements

Repetition Syntax	Meaning
{n,m}	Match the preceding element at least n times but no more than m times.
{n,}	Match the preceding element n or more times.
{n}	Match the preceding element exactly n times.
?	Match the preceding element zero or one times—in other words, the element is optional; equivalent to {0,1}.
+	Match one or more occurrences of the preceding element; equivalent to {1,}.
*	Match zero or more occurrences of the preceding element—in other words, the element is optional, but can also appear multiple times; equivalent to {0,}.

As we've already seen, to match a number with one to three digits, you can use the regular expression \d{1,3}. Another example is that you can match a word surrounded by space characters by creating a pattern that sandwiches the word between \s+ sequences. For example,

    \s+love\s+

matches "I love you!" but not "Iloveyou!".

Organizing Patterns

Regular expression syntax provides special characters that allow you to organize patterns. These characters are shown in Table 9.9 and discussed below.

TABLE 9.9: Alternation, Grouping, and Reference Characters

Character	Meaning
|	Alternation. Matches the character or subexpression to the left or right of the | character.
(...)	Grouping. Groups several items into a unit, or subexpression, that can be used with repeated syntax and referred to later in an expression.
\\n	Referenced subexpression match. Matches the same characters that were matched when the subexpression \\n was first matched.

Alternation

The pipe character (|) is used to indicate an alternative. For example, the regular expression jaws|that|bite matches the three strings *jaws*, *that*, or *bite*. In another example, \d{2}|[A-Z]{4} matches either two digits or four capital letters.

Grouping

Parentheses are used to group elements in a regular expression. Once items have been grouped into *subexpressions*, they can be treated as a single element using repetition syntax. For example, chocolate(donut)? matches *chocolate* with or without the optional *donut*.

Referring to Subexpressions

Parentheses are also used to refer back to a subexpression that is part of a regular expression. Each subexpression that has been grouped in parentheses is internally assigned an identification number. The subexpressions are numbered from left to right, using the position of the left parenthesis to determine order. Nesting of subexpressions is allowed.

Subexpressions are referred to using a backslash followed by a number. So \1 means the first subexpression, \2 the second, and so on.

A reference to a subexpression matches the same characters that were originally matched by the subexpression. For example, the regular expression

    ['"][^'"]*['"]

matches a string that starts with a single or double quote and ends with a single or double quote. (The middle element, [^'"]*, matches any number of characters, provided they are not single or double quotes.)

However, this expression doesn't distinguish between the two kinds of quotes. A comparison string that started with a double quote and ended with a single quote would match this expression. For example, the string

    "We called him Tortoise because he taught us'

which starts with a double quote and ends with a single quote, matches the regular expression pattern.

A better result would be to have a match depend on which kind of quote the match began with. If it begins with a double quote, it should end with a double quote; likewise, if it starts with a single quote, it should end with a single quote.

This can be accomplished by referring to the earlier subexpression so that the same kind of quote that the string starts with is required for a match. Here's the regular expression pattern to accomplish this:

```
(['"])[^'"]*\1
```

As you'll see if you try running this in the test bed program, it matches *"CSharp"* but not *"CSharp'*.

Specifying a Position for a Match

Finally, you should know about the regular expression characters that are used to specify a match position. These characters, shown in Table 9.10, do not match characters; rather, they match boundaries, typically the beginning or end of a word or a string.

TABLE 9.10: Regular Expression Position-Matching Characters

Character	Matching Position
^	The beginning of a string; in multiline searches, the beginning of a line.
$	The end of a string; in multiline searches, the end of a line.
\b	A word boundary. In other words, it matches the position between a \w character and a \W character. Also see the note about \b in the "Literal Characters" section of this chapter.
\B	Not a word boundary.

You'll find that many regular expressions use positioning characters. It's easier to get a sense of how to use them in the context of actual tasks. Here are two examples of regular expressions that match positions.

To match a word, you can use the regular expression

```
\b[A-Za-z'-]+\b
```

NOTE You have to think carefully about what exactly a "word" is and what you need to accomplish in a given programming context. This regular expression defines a word to include apostrophes and hyphens but not digits or underscores (so *85th* would fail the match).

To match a string by itself on a line, start the regular expression with a caret (^) and end with a dollar sign. For example, the regular expression

```
^Prospero$
```

matches the string *Prospero* if it is alone on a line, but not if any other characters (even spaces) are on the line.

Regular Expression Examples

The full power of regular expressions becomes apparent when you start to use their pattern-matching abilities in combination with string and regular expression class methods in your programs.

But regular expressions can do a lot for you more or less on their own. So I'll start by showing you a few somewhat complicated regular expression patterns that may be useful—and that you can use to test your understanding of the syntax of regular expressions.

Pattern Matches

To match a date in *mm/dd/yyyy* format, use the pattern:

```
\b(\d{2})\/(\d{2})\/(\d{4})\b
```

To match a number in Roman notation, use the pattern:

```
(?i:^m*(d?c{0,3}|c[dm])(l?x{0,3}|x[lc])(v?i{0,3}|i[vx])$)
```

MDCCLXXVI, or 1776, is shown matching this pattern in Figure 9.13.

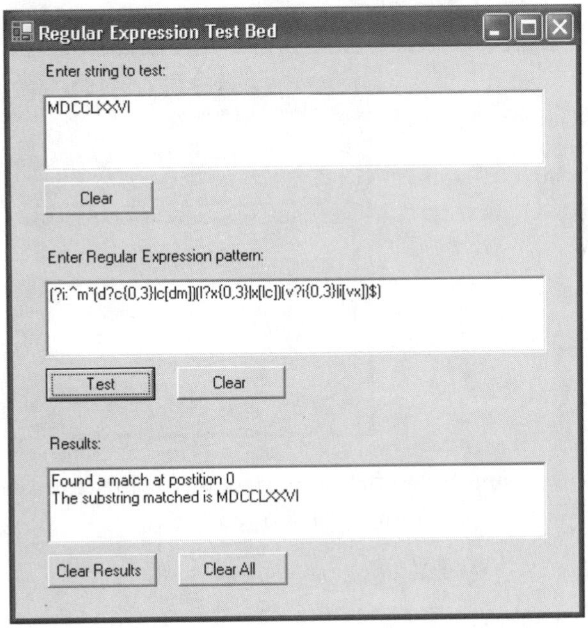

FIGURE 9.13:

The regular expression shown here matches a Roman number.

Note that the pattern used in the Roman number example includes the i (case-insensitivity) attribute. As explained earlier in this chapter, this could have been accomplished using the RegexOptions enumeration and the Regex constructor rather than as part of the pattern string.

To match a URL, use the following regular expression:

```
\w+:\/\/[\w.]+\/?\S*
```

This will match any standard URL that includes a protocol, e.g., http:// or ftp://. Path information following the domain is allowed, but optional. So both http://www.bearhome.com/cub/ and http://www.sybex.com match this pattern.

Matching Substrings in an Expression

The preceding pattern that matches a URL is all very well and good, but what if you need only part of the URL? For instance, you might need to know the protocol used, or the domain. In this example, I'll show you how to use regular expressions to "decompose" a URL into its constituent parts. Obviously, you could also do this with string methods—there's no real need for regular expressions—but following this example should help you to understand how the .NET Framework regular expression classes are related.

For a user interface, I've used a TextBox for entering the URL (which is to, once again, include protocol followed by ://), a ListBox to display the URL's decomposed parts, and a Button whose click event will process the decomposition (Figure 9.14).

FIGURE 9.14:

Regular expressions can be used to decompose a URL into constituent parts.

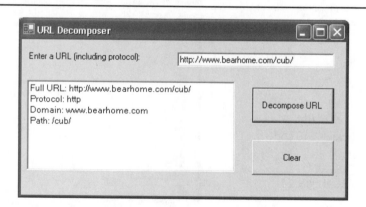

The first step in the click event is to rewrite the regular expression pattern a bit. The original URL-matching pattern that I showed you is

```
\w+:\/\/[\w.]+\/?\S*
```

To do substring matches on this, we need to break it up into groups using parentheses:

(\w+):\/\/([\w.]+)(\/?\S*)

In order to assign the pattern to a string variable, we need to use the verbatim symbol (otherwise the compiler thinks the string includes an invalid escape character):

```
string pattern = @"(\w+):\/\/([\w.]+)(\/?\S*)";
```

Now that we have our regular expression, we have to use it to retrieve the substring values. First, we start a counter and a string array to hold the results:

```
int k = 0;
string [] results = new string[4];
```

Next, create a Regex instance using the "ignore case" option:

```
Regex regex = new Regex (pattern, RegexOptions.IgnoreCase);
```

Use the instance's Match method to assign the match with the URL entered by the user to a Match object:

```
Match match = regex.Match(txtURL.Text);
```

Use the Match instance's Groups property to populate a GroupCollection object:

```
GroupCollection gc = match.Groups;
```

Cycle through the GroupCollection instance. For each item in it (each Group), use the Group instance's Captures property to populate a CaptureCollection instance. Cycle through each CaptureCollection instance, and use each item's Value property to add a substring match to the *results* array and increase the array counter:

```
for (int i = 0; i < gc.Count; i++) {
    CaptureCollection cc = gc [i].Captures;
    for (int j = 0; j < cc.Count ; j++) {
        results[k] = cc[j].Value;
        k++;
    }
}
```

Finally, add the text in the *results* array to the ListBox Items collection for display. The complete code for the URL decomposition is shown in Listing 9.14.

Listing 9.14   Decomposing a URL into Groups

```
using System.Text.RegularExpressions;
...
private void btnDecomp_Click_1(object sender, System.EventArgs e) {
    lstURL.Items.Clear();
    string pattern = @"(\w+):\/\/([\w.]+)(\/?\S*)";
    int k = 0;
```

```
string [] results = new string[4];
Regex regex = new Regex (pattern, RegexOptions.IgnoreCase);
Match match = regex.Match(txtURL.Text);
GroupCollection gc = match.Groups;
for (int i = 0; i < gc.Count; i++) {
   CaptureCollection cc = gc [i].Captures;
   for (int j = 0; j < cc.Count ; j++) {
      results[k] = cc[j].Value;
      k++;
   }
}
lstURL.Items.Add ("Full URL: " + results[0]);
lstURL.Items.Add ("Protocol: " + results[1]);
lstURL.Items.Add ("Domain: " + results[2]);
lstURL.Items.Add ("Path: " + results[3]);
}
```

Conclusion

This chapter has covered a lot of ground. If string manipulation is, indeed, "everything," it is fair to say that you've been—at least—introduced to everything you need to know to work with strings.

We started with the various string-related types: string, char, and the StringBuilder class. I explained how to create instances of the types, and how to use the instance and static methods related to these classes. I also showed you how to implement ToString methods in your own classes.

Moving on, we touched on the fact that the string type implements IComparable. I showed you how to implement IComparable in your own classes, and how to create a custom interface for use with Dinosaur and its derived classes, dubbed ICarnivore.

The final part of this chapter explained working with regular expressions. While regular expressions are not unique to C# or .NET, successfully using them can add a great deal of ease and power to your programs. You do need to understand how the .NET regular expression classes and collections interact—I concluded the chapter with an example showing this.

It's time to move on. Chapter 10 will show you how to work with files, input, and output.

PART IV

Gigue: Leaping to Success

Working with Streams and Files

- Files and directories

- Using the *Environment* and *Path* classes

- Finding files

- Working with the system Registry

- Using isolated storage

- Understanding streams

- Reading and writing files

- Web streams

- Using a *FileStream* asynchronously

I t's an unusual program of any size that doesn't save and retrieve values for initialization purposes. Most programs also need to work with files. In other words, to accomplish many tasks, along the way you'll need to obtain information about the file system a program is operating in, read (and write) configuration data, and read from and write to files.

This chapter explains how to work with files and directories. Next, I'll show you how to save initialization information—using both the system Registry and isolated storage. I'll explain streams and how the stream classes interrelate, and show you how to read and write both text and binary files. We'll also take a look at web streams and at invoking `FileStreams` asynchronously.

Files and Directories

You'll find the `Environment`, `Path`, `Directory`, `DirectoryInfo`, `File`, and `FileInfo` classes essential for obtaining information about local systems, paths, directories, and files—and for manipulating them.

Environment Class

The `Environment` class, part of the `System` namespace, contains properties and methods that let you get information about the system on which a program is running, the current user logged on to a system, and the *environment strings*—or, variables that are used to maintain information about the system environment. Using the `Environment` class, besides information about environment variables, you can retrieve command-line arguments, exit codes, the contents of the call stack, the time since the last system boot, the version of the CLR that is running, and more. For a full list of `Environment` members, look up "Environment Members" in online help.

Table 10.1 shows some of the static `Environment` methods and properties that are related to the file system.

TABLE 10.1: *Environment* Class Members Related to Files and Directories

Member	What It Does
CurrentDirectory	Property gets (or sets) the fully qualified path for the current directory.
GetFolderPath	Method gets the fully qualified path to the special folder identified in the `Environment.SpecialFolder` enumeration (see Table 10.2).
GetLogicalDrives	Method returns an array of strings containing the names of the logical drives on the system.
SystemDirectory	Property gets the fully qualified path of the system directory.

Table 10.2 shows the possible values of the `Environment.SpecialFolder` enumeration. It is unusual that this enumeration is defined within the `Environment` class, as you can see in the

Object Browser in Figure 10.1 (it is more common to define the enumeration directly within the namespace, e.g., System).

FIGURE 10.1:

The SpecialFolder enumeration is defined within the Environment class.

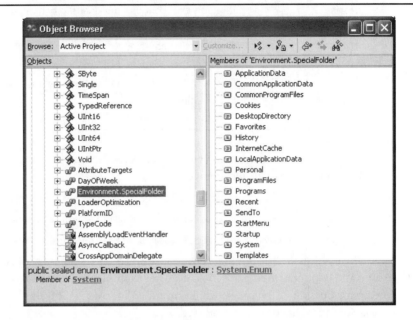

TABLE 10.2: Values of the *Environment.SpecialFolder* Enumeration

Constant	Special Folder Description
ApplicationData	Directory that serves as a common repository for application-specific data for the current roaming user
CommonApplicationData	Directory that serves as a common repository for application-specific data that is used by all users
CommonProgramFiles	Directory for components that are shared across applications
Cookies	Directory that serves as a common repository for Internet cookies
DesktopDirectory	Directory used to physically store file objects shown on the Desktop
Favorites	Directory that serves as a common repository for the user's favorite items
History	Directory that serves as a common repository for Internet history items
InternetCache	Directory that serves as a common repository for temporary Internet files
LocalApplicationData	Directory that serves as a common repository for application-specific data that is used by the current, non-roaming user
Personal	Directory that serves as a common repository for documents (My Documents)
ProgramFiles	Program files directory

Continued on next page

TABLE 10.2 CONTINUED: Values of the *Environment.SpecialFolder* Enumeration

Constant	Special Folder Description
Programs	Directory that contains the user's program groups
Recent	Directory that contains the user's most recently used documents
SendTo	Directory that contains Send To menu items
StartMenu	Directory that contains Start menu items
Startup	Directory that corresponds to the user's Startup program group
System	System directory
Templates	Directory that serves as a common repository for document templates

Being defined within the Environment class implies that the enumeration must be referenced with the class as a qualifier. Hence

```
String str = Environment.GetFolderPath(SpecialFolder.ProgramFiles);
```

produces a compile-time syntax error. The correct formulation is

```
String str = Environment.GetFolderPath(Environment.SpecialFolder.ProgramFiles);
```

The fully qualified path that these constants refer to depends, of course, on the operating system and configuration. Let's look at a brief example, shown in Listing 10.1, namely getting the current Personal directory—which on my Windows XP system happens to be C:\Documents and Settings\harold\My Documents.

Listing 10.1   Getting the Personal Directory

```
private void btnMyDocs_Click(object sender, System.EventArgs e) {
    try {
        txtStartDir.Text = Environment.GetFolderPath
            (Environment.SpecialFolder.Personal);
    }
    catch (Exception excep) {
        MessageBox.Show (excep.Message);
    }
}
```

If you run this code, the current Personal directory will be displayed in a TextBox. (I'll be using the contents of this TextBox as the starting place for a recursive scan of a computer's directories—shown in an example a little later in this chapter.)

Enter a starting directory: C:\Documents and Settings\harold\My Documents

My Documents

NOTE In the examples in this chapter, I have been rigorous about always using some variant of the `try...catch`, `try...catch...finally`, or `try...finally` exception handling syntax explained in Chapter 6, "Zen and Now: The C# Language." The reason is that when it comes to files and file systems, one just never knows. Files can be moved or deleted. Drives can be unavailable. Permission levels may be required to access certain information, and so on. This is an arena in which, realistically, you can never assert perfect control—and should therefore embed program statements within exception handling blocks.

Path Class

The `Path` class, defined in the `System.IO` namespace, provides static methods that perform string manipulations on file and path information stored in `string` instances. Note that these methods do not interact with the file system and do not verify the existence of specified files or paths—with the interesting implication that a path string does not have to represent an existing path in order to be used with the members of this class. So you could use `Path` class methods to construct a `string` representing a path and file, and then check to see whether the file actually exists before using the string. As another example, the `Path.GetExtension` method returns a file extension. So the following code stores the value "sybex" in the variable *extension*:

```
string fileName = @"C:\theDir\myfile.sybex"
string extension;
extension = Path.GetExtension(fileName);
```

But nothing about this code snippet guarantees that "sybex" is a valid file extension—or, for that matter, that the specified file name and path in the *fileName* variable represents an existing file.

The methods of the `Path` class, all of which are static, are shown in Table 10.3.

TABLE 10.3: *Path* Class Methods

Method	What It Does
ChangeExtension	Changes the extension of a path string.
Combine	Joins a path name (on the left) with a path and/or file name (on the right). This is like string concatenation, except you do not have to worry about whether a backslash is the end of the left part or the beginning of the right part.
GetDirectoryName	Returns the directory information for the specified path string.
GetExtension	Returns the extension of the specified path string.
GetFileName	Returns the file name and extension of the specified path string.
GetFileNameWithoutExtension	Returns the file name of the specified path string without the extension.
GetFullPath	Returns the absolute path for the specified path string.
GetPathRoot	Gets the root directory information of the specified path.

Continued on next page

TABLE 10.3 CONTINUED: *Path* Class Methods

Method	What It Does
GetTempFileName	Returns a unique temporary file name and creates an empty file by that name on disk.
GetTempPath	Returns the path of the current system's temporary folder.
HasExtension	Determines whether a path includes a file name extension.
IsPathRooted	Gets a value indicating whether the specified path string contains absolute or relative path information.

Directory and *File* Classes

Four parallel classes are designed to let you work with (and perform discovery on) directories and files. The classes—all members of the System.IO namespace and all sealed so they can't be inherited—are Directory, DirectoryInfo, File, and FileInfo. Here's some more information about these classes:

- Directory contains only static members for manipulating directories, which require an argument that is a directory, such as a Path string (see Table 10.4 for class methods).

- DirectoryInfo contains no static members, so you must instantiate a DirectoryInfo object to use it. DirectoryInfo inherits from the abstract class FileSystemInfo (as does FileInfo). The GetFiles method of DirectoryInfo returns an array of FileInfo objects that are the files in a given directory. Selected members of the DirectoryInfo class are shown in Table 10.5.

- File, like Directory, provides static methods used for manipulating files, which require a string argument representing a file name. Selected File members are shown in Table 10.6.

- FileInfo contains no static members, so you must obtain an instance to use it. The Directory method returns a DirectoryInfo object that is an instance of the parent directory of the FileInfo object. Selected members of FileInfo are shown in Table 10.7.

It is more or less the case that one can achieve comparable functionality using either parallel pair—Directory and File, or DirectoryInfo and FileInfo. If you need only a few items of information or to perform only a few operations, it's probably easiest to use the static classes, Directory and File. However, if you expect to use members multiple times, it probably makes more sense to instantiate DirectoryInfo and FileInfo objects—which is my stylistic preference in any case.

TABLE 10.4: *Directory* Class Static Methods

Method	What It Does
CreateDirectory	Creates a directory or subdirectory
Delete	Deletes a directory and its contents

Continued on next page

TABLE 10.4 CONTINUED: *Directory* Class Static Methods

Method	What It Does
Exists	Returns a Boolean value indicating whether the specified path corresponds to an actual existing directory on disk
GetCreationTime	Gets the creation date and time of a directory
GetCurrentDirectory	Gets the current working directory of the application
GetDirectories	Gets the names of subdirectories in the specified directory
GetDirectoryRoot	Returns the volume information, root information, or both for the specified path
GetFiles	Returns the names of files in the specified directory
GetFileSystemEntries	Returns the names of all files and subdirectories in the specified directory
GetLastAccessTime	Returns the date and time that the specified file or directory was last accessed
GetLastWriteTime	Returns the date and time that the specified file or directory was last written to
GetLogicalDrives	Retrieves the names of the logical drives on the current computer (in the form "*<drive letter>*:\")
GetParent	Retrieves the parent directory of the specified path, including both absolute and relative paths
Move	Moves a file or a directory and its contents to a specified location
SetCreationTime	Sets the creation date and time for the specified file or directory
SetCurrentDirectory	Sets the application's current working directory to the specified directory
SetLastAccessTime	Sets the date and time that the specified file or directory was last accessed
SetLastWriteTime	Sets the date and time a directory was last written to

TABLE 10.5: Selected *DirectoryInfo* Class Instance Members

Member	What It Does
Attributes	Property gets or sets the FileAttributes of the current FileSystemInfo
CreationTime	Property gets or sets the creation time of the current FileSystemInfo object
Create	Method creates a directory
CreateSubdirectory	Method creates a subdirectory or subdirectories
Delete	Method deletes a DirectoryInfo and its contents from a path
Exists	Property returns a Boolean value indicating whether a DirectoryInfo instance corresponds to an actual existing directory on disk

Continued on next page

TABLE 10.5 CONTINUED: Selected *DirectoryInfo* Class Instance Members

Member	What It Does
Extension	Property gets the string representing the extension part of the file
FullName	Property gets the full path of the directory or file
GetDirectories	Method returns the subdirectories of the current directory
GetFiles	Method returns an array of FileInfo objects representing the files in the current directory
GetFileSystemInfos	Method retrieves an array of FileSystemInfo objects
LastAccessTime	Property gets or sets the time that the current file or directory was last accessed
LastWriteTime	Property gets or sets the time when the current file or directory was last written to
MoveTo	Method moves a DirectoryInfo instance and its contents to a new path
Parent	Property gets the parent directory of a specified subdirectory
Root	Property gets the root portion of a path

TABLE 10.6: *File* Class Static Methods

Method	What It Does
AppendText	Creates a StreamWriter that appends text to an existing file (see "Streams" later in this chapter for more information about StreamWriters)
Copy	Copies a file
Create	Creates a file in the specified fully qualified path
CreateText	Creates or opens a new file for writing text
Delete	Deletes the file specified by the fully qualified path (an exception is not thrown if the specified file does not exist)
Exists	Determines whether the specified file exists
GetAttributes	Gets the FileAttributes of the file on the fully qualified path
GetCreationTime	Returns the creation date and time of the specified file or directory
GetLastAccessTime	Returns the date and time that the specified file or directory was last accessed
GetLastWriteTime	Returns the date and time that the specified file or directory was last written to
Move	Moves a specified file to a new location, providing the option to specify a new file name
Open	Opens a FileStream on the specified path (see "Streams" later in this chapter for more information about FileStreams)

Continued on next page

TABLE 10.6 CONTINUED: *File* Class Static Methods

Method	What It Does
OpenRead	Opens an existing file for reading
OpenText	Opens an existing text file for reading
OpenWrite	Opens an existing file for writing
SetAttributes	Sets the specified FileAttributes of the file on the specified path
SetCreationTime	Sets the date and time that the file was created
SetLastAccessTime	Sets the date and time that the specified file was last accessed
SetLastWriteTime	Sets the date and time that the specified file was last written to

TABLE 10.7: Selected *FileInfo* Class Instance Members

Member	What It Does
AppendText	Method creates a StreamWriter that appends text to the file
Attributes	Property gets or sets a FileAttributes object that represents the file's attributes
CopyTo	Method copies an existing file to a new file
Create	Method creates a file
CreateText	Creates a StreamWriter that writes a new text file
CreationTime	Property gets or sets the creation time of the current object
Delete	Method permanently deletes a file
Directory	Property gets an instance of the parent directory
DirectoryName	Property gets a string representing the directory's full path
Exists	Property gets a Boolean value indicating whether a file exists
Extension	Property gets the string representing the extension part of the file
FullName	Property gets the full path of the file
LastAccessTime	Property gets or sets the time that the file was last accessed
LastWriteTime	Property gets or sets the time when the file was last written to
Length	Property gets the size of the current file or directory
MoveTo	Method moves a file to a new location, providing the option to specify a new file name
Open	Method opens a file with various read/write and sharing privileges
OpenRead	Method creates a read-only FileStream
OpenText	Method creates a StreamReader that reads from a text file
OpenWrite	Method creates a write-only FileStream

Finding the Files in (or Under) a Directory

It's really pretty simple to use these classes, and they provide a tremendous amount of power in manipulating files and directories.

Let's put together a sample application that works with `DirectoryInfo` and `FileInfo`, my preferred pair of these classes, to show how this can work. I don't want to belabor the point, but it bears repeating that you could replace the instance members of `DirectoryInfo` and `FileInfo` with static members of `Directory` and `File`.

This application searches, recursively through the user-selected directory and all its contents, to find files that match the specifications given. A `DirectoryInfo` instance is created using the initial directory. An array of `FileInfo` objects is created in the directory, and each is checked for a match. Next, an array of `DirectoryInfo` objects is created based on the subdirectories within the directory. The whole procedure starts over with each `DirectoryInfo` instance.

In a little more detail, the sample application lets the user enter a starting path that is anywhere in your file system. (Alternatively, a button lets you set the starting path to your My Documents folder, using the `Environment.Personal` enumeration explained earlier in this chapter.)

Next, the user enters a file name to be searched for. Because Chapter 9, "Everything Is String Manipulation," explained regular expressions, I put a regular expression pattern match behind the file text entry box—so you can just enter a name, for example `mytext.txt`, or enter a pattern using regular expression wildcards, such as `mytext.*`.

When the user clicks Start, the application moves recursively though all directories "below" the initially selected directory. Each directory—and its time of last access—is displayed in a multiline TextBox, indented to show its level in the hierarchy. If a file is found that matches the file input specification, the fully qualified name of the file, along with its size and attributes, is displayed in another TextBox.

Figure 10.2 shows the user interface for this application (searching through a subdirectory of My Documents for all files matching the specification `mytext.*`).

FIGURE 10.2:

The application recursively moves through the directory structure.

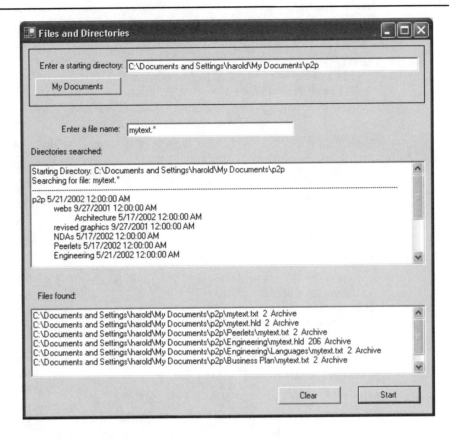

Let's start with the first and last things that happen when the user clicks the Start button. Here's what happens first.

A `DirectoryInfo` object is created based on the user's input:

```
DirectoryInfo dir = new DirectoryInfo (txtStartDir.Text);
```

The `Regex` instance is created based on the user's file name input (as explained in Chapter 9):

```
Regex regex = new Regex (txtFileName.Text);
```

Next, the `DirectoryInfo` instance is checked to see whether it really is an existing directory:

```
if (dir.Exists == true)...
```

If it is, some initial text is displayed, the cursor is set to an hourglass, and the recursive `FindFile` method is called, with the `DirectoryInfo` object and the pattern specification string passed as arguments to it:

```
...
this.Cursor = Cursors.WaitCursor;
FindFile (dir, regex);
...
```

Here's what happens last (and we can be sure that this will be executed last, because it is within a finally block). The cursor is restored to its normal state, and if no matching files were found, an appropriate message is displayed:

```
finally {
    this.Cursor = Cursors.Default;
    if (txtFilesFound.Text == String.Empty)
        txtFilesFound.Text = "No matching files found!";
}
```

Before we get to the FindFile method, note the static variable *indent*, used to control the hierarchal display of each directory:

```
static int indent = -10;
```

I started this variable at –10 so that the increment that is used within the recursive method would bring it back up to 0 for the highest-level directory.

Within FindFile, the indentation is incremented and information about the current DirectoryInfo instance is displayed:

```
private void FindFile (DirectoryInfo dir, string fn) {
    indent += 10;
    txtResults.Text += new String (' ', indent) + dir.Name + " " +
        dir.LastAccessTime + "\r\n";
    ...
```

The GetFiles method of the DirectoryInfo instance is used to read the files in the current directory into an array of FileInfo objects:

```
FileInfo[] filesInDir = dir.GetFiles();
```

Next, the foreach syntax is used to cycle through the array of FileInfo objects. Each time there is a match, the fully qualified file name, size, and attributes are added to a TextBox for display:

```
foreach (FileInfo fi in filesInDir){
    Match match = regex.Match (fi.Name);
    if (match.Success){
        if (txtFileName.Text != String.Empty){
            txtFilesFound.Text += fi.FullName + "  " + fi.Length + "  " +
                fi.Attributes + "\r\n";
        }
    }
}
```

Once the files in the current directory have been checked, and the resulting matches displayed, the GetDirectories method of the DirectoryInfo object is used to read the subdirectories of the current directory into an array of DirectoryInfo objects:

```
DirectoryInfo[] dirs = dir.GetDirectories();
```

The array of `DirectoryInfo` objects is cycled through. For each subdirectory, the `FindFile` method is called recursively:

```
foreach (DirectoryInfo di in dirs){
    FindFile(di, regex);
}
```

Finally, after returning from the recursive call, the indent is decremented to mark the appropriate hierarchal level:

```
indent -= 10;
```

The complete code for the recursive `FindFile` method and the Start click event is shown in Listing 10.2.

Listing 10.2   **Recursing through Directories and Matching a Specified File**

```
using System.IO;
using System.Text.RegularExpressions;
...
private void btnStart_Click(object sender, System.EventArgs e) {
    txtResults.Text = String.Empty;
    txtFilesFound.Text = String.Empty;
    try {
        DirectoryInfo dir = new DirectoryInfo (txtStartDir.Text);
        Regex regex = new Regex (txtFileName.Text);
        if (dir.Exists == true) {
            txtResults.Text = "Starting Directory: " + txtStartDir.Text + "\r\n";
            txtResults.Text += "Searching for file: " + txtFileName.Text + "\r\n";
            txtResults.Text += new String ('-',170) + "\r\n";;
            this.Cursor = Cursors.WaitCursor;
            FindFile (dir, regex);
        }
        else {
            txtResults.Text =
                "Please start your search from an existing directory!";
        }
    }
    catch (Exception excep) {
        MessageBox.Show (excep.Message);
    }
    finally {
        this.Cursor = Cursors.Default;
        if (txtFilesFound.Text == String.Empty)
            txtFilesFound.Text = "No matching files found!";
    }
}
static int indent = -10;

private void FindFile (DirectoryInfo dir, Regex regex) {
    indent += 10;
    txtResults.Text += new String (' ', indent) + dir.Name + " " +
        dir.LastAccessTime + "\r\n";
```

```
      FileInfo[] filesInDir = dir.GetFiles();
      foreach (FileInfo fi in filesInDir){
         Match match = regex.Match (fi.Name);
         if (match.Success){
            if (txtFileName.Text != String.Empty){
               txtFilesFound.Text += fi.FullName + "   " + fi.Length + "   " +
                  fi.Attributes + "\r\n";
            }
         }
      }
      DirectoryInfo[] dirs = dir.GetDirectories();
      foreach (DirectoryInfo di in dirs){
         FindFile(di, regex);
      }
      indent -= 10;
   }
```

Working with Initialization Information

It's often the case that a program needs initialization information. Usually, this does not involve lengthy pieces of data. The data may have to do with a user preference—for example, "start the application with a red background, and only show this year's data." Other pieces of initialization information may be more oriented towards the internal needs of a program—for example, the location of a required file, or the data needed to connect with a database.

This kind of information is usually stored in *key=value* pairs. It is used to be conventional to store this kind of data in *private profile files* (also called INI files)—text files consisting of key/value pairs named with a .ini suffix (see the sidebar).

INI Files

Although the classes provided under the .NET Framework no longer explicitly support private profile files, there are some cases in which INI files provide a more convenient mechanism for saving and retrieving initialization data than the system Registry or isolated storage. For example, INI files are easier to use for application-global settings such as database connections (since the settings for all users can be changed simply by distributing a new INI file if the server information changes).

Isolated storage is on a per-user basis. Best-practices use of the Registry is also per-user (generally under the HKEY_CURRENT_USER node)—although you can also store information on a "per–local system" basis in the Registry. This kind of per-user—or, at best, per–local system—arrangement is not very convenient when updating hundreds of systems at once; it is much easier to just send out a new initialization file to all the users of your application.

I bring this up because, supported classes or no, it's clearly easy enough to construct your own key/value initialization files to be placed in the same directory as your application. (You can use the technique shown in the isolated storage example in this section to parse the file.) There's no need to name the file with a .ini suffix; you might want to name it something like myapp.cfg.

NOTE   Win.ini and System.ini were examples of public INI files. It was really considered bad form to save private initialization information in these public files—but it could also be done.

In the due fullness of time, the system Registry came along. The Registry is actually a small database, and it is generally preferred to INI files for reading and writing initialization information. Classes provided by the .NET Framework support the Registry, and I'll show you how to use them later in this section.

There's always a next new, new thing in technology, and that's certainly the case in working with initialization information. .NET supports a concept called *isolated storage*. Using isolated storage, applications save data to a per-user data compartment. The CLR implements this data compartment as a directory in the file system, and the application is free to store whatever data it would like in files—of any kind—within the directory. Administrators can limit the amount of isolated storage available to applications.

In other words, isolated storage provides a place to save initialization data, but it does not impose a structure as to how that data is saved. It's nonetheless still common, even when using isolated storage, to store initialization data as key/value pairs. I'll show you an example later in this section.

Using the Registry

The Registry and RegistryKey classes, used for accessing the system Registry, are located in the Microsoft.Win32 namespace.

The static public fields of the Registry class, shown in Table 10.8, correspond to the nodes that are the standard roots in the Windows system Registry.

TABLE 10.8: *Registry* Class Fields

Field	Registry Key Equivalent	Typically Used For
ClassesRoot	HKEY_CLASSES_ROOT	Information about types and classes and their properties
CurrentConfig	HKEY_CURRENT_CONFIG	Per-system local hardware information
CurrentUser	HKEY_CURRENT_USER	Per-user preference information (organized per application)
DynData	HKEY_DYN_DATA	Dynamic data, such as real-time information provided by virtual device drivers (VxDs)
LocalMachine	HKEY_LOCAL_MACHINE	Per-system local configuration information
PerformanceData	HKEY_PERFORMANCE_DATA	Per-application performance counters
Users	HKEY_USERS	Contains a branch for each user of the local system, as well as a default user configuration for new users

In the example shown in Listing 10.3, an instance of the `RegistryKey` class is created by using the `Registry.CurrentUser` field (giving the Registry key a starting value of `HKEY_CURRENT_USER`):

```
RegistryKey theKey;
...
theKey = Registry.CurrentUser;
```

Returning the static Registry field creates an instance of `RegistryKey` without having to explicitly instantiate it.

Next, a new subkey named `SybexCSharp` is created under the `CurrentUser` key (and assigned back to the *theKey* variable):

```
theKey = theKey.CreateSubKey("SybexCSharp");
```

The key/value pair is written under the `SybexCSharp` node:

```
theKey.SetValue(txtKey.Text, txtValue.Text);
```

The `Close` method of the `RegistryKey` object, which closes it and flushes its contents to disk if they have been modified, is called in the `finally` clause of the code, so that it is sure to execute:

```
...
finally {
    theKey.Close();
}
```

If you run this code, you can enter a key pair to test that it works (Figure 10.3).

FIGURE 10.3:

The key/value pair shown will be saved under the SybexCSharp node, under HKEY_ CURRENT_USER.

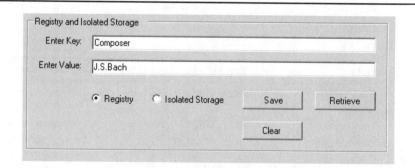

To verify that this has all worked as planned, open the Registry Editor (by selecting Run from the Windows Start menu, and opening `regedit` in the Run dialog). Find the `HKEY_ CURRENT_USER` node, locate `SybexCSharp`, and make sure that the key and value have been written to the Registry (Figure 10.4).

FIGURE 10.4:

Open the Registry Editor to verify that the key/value pair has been written to the Registry.

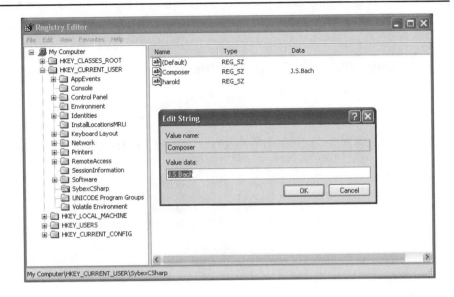

If your application is run by a user that does not have the right level of privileges under Windows XP, NT, and 2000 (the user should be a member of the Administrator group), it will not be able to write to the Registry.

Listing 10.3   Saving a Key/Value Pair to the Registry

```
using Microsoft.Win32;
...
RegistryKey theKey;

private void btnSave_Click(object sender, System.EventArgs e) {
    try {
        theKey = Registry.CurrentUser;
        theKey = theKey.CreateSubKey("SybexCSharp");
        theKey.SetValue(txtKey.Text, txtValue.Text);
    }
    catch (Exception excep) {
        MessageBox.Show (excep.Message);
    }
    finally {
        theKey.Close();
    }
}
```

Retrieving the value, presuming you know the key, follows the same general course, as shown in Listing 10.4.

Listing 10.4 **Retrieving a Value Using a Key from the Registry**

```
using Microsoft.Win32;
...
RegistryKey theKey;

private void btnRetrieve_Click(object sender, System.EventArgs e) {
    if (txtKey.Text != String.Empty){
        try {
            txtValue.Text = String.Empty;
            theKey = Registry.CurrentUser;
            theKey = theKey.CreateSubKey("SybexCSharp");
            txtValue.Text = (string)theKey.GetValue(txtKey.Text, String.Empty);
        }
        catch (Exception excep) {
            MessageBox.Show (excep.Message);
        }
        finally {
            theKey.Close();
            if (txtValue.Text == String.Empty)
                txtValue.Text = "Could not get value!";
        }
    }
}
```

First, a RegistryKey instance containing the SybexCSharp node is created:

```
RegistryKey theKey;
...
theKey = Registry.CurrentUser;
theKey = theKey.CreateSubKey("SybexCSharp");
```

The RegistryKey's GetValue method is used to retrieve the value:

```
txtValue.Text = (string)theKey.GetValue(txtKey.Text, String.Empty);
```

NOTE The return type of the GetValue method is object, so it needs to be explicitly cast to string. If the value doesn't exist, the second argument passed to GetValue is returned (in this case, the empty string). You can omit the second argument, in which case it will return null if no value is returned (either because the key doesn't exist, or because the value is empty).

In the `finally` clause, the `RegistryKey` is closed, and a message is displayed if a value cannot be obtained:

```
finally {
    theKey.Close();
    if (txtValue.Text == String.Empty)
        txtValue.Text = "Could not get value!";
}
```

If you take the sample program for a test spin, you'll see that if the key/value pair doesn't exist, you won't be able to obtain a value, whereas if there is a value associated with an existing key in the specified location, it will be returned in the Enter Value box.

Enter Key:	NotReallyAKey
Enter Value:	Could not get value!

Enter Key:	Palindrome
Enter Value:	a man a plan a canal panama

Isolated Storage

In discussing isolated storage, I am getting a little ahead of myself. To work with isolated storage, you'll need to use the `IsolatedStorageFileStream` class, which is derived from the `FileStream` class. The isolated storage example also shows one way to use `StreamWriter`s and `StreamReader`s. The `FileStream`, `StreamWriter`, and `StreamReader` classes are discussed in the subsequent sections of this chapter.

This apparent back-to-front order is okay. When you get to the discussion of how the `Stream` classes interrelate, it will be a little less theoretical since you'll have already seen them in action once.

To start with, `IsolatedStorageFileStream` is part of the `System.IO.IsolatedStorage` namespace, and `StreamWriter` and `StreamReader` belong to the `System.IO` namespace, so you'll need to include a `using` directive to both these namespaces:

```
using System.IO;
using System.IO.IsolatedStorage;
```

Next, use the constructor of the `IsolatedStorageFileStream` class to create an instance of the class:

```
IsolatedStorageFileStream isfs;
...
isfs = new IsolatedStorageFileStream ("isfs.hld", FileMode.Append);
```

The constructor is given a file name, which can be named anything you'd like (in this case, isfs.hld). This is the simplest of the IsolatedStorageFileStream constructors, and it also requires a System.IO.FileMode enumeration value. The FileMode enumeration specifies how the operating system should open a file. The values of this enumeration are shown in Table 10.9.

TABLE 10.9: *FileMode* Enumeration Values

Constant	How File Is Opened
Append	Opens the file if it exists and moves to the end of the file. If the file doesn't exist, a new file is created.
Create	Creates a new file. If the file already exists, it will be overwritten.
CreateNew	Creates a new file. If the file already exists, an IOException is thrown.
Open	Opens an existing file. A System.IO.FileNotFoundException is thrown if the file does not exist.
OpenOrCreate	Opens a file if it exists; if it does not, a new file is created.
Truncate	Opens an existing file and deletes the contents. An attempt to read from a file opened with Truncate throws an exception.

Next, use a StreamWriter constructor, with the IsolatedStorageFileStream instance as an argument, to create a StreamWriter:

```
writer = new StreamWriter (isfs);
```

Add a key/value pair to the isolated storage file using the WriteLine method of the StreamWriter:

```
string str = txtKey.Text + "=" + txtValue.Text;
writer.WriteLine (str);
```

In the finally block, flush and close the StreamWriter, and close the IsolatedStorageFileStream:

```
finally {
   writer.Flush();
   writer.Close();
   isfs.Close();
}
```

The code for saving a key/value pair to an isolated storage text file is shown in Listing 10.5. If you run it and add a few key/value pairs, you can then use the Windows Search facility to locate the file using the name specified in the code. Figure 10.5 shows where it turned up on my system, along with the contents of the file with a few key/value pairs.

FIGURE 10.5:

You can find where
your isolated storage is
by using the Windows
Search facility.

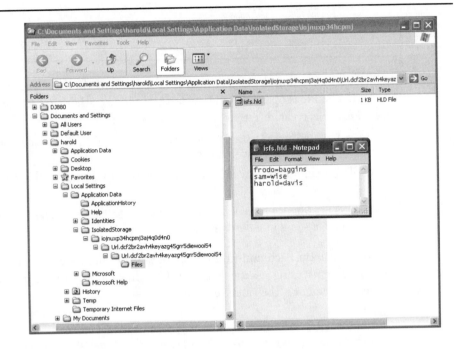

Listing 10.5   **Saving a Key/Value Pair to a Text File in Isolated Storage**

```csharp
using System.IO;
using System.IO.IsolatedStorage;
...
IsolatedStorageFileStream isfs;
StreamWriter writer;
StreamReader reader;

private void btnSave_Click(object sender, System.EventArgs e) {
    try {
        isfs = new IsolatedStorageFileStream ("isfs.hld", FileMode.Append);
        writer = new StreamWriter (isfs);
        string str = txtKey.Text + "=" + txtValue.Text;
        writer.WriteLine (str);
    }
    catch (Exception excep) {
        MessageBox.Show (excep.Message);
    }
    finally {
        writer.Flush();
```

```
        writer.Close();
        isfs.Close();
    }
}
```

Once again, reading the key/value pairs is essentially the same process as writing them, but reversed. The file is opened in `FileMode.Open` mode (rather than `FileMode.Append`), and a `StreamReader` is created (rather than a `StreamWriter`):

```
isfs = new IsolatedStorageFileStream ("isfs.hld", FileMode.Open);
reader = new StreamReader (isfs);
```

The file is read line by line in a `do...while` loop that runs until it hits a null line.

TIP   Reading a file within a loop until a null character (or line) is reached—which indicates the end of the file—is a standard technique.

Within the loop, each non-null line is split, using the static `String.Split` method, into an array of elements, using = as the delimiter. If the first element of the array matches the key, then the second element is the value returned:

```
do {
    lineOfText = reader.ReadLine();
    if ((lineOfText != null) && (lineOfText.IndexOf('=') != -1)) {
        string [] subStrs = lineOfText.Split('=');
        if (subStrs[0] == txtKey.Text){
            txtValue.Text = subStrs[1];
            break;
        }
    }
} while (lineOfText != null);
```

NOTE   You should be aware that there are some limitations to this parse for key/value pairs. If the value string itself contains an equal sign, the second equal sign and anything following it will not be returned. In addition, only the first occurrence of a key is matched. In other words, in a production situation, you should modify this code to fit your specific needs.

The complete click event procedure for retrieving a value using a key is shown in Listing 10.6.

Listing 10.6　　**Retrieving a Value Using a Key from a Text File in Isolated Storage**

```
using System.IO;
using System.IO.IsolatedStorage;
...
```

```
IsolatedStorageFileStream isfs;
StreamWriter writer;
StreamReader reader;

private void btnRetrieve_Click(object sender, System.EventArgs e) {
    try {
        txtValue.Text = String.Empty;
        isfs = new IsolatedStorageFileStream ("isfs.hld", FileMode.Open);
        reader = new StreamReader (isfs);
        string lineOfText = null;
        do {
            lineOfText = reader.ReadLine();
            if ((lineOfText != null) && (lineOfText.IndexOf('=') != -1)) {
                string [] subStrs = lineOfText.Split('=');
                if (subStrs[0] == txtKey.Text){
                    txtValue.Text = subStrs[1];
                    break;
                }
            }
        } while (lineOfText != null);
    }
    catch (Exception excep) {
        MessageBox.Show (excep.ToString());
    }
    finally {
        reader.Close();
        isfs.Close();
        if (txtValue.Text == String.Empty)
            txtValue.Text = "Could not get value!";
    }
}
```

XML Configuration Files

Yet another way to store initialization information is in XML configuration files. These files are stored in the same directory as a corresponding .NET executable, and have the same name as the executable with a `.config` extension added. For example, if an application were named `theApp.exe`, then its XML configuration file would be named `theApp.exe.config`.

It's easy to store information in an XML configuration file that is both human- and machine-readable. The classes in the `System.Configuration` namespace make it easy to access this data, which can include key/value pairs, from within a running application.

XML configuration files have the same advantage as INI files over mechanisms like the Registry or isolated storage: that is, if global changes are made to an application's startup data, many users can be updated all at once just by distributing a new file.

Continued on next page

A caveat is that there are no intrinsic .NET Framework methods for writing to XML configuration files. However, they can easily enough be edited by hand or by using some of the techniques described in Chapter 12, "Working with XML and ADO.NET."

For more information about XML configuration files, look up "Configuration Files" in online help.

Streams

In his great novel *The History of Henry Esmond*, the Victorian author William Makepeace Thackeray wrote:

> *What! does a stream rush out of a mountain free and pure, to roll through fair pastures, to feed and throw out bright tributaries, and to end in a village gutter?*

In our context, this quotation does to some degree convey the idea of *stream*. A digital stream is an abstract concept representing flows of information, or—a little less abstractly—flows of bytes. The stream comes from somewhere. A stream could come over the Web, transfer across a network, or be created in memory. When a file is opened for reading or writing, it becomes a stream.

In the .NET Framework, Stream is an abstract base class representing this concept. Various classes derive from Stream, the most important of which is FileStream (you've already seen IsolatedStorageFileStream, which derives from FileStream). Stream, and the classes that derive from it, are shown in Table 10.10 (unless otherwise noted, these classes can be found in the System.IO namespace).

TABLE 10.10: *Stream* and Its Derived Classes

Class	Purpose
BufferedStream	A stream that adds buffering to another stream. (FileStream already supports buffering.)
CryptoStream	A stream that is used to link data stream to cryptographic transformations. Located in the System.Security.Cryptography namespace.
FileStream	Supports reading and writing to files.
IsolatedStorageFileStream	Supports reading and writing to files in isolated storage (see example in previous section). Located in the System.IO.IsolatedStorage namespace.
MemoryStream	A stream whose data is available in memory. Not buffered, and primarily used for short-term storage.
NetworkStream	A stream across a network. Located in the System.Net.Sockets namespace.
Stream	Abstract base class that supports reading and writing bytes.

Streams—which, as you'll see later in this chapter, support both synchronous and asynchronous action—are used for reading, writing, random access, and searching (called "seeking") though a stream source. In truth, the bulk of streaming operations involve files—explaining why FileStream is the most important of the Stream classes.

How do you create a FileStream? There are two different routes. An instance of the class can be created using one of the class constructors. The constructor is passed the file name and enumeration values that indicate how the file should be opened.

Alternatively, some of the methods of the File and FileInfo classes—such as the Open method—return a FileStream object.

FileStream itself supports reading and writing bytes—and not much more. But once you have a FileStream, you can use it to instantiate objects used to make specific kinds of file operations easier. You do this by using an instance of a FileStream to create an object of the right class for the type of file and operation you want. (You can, in fact, use an instance of any class derived from Stream, but unless you have specific requirements for something like buffering or cryptography, you'll find yourself using FileStream most of the time.) The specific classes come generally in pairs, matched up as *type*Reader and *type*Writer:

- Although it is wise—when in doubt—to assume that a file is just plain binary, many times one knows that one is operating on a text file. Two different pairs of classes, derived from the abstract TextReader/TextWriter pair, make reading and writing text files a breeze:

  - The most commonly used of these two class pairs for text files is StreamReader/ StreamWriter, which reads characters from and writes them to a stream (see the example in the next section).

  - The StringReader/StringWriter class pair is an alternative—it reads from and writes to a file using the StringBuilder class as the underlying data type.

- On the other side of the fence, the BinaryReader/BinaryWriter classes extend the FileStream facilities available for working with binary files by allowing you to read and write encoded strings and primitive data types to a stream.

The relationships between objects based on the classes derived from Stream and the "Readers/ Writers" can be a bit confusing at first—but the diagram in Figure 10.6 should help to make it clearer.

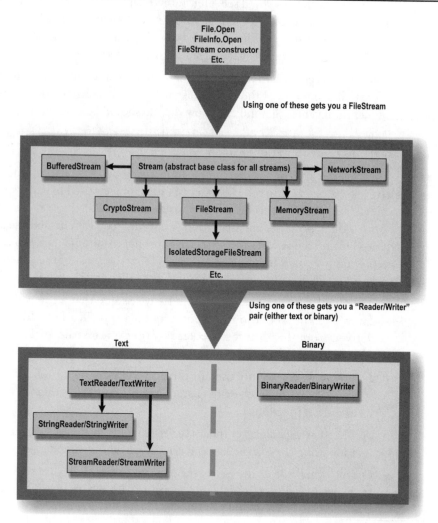

© Phyllis Davis 2002

Reading and Writing Text Files

The simplest way to deploy a StreamWriter is to use its Write method to save a block of text to a file. Similarly, the ReadToEnd method of a StreamReader can be used to retrieve a block of text from a file.

As an example, I'll show you how to save the contents of a multiline TextBox to a file selected by the user. The contents of a text file—including the one just saved—can then be retrieved by the user back into the TextBox. Common dialog controls (explained in Chapter 4, "Building a Better Windows Interface") are used to allow the user to choose a file for reading or writing.

Let's start with saving a block of text. A common dialog control is used to allow the user to select a file (Figure 10.7), and the file in which to save the text is stored in the variable *theFile*:

```
theFile = saveFileDialog1.FileName;
```

FIGURE 10.7:

Common dialog controls are used to choose a file for reading or writing.

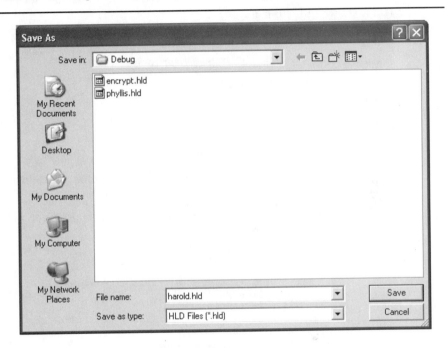

Next, within the `try` block, a `FileStream` is created:

```
fs = new FileStream(theFile, FileMode.Create);
```

NOTE See Table 10.9 earlier in this chapter for the meanings of the `FileMode` enumeration values.

The `FileStream` is used to create a `StreamWriter`:

```
writer = new StreamWriter(fs);
```

The `Write` method of the `StreamWriter` is used to save the text in the multiline TextBox to the file:

```
writer.Write (txtToSave.Text);
```

In the `finally` block, the `StreamWriter` and `FileStream` are closed:

```
finally {
    writer.Flush();
    writer.Close();
    fs.Close();
}
```

That's all, folks! The complete click procedure that lets a user select a file and then saves the text is shown in Listing 10.7.

Listing 10.7   **Using a *StreamWriter* to Save Text**

```
using System.IO;
...
StreamWriter writer;
FileStream fs;

private void btnSaveStream_Click(object sender, System.EventArgs e) {
    string theFile;
    saveFileDialog1.InitialDirectory = Application.ExecutablePath;
    saveFileDialog1.DefaultExt = "hld"; //custom format
    saveFileDialog1.FileName = "harold";
    saveFileDialog1.Filter = "HLD Files (*.hld)|*.hld|All Files (*.*) | *.*";
    saveFileDialog1.OverwritePrompt = true;
    saveFileDialog1.ShowDialog();
    theFile = saveFileDialog1.FileName;
    try {
        fs = new FileStream(theFile, FileMode.Create);
        writer = new StreamWriter(fs);
        writer.Write (txtToSave.Text);
    }
    catch (Exception excep) {
        MessageBox.Show (excep.Message);
    }
    finally {
        writer.Flush();
        writer.Close();
        fs.Close();
    }
}
```

Retrieving the text is just about as simple. With a user-selected file, once again a `FileStream` is created (this time in `Open` mode). Next, a `StreamReader` is created. The `StreamReader`'s `ReadToEnd` method is used to assign the entire contents of the opened text file to the `TextBox`:

```
theFile = openFileDialog1.FileName;
try {
    fs = new FileStream(theFile, FileMode.Open);
```

```
    reader = new StreamReader(fs);
    txtToSave.Text = reader.ReadToEnd();
}
```

In the finally block, the StreamReader and FileStream are closed:

```
finally {
    reader.Close();
    fs.Close();
}
```

When the user runs the complete program (Listing 10.8), the text in the file that the user selects is displayed in the TextBox (Figure 10.8).

FIGURE 10.8:

The StreamReader reads the text in the selected file into the multiline TextBox.

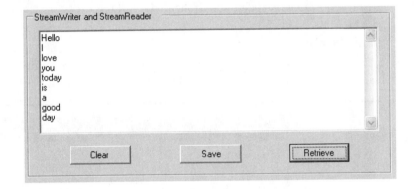

Listing 10.8   **Using a *StreamReader* to Retrieve Text**

```
using System.IO;
...
StreamReader reader;
FileStream fs;

private void btnRetrieveStr_Click(object sender, System.EventArgs e) {
    string theFile;
    openFileDialog1.InitialDirectory = Application.ExecutablePath;
    openFileDialog1.DefaultExt = "hld"; //custom format
    openFileDialog1.FileName = "harold";
    openFileDialog1.Filter = "HLD Files (*.hld)|*.hld|All Files (*.*) | *.*";
    if (openFileDialog1.ShowDialog() == DialogResult.OK){
        theFile = openFileDialog1.FileName;
        try {
            fs = new FileStream(theFile, FileMode.Open);
            reader = new StreamReader(fs);
            txtToSave.Text = reader.ReadToEnd();
        }
        catch (Exception excep) {
```

```
            MessageBox.Show (excep.ToString());
        }
        finally {
            reader.Close();
            fs.Close();
        }
    }
}
```

NOTE   Listing 10.8 shows a check for the DialogResult value (if (openFileDialog1...)), and Listing 10.7 does not. There's no practical reason in these particular procedures to do it one way rather than the other, but I thought I'd show you both. For stylistic reasons, I slightly prefer including the explicit check of the dialog's result.

Binary Files

The user interface shown in Figure 10.9 is used to demonstrate reading and writing binary files. Once again, common dialogs let the user select files for reading or writing.

FIGURE 10.9:

Text is saved and retrieved using binary files.

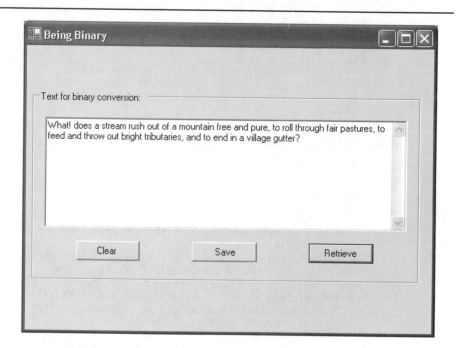

Out of pure orneriness, I've elected to demonstrate saving and retrieving text to and from binary files. If you knew it was text, you probably wouldn't want to do it this way, since working with StreamReaders and StreamWriters is easier. But then again, what if you aren't sure it's a text file?

The BinaryWriter class Write method is overloaded. You can use variants of it to write many different kinds of simple types to binary files. Many of these overloads are shown in the Object Browser in Figure 10.10.

FIGURE 10.10:

The overloaded variants of the BinaryWriter .Write method allow you to easily write a variety of primitive types to a binary file.

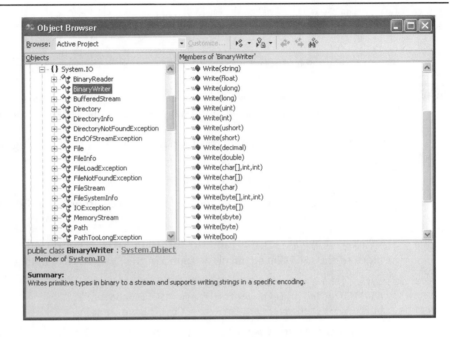

But before we get to the BinaryWriter, let's have a look at what it takes to write the contents of the TextBox to a binary file using a raw FileStream (the code is shown in Listing 10.9).

Listing 10.9   Writing Text to a Binary File Using a *FileStream*

```
using System.IO;
using System.Text;
...
Stream theStream;
const int SizeBuff = 2048;
...
private void btnSaveStream_Click(object sender, System.EventArgs e) {
    string theFile;
    ... // Common dialog stuff
    theFile = saveFileDialog1.FileName;
    try {
        theStream = File.OpenWrite(theFile);
        byte [] buffer = new Byte[SizeBuff];
        ASCIIEncoding byteConverter = new ASCIIEncoding();
        buffer = byteConverter.GetBytes (txtToSave.Text);
```

```
        theStream.Write (buffer, 0, buffer.Length);
    }
    catch (Exception excep) {
        MessageBox.Show (excep.Message);
    }
    finally {
        theStream.Close();
    }
}
```

In the code shown in Listing 10.9, it is assumed that the user has selected a file to write to, using a common dialog, with the name saved in the variable *theFile*.

First, a stream is instantiated, this time for the sake of variety using the File.OpenWrite method:

```
theStream = File.OpenWrite(theFile);
```

Using a FileStream, the only type we get to work with is bytes. So let's change our text to bytes!

An array of bytes is created, and the text to be saved is converted into the array using an instance of the ASCIIEncoding class (found in the System.Text namespace):

```
byte [] buffer = new Byte[SizeBuff];
ASCIIEncoding byteConverter = new ASCIIEncoding();
buffer = byteConverter.GetBytes (txtToSave.Text);
```

Finally, the byte array is written to the stream:

```
theStream.Write (buffer, 0, buffer.Length);
```

and the stream closed:

```
theStream.Close();
```

This is actually considerably simpler using a BinaryWriter—we can just directly write the string type to the file:

```
theStream = File.OpenWrite(theFile);
bw = new BinaryWriter (theStream);
bw.Write (txtToSave.Text);
```

Listing 10.10 shows the click event (once again, without the common dialog portion) that uses a BinaryWriter to save text to a binary file.

Listing 10.10   **Writing Text to a Binary File Using a *BinaryWriter***

```
using System.IO;
...
Stream theStream;
```

```
BinaryWriter bw;
const int SizeBuff = 2048;
...
private void btnSaveStream_Click(object sender, System.EventArgs e) {
   string theFile;
   ... // Common dialog stuff
   theFile = saveFileDialog1.FileName;
   try {
      theStream = File.OpenWrite(theFile);
      bw = new BinaryWriter (theStream);
      bw.Write (txtToSave.Text);
   catch (Exception excep) {
      MessageBox.Show (excep.Message);
   }
   finally {
      bw.Flush();
      bw.Close();
      theStream.Close();
   }
}
```

Listing 10.11 shows how you can use a BinaryReader's ReadString method to read a binary file containing string data (once again, the material related to the common dialog is left out of the listing for clarity).

Listing 10.11   Reading String Data from a Binary File Using a *BinaryReader*

```
using System.IO;
...
Stream theStream;
BinaryReader br;
const int SizeBuff = 2048;

private void btnRetrieveStr_Click(object sender, System.EventArgs e) {
   string theFile;
   ... // Common Dialog code omitted
   theFile = openFileDialog1.FileName;
   try {
      theStream = File.OpenRead(theFile);
      br = new BinaryReader (theStream);
      txtToSave.Text = br.ReadString();
   }
   catch (Exception excep) {
      MessageBox.Show (excep.Message);
   }
   finally {
      br.Close();
      theStream.Close();
   }
}
```

Listing 10.12 shows how you could achieve the same thing using the `FileStream` without the `BinaryReader`, and reading the text into a byte array and then converting it to a string.

Listing 10.12   **Using a *FileStream* to Read a Byte Array, and Converting It to String**

```csharp
using System.IO;
using System.Text;
...
Stream theStream;
const int SizeBuff = 2048;
private void btnRetrieveStr_Click(object sender, System.EventArgs e) {
    string theFile;
    ... // Common Dialog code omitted
    theFile = openFileDialog1.FileName;
    try {
        theStream = File.OpenRead(theFile);
        byte [] buffer = new Byte[SizeBuff];
        FileInfo fi = new FileInfo (theFile);
        int byteCount = (int) fi.Length;
        theStream.Read (buffer, 0, byteCount);
        ASCIIEncoding byteConverter = new ASCIIEncoding();
        txtToSave.Text = byteConverter.GetString (buffer);
    }
    catch (Exception excep) {
        MessageBox.Show (excep.Message);
    }
    finally {
        theStream.Close();
    }
}
```

Web Streams

It's quite easy to read a web page as a stream using the classes in the `System.Net` namespace and a `StreamReader`. (This is a process sometimes called "screen scraping.")

To start with, use the `WebRequest.Create` method to create an `HttpWebRequest` object (using a URL as an argument):

```csharp
HttpWebRequest wreq = (HttpWebRequest) WebRequest.Create(theURL);
```

NOTE   WebRequest.Create is a static method that returns different object instances depending on what is passed in. Since the return type of the method is WebRequest, it must be cast to HttpWebRequest.

The `HttpWebRequest` statement establishes a connection to a web page. Next, the `GetResponse` method of the `HttpWebRequest` object is used to load the connected page into an `HttpWebResponse`:

```csharp
HttpWebResponse wres = (HttpWebResponse) wreq.GetResponse();
```

Using the `HttpWebResponse` object, a `StreamReader` can be created:

```
sr = new StreamReader (wres.GetResponseStream(), Encoding.Default);
```

This `StreamReader` can be used like any other `StreamReader`. Specifically, its `ReadToEnd` method can be used to load the contents of the web page into a TextBox:

```
txtResults.Text = sr.ReadToEnd()
```

The results of reading a web page into the TextBox are shown in Figure 10.11, and the complete click event code for doing so is shown in Listing 10.13.

FIGURE 10.11:

You can use a `FileStream` to read the contents of a web page.

Listing 10.13   **Reading a Web Page as a Stream**

```
using System.IO;
using System.Net;
using System.Text;
...
StreamReader sr;
HttpWebRequest wreq;
```

```
private void btnEngage_Click(object sender, System.EventArgs e) {
   string theURL = txtURL.Text;
   txtResults.Text = String.Empty;
   try {
      HttpWebRequest wreq = (HttpWebRequest) WebRequest.Create(theURL);
      HttpWebResponse wres = (HttpWebResponse) wreq.GetResponse();
      sr = new StreamReader (wres.GetResponseStream(), Encoding.Default);
      txtResults.Text = sr.ReadToEnd();
   }
   catch (Exception excep) {
      MessageBox.Show (excep.Message);
   }
   finally {
      sr.Close();
   }
}
```

WARNING   Obviously, using this technique, you can "screen scrape" any web page. I generally hate hectoring adults. However, please be sure that you have copyright permission to use the text and HTML of any page that you choose to retrieve this way.

Asynchronous I/O

In Chapter 3, "Windows Uses Web Services, Too!," I showed you the general design pattern for asynchronous invocation, in the context of web services.

You'll probably not be surprised to learn that the FileStream class supports asynchronous invocation as well—using the same design pattern explained in Chapter 3. This means that FileStream provides BeginRead and BeginWrite methods that reference an AsyncCallback object. These methods return an IAsyncResult object that can be queried to determine the status of the asynchronous operation.

Asynchronous I/O operations can be performed using any class derived from Stream. In particular, you might want to initiate asynchronous invocation of a FileStream if you had a big file to read and wanted your program to be able to do other things while reading besides twiddling its virtual thumbs.

Listing 10.14 shows an example of asynchronous use of a FileStream in the context of the web streaming example from the last section. While the web page is being read by the FileStream, a display counter is incremented. As shown in Figure 10.12, when the asynchronous read operation completes, a message box is displayed.

FIGURE 10.12:

FileStreams support
asynchronous as well as
synchronous operation.

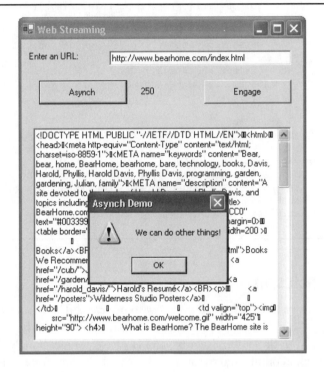

Listing 10.14   **Asynchronously Using a *FileStream* to Read a Web Page**

```
using System.IO;
using System.Net;
using System.Text;
...
StreamReader sr;
HttpWebRequest wreq;

private void btnAsynch_Click(object sender, System.EventArgs e) {
    string theURL = txtURL.Text;
    long counter = 0;
    txtResults.Text = String.Empty;
    try {
        AsyncCallback cb = new AsyncCallback (IOCallback);
        wreq = (HttpWebRequest) WebRequest.Create(theURL);
        IAsyncResult ar = wreq.BeginGetResponse(cb, null);
        while (!ar.IsCompleted){
            Application.DoEvents();
            counter ++;
```

```
            lblCounter.Text = counter.ToString();
        }
        MessageBox.Show ("We can do other things!", "Asynch Demo",
            MessageBoxButtons.OK, MessageBoxIcon.Exclamation);
    }
    catch (Exception excep) {
        MessageBox.Show (excep.Message);
    }
    finally {
        sr.Close();
    }
}
private void IOCallback (IAsyncResult ar){
    HttpWebResponse wres = (HttpWebResponse) wreq.EndGetResponse(ar);
    sr = new StreamReader (wres.GetResponseStream(), Encoding.Default);
    txtResults.Text = sr.ReadToEnd();
    sr.Close();
}
```

Conclusion

In this chapter, I showed you how to use the .NET Framework classes that provide information about files and the file system. Next, I showed you how to store and retrieve initialization data from the system Registry and isolated storage. Finally, I moved on to the large topic of input and output and streams, and showed you how to read and write information to and from files and other sources.

These topics may not be the most exciting on the planet, but the relationship of your programs to files, the file system, and other sources of streaming data is very important. In addition, use of appropriate initialization information gives you a chance to get your program going with the "right foot forward" and give a good first impression.

Almost every program needs these things. So I've included this chapter as a good first step towards connecting your projects with the rest of the world.

CHAPTER 11

Messaging

- Subclassing Windows messages

- Understanding *MessageQueues*

- Creating queues and messages

- Receiving and replying to messages

- Message queues and application architecture

- Asynchronous peeking and receiving

With a nod to the singer Madonna, we live in a world that is both material and asynchronous. This is probably a good thing; who among us would want their every activity dictated by a central mechanism, comparable to linear, top-down code execution? At the same time, mechanisms *are* needed to keep us in touch and to facilitate teamwork. These distributed, peer-to-peer mechanisms are usually asynchronous in real life (for example, you call someone and ask them if they would do something for you).

Successful software starts by mimicking the real-world activity it is intended to aid or replace. (Put differently, if you don't understand the real-world problem, you certainly can't write good programs to help with it.) This leads to the supposition that programs of any complexity—or groups of programs—ought to operate asynchronously, as real-life processes do. Only the simplest linear, non-event-driven program can really be expected to behave synchronously—meaning, to always execute commands in a predictable, top-to-bottom fashion, waiting for one command to finish processing before embarking on the next.

Under Windows and .NET, you have several tools that enable asynchronous intra-program design. The principal mechanism is firing events and writing the code that responds to these events. (A less-optimal mechanism is to throw and respond to exceptions, but this is not a recommended practice.)

As you probably know, the mechanism behind Windows itself—and any form that you use to create a Windows application—is a giant, asynchronous messaging loop. When the user moves the mouse, this causes a message to be sent. All the messages that are floating around a Windows application are processed in a giant switch statement, which is always asynchronously waiting for messages—with appropriate action taken when a particular message is encountered.

As an illustration of how a complex program can use messaging to enable asynchronous execution, I'll start this chapter by showing you how to look at the Windows message stream. I'll briefly show you how to intercept these messages—a process called *subclassing*, although it should not be confused with deriving a class via inheritance.

The main topic of this chapter, then, is how to use the classes in the System.Messaging namespace to add messages to a queue, to retrieve messages from a queue, and, generally, to facilitate asynchronous program design, both intra- and inter-program.

Observing Windows Messages

Subclassing is a technique that lets you intercept, observe, and process messages going from Windows to a form or windowing control.

NOTE   The Message class used with Windows, System.Windows.Forms.Message, is different from the Message class used with message queues, System.Messaging.Message, discussed in other sections of this chapter. To avoid an ambiguous reference, you'll need to qualify the Message class when you use it, so the compiler knows which one you are talking about if both the System.Windows.Forms and System.Messaging namespaces are referenced in your project.

In earlier versions of Visual Basic, subclassing was needed as a "down and dirty" tool to get around limitations of the language. Many things could not be accomplished without subclassing; for example, it was required in order to enforce limits on form size.

There should rarely be a need to use subclassing in the more powerful and rigorous Visual Basic .NET; for example, form size limits can be enforced using the form class MinimumSize and MaximumSize properties. But in some languages and in some situations, subclassing is still an instructive technique for having a look at what is going on behind the curtains in Windows.

The System.Windows.Forms.Form class exposes the WndProc method, which is invoked for every message sent by Windows to the form. Using the Object Browser, as shown in Figure 11.1, we can determine that WndProc is a member of Control, the class from which Form is ultimately derived, and that it is marked protected and virtual—meaning that you can override it in any class derived from Form.

FIGURE 11.1:

Using the Object Browser, one can see that the WndProc procedure has been marked with the protected and virtual attributes.

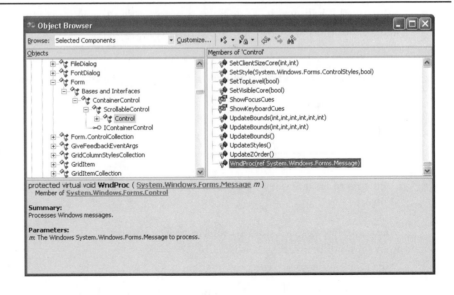

The Object Browser also tells us (Figure 11.2) that the `Message` object that is the parameter of `WndProc` exposes properties. These include `Msg`, which is a numerical ID; `HWnd`, which is the handle—or identification—of the window; and `LParam` and `WParam`, which are message-specific arguments. (Another property, `Result`, is the value that will be returned to Windows.)

FIGURE 11.2:

The members of the `System.Windows.Forms.Message` class include an ID number.

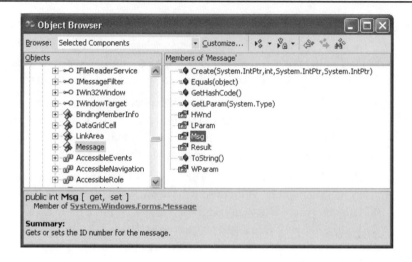

Listing 11.1 shows the code necessary to display the Windows messages sent to a form's `WndProc` method in the Output window.

Listing 11.1   **Viewing Windows Messages in the Output Window**

```
protected override void WndProc(ref Message m){
    base.WndProc(ref m);
    Debug.WriteLine(m);
}
```

NOTE   Be sure to include a `using System.Diagnostics` directive so that you can use the `Debug` object.

In most cases, you'll want to start with a call to the base class `WndProc` method, so that the messages will be processed normally:

```
base.WndProc(ref m);
```

If you start this code in debug mode, and open the Output window if it isn't already visible, you'll see many Windows messages (Figure 11.3)—for example, one for every time you move the mouse over the form.

FIGURE 11.3:

Windows messages
sent by the application
can be viewed in the
Output window.

Subclassing a Message

Supposing you do want to do something with a Windows message, it is easy enough. To
see how, let's write a very short override to WndProc that intercepts the WM_MOUSEMOVE and
WM_MOUSELEAVE messages. (The first of these is sent when the mouse moves on a window, the
second when the mouse cursor leaves a window.)

The value of the ID stored in the Msg parameter for WM_MOUSEMOVE is hexadecimal 0x200, and
WM_MOUSELEAVE is 0x2a3. (This can be seen in the Debug output shown in Figure 11.3.) Trans-
lating these values to decimals, I can set up constants that are their equivalent:

```
const int WM_MOUSEMOVE = 512;
const int WM_MOUSELEAVE = 675;
```

It's no problem now to write our own switch statement that intercepts each message, changing the form's text and cursor on a mouse movement (WM_MOUSEMOVE) and changing them once
again when a WM_MOUSELEAVE is intercepted, as shown in Listing 11.2. If you run this code, you'll
see that the text and cursor do, indeed, change back and forth to reflect the message subclassing.

Listing 11.2   **Subclassing Mouse-Move and Mouse-Leave Messages**

```
protected override void WndProc(ref Message m) {
    base.WndProc(ref m);
    const int WM_MOUSEMOVE = 512;
    const int WM_MOUSELEAVE = 675;
    switch (m.Msg) {
        case WM_MOUSEMOVE:
            this.Text = "Mouse is moving...";
            this.Cursor = Cursors.Hand;
            break;
        case WM_MOUSELEAVE:
            this.Text = "Hello, again!";
            this.Cursor = Cursors.Default;
            break;
    }
}
```

WARNING   Once again, the code shown in Listing 11.2 started by invoking the base class WndProc method, so that messages could get processed normally. If you don't invoke the base class method, the window won't even display, and attempting to open the window by running the form class will throw an exception ("Error creating window handle").

NOTE   Since both MouseLeave and MouseMove are events supplied with a form, you could place code in the related event handler procedures—implying that there is no reason you'd ever need to subclass for these two messages.

If messaging works to organize a program that is as complex as Windows, why not consider it as architecture for your own solutions?

MessageQueue Preliminaries

As you'll recall from the discussion of the Queue class in Chapter 7, "Arrays, Indexers, and Collections," a queue is a first in, first out data structure. An object can be *enqueued* (or *pushed*), in which case it is placed on the end of the queue. An object can be *dequeued* (or *popped*), which means it is retrieved—and removed—from the front of the queue. Alternatively, *peeking* at a queue means to have a look at the front object on the queue without removing it.

Message queues, as implemented in the System.Messaging.MessageQueue class, work in exactly this fashion—although, as you'll see, the terminology differs a bit. The objects on the queue are messages as implemented in the System.Messaging.Messages class. (As noted earlier, these are quite different from objects of the System.Windows.Forms.Message class.)

A good way to think of these messages is as an analog to e-mail (or instant messaging) that people use to communicate—except that these messages are used for communication within or between software applications.

Message queues under the Windows operating systems come in three varieties:

Public queues   Allow machines on a network to send and receive messages across the network.

Private queues   Visible only on a local machine.

System queues   Primarily used for administrative purposes, although applications that need access to a journal queue (which saves copies of messages as they are processed), acknowledgment, and auditing facilities can use these queues.

Formerly a separate product called MSMQ, message queuing is now part of Windows XP and Windows 2000 (however, as I'll show you shortly, you may need to install it). It is additionally available to Windows NT users as part of the NT4 Options Pack. MSMQ services are not available for the Windows 98 or Windows Me family of products. In addition, public (as opposed to private) message queuing cannot be run using non-Server versions of NT or 2000.

NOTE   The examples in this chapter use private queues but would essentially be the same if public queues were involved. (You can substitute one of the GetPublicQueues methods for the GetPrivateQueuesByMachine method shown in one of the examples.)

Before we move on to making sure that you have message queuing installed, let's back up for a second and ask, what is message queuing likely to be good for?

First, one could easily see how messaging could be used as an architecture to divide up computationally intensive tasks. This could happen within a single large application or across multiple applications.

NOTE   In some cases, you may need to consider issues around giving multiple programs access to the same resource, such as a file. In this case, you may need to apply specific locking conditions to the resource to prevent conflicts using synchronization objects. For more information, look up "Synchronization" in online help.

An application might send out messages saying what it is doing and providing interim results that could be used by other applications performing related tasks. One of the tasks might be to find certain text on the Internet; a vast army of "crawlers" might go out to parse the text behind web pages—for example, using the screen scraping technique explained at the end of Chapter 10, "Working with Streams and Files." A crawler might send out messages like "I found it" or "Completed assignment without finding requested text."

Workflow like this facilitates peer-to-peer divisions of load. It also makes conceivable a scenario like the one proposed by David Gerlernter in his seminal book about the future of computing, *Mirror Worlds* (Oxford University Press, 1992), in which myriad applications are set loose to create their own world within a world in the computer as part of the ultimate object-oriented paradigm.

On a more mundane level, message queues encourage self-reporting. An application could cause each server in a large network to send out messages with traffic and status statistics. An automated administrative program could use these messages to route incoming traffic.

NOTE   Microsoft message queuing is somewhat limited for this kind of activity, because it is limited to servers using Microsoft operating systems. Most large networks are Unix-only or are *heterogeneous*—that is, they include servers using a variety of operating systems, such as Linux, Unix, and Windows.

Making Sure Message Queuing Is Installed

To begin with, you should verify that messaging is installed on a server that you are connected to, or you should use the Services applet to make sure that the Message Queuing service has been installed and is started (Figure 11.4). (To open the Services applet in Windows XP, select Control Panel from the Start menu, double-click Administrative Tools, and double-click the Services shortcut.)

FIGURE 11.4:

You can check the Services application to make sure that Message Queuing is installed and started.

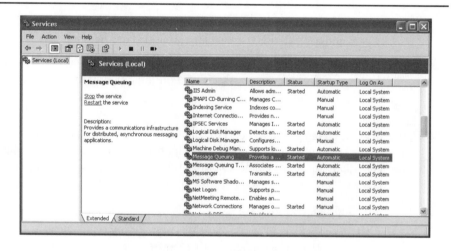

In the Services applet, if the Message Queuing service is not shown as running, click the Start link to start the service. You can also right-click the Message Queuing service, select Properties from the context menu, and set it for Automatic startup (if the service hasn't already been configured this way).

If you don't see the Message Queuing service in the Services applet, then it probably has not been installed. To remedy this under Windows XP, double-click the Add or Remove Programs link in the Control Panel. In the Add or Remove Programs dialog, click Add/Remove Windows Components. The Windows Components Wizard will open. As shown in Figure 11.5, make sure that Message Queuing is selected, click Next, and follow the instructions to complete the installation.

FIGURE 11.5:

The Windows
Component Wizard
is used to install the
Message Queuing
application on
a system.

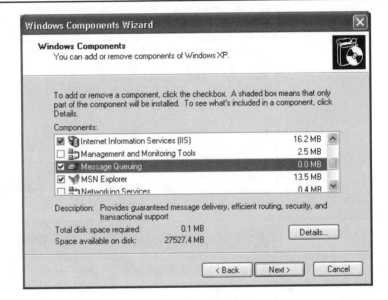

If you open a new Visual C# .NET project in the Visual Studio development environment, you won't see the System.Messaging namespace in the Object Browser, and the classes in that namespace will not be usable. As a preliminary, you must add a reference to System.Messaging .dll. To do this, select Project ➤ Add Reference (alternatively, highlight the project in Solution Explorer, right-click, and select Add Reference from the context menu). The Add Reference dialog will open.

Using the .NET tab of the Add Reference dialog, highlight System.Messaging.dll and click Select. The DLL will appear in the Selected Components list at the bottom of the Add Reference dialog (Figure 11.6). Click OK to add the reference. The classes in the System.Messaging namespace will then appear in the Object browser (Figure 11.7).

FIGURE 11.6:

A reference to the
selected component
(System.Messaging)
will be added to the
current project.

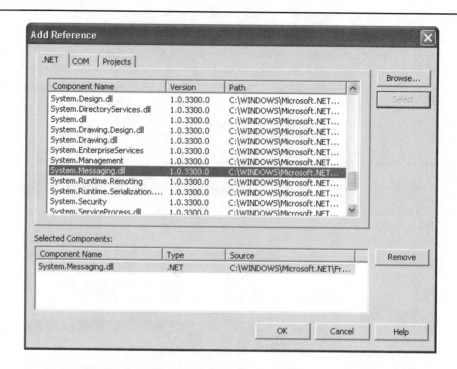

FIGURE 11.7:

With Message Queuing
installed and a reference
to the System.Messaging
component added, the
System.Messaging
namespace and the
Messaging classes
appear in the Object
Browser.

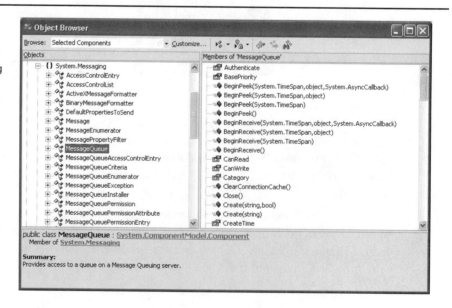

NOTE   Code that uses the `System.Messaging` namespace should include a `using System.Messaging` directive. In the interests of clarity, I've omitted these directives from the program listings in the remainder of this chapter.

In most cases, by their very nature, applications organized around message queues are, in fact, asynchronous. (If I'm going about my business doing things but waiting to get a message from you that you've completed a task, and providing a result, then I am behaving asynchronously.) But as you'll see in the examples in this chapter, messages can be popped off a queue—or peeked at—either synchronously or asynchronously. In other words, even though the whole process of message queuing is essentially asynchronous by definition, it is possible to add another level of asynchronism on top of this.

NOTE   The examples in this chapter show creating and using message queues in code. You should know, however, that the Message Queue item on the components tab of the Toolbar makes it easy to set the properties of public queues using the Properties window (rather than code), provided you are connected to a server that supports public queues. I'll leave it to your personal taste whether you prefer to set properties using code or in the Properties window.

Working with Message Queues and Messages

In order to work with `MessageQueue` objects, you need to know how to create or join a queue. Next, you need to know how to push a `Message` object onto the queue (by *sending* it) and how to pop one off the front of the queue (by *receiving* it).

NOTE   In this section, I'll show you how to receive messages synchronously. In the example toward the end of the chapter, I'll show you how to receive—and peek—asynchronously.

You also might want to retrieve a list of all the current queues and—with a queue from this list selected—to retrieve all the messages on one queue.

This is a lot of programmatic ground to cover, so let's get started. The first example shows an application that sends and receives messages to itself. From a coding standpoint, it doesn't make much difference if the message is received by the application that sent it or by another application.

Creating or Joining a Queue

Listing 11.3 shows joining a queue—or creating a queue if it doesn't already exist—using the name supplied by the user in a TextBox.

Listing 11.3 **Creating or Joining a Queue**

```
MessageQueue mq;
private void btnCreate_Click(object sender, System.EventArgs e) {
    if (txtQName.Text != String.Empty) {
        string qpath = @".\Private$\" + txtQName.Text;
        if (!MessageQueue.Exists(qpath))
            MessageQueue.Create (qpath);
        mq = new MessageQueue(qpath);
    }
    else
        MessageBox.Show ("Please enter a Queue name!", "No path",
            MessageBoxButtons.OK, MessageBoxIcon.Error);
}
```

The name of the queue is built up by appending the name supplied by the user to the verbatim string `@".\Private$\"` (which specifies that a private queue on the current machine is being created):

```
string qpath = @".\Private$\" + txtQName.Text;
```

NOTE For an explanation of verbatim strings, see Chapter 9, "Everything Is String Manipulation."

It's then an easy matter to create the `MessageQueue` if it doesn't already exist, as determined by the `MessageQueue.Exists` property:

```
if (!MessageQueue.Exists(qpath))
    MessageQueue.Create (qpath);
```

One way or another, a `MessageQueue` with the requisite name now exists, and we can instantiate it in our class-level variable *mq*:

```
mq = new MessageQueue(qpath);
```

If you run this code and enter a queue name (as shown in Figure 11.8), you can use Server Explorer to verify that it has been created (I'll show you Server Explorer in just a moment).

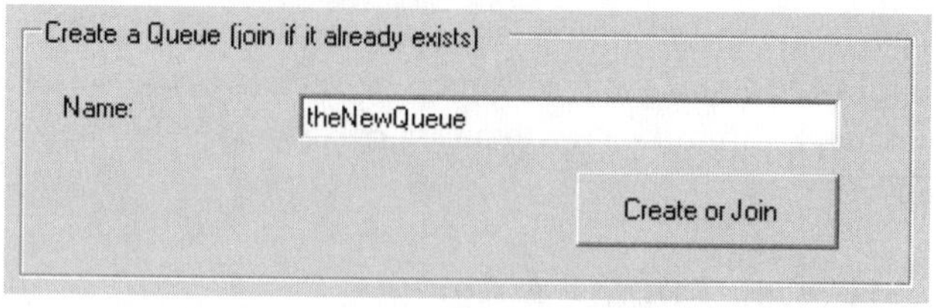

FIGURE 11.8:

It's easy to join an existing queue (or create the queue if it doesn't already exist).

Sending a Message

To send a message—that is, to push a `Message` object onto the queue—is pretty easy. The first step is to apply a *formatter* to the `MessageQueue`:

```
mq.Formatter = new BinaryMessageFormatter();
```

Message Formatters

Message formatters, which implement the `IMessageFormatter` interface, can be applied to Messages or to a `MessageQueue` as whole. The job of the message formatter is to produce a stream to be written to or read from a message body. Clearly, you want to deformat a message with the same formatter used to add it to the queue.

There are three formatters to choose from, supplied in the `System.Messaging` namespace:

ActiveXMessageFormatter   Used when sending or receiving COM components.

BinaryMessageFormatter   Used to serialize the message into a binary representation.

XMLMessageFormatter   The default formatter; serializes the message to and from XML.

Although XMLMessageFormatter is a little slower than `BinaryMessageFormatter`, one can do some pretty cool things with XMLMessageFormatter (for example, it is standard practice to deserialize a message using XMLMessageFormatter into specified elements of an XML schema). For further information, look up "XMLMessageFormatter" in online help.

Next, the `MessageQueue`'s Send method is used to push a message onto the queue:

```
mq.Send (txtMsg.Text, txtSubject.Text);
```

In the example shown, an optional subject heading, called the *label*, has been sent along with the text of the message.

NOTE   Since the first parameter of the Send method is of type `object`, the example implicitly constructs a Message object, using the text string entered by the user to instantiate it (the string becomes the *body* of the message). But if you needed to, you could explicitly instantiate a Message object using one of the Message class constructors and then set Message instance properties, such as `DigitalSignature`, `Priority`, `UseTracing`, etc.

TIP   It's important to understand that you can send any object as a message, not limited to just text. This includes the possibility of sending objects based on classes you have designed yourself.

Listing 11.4 shows the code for sending the relatively simple message.

Listing 11.4 **Sending a Message**

```
MessageQueue mq;
...
private void btnSend_Click(object sender, System.EventArgs e) {
    if (txtMsg.Text != String.Empty){
        if (mq != null){
            mq.Formatter = new BinaryMessageFormatter();
            mq.Send (txtMsg.Text, txtSubject.Text);
            txtMsg.Text = String.Empty;
            txtSubject.Text = String.Empty;
        }
        else
            MessageBox.Show ("Please create or select a Queue!", "No queue",
                MessageBoxButtons.OK, MessageBoxIcon.Error);
    }
    else
        MessageBox.Show ("Please enter a Message!", "No text",
            MessageBoxButtons.OK, MessageBoxIcon.Error);
}
```

If you run the code, you can enter a message and a subject line (Figure 11.9).

FIGURE 11.9:

When you send a message, it is placed at the end of the queue.

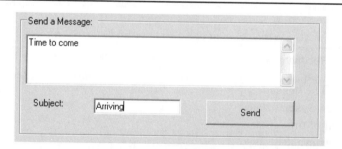

Next, click Send, and open Server Explorer (View ➢ Server Explorer). Expand the node for the server hosting the message queue. You'll find Private Queues beneath the Message Queues node. Within Private Queues, there will be a node for the newly created queue, and each message on the queue will be listed by subject label (Figure 11.10).

FIGURE 11.10:

If you open Server Explorer, the messages in a queue will be labeled with their subject.

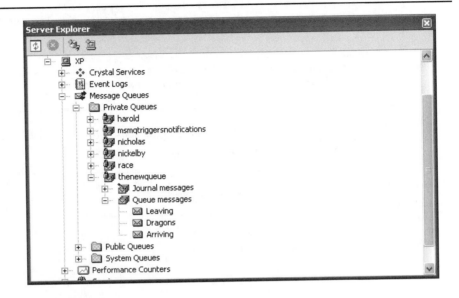

Retrieving a Message

To retrieve the first message on the queue synchronously, use the Receive method of the MessageQueue object with a TimeSpan instance:

```
System.Messaging.Message msg = mq.Receive (new TimeSpan(0,0,5));
```

> **NOTE** Receiving a message asynchronously is covered later in this chapter.

The MessageQueue Receive method stores a reference to the first message on the queue in a new System.Messaging.Message instance. The System.TimeSpan instance represents an interval of time—TimeSpan(0,0,5) means five seconds—that execution will wait for the message retrieval (this is sometimes referred to as a *timeout* parameter). If a timeout is not supplied, the execution will wait indefinitely for the message.

The code shown in Listing 11.5 starts with a check to make sure that there are some messages on the queue in question, using the Length property of the array of Message instances returned by the GetAllMessages method.

Listing 11.5   **Retrieving the Message at the Head of the Queue**

```
MessageQueue mq;
...
private void btnRetrieve_Click(object sender, System.EventArgs e) {
    if (mq.GetAllMessages().Length > 0) {
```

```
        mq.Formatter = new BinaryMessageFormatter();
        System.Messaging.Message msg = mq.Receive (new TimeSpan(0,0,5));
        txtRetrieve.Text = msg.Body.ToString();
    }
    else
        MessageBox.Show ("Nothing on the queue!", "No messages",
            MessageBoxButtons.OK, MessageBoxIcon.Error);
}
```

The code shown in Listing 11.5 converts the Body property of the Message instance to string and displays it, as shown in Figure 11.11.

FIGURE 11.11:

The Receive method retrieves the message at the "head" of the queue.

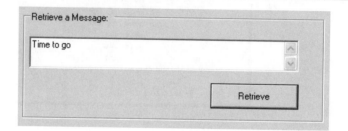

NOTE Windows message queuing is designed to automatically handle connection problems and issues of transient connectivity (such as a dial-up connection between two machines). If you send a message to a machine—normally a server—that you are not currently connected with, the message will wait in a queue on the source machine until the connection is established, when it will be sent.

Getting a List of Message Queues

Let's move on to a new application. Perhaps this application would like to receive and reply to messages sent by the first application, but it isn't quite sure of the name of the queue. It's easy to list all the MessageQueues on a machine, as shown in Listing 11.6.

Listing 11.6 **Retrieving All the Private Queues on a Machine**

```
MessageQueue [] msq;
private void btnGet_Click(object sender, System.EventArgs e) {
    lstQ.Items.Clear();
    msq = MessageQueue.GetPrivateQueuesByMachine(".");
    foreach (MessageQueue m in msq) {
        lstQ.Items.Add(m.FormatName);
    }
}
```

The code in Listing 11.6 uses the `GetPrivateQueuesByMachine` method to read the existing `MessageQueues` into an array declared at the class level, *msq*. The argument passed to the method, ".", is shorthand for the current machine. Once the `MessageQueues` are retrieved into the array, each instance's `FormatName` property is displayed in a ListBox, as shown in Figure 11.12.

FIGURE 11.12:

You can easily retrieve all the queues on a machine.

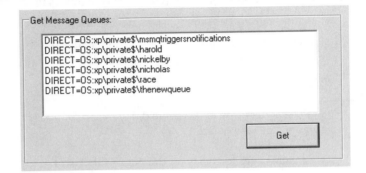

Get Message Queues:

```
DIRECT=OS:xp\private$\msmqtriggersnotifications
DIRECT=OS:xp\private$\harold
DIRECT=OS:xp\private$\nickelby
DIRECT=OS:xp\private$\nicholas
DIRECT=OS:xp\private$\race
DIRECT=OS:xp\private$\thenewqueue
```

Get

Getting All Messages in a Queue

It's not a whole lot harder to display all the messages on a queue selected by the user; most of the programmatic work involves determining which `MessageQueue` the user selected. As a preliminary before doing this, I decided to set up a property at the class (or form) level to store the index in the array of the selected `MessageQueue`, so that this could easily be used to reply to a message in the queue. Here's the property:

```
private int m_MsgIndex = 0;
public int MsgIndex {
    get {
        return m_MsgIndex;
    }
    set {
        m_MsgIndex = value;
    }
}
```

NOTE I could have used a variable declared with a class-level scope to accomplish the same purpose (as with *msq*, the variable holding the array of MessageQueues), but I decided to use a property for the sake of variety. Properties are wonderful agents of encapsulation, and it is good to get in the habit of using them.

I compared the `FormatName` property of each `MessageQueue` in the *msq* array with the contents of the `ListBox.SelectedItem` property cast to `string`, to determine which `MessageQueue` was selected:

```
if (msq[i].FormatName == (string) lstQ.SelectedItem)
```

When a match is made, we have the MessageQueue that was selected by the user and can save the index in the property created for that purpose:

```
this.MsgIndex = i;
```

An array of System.Message.Message objects named *messages* is declared, and populated using the GetAllMessages method of the selected MessageQueue:

```
System.Messaging.Message [] messages = msq[i].GetAllMessages();
```

The messages on this queue are now eliminated using the Purge method, since, unlike the MessageQueue.Receive method, MessageQueue.GetAllMessages does not delete the messages obtained.

NOTE   You will have to decide in the context of a particular application whether it is appropriate to purge a message queue or not.

With the messages formerly on the queue safely stored in the *messages* array, it is now time to display the message subject line—using the Label property—and its body text—using the Body property and the ToString method:

```
for (int j = 0; j < messages.Length; j++) {
    lstMessages.Items.Add
        (messages[j].Label + ": " +messages[j].Body.ToString());
}
```

When the code is run, the subject and body of each message, separated by a colon, is displayed (Figure 11.13).

FIGURE 11.13:

You can use an array
of messages to retrieve
the subject and text
of all messages in
a queue.

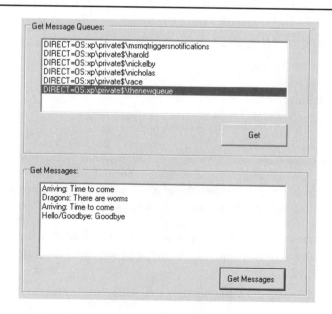

The complete code for retrieving all the messages in a queue is shown in Listing 11.7.

Listing 11.7   **Getting All the Messages in a Queue**

```
MessageQueue [] msq;
...
private void btnGetMessages_Click(object sender, System.EventArgs e) {
    lstMessages.Items.Clear();
    for (int i = 0; i < msq.Length; i++) {
        if (msq[i].FormatName == (string) lstQ.SelectedItem) {
            this.MsgIndex = i;
            msq[i].Formatter = new BinaryMessageFormatter();
            System.Messaging.Message [] messages = msq[i].GetAllMessages();
            msq[i].Purge();
            for (int j = 0; j < messages.Length; j++) {
                lstMessages.Items.Add
                    (messages[j].Label + ": " +messages[j].Body.ToString());
            }
        }
    }
}
private int m_MsgIndex = 0;
public int MsgIndex {
    get {
        return m_MsgIndex;
    }
    set {
        m_MsgIndex = value;
    }
}
```

Replying to a Message

In the interests of completeness, let's reply to a message selected by the user in the Get Messages ListBox. This time, however, instead of letting the user select a subject for the message, we'll automatically give it the subject "REPLY"—so Figure 11.14 shows no room for the message reply subject.

Here's how we get the right MessageQueue in the *msq* array:

```
MessageQueue theQ = msq[this.MsgIndex];
```

FIGURE 11.14:

The message sent
in the box shown is
automatically labeled
REPLY.

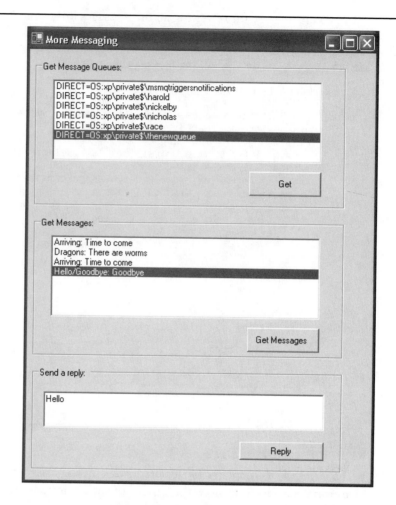

Here's sending back the message with the REPLY subject line:

```
theQ.Send("You said, \"" + lstMessages.SelectedItem.ToString() +
    ",\"and I say: \"" + txtReply.Text + "\"", "REPLY");
```

Going back to the application that started this section, if you make sure that the queue that
is joined is the one that was used to display messages in Figure 11.14, then when you click
Retrieve, the reply to the original message will be displayed (Figure 11.15). The code for replying
to the selected message is shown in Listing 11.8.

FIGURE 11.15:

The Receive method takes the first message off the queue, regardless of what program sent it.

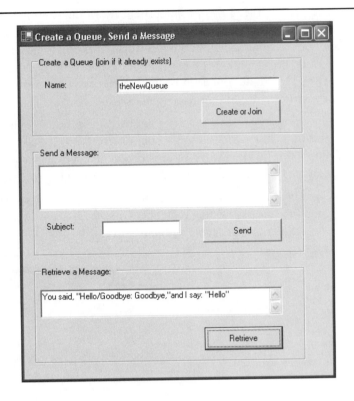

⤶ **Listing 11.8**   **Replying to a Message**

```
MessageQueue [] msq;
...
private void btnReply_Click(object sender, System.EventArgs e) {
    MessageQueue theQ = msq[this.MsgIndex];
    theQ.Formatter = new BinaryMessageFormatter();
    theQ.Send("You said, \"" + lstMessages.SelectedItem.ToString() +
        ",\"and I say: \"" + txtReply.Text + "\"", "REPLY");
    txtReply.Text = String.Empty;
}
```

Messaging as Architecture

Of course, to really get power out of messaging, software needs to be sending messages and responding to them. (If the idea were to have a human select a MessageQueue, and then select a message, and then type out a response, we could use e-mail or instant messaging and save some programming time.)

I've put together a pair of small applications that simulate how messaging might be used as architecture to create a distributed application. Please bear in mind that these applications don't do anything much. In the real world, they might be performing extensive numerical calculations, crawling through text, or mimicking complex systems such as a tornado or the stock market. My simple applications simulate the parts of a more complex organization that might be constructed around message queuing.

One of my applications, which I've called "Gigantic," counts down from 100 to 1. The other application, dubbed "Colossal," counts up from 1 to 100. A target number (between 1 and 100) is supplied. The idea is that the application that gets to the target number first sends a message out saying that it is done. When the "done" message is received, the other node stops working.

Gigantic, the (top-down) first node, serves as a kind of controller for the whole thing, since it sends out a message telling both nodes (itself and Colossal) to start. The start message includes the target number, as shown in Figure 11.16.

FIGURE 11.16:

The initial program serves as a kind of controller, since it sends the message that starts the race.

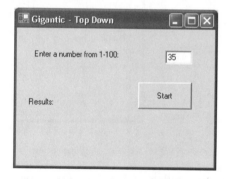

Colossal, the (bottom-up) other node, is intended as the prototype for many distributed objects where something more complex than counting from 1 to 100 would be involved. The only action the user can take with respect to Colossal is to initialize it by clicking the Start button. The initialization code, shown in Listing 11.9, causes Colossal to go into standby mode, wait for a message, and display a Ready status indication (Figure 11.17).

FIGURE 11.17:

After the other program has been initialized, it signals that it is asynchronously waiting in standby mode for the start message.

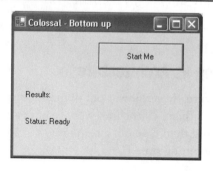

Listing 11.9   **Initializing a "Node" and Asynchronously Waiting to Peek**

```
MessageQueue mq;
private void btnStartMe_Click(object sender, System.EventArgs e) {
    lblResults.Text = String.Empty;
    string qpath = @".\Private$\Race";
    if (!MessageQueue.Exists(qpath))
        MessageQueue.Create (qpath);
    mq = new MessageQueue(qpath);
    mq.Purge();
    mq.Formatter = new BinaryMessageFormatter();
    mq.PeekCompleted += new PeekCompletedEventHandler(MyPeekCompleted);
    lblResults.Text = "Status: Ready";
    mq.BeginPeek();
    // Can do stuff here while waiting for asynch event to complete
}
```

I picture the competition between Gigantic counting down and Colossal counting up as a kind of race, so I named the message queue *Race*. The code shown in Listing 11.9 uses the familiar syntax to create or join that queue.

NOTE   The MessageQueue also is purged so that any old messages that may be sitting in it don't lead to erroneous results.

Next, the event handler for the asynchronous MyPeekCompleted event procedure is added, and the BeginPeek method is invoked to start an asynchronous peek operation with no timeout:

```
mq.PeekCompleted += new PeekCompletedEventHandler(MyPeekCompleted);
...
mq.BeginPeek();
```

If this asynchronous code looks familiar, it should: it is based on the same asynchronous design pattern shown used with web services in Chapter 3, "Windows Uses Web Services, Too!," and to perform FileStream operations in Chapter 10, "Working with Streams and Files."

The code in the MyPeekCompleted event handler, which gets invoked when a peek completes, is really pretty simple (see Listing 11.10).

Listing 11.10   **Responding to the "Peeked" Message**

```
MessageQueue mq;
...
public void MyPeekCompleted (Object source, PeekCompletedEventArgs ar){
    System.Messaging.Message msg = mq.EndPeek (ar.AsyncResult);
```

```
    if (msg.Label == "DONE"){
        return;
    }
    if (msg.Label == "START"){
        CountUp (Convert.ToInt32(msg.Body));
        return;
    }
}
public void CountUp (int target){
    this.lblResults.Text = "START: " + this.Text;
    if (target < 0)
        target = 0;
    if (target > 100)
        target = 100;
    int i = 0;
    while (i <= target){
        this.lblResults.Text += " " + i.ToString();
        if (i == target){
            mq.Send (this.Text, "DONE");
            this.lblResults.Text += " Status: Not Ready";
            break;
        }
        i++;
    }
    return;
}
```

A `System.Messaging.Message` object is created using the *mq* EndPeek event, with the `AsyncResult` object passed into the event handler:

```
System.Messaging.Message msg = mq.EndPeek (ar.AsyncResult);
```

Note that, in this code, I've used the fact that I know what `MessageQueue` is involved (and it is available as a class-level variable). The *source* parameter of the event procedure is the object that fired the event—e.g., the `MessageQueue` causing it—so *source* can be cast to `MessageQueue` and used like so:

```
public void MyPeekCompleted (Object source, PeekCompletedEventArgs ar){
    MessageQueue mq = (MessageQueue) source;
    ...
```

However the `MessageQueue` is obtained, its purpose is to use its EndPeek method to obtain a look at the message at the front of the queue. If the message is labeled "DONE", then work ceases. If the message is labeled "START", then the count-up method is called, using the number passed in the body of the message:

```
if (msg.Label == "START"){
    CountUp (Convert.ToInt32(msg.Body));
    ...
```

In the CountUp method, when the target is reached, a DONE message is sent:

```
mq.Send (this.Text, "DONE");
```

and the status message is put back to "Not Ready":

```
this.lblResults.Text += " Status: Not Ready";
```

Moving back to the Gigantic controller node, you can see from Listing 11.11 that its initialization process is pretty much the same as a normal node, except that it also sends a START message using the number input in a TextBox:

```
mq.Send (txtNum.Text, "START");
```

In addition, the controller node is asynchronously waiting for a Receive (rather than a Peek), the difference being that Receive will delete the message from the queue, and Peek won't.

Listing 11.11   Starting the "Race" and Waiting for an Asynchronous Receive

```
MessageQueue mq;
private void btnStart_Click(object sender, System.EventArgs e) {
    lblResults.Text = String.Empty;
    string qpath = @".\Private$\Race";
    if (!MessageQueue.Exists(qpath))
        MessageQueue.Create (qpath);
    mq = new MessageQueue(qpath);
    mq.Purge();
    mq.Formatter = new BinaryMessageFormatter();
    mq.Send (txtNum.Text, "START");
    mq.ReceiveCompleted += new ReceiveCompletedEventHandler(MyReceiveCompleted);
    mq.BeginReceive();
    // Can do stuff here while waiting for asynch event to complete
}
```

Gigantic responds to messages in the MyReceiveCompleted event handler in a similar way to the Colossal node (see Listing 11.12). When a DONE message is received, a display is created that uses the text of the message to display the "winner," the queue is purged, and work stops. When the START message is received, the CountDown method is called.

Listing 11.12   Responding to the Received Messages

```
MessageQueue mq;
...
public void MyReceiveCompleted (Object source,
    ReceiveCompletedEventArgs ar){
    System.Messaging.Message msg = mq.EndReceive (ar.AsyncResult);
    if (msg.Label == "DONE"){
```

```
          this.lblResults.Text += " " + msg.Body.ToString() + " is done first.";
          mq.Purge();
          return;
      }
      if (msg.Label == "START"){
          CountDown (Convert.ToInt32(msg.Body));
      }
   }
   public void CountDown (int target){
      this.lblResults.Text = "START: " + this.Text;
      if (target < 0)
          target = 0;
      if (target > 100)
          target = 100;
      int i = 100;
      // Delay it a little, since it gets the message first
      System.Threading.Thread.Sleep(200);
      while (i >= target){
          this.lblResults.Text += " " + i.ToString();
          if (i == target){
             mq.Send (this.Text, "DONE");
             mq.BeginReceive();
             break;
          }
          i--;
      }
   }
}
```

NOTE I've added a short delay within the CountDown method by putting the thread to sleep for 0.2 of a second—System.Threading.Thread.Sleep(200)—because Gigantic, as the originator of the START message, seemed to have an unfair head start.

Within the CountDown method, when the target is reached, a DONE message is sent. In addition, the BeginReceive method is invoked another time—so that the DONE message can be responded to:

```
if (i == target){
   mq.Send (this.Text, "DONE");
   mq.BeginReceive();
   break;
}
```

To experiment with Gigantic and Colossal, run both programs. Click Colossal's Start button to initialize it. When its display indicates that it is ready, enter a number in Gigantic and click Start. The display will indicate which node completed first, as shown in Figure 11.18.

FIGURE 11.18:

Each program sends a message when it is done with its task; the first DONE message is displayed.

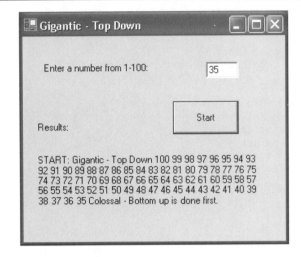

Messaging Architectures and Non-Determinism

You should be aware that application architectures that use message queues have some issues with non-determinism. There's really no way to say exactly when a given node will receive a given message, or even in what order nodes will receive a particular message. (This may depend to some degree on network loads.) So your applications should not depend on the timing or order of message delivery.

In addition, just like in real life, it is possible that messages may get dropped or lost. In a rigorous architecture that depends on message queues, you should plan for this and use a system that relies on acknowledgments and redundant messaging.

Conclusion

Although the logic of applications built around sending and receiving messages can be confusing, using .NET, message queues and messaging do not demand much in the way of programmatic infrastructure. The technology creates powerful opportunities for distributed and peer-to-peer applications. One can easily imagine scenarios in which applications are objects that interoperate solely using a messaging infrastructure.

This chapter touched very briefly on messages formatted using XML. Chapter 12, "Working with XML and ADO.NET," explores the exciting and important world of XML—and shows you how to effectively use data with your applications.

CHAPTER 12

Working with XML and ADO.NET

- Understanding and serializing XML

- The *XmlSchema* class and XSD schemas

- *XmlTextReader* and *XmlTextWriter* classes

- The XML Document Object Model (DOM)

- XSL transformations (XSLT)

- Understanding ADO.NET and databases

- Connection strings

- Managed providers and data components

- Working with *DataSet*s

U nder the hood, the .NET Framework, .NET languages, and Visual Studio rely on XML as the underlying facilitator of interoperability, configuration, and much more. In large part, the developer has no great need to be concerned with these uses of XML—you certainly don't need to know how to program XML to run the Visual Studio IDE—except that if the .NET programming structure finds XML the best tool to use for application integration, why not use it in your own applications as well?

NOTE   For more information about many of the ways XML is used within the .NET Framework and development environment, look up "XML in Visual Studio" in online help.

A great deal of XML and XML-related capabilities are built into the .NET Framework. There are literally hundreds of classes you can use to generate and manipulate XML in C# .NET. This chapter provides an overview of some of the ways you can work with XML using C# .NET. By starting the chapter in this book that treats data with a discussion of XML, I am emphasizing the fact that in today's world it is an intelligent move to regard data from an XML-centric viewpoint whenever this is a plausible approach.

In the long run, you can't do anything very sophisticated or useful without the ability to save and retrieve data between program sessions. While there are a variety of ways you could go about doing this—for example, reading and writing to files as explained in Chapter 10, "Working with Streams and Files"—for many developers today, input/output essentially means working with a database.

In effect, the great majority of real-world programs are designed to query databases to populate the programs' objects. Programs that perform jobs such as managing accounts receivable or hotel reservations must also be able to save their work and pick up where they left off. In addition, users need to be able to query stored data and to update it.

This chapter is not concerned with programming databases—and, indeed, it would take at least an entire book to do justice to the topic. As a general matter of contemporary application architecture, a *connectivity layer* usually is interposed between an application and a database. The chapter's primary focus is the tools available to help you create the database connectivity layer in .NET, and how to use XML to facilitate interoperability.

Understanding XML

Of all the tools, technologies, and languages that have emerged in the past few years, none has had a greater impact on the interoperability of applications and data than XML (short for Extensible Markup Language). XML is deceptively simple. It's easy to understand, it can be read by both humans and machines, and constructing XML documents and schemas is easy.

This simplicity belies a great deal of power and sidesteps the occasional complexity of using XML.

As you probably know, HTML and XML are both markup languages, meaning that they consist of tags that describe content. That's about where the similarity ends. HTML tags are fixed in nature (at least in each version of HTML) and used to describe the elements that make up an HTML page. HTML elements are usually visual. In contrast, XML tags are custom in nature and are used to describe data.

In other words, an HTML tag, such as `<h1></h1>`, is used to describe the appearance of the contents within the tag. (The `<h1>` tag means that the tag content is a level 1 heading.) The meaning of the `<h1>` tag is fixed, and it means the same thing to everybody.

On the other hand, an XML tag such as `<phone_num></phone_num>` identifies the contents as a phone number. XML tags can be used for anything that you might logically use when structuring data. You can invent your own XML tags and use them to mark data as you'd like. In other words, the meaning of an XML tag is not fixed for all users the way an HTML tag is. For example, in your XML a `<name>` tag might identify a first name, and in my XML the `<name>` tag might mean first, middle, and last names.

For example, in the last novel that Charles Dickens completed, *Hard Times*, the aptly-named teacher Thomas Gradgrind—only interested in realities, and a man of "facts and calculations"—asks his student Sissy Jupe, whom he refers to as "girl number twenty," to define a horse. Sissy, put on the spot, is unable to produce a definition, so Gradgrind turns to one of his pet students, a boy named Bitzer:

> *"Bitzer," said Thomas Gradgrind. "Your definition of a horse."*

> *"Quadruped. Graminivorous. Forty teeth, namely twenty-four grinders, four eye-teeth, and twelve incisive. Sheds coat in the spring; in marshy countries, sheds hoofs, too. Hoofs hard, but requiring to be shod with iron. Age known by marks in mouth." Thus (and much more) Bitzer.*

> *"Now girl number twenty," said Mr Gradgrind. "You know what a horse is."*

Bitzer's definition of a horse is actually a kind of pidgin XML. If rendered into XML, it might begin something like this:

```
<?xml version="1.0"?>
<horse>
   <legs>
      Quadruped
   </legs>
   <diet>
      Graminivorous
   </diet>
```

```
<teeth>
    <totalnumber>
        40
    </totalnumber>
    <grinders>
        24
    </grinders>
    <eye-teeth>
        4
    </eye-teeth>
    <incisive>
        12
    </incisive>
</teeth>
    ...
</horse>
```

The point of this XML description of a horse is that almost anything can be described using XML. However, in the real world there is little use for data description—such as XML—without the ability to communicate. So a more realistic use of XML in connection with a horse would not be a description of where the horse fits into a Linnaean genus (which is essentially what Bitzer's description is about: what kind of animal is this?) but rather one that has to do with horse transactions and affairs for specific horses. This XML description might include elements such as `<name>`, `<sire>`, `<dame>`, `<weight>`, `<cost>`, and so on. (And sure, while we're at it, why not a `<teeth>` section?)

Business communities create meta-XML structures specific to that community. These structures, called *schemas*—in the same spirit that the tabular structure of relational databases are also called schemas (and convertible to and from database schemas)—are used to standardize XML communications. As long as you mark your data as elements following a specific schema, all participants will know what you are talking about.

Whether specified by an industry group or created on an ad hoc basis, schemas are themselves written in XML and saved as XSD files. (DTD, or Document Type Definition, and XDR, a proprietary Microsoft schema specification, are both older schema definition formats, replaced in .NET by XSD.) An example of an XSD schema is shown later in this chapter in Listing 12.1.

NOTE   XSD is a standard specified by the World Wide Web Consortium (W3C; www.w3c.org). In keeping with the role of the W3C, it is vendor-neutral and not controlled by any one company.

As I'll show you in this chapter, the tools built into the development environment, and the XML classes in the .NET Framework, make it easy to create XML schemas and to validate XML documents—which means, to make sure that the elements in the documents comply with the schema.

XML Namespaces

Some of the most important namespaces that contain classes related to XML development are shown in Table 12.1.

TABLE 12.1: Namespaces Related to XML

Namespace	Description
System.Xml	Provides primary support for a variety of XML functions.
System.Xml.Schema	Contains the XML classes that provide support for XML Schemas Definition (XSD) schemas.
System.Xml.Serialization	Contains the classes used to serialize and deserialize XML and XML schemas to and from SOAP (Simple Object Access Protocol). SOAP is an open-standard mechanism for wrapping XML and other content so that it can be transmitted over HTTP. SOAP is used as a mechanism for invoking methods on a remote server using XML documents.
System.Xml.XPath	Provides an XPath parser and evaluation engine. XPath (XML Path Language) enables you to easily write queries that retrieve particular subsets of XML data.
System.Xml.Xsl	Provides the tools needed to work with XSLT (Extensible Stylesheet Language Transformations). Essentially, XSLT lets you create templates that can be used to manipulate XML documents into other formats and/or to tweak the XML. One use of XSLT is to transform XML into HTML so that it can be rendered in a web browser, as explained later in this chapter.

Creating an XML Schema

To create an XML schema using the Visual Studio .NET Schema Designer, choose Project ➢ Add New Item from the Project menu. When the Add New Item dialog opens, select XML Schema, as shown in Figure 12.1, and click Open.

FIGURE 12.1:

You can create an XML
schema by adding an
XML Schema module
to your project.

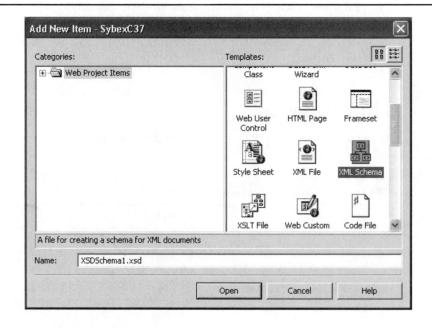

NOTE   In Figure 12.1, you can also see the templates you would select to open an XML Designer
(XML File) and an XSLT Designer (XSLT File).

The XML Schema Designer will open, as shown in Figure 12.2. The designer is empty when
it first opens.

FIGURE 12.2:

The XML Designer is
empty when it opens.
To add elements and
attributes to your schema,
right-click the designer
and choose Add.

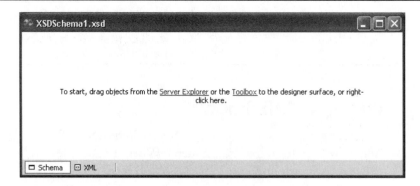

At this point, with the XML Schema Designer open, there are many ways you can go about
adding elements, attributes, and other items to the schema. The techniques, some of which will
be covered later in this chapter, include:

- Right-clicking the surface of the designer, choosing Add from the context menu, and selecting a new item from the submenu.

- Dragging-and-dropping any of the items from the XML Schema tab of the Toolbox to the designer. The XML Schema tab of the Toolbox, which is shown in Figure 12.3, will be available when the XML Designer is open.

- Using the Server Explorer to drill down into a database and its tables. You can then simply drag and drop a table onto the Schema Designer. The schema will be generated automatically based on the database table elements.

- Using the XML Designer to generate a schema based on specific XML in the designer.

- Clicking the XML tab of the designer, and editing the XML that constitutes the schema by hand.

NOTE   In addition, you can create a schema programmatically using the Items collection of the XmlSchema class, as I'll show you shortly.

The items in the XML Schema tab—and the XML Designer Add context menu—correspond to the standard elements of a XSD schema as approved by the World Wide Web Consortium (W3C). They also correspond to classes and members within the System.XML.Schema namespace, which are collectively called the Schema Object Model (SOM). For example, objects of the XmlSchema class are each elements in a schema.

Put differently, the SOM implements W3C-approved XSD schemas within the .NET Framework. The SOM can be used to programmatically create and edit schemas in much the same way that the Document Object Model (DOM), discussed later in this chapter, can be used to edit XML documents themselves. The XmlSchema class can also be used to validate the syntactic and semantic structure of a programmatically built schema.

Table 12.2 shows the meanings of the items that appear on the XML Designer context menu and on the XML Schema tab of the Toolbox.

NOTE   You can also learn more about XSD schemas by looking up the topics "XML Schema Reference" and "XML Schema Elements" in online help. You can also have a look at the information published by the W3C regarding XML schemas at www.w3.org/2001/XMLSchema.

TABLE 12.2: XSD Schema Items

Toolbox Item	What It Does
element	Creates an element, which associates a name with a type. The element can be global, added to other elements, added to groups, or used to construct complexTypes.
attribute	Creates an attribute, which associates a name with a type and is associated with an element or complexType. Attributes can be global, added to elements, or added to groups.
attributeGroup	Creates an attributeGroup (a group of attributes) that can be global, added to elements, or used in the construct of complexTypes.
complexType	Creates a complexType to which you can add elements, attributes, attributeGroups, anys, and anyAttributes.
simpleType	Creates a simpleType to which you can add facets.
group	Creates groups that can be global, added to other groups, elements, or complexTypes.
any	Creates an any element (meaning any element, or sequence of elements, from a specified namespace) that can be added to elements, complexTypes, or groups.
anyAttribute	Creates an anyAttribute element (meaning any attribute element, or sequence of attribute elements, from a specified namespace) that can be added to elements, attribute groups, or complex types.
facet	Sets limits on the type of content a simpleType can contain (for an example using facets, see "Create It in Code" later in this chapter).
key	Launches the Edit Key dialog box, which is used to create keys when added to an element. Keys are the primary fields that tie relations together (see "Database Basics" later in this chapter).
Relation	Launches the Edit Relation dialog box, which is used to define relationships between elements.

Whichever method you use with the Schema Designer to create a schema, the schema appears in the designer in tabular form (can we all say together, "just like a database schema"?) as you can see in Figure 12.4.

FIGURE 12.4:

When you add items from the Toolbox, context menu, or Server Explorer, the schema appears in tabular form in the designer.

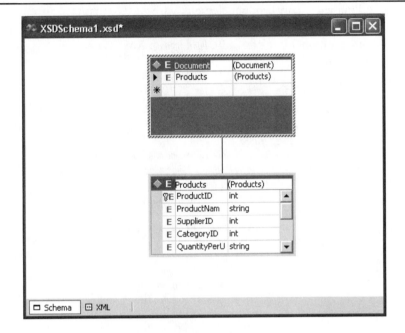

Programmatically Creating and Validating a Schema

Before I show you how to use the Xml Schema class to create and validate a schema, let's define the schema manually. To put the cart even further before the horse, let's first create some XML that we'd like to be the basis for the schema, and describe how we'd like the XML to work (in fact, this is likely to be the way schemas are created in the real world).

One If by Hand

My XML excerpt describes a product, which is an element that is a complex type. Each product must have an integer product identification number and a product type chosen from the enumeration "Candy", "Toy", or "Gadget". In addition, each product should have a name, a description, and as many or few subparts as one would like. Here's an XML rendering of this element for a candy named a "Purple Wheeler":

```
<?xml version="1.0" encoding="utf-8" ?>
<Product ProdId="123" ProdType="Candy">
    <Name>Purple Wheeler</Name>
    <Desc>Tastes like grape</Desc>
```

```
        <SubPart>Wheel</SubPart>
        <SubPart>Purple</SubPart>
    </Product>
```

To enforce the conditions I'd like for the XML, I must create a sequence of simple elements falling within my product element, with zero to many occurrences of the SubPart element. In addition, two required attributes must be specified, with one of them taking values from an enumeration. Here's how this looks as an XML schema with the xs schema item prefix omitted for clarity:

```
<?xml version="1.0" ?>
<schema xmlns="http://www.w3.org/2001/XMLSchema">
    <element name="Product">
        <complexType>
            <sequence>
                <element name="Name" type="string" />
                <element name="Desc" type="string" />
                <element name="SubPart" minOccurs="0"
                    maxOccurs="unbounded" />
            </sequence>
            <attribute name="ProdId" use="required" type="integer" />
            <attribute name="ProdType" use="required" >
                <simpleType>
                    <restriction base = "string">
                        <enumeration value="Candy" />
                        <enumeration value="Toy" />
                        <enumeration value="Gadget" />
                    </restriction>
                </simpleType>
            </attribute>
        </complexType>
    </element>
</schema>
```

Listing 12.1 shows the same XML schema rendered a little more formally.

NOTE   The xs:schema declaration says that the text represents a schema, and that the xs prefix will be used before elements. The xmlns:xs="http://www.w3.org/2001/XMLSchema" declaration says that all tags should be interpreted according to the W3C defaults. The targetNamespace declaration names the schema and provides a URI as its default namespace (the same purpose is also achieved using xmlns and xmlns:mstns declarations). If you create a schema within Visual Studio using one of the tools available (such as the Create Schema menu item available from the XML Designer), you'll probably find that some additional attribute declarations, many of them Microsoft-specific, have been added to the schema tag.

Listing 12.1   An XSD XML Schema

```xml
<?xml version="1.0" ?>
<xs:schema targetNamespace="http://www.tempuri.org/XMLFile1.xsd"
    xmlns:xs="http://www.w3.org/2001/XMLSchema">
    <xs:element name="Product">
        <xs:complexType>
            <xs:sequence>
                <xs:element name="Name" type="xs:string" />
                <xs:element name="Desc" type="xs:string" />
                <xs:element name="SubPart" minOccurs="0"
                    maxOccurs="unbounded" type="xs:string" />
            </xs:sequence>
            <xs:attribute name="ProdId" use="required"
                type="xs:integer" />
            <xs:attribute name="ProdType" use="required">
                <xs:simpleType>
                    <xs:restriction base="xs:string">
                        <xs:enumeration value="Candy" />
                        <xs:enumeration value="Toy" />
                        <xs:enumeration value="Gagdet" />
                    </xs:restriction>
                </xs:simpleType>
            </xs:attribute>
        </xs:complexType>
    </xs:element>
</xs:schema>
```

Next, if the XML schema shown in Listing 12.1 is copied into an XML Schema Designer in Visual Studio, it can be validated by giving the designer the focus and selecting Schema ≻ Validate. If you've left something off—for instance, a closing bracket—validation will tell you. If there are no validation errors, then the schema is "well-formed" and usable.

Going back to our original XML fragment, we can now enter it in an XML Designer and connect it to its intended schema:

```xml
<?xml version="1.0" encoding="utf-8" ?>
<Product xsi:ProdId="123" xsi:ProdType="Candy"
    xmlns="http://www.tempuri.org/XMLFile1.xsd"
    xmlns:xsi="http://www.tempuri.org/XMLFile1.xsd">
    <Name>Purple Wheeler</Name>
    <Desc>Tastes like grape</Desc>
    <SubPart>Wheel</SubPart>
    <SubPart>Purple</SubPart>
</Product>
```

To open a new, empty XML Designer in Visual Studio, select Project ➤ Add New Item, and then select XML File in the Add New Item dialog.

Note that connecting XML and target schemas within Visual Studio that have not been created using auto-generation tools can be a little tricky. In addition to the internal namespace declaration (xmlns="http://www.tempuri.org/XMLFile1.xsd"), you may need to use the Properties window to point an XML Designer at its target schema.

If the XSD schema isn't qualified by a namespace, you can link an XML document to it using a noNameSpaceSchema declaration.

The whole point of creating a well-formed XSD schema and linking XML to it is that the schema can enforce conditions on the XML. Let's try this out in the example. In the XML Designer, change the value of the ProdType enumeration to a value not included in the enumeration—for example, "Game". If you now try to validate the XML against the schema (by selecting XML ➤ Validate XML Data), you'll get an error message, as shown in Figure 12.5.

FIGURE 12.5:

An XSD schema is used to enforce typing and conditions within an XML document.

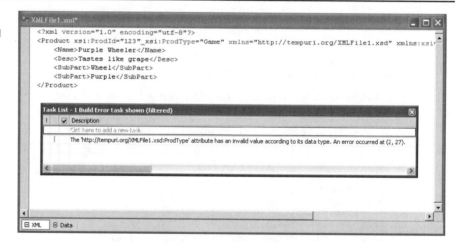

Create It in Code

The XmlSchema and related classes are used to construct and validate an XSD schema programmatically. XmlSchema is a member of the System.Xml.Schema namespace.

To see how this works, let's construct the same schema (for the Product defined earlier in this chapter) one more time using code mechanisms.

NOTE   The code for creating the schema may seem like a great deal of trouble, considering the excellent tools available in Visual Studio for creating schemas without programming. But if you need to work with XML, you'll want to know the classes, objects, and relationships involved in a programmatic construction of a schema. Often, no human being is available to build the schema.

First, create a new schema and the `Product` schema element:

```
XmlSchema schema = new XmlSchema();
XmlSchemaElement eProduct = new XmlSchemaElement();
eProduct.Name = "Product";
schema.Items.Add (eProduct);
```

Next, establish the `Product` element as a complex type that includes a sequence:

```
XmlSchemaComplexType ct = new XmlSchemaComplexType();
eProduct.SchemaType = ct;
XmlSchemaSequence ss = new XmlSchemaSequence();
ct.Particle = ss;
```

For each simple element in the schema sequence, add it to the sequence by adding it to the schema sequence `Items` collection:

```
XmlSchemaElement eName = new XmlSchemaElement();
eName.Name = "Name";
eName.SchemaTypeName = new XmlQualifiedName("string",
    "http://www.w3.org/2001/XMLSchema");
ss.Items.Add (eName);
...
```

As you'll recall, the `SubPart` element can occur no times, or many times, in the sequence. This is coded using the element's `MinOccurs` and `MaxOccursString` properties:

```
XmlSchemaElement eSubPart = new XmlSchemaElement();
eSubPart.Name = "SubPart";
eSubPart.SchemaTypeName = new XmlQualifiedName("string",
    "http://www.w3.org/2001/XMLSchema");
eSubPart.MinOccurs = 0;
eSubPart.MaxOccursString = "unbounded";
ss.Items.Add (eSubPart);
```

Next, the attributes are added to the complex type's `Attributes` collection:

```
XmlSchemaAttribute aProdId = new XmlSchemaAttribute();
aProdId.Name = "ProdId";
aProdId.SchemaTypeName = new XmlQualifiedName("integer",
    "http://www.w3.org/2001/XMLSchema");
aProdId.Use = XmlSchemaUse.Required;
ct.Attributes.Add(aProdId);
```

The ProdType attribute is a little more complicated, since it uses a type restriction and facets on a simple type to achieve its goal of restricting user choice to an enumeration:

```
XmlSchemaSimpleType st = new XmlSchemaSimpleType();
aProdType.SchemaType = st;
XmlSchemaSimpleTypeRestriction res = new XmlSchemaSimpleTypeRestriction();
res.BaseTypeName = new XmlQualifiedName ("string",
    "http://www.w3.org/2001/XMLSchema");
st.Content = res;
XmlSchemaEnumerationFacet f1 = new XmlSchemaEnumerationFacet();
XmlSchemaEnumerationFacet f2 = new XmlSchemaEnumerationFacet();
XmlSchemaEnumerationFacet f3 = new XmlSchemaEnumerationFacet();
f1.Value = "Candy";
f2.Value = "Toy";
f3.Value = "Gadget";
res.Facets.Add(f1);
res.Facets.Add(f2);
res.Facets.Add(f3);
ct.Attributes.Add(aProdType);
```

With the schema elements complete, the remaining step is to use the XmlSchema's Compile method, assigning it a callback method for reporting any validation errors:

```
...
    schema.Compile(new ValidationEventHandler(SOMHandler));
    if (txtValidate.Text == "")
        txtValidate.Text = "Schema validates without problems.";
...
}
private void SOMHandler(object sender, ValidationEventArgs e){
    txtValidate.Text += e.Message;
}
```

NOTE If no validation errors are reported, the code after the Compile method is invoked displays a "validates without problems" message.

I used a FileStream along with an XMLTextWriter to write the schema to a file:

```
file = new FileStream("Product.xsd", FileMode.Create, FileAccess.ReadWrite);
XmlTextWriter xwriter = new XmlTextWriter(file, new UTF8Encoding());
xwriter.Formatting = Formatting.Indented;
schema.Write (xwriter);
```

I chose to read the file as plain text back into a multiline TextBox:

```
nfile = new FileStream("Product.xsd", FileMode.Open, FileAccess.ReadWrite);
reader = new StreamReader(nfile);
txtSchema.Text = reader.ReadToEnd();
```

The complete code for creating and validating the schema is shown in Listing 12.2. If you run the program, the schema will be displayed (Figure 12.6).

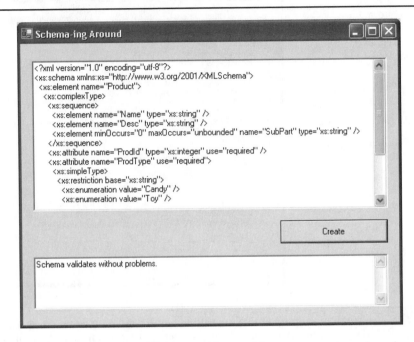

It's worth experimenting to see what will happen if you add some errors into the schema. Doing this involves walking a fine line, because your "error" has to pass syntax compilation, which not just any old error will do.

For example, the following "bogus" element type is not "really" part of the W3C schema specification, but it does not cause a C# syntax error because the syntaxes of the statements creating the element are legal:

```
XmlSchemaElement eBogus = new XmlSchemaElement();
eBogus.Name = "Bogus";
eBogus.SchemaTypeName = new XmlQualifiedName("bogus",
    "http://www.w3.org/2001/XMLSchema");
ss.Items.Add (eBogus);
```

If you add the "bogus" element type to the code, you'll get an appropriate error message (Figure 12.7).

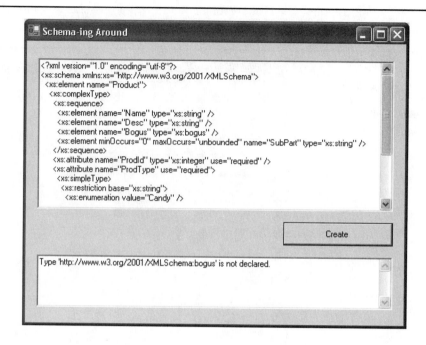

FIGURE 12.7:

A schema validation error is thrown because "bogus" is not a recognized element type.

NOTE   If you find yourself struggling with schema validation issues, it's a good idea to copy the schema into the Schema Designer, which has much more helpful validation error messages (including line and character numbers) than the XmlSchema.Compile method.

Listing 12.2   **Creating and Validating the Schema in Code**

```
using System.Xml;
using System.Xml.Schema;
using System.IO;
using System.Text;
...
FileStream file;
FileStream nfile;
StreamReader reader;

private void btnCreate_Click(object sender, System.EventArgs e) {
    Cursor = Cursors.WaitCursor;
    try{
        XmlSchema schema = new XmlSchema();
        XmlSchemaElement eProduct = new XmlSchemaElement();
        eProduct.Name = "Product";
        schema.Items.Add (eProduct);
```

```
XmlSchemaComplexType ct = new XmlSchemaComplexType();
eProduct.SchemaType = ct;
XmlSchemaSequence ss = new XmlSchemaSequence();
ct.Particle = ss;

XmlSchemaElement eName = new XmlSchemaElement();
eName.Name = "Name";
eName.SchemaTypeName = new XmlQualifiedName("string",
    "http://www.w3.org/2001/XMLSchema");
ss.Items.Add (eName);

XmlSchemaElement eDesc = new XmlSchemaElement();
eDesc.Name = "Desc";
eDesc.SchemaTypeName = new XmlQualifiedName("string",
    "http://www.w3.org/2001/XMLSchema");
ss.Items.Add (eDesc);

XmlSchemaElement eSubPart = new XmlSchemaElement();
eSubPart.Name = "SubPart";
eSubPart.SchemaTypeName = new XmlQualifiedName("string",
    "http://www.w3.org/2001/XMLSchema");
eSubPart.MinOccurs = 0;
eSubPart.MaxOccursString = "unbounded";
ss.Items.Add (eSubPart);

XmlSchemaAttribute aProdId = new XmlSchemaAttribute();
aProdId.Name = "ProdId";
aProdId.SchemaTypeName = new XmlQualifiedName("integer" ,
    "http://www.w3.org/2001/XMLSchema");
aProdId.Use = XmlSchemaUse.Required;
ct.Attributes.Add(aProdId);

XmlSchemaAttribute aProdType = new XmlSchemaAttribute();
aProdType.Name = "ProdType";
aProdType.Use = XmlSchemaUse.Required;

XmlSchemaSimpleType st = new XmlSchemaSimpleType();
aProdType.SchemaType = st;
XmlSchemaSimpleTypeRestriction res = new
    XmlSchemaSimpleTypeRestriction();
res.BaseTypeName = new XmlQualifiedName ("string",
    "http://www.w3.org/2001/XMLSchema");
st.Content = res;
XmlSchemaEnumerationFacet f1 = new XmlSchemaEnumerationFacet();
XmlSchemaEnumerationFacet f2 = new XmlSchemaEnumerationFacet();
XmlSchemaEnumerationFacet f3 = new XmlSchemaEnumerationFacet();
f1.Value = "Candy";
f2.Value = "Toy";
f3.Value = "Gadget";
res.Facets.Add(f1);
res.Facets.Add(f2);
res.Facets.Add(f3);
ct.Attributes.Add(aProdType);
```

```
        schema.Compile(new ValidationEventHandler(SOMHandler));
        if (txtValidate.Text == "")
            txtValidate.Text = "Schema validates without problems.";
        file = new FileStream("Product.xsd", FileMode.Create,
            FileAccess.ReadWrite);
        XmlTextWriter xwriter = new XmlTextWriter(file, new UTF8Encoding());
        xwriter.Formatting = Formatting.Indented;
        schema.Write (xwriter);
        xwriter.Close();
        nfile = new FileStream("Product.xsd", FileMode.Open,
            FileAccess.ReadWrite);
        reader = new StreamReader(nfile);
        txtSchema.Text = reader.ReadToEnd();
    }
    finally {
        file.Close();
        nfile.Close();
        reader.Close();
        Cursor = Cursors.Default;
    }

private void SOMHandler(object sender, ValidationEventArgs e){
    txtValidate.Text += e.Message;
}
```

Validating Against the Schema

It's a good thing to go with the flow, go with the tide, and not to cut against the grain. Similarly, you don't want to go against the schema—which is all a roundabout way of saying that the next logical step is to validate XML programmatically against the programmatically created schema. That is normally, after all, the point of a schema. So the application allows the user to enter some XML in the TextBox that can be programmatically validated against the schema.

As in the previous example, the contents of a TextBox are saved using normal `FileStream` mechanisms as a text file:

```
...
FileStream fs = new FileStream("Product.xml", FileMode.Create,
    FileAccess.ReadWrite);
try {
    sw.Write (txtXML.Text);
}
finally {
    sw.Flush();
    sw.Close();
```

```
        fs.Close();
    }
    ...
```

NOTE As usual when writing to a file, be sure to flush the `StreamWriter` when creating file; otherwise text may not get written from the buffer to the file. If you flush and close the `StreamWriter` within the `finally` clause of a `try...finally` construct, you can be sure it will get executed.

Next, another `FileStream` is used to create an `XmlValidatingReader`, opening the XML file that we just created:

```
FileStream  nfs = new FileStream("Product.xml", FileMode.Open,
    FileAccess.ReadWrite);
XmlValidatingReader vr = new XmlValidatingReader (nfs,
    XmlNodeType.Element, null);
```

The file containing the `Product.xsd` schema is added to the schemas collection of the `XmlValidatingReader`:

```
vr.Schemas.Add(null, "Product.xsd");
```

The `ValidationType` of the `XmlValidatingReader` is set to `ValidationType.Schema`:

```
vr.ValidationType = ValidationType.Schema;
```

NOTE A `XmlValidatingReader` can also be used to validate XML with older schema formats—such as DTD and XDR—by changing the `ValidationType` setting.

As with the schema validation code, a callback is set up to handle validation errors:

```
    vr.ValidationEventHandler += new ValidationEventHandler(XmlValidHandler);
...
}
private void XmlValidHandler(object sender, ValidationEventArgs e){
    txtValidate.Text += e.Message;
}
```

The only thing that remains is to read through the entire `XmlValidatingReader`—and display an appropriate message if there are no validation problems:

```
while (vr.Read());
if (txtValidate.Text == "")
    txtValidate.Text = "XML validates without problems.";
```

The complete code for validating a piece of XML against an XSD schema is shown in Listing 12.3.

Listing 12.3   **Validating XML Against the XSD Schema**

```
using System.Xml;
using System.Xml.Schema;
using System.IO;
...
private void btnValXML_Click(object sender, System.EventArgs e) {
    if (txtXML.Text == String.Empty){
        MessageBox.Show("Please enter some XML to validate!");
        return;
    }
    txtValidate.Text = String.Empty;
    FileStream fs = new FileStream("Product.xml", FileMode.Create,
        FileAccess.ReadWrite);
    StreamWriter  sw = new StreamWriter(fs);
    try {
        sw.Write (txtXML.Text);
    }
    finally {
        sw.Flush();
        sw.Close();
        fs.Close();
    }
    FileStream  nfs = new FileStream("Product.xml", FileMode.Open,
        FileAccess.ReadWrite);
    XmlValidatingReader vr = new XmlValidatingReader (nfs,
        XmlNodeType.Element, null);
    vr.Schemas.Add(null, "Product.xsd");
    vr.ValidationType = ValidationType.Schema;
    vr.ValidationEventHandler += new ValidationEventHandler(XmlValidHandler);
    while (vr.Read());
        if (txtValidate.Text == "")
            txtValidate.Text = "XML validates without problems.";
    vr.Close();
}
private void XmlValidHandler(object sender, ValidationEventArgs e){
    txtValidate.Text += e.Message;
}
```

To test it, run the program, and enter the original Product XML in the TextBox:

```
<?xml version="1.0" encoding="utf-8" ?>
<Product ProdId="123" ProdType="Toy">
    <Name>Purple Wheeler</Name>
    <Desc>Tastes like grape</Desc>
    <SubPart>Wheel</SubPart>
    <SubPart>Purple</SubPart>
</Product>
```

Next, click Validate XML. The message will indicate that there have been no validation problems (Figure 12.8).

FIGURE 12.8:

Well-formed XML that matches the schema file is validated without problems.

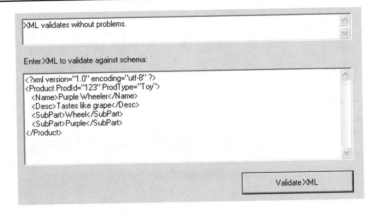

In the interests of science, try making some changes, such as entering a ProdType value that is not part of the enumeration and a "Bogus" element. Both things will be reported as validation problems (Figure 12.9).

FIGURE 12.9:

The XmlValidatingReader has found some problems in the XML.

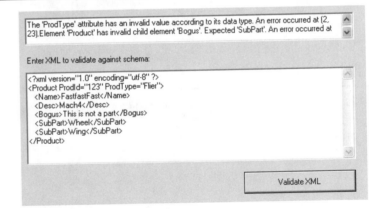

Creating an XML Data File

Before we get to some more of the interesting things you can do reading and writing XML, it's worth emphasizing that you can use the Data tab of the Visual Studio XML Designer to add element data against XML.

In order to use this feature, you must first create the XML for a table using the XML tab of the XML Designer. For example, the XML for a simplified Product table might look like this:

```
<Product ProdId="" ProdType="">
    <Name></Name>
```

```
   <Desc></Desc>
   <SubPart></SubPart>
</Product>
```

With this in place, if you switch to the Data tab of the XML Designer, shown in Figure 12.10, you can start entering your data using the table provided. This approach is a great deal faster than hand-constructing each XML data element—although in real life, you'll probably prefer to get your XML data from databases, files, or code generation.

FIGURE 12.10:

XML data can be entered using a table once the element has been constructed.

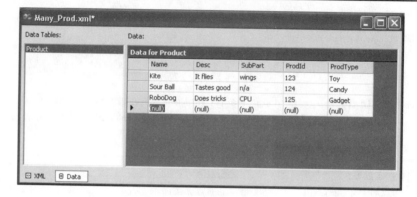

Once you have entered your data in tabular fashion, you can view it as straight XML by clicking the XML tab, as shown in Figure 12.11.

FIGURE 12.11:

Data entered in the table can be viewed as "straight" XML.

```
Many_Prod.xml
<?xml version="1.0" encoding="utf-8" ?>
<NewDataSet>
    <Product ProdId="123" ProdType="Toy">
        <Name>Kite</Name>
        <Desc>It flies</Desc>
        <SubPart>wings</SubPart>
    </Product>
    <Product ProdId="124" ProdType="Candy">
        <Name>Sour Ball</Name>
        <Desc>Tastes good</Desc>
        <SubPart>n/a</SubPart>
    </Product>
    <Product ProdId="125" ProdType="Gadget">
        <Name>RoboDog</Name>
        <Desc>Does tricks</Desc>
        <SubPart>CPU</SubPart>
    </Product>
</NewDataSet>
```

As I mentioned earlier in this chapter, you don't need to create an XML schema. If you don't set up a schema, the DataSet will do the best it can to create a schema on the fly from an XML data file. The reasons to first create an XML schema are to ensure consistency and to make the schema available to remote applications that may communicate with your application.

It's a neat feature that you can auto-generate an XML schema based on your XML data file. To do this, right-click in the XML Designer and choose Create Schema from the context menu. The newly generated XSD file will appear in the Solution Explorer with the same name as the original XML file but with a `.xsd` file extension. The XML required to connect the XML file to the schema will automatically be added to the XML file.

NOTE   In many cases, you might want to mirror the sequence I've used in this chapter. First, create an XML fragment. Use it to auto-generate a schema. Tweak the schema. Then distribute the schema for validation of longer XML documents.

Serializing XML

Let's have some fun with serializing a class to XML! Actually, it's quite easy to use the `Serialize` method of `XmlSerializer` objects to turn the fields and properties of a class into XML (methods are ignored). The `Deserialize` method lets one "re-hydrate" the serialized XML and access it by the name of each element—just as though you were accessing a property belonging to an instance of a class.

It is a little bit harder to serialize multiple elements of the same type under a single root node—but not that difficult. Here's how it works.

Let's start with the `Employee` class shown in Listing 12.4. This will be the member information used for serialization into XML. The class provides first name, last name, and title properties for each employee. For convenience sake, it has a class constructor that supplies these values, as well as a parameter-less constructor.

NOTE   I went to the trouble of implementing properties in this class because it is good programming practice to use properties for access combined with private variables to maintain property state. It would have worked just as well from the viewpoint of serialization to use public class fields.

Listing 12.4   **A Class Ripe for Serialization to XML**

```
public class Employee {
    public Employee(string fname, string lname, string title)
    {
        m_Fname = fname;
        m_Lname = lname;
        m_Title = title;
    }
```

```
public Employee(){
}
private string m_Fname = String.Empty;
private string m_Lname = String.Empty;
private string m_Title = String.Empty;

public string Fname {
    get {
        return m_Fname;
    }
    set {
        m_Fname = value;
    }
}
public string Lname {
    get {
        return m_Lname;
    }
    set {
        m_Lname = value;
    }
}
public string Title {
    get {
        return m_Title;
    }
    set {
        m_Title = value;
    }
}
}
}
```

NOTE   Many aspects of how an object is serialized to XML can be controlled with attributes. For more information, see the topic "Controlling XML Serialization Using Attributes" in online help.

The next step is to "wrap" the Employee class in a collection class named OurTeam that implements the ICollection interface, shown in Listing 12.5. ICollection defines size, enumerators, and synchronization for all collection classes. In addition, the XmlSerializer needs the class to have an Add method and an Indexer. For my own convenience, I also added a Clear method to the class.

Listing 12.5   **Implementing the *ICollection* Interface Around the *Employee* Class**

```
using System.Collections;
...
public class OurTeam: ICollection {
    public OurTeam(){
    }
```

```
   private ArrayList empArray = new ArrayList();
   public Employee this[int index]{
      get{return (Employee) empArray[index];}
   }
   public int Count{
      get{return empArray.Count;}
   }
   public void CopyTo(Array a, int index){
      empArray.CopyTo(a, index);
   }
   public object SyncRoot{
      get{return this;}
   }
   public bool IsSynchronized{
      get{return false;}
   }
   public IEnumerator GetEnumerator(){
      return empArray.GetEnumerator();
   }
   public void Add(Employee newEmployee){
      empArray.Add(newEmployee);
   }
   public void Clear(){
      empArray.Clear();
   }
}
```

The preliminaries are now in place. The user interface can be implemented in a Windows form.

The user will enter a first name, last name, and title for each employee. When the Add Employee button is clicked, the employee will be added to the OurTeam collection. When all the employees have been added, the Serialize button is used to serialize the class to a file. The Deserialize button recovers the information from the XML and reads it into ListBoxes.

To get started in the form, a variable needs to be declared to hold the OurTeam instance at the form level, and the object is instantiated in the form constructor—both are done so that the instance of the collection class is available while the form is running:

```
OurTeam ourteam; //at the form level
...
ourteam = new OurTeam(); // in the form constructor
```

Listing 12.6 shows the code for adding `Employee` instances, based on user input, to the collection class.

Listing 12.6   Adding *Employee* Instances to the Collection Class

```
private void btnAdd_Click(object sender, System.EventArgs e) {
    Employee employee = new Employee(txtFname.Text, txtLname.Text,
        txtTitle.Text);
    ourteam.Add (employee);
    txtFname.Text = String.Empty;
    txtLname.Text = String.Empty;
    txtTitle.Text = String.Empty;
}
```

To serialize the collection class, you need to add directives to `System.IO` and `System.Xml .Serialization`. Listing 12.7 shows the code required to serialize the class.

Listing 12.7   Serializing the Collection Class

```
using System.IO;
using System.Xml.Serialization;
...
StreamWriter sw;

private void btnSerial_Click(object sender, System.EventArgs e) {
    try {
        XmlSerializer theSerial = new XmlSerializer (typeof(OurTeam));
        sw = new StreamWriter("employee.xml",false);
        theSerial.Serialize(sw, ourteam);
    }
    catch (Exception excep){
        MessageBox.Show (excep.Message);
    }
    finally{
        sw.Flush();
        sw.Close();
        ourteam.Clear();
    }
}
```

This code is pretty straightforward. A new `XmlSerializer` is created, using the `typeof` method to pass it the type of the `OurTeam` collection. A `StreamWriter` is connected to the file `employee.xml` in the application directory.

NOTE   The second argument to the `StreamWriter` constructor, the Boolean `false`, tells the `StreamWriter` to overwrite a file with the given path (rather than append to it).

Finally, the XmlSerializer's Serialize method is used to connect the collection class and the StreamWriter.

If you try this out and examine the file that results, you'll see that it produces multiple XML elements of this sort:

```
<Employee>
    <Fname>Frodo</Fname>
    <Lname>Baggins</Lname>
    <Title>Hobbit</Title>
</Employee>
```

All the <Employee> elements are contained within a single root <ArrayOfEmployee> </ArrayOfEmployee> node. If you open the file created by the XmlSerializer in an XML editor, it will appear along the lines of Figure 12.12.

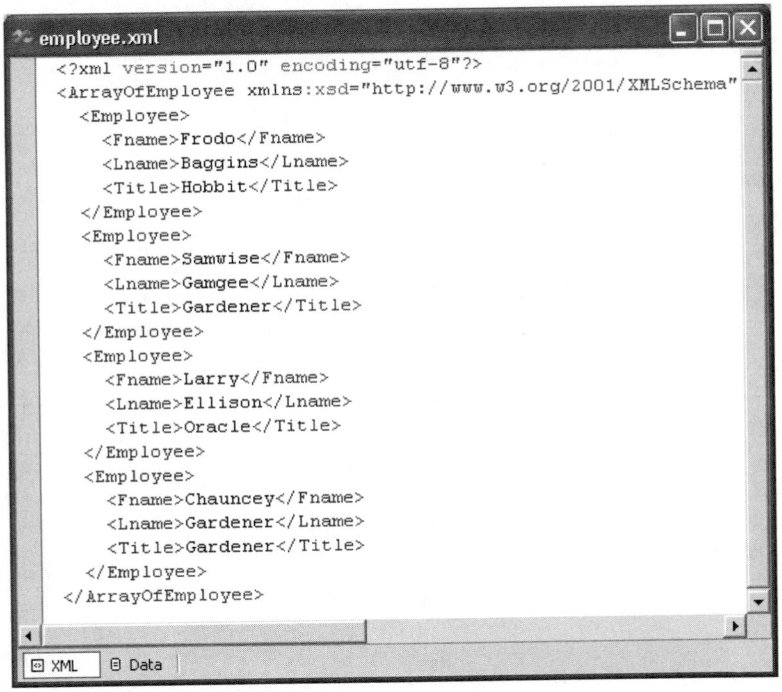

FIGURE 12.12:

The <Employee> elements are contained within one <ArrayOfEmployee> root node tag.

```
<?xml version="1.0" encoding="utf-8"?>
<ArrayOfEmployee xmlns:xsd="http://www.w3.org/2001/XMLSchema"
    <Employee>
        <Fname>Frodo</Fname>
        <Lname>Baggins</Lname>
        <Title>Hobbit</Title>
    </Employee>
    <Employee>
        <Fname>Samwise</Fname>
        <Lname>Gamgee</Lname>
        <Title>Gardener</Title>
    </Employee>
    <Employee>
        <Fname>Larry</Fname>
        <Lname>Ellison</Lname>
        <Title>Oracle</Title>
    </Employee>
    <Employee>
        <Fname>Chauncey</Fname>
        <Lname>Gardener</Lname>
        <Title>Gardener</Title>
    </Employee>
</ArrayOfEmployee>
```

employee.xml |⊡ XML   ⊟ Data|

The code for deserializing the XML in the file is shown in Listing 12.8. To deserialize the XML contained in the file into Employee instances of an instance of the OurTeam class, first instantiate an XmlSerializer and a FileStream. Next, use the Deserialize method of the XmlSerializer to connect with the FileStream, and cast the result to type OurTeam:

```
newteam = (OurTeam) theSerial.Deserialize(fs);
```

Listing 12.8   **Deserializing XML from a File to Class Instances**

```
using System.IO;
using System.Xml.Serialization;
...
FileStream fs;

private void btnDeserial_Click(object sender, System.EventArgs e) {
    try{
        XmlSerializer theSerial = new XmlSerializer (typeof(OurTeam));
        fs = new FileStream("employee.xml",FileMode.Open);
        OurTeam newteam = new OurTeam();
        newteam = (OurTeam) theSerial.Deserialize(fs);
        foreach (Employee emp in newteam){
            lstFname.Items.Add(emp.Fname);
            lstLname.Items.Add(emp.Lname);
            lstTitle.Items.Add(emp.Title);
        }
    }
    catch (Exception excep){
        MessageBox.Show (excep.Message);
    }
    finally{
        fs.Close();
    }
}
```

Finally, the `Employee` items in the collection class can be cycled through, and their XML elements accessed like instance members. The results of adding the XML elements, using instance member syntax, to ListBoxes, is shown in Figure 12.13.

FIGURE 12.13:

Once the XML has been deserialized from the file back to class instances, it can be accessed normally.

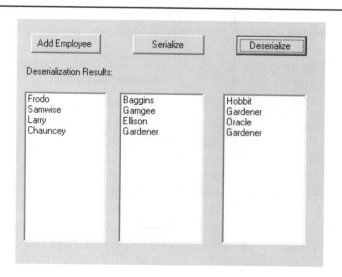

Reading and Writing XML

You don't need to serialize XML content to write (and read) XML documents to and from files. The XmlTextWriter class allows you to write whatever XML you care to generate, and XmlTextReader lets you read the contents of an XML document. Using the XMLTextWriter, an XML document is written from top to bottom. In other words, you get a single forward pass at creating the XML document.

To see this in action, I've set up a simple interface, shown in Figure 12.14, which lets the user decide the name for XML nodes and the values that those nodes enclose. The text entered by the user in the Element text box will become the XML tag, and the text entered in the Value text box will become its value:

```
<element>
    value
</element>
```

FIGURE 12.14:

Users can enter as many element/value pairs as they want; when all the pairs have been entered, the XML document is created.

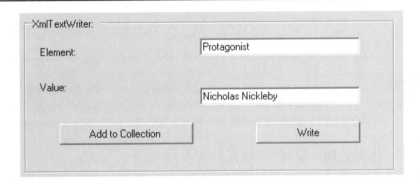

In the interests of simplicity, all the element/value pairs entered by the user will fall under one root XML node, <UserChoice>. So the structure of the XML document will look like this, with each element/value combination chosen by the user:

```
<UserChoice>
    <element>
        value
    </element>
    <element>
        value
    </element>
    ...
</UserChoice>
```

Creating the Class and Collection Class

If the user can enter multiple element/value pairs before the XML document is generated, the application must have some way to store the information. Once again, we'll use a class that is based on ArrayList to handle this (this time inheriting directly from ArrayList rather than using ArrayList functionality via encapsulation as in the example in the previous section).

Listing 12.9 shows the bare-bones class that will be used for each element/value pair and the collection class that will be used to store the user's XML choices until the XML document is ready to be generated.

Listing 12.9   **An Element/Value XML Class and a Collection Class Used to Store Element/Value Pairs**

```
using System.Collections;
...
public class Xml {
    public string element;
    public string @value;
}
public class XmlCollection : ArrayList {
    public void Add (Xml aXml){
        base.Add (aXml);
    }
}
```

NOTE   I really wanted to use the identifier *value* for the variable holding the value of an element, but, of course, value is a reserved keyword in C#. So I marked the variable name with the @ literal identifier, *@value*, which can be used as a variable.

Using the Class and Collection

After you've set up the class and collection, create an interface with text boxes for the user input of elements and values, like that shown in Figure 12.14. The Add button will be used to add an element/value pair to the collection, and the Write button will be used to generate the relevant XML document.

At the top of the form module, import the System.Xml namespace (it contains the XmlTextReader and XmlTextWriter classes):

```
using System.Xml;
```

Next, declare at the form level and instantiate in Form1's constructor a collection object based on the collection class defined in Listing 12.9:

```
XmlCollection theXml; // Declared at form level
...
theXml = new XmlCollection(); // in Form1 constructor
```

In the click event procedure of the Add button, instantiate an element/value object, assign the values of the text boxes to it, and add it to the collection:

```
private void btnAdd_Click(object sender, System.EventArgs e) {
    Xml aXml = new Xml();
    aXml.element = txtElement.Text;
    aXml.@value = txtValue.Text;
    theXml.Add (aXml);
    txtElement.Text = String.Empty;
    txtValue.Text = String.Empty;
}
```

That takes care of adding element/value pairs to the collection. Now let's write an XML document based on the contents of the collection!

In the click event procedure for the Write button, declare and instantiate a XmlTextWriter, specifying a file (including path) and the encoding to use:

```
XmlTextWriter myXmlTextWriter = new XmlTextWriter("doc.xml", null);
```

Setting the encoding to null causes it to be written out as UTF-8. If no path is provided, by default the file will be written to the executable, or bin, directory of the project.

WARNING   The XmlTextWriter will overwrite the specified file if it already exists. There's nothing to stop you from using the common dialogs (or other mechanism) to allow the user to select a file.

Next, declare an element/value XML object based on the class defined in Listing 12.9.

Use the methods and properties of the XmlTextWriter object to tell the XmlTextWriter to format the XML with three spaces for indentation, place a comment at the start of the document, and create a root XML element called <UserChoice>:

```
myXmlTextWriter.Formatting = Formatting.Indented;
myXmlTextWriter.Indentation = 3;
myXmlTextWriter.IndentChar = ' ';
myXmlTextWriter.WriteStartDocument();
myXmlTextWriter.WriteComment("This is a sample XML document" +
    " generated using an XmlTextWriter object.");
myXmlTextWriter.WriteStartElement("UserChoice");
```

Next, use the foreach syntax to cycle through the collection to write each item in the collection:

```
foreach (Xml aXml in theXml){
    myXmlTextWriter.WriteElementString(aXml.element, aXml.@value);
}
```

Finally, close the root element and document:

```
myXmlTextWriter.WriteEndElement();
myXmlTextWriter.Close();
```

NOTE   I just wrote "finally" close the root element and document. Well, as you may be thinking, the closure code in this example (and in some others in this chapter) should be placed in the `finally` block of a `try...finally` structure. I haven't done this here to make the code more readable—but you should place this kind of closure code within `finally` blocks in all real-world applications.

The complete code for adding XML element/value pairs to the collection and writing an XML document based on the collection items that have been added is shown in Listing 12.10.

Listing 12.10   **Creating a Collection of Element/Value Pairs and Writing Them to an XML Document**

```
using System.Xml;
...
XmlCollection theXml; // Declared at form level
...
theXml = new XmlCollection(); // in Form1 constructor
...
private void btnAdd_Click(object sender, System.EventArgs e) {
    Xml aXml = new Xml();
    aXml.element = txtElement.Text;
    aXml.@value = txtValue.Text;
    theXml.Add (aXml);
    txtElement.Text = String.Empty;
    txtValue.Text = String.Empty;
}
private void btnWrite_Click(object sender, System.EventArgs e) {
    XmlTextWriter myXmlTextWriter = new XmlTextWriter("doc.xml", null);
    myXmlTextWriter.Formatting = Formatting.Indented;
    myXmlTextWriter.Indentation = 3;
    myXmlTextWriter.IndentChar = ' ';
    myXmlTextWriter.WriteStartDocument();
    myXmlTextWriter.WriteComment("This is a sample XML document" +
        " generated using an XMLTextWriter object.");
    myXmlTextWriter.WriteStartElement("UserChoice");
    foreach (Xml aXml in theXml){
        myXmlTextWriter.WriteElementString(aXml.element, aXml.@value);
    }
    myXmlTextWriter.WriteEndElement();
    myXmlTextWriter.Close();
}
```

Run the project and enter some element/value pairs, clicking Add each time. Next, click the Write button. You'll find that an XML document, containing the elements and values you added, has been created along these lines:

```
<?xml version="1.0"?>
<!--This is a sample XML document generated using an XmlTextWriter object.-->
<UserChoice>
    <Protagonist>Nicholas Nickleby</Protagonist>
    <Schoolmaster>Wackford Squeers</Schoolmaster>
    <InfantPhenomenon>Ninetta Crummles</InfantPhenomenon>
</UserChoice>
```

NOTE   You could certainly extend this application if you were interested or needed to. For example, this simple application doesn't check to make sure that each element added is unique. Duplicate checking could be implemented by calling the Exists method of the XmlCollection class before adding an element to the collection.

Reading XML with *XmlTextReader*

The counterpart to the XmlTextWriter class is the XmlTextReader class. Realize that this is by no means the only class available in .NET to read (or parse) XML files; XmlNodeReader and XmlValidatingReader (used in the example in the previous section of this chapter) are also powerful classes.

Much of the time, you will know a great deal about the formatting of the XML file you want to read. That's certainly the case with the example that I'll show you, in which we know that the root element is named <UserChoice> and is followed by elements and values:

```
<UserChoice>
    <element>
        value
    </element>
    <element>
        value
    </element>
    ...
</UserChoice>
```

If you are interested in only the elements and values, it's an easy thing to instantiate a new XmlTextReader object and start it past the root element:

```
XmlTextReader myXmlTextReader = new XmlTextReader("doc.xml");
myXmlTextReader.ReadStartElement("UserChoice");
```

You could then set up a loop reading the rest of the document, and exiting only when the end of the document or the </UserChoice> tag is reached:

```
while (myXmlTextReader.Read()){
    if (myXmlTextReader.Name == "UserChoice")
        break;
    ...
}
```

Within the loop, you can use the ReadOuterXml method to read tags and values into a multiline text box:

```
while (myXmlTextReader.Read()){
    if (myXmlTextReader.Name == "UserChoice")
        break;
    txtReader.Text += myXmlTextReader.ReadOuterXml() + "\r\n";
}
```

Finally, the XmlTextReader should be closed:

```
myXMLTextReader.Close()
```

The code, placed in the Display button's click event, is shown in Listing 12.11.

Listing 12.11   Reading an XML File

```
private void btnDisplay_Click(object sender, System.EventArgs e) {
    txtReader.Text = String.Empty;
    XmlTextReader myXmlTextReader = new XmlTextReader("doc.xml");
    myXmlTextReader.ReadStartElement("UserChoice");
    while (myXmlTextReader.Read()){
        if (myXmlTextReader.Name == "UserChoice")
            break;
        txtReader.Text += myXmlTextReader.ReadOuterXml() + "\r\n";
    }
    myXmlTextReader.Close();
}
```

If you run the project and click the Display button, the elements and values in the doc.xml file contained between the beginning <UserChoice> tag and the ending </UserChoice> tag will be shown in the text box (Figure 12.15).

I leave it, as they say, as an exercise for the reader to refine this project by adding exception handling and dealing with white space entered by the user for an element tag (as things stand, this will cause the program to throw an exception when XmlTextReader tries to retrieve the tag with white space)—and to customize the application for your particular needs.

The XmlTextReader is programmed to retrieve the tags and values between the <UserChoice> and </UserChoice> tags.

The Document Object Model (DOM)

The XmlTextWriter and XmlTextReader classes described in the last section are great if all you need to do is make a single pass through an XML document—and read or write it to a file. However, they don't help you that much with adding, editing, and deleting members of an XML document. Other mechanisms exist that do a better job of this, including SAX (see sidebar) and the Document Object Model (DOM)—implemented by the XmlDocument class and related classes—which is discussed in this section.

Simple API for XML (SAX)

Simple API for XML (SAX) is an alternative to DOM that is not supported explicitly by any .NET classes. (As a publicly developed interface, SAX could fairly easily be implemented in a class derived from XmlReader.)

Continued on next page

> The SAX interface reads an XML document using an events-based model. A SAX reader is fast, read-only, and only moves in one direction: forward.
>
> SAX requires less overhead than DOM, so it might make sense to use it if resources are an issue and you have a large number of XML documents to parse (or a single, very large document). SAX can be configured to read only the information you need (unlike DOM, which reads the entire XML document into memory). In addition—unlike DOM—a SAX parse can be stopped when you find what you need.

Once an XML document has been loaded into an instance of the Xml Document class, it is available in memory and can be traversed backwards and forwards. The parts of the XML document are represented by node classes, some of which are shown in Table 12.3. These classes represent elements, attributes, and so on. You can add, edit, or delete node classes belonging to an active Xml Document instance.

TABLE 12.3: Types of *XmlDocument* Nodes

DOM Node	.NET Class	Description
Document	Xml Document	The container of all the nodes in the tree. It is also known as the document root (not always the same as the root element).
DocumentFragment	Xml DocumentFragment	Temporary XML storage containing one or more nodes without any tree structure.
DocumentType	Xml DocumentType	Represents the <!DOCTYPE...> node.
Element	Xml Element	Represents an element node.
Attr	Xml Attribute	An attribute of an element.
ProcessingInstruction	Xml ProcessingInstruction	A processing instruction node.
Comment	Xml Comment	A comment node.
Text	Xml Text	Text belonging to an element or attribute.

NOTE For a complete list of XML nodes, look up "Types of XML Nodes" in online help. The topic describes nodes (not shown in Table 12.3) that can be used in .NET but are not approved by W3C.

Figure 12.16 shows how the DOM classes interact. As you can see in the figure, nodes in an Xml Document can be accessed and managed using the Xml Node class. They can also be accessed and managed using a class that depends on the specific type of the node, e.g., Xml Attribute and Xml Element.

FIGURE 12.16:

Interaction of the XML Document Object Model (DOM) classes.

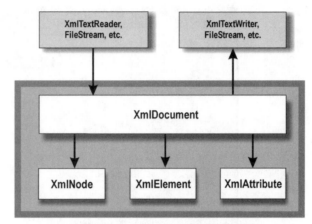

XML Document Object Model (DOM)

NOTE   You may also be interested in the XmlDataDocument class, which is derived from XmlDocument. XmlDataDocument allows you to load relational data and manipulate it as XML using the DOM.

As you can see, the classes and mechanisms related to DOM and the XmlDocument class are complex and powerful. It would take at least a chapter to cover them all—actually, more like a book, a big fat book.

Obviously, I don't have space to explain all the DOM-related .NET classes and how they work. But I can provide a demonstration that allows you to load an XmlDocument object from a file, and then move recursively through the nodes in the XmlDocument, displaying representations of them in a TreeView control. (The complete code will be shown in Listing 12.12.)

To start with, I added a Button, an OpenFileDialog, and a TreeView control to a form. At the form level, I declared some variables to hold the TreeView nodes, the XMLDocument nodes, and an XmlTextReader:

```
TreeNode tn;
XmlNode xn;
XmlTextReader xr;
```

Next, within the button's click event, I added the standard common-dialog code to allow the user to select an XML file. Note that not all XML files end with a .xml suffix; in Figure 12.17, the user is shown selecting a Web.config XML file. However, if a non-XML file is selected (whatever the suffix), the program will throw an exception.

FIGURE 12.17:

The user can select an XML file for parsing.

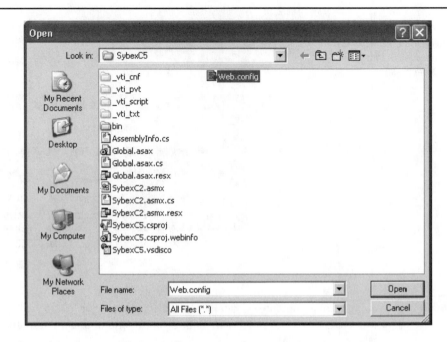

With a file selected, an `XmlTextReader` and an `XmlDocument` are instantiated:

```
xr = new XmlTextReader(theFile);
...
XmlDocument xDoc = new XmlDocument()
```

The `Load` method of the `XmlDocument` is used to connect the selected file to the `XmlDocument`:

```
xDoc.Load (xr);
```

The top node of the `TreeView` is created and the `WalkTheTree` method invoked:

```
tn = new TreeNode("XML Document");
tView.Nodes.Add(tn);
xn = xDoc.DocumentElement;
WalkTheTree (xn, tn);
```

Within `WalkTheTree`, a node is added to the topmost node, using the XML name and value of the node for display purposes:

```
XmlNode tmpXn;
TreeNode tmpTn;
TreeNode tmpTnAttr;
tmpTn = new TreeNode (xn.Name + " " + xn.Value);
tn.Nodes.Add(tmpTn);
```

Attributes need special handling:

```
if (xn.NodeType == XmlNodeType.Element){
```

```
        foreach (XmlNode xnAttr in xn.Attributes){
            tmpTnAttr = new TreeNode(xnAttr.Name + " = " + xnAttr.Value);
            tmpTn.Nodes.Add(tmpTnAttr);
        }
    }
```

If the node has children, then process them, and their children and siblings, by recursively calling WalkTheTree:

```
    if (xn.HasChildNodes){
        tmpXn = xn.FirstChild;
        while (tmpXn != null){
            WalkTheTree(tmpXn, tmpTn);
            tmpXn = tmpXn.NextSibling;
        }
    }
```

If you try this on an XML file, such as the Web.config file selected earlier, you'll have to expand the nodes in the TreeView. With the nodes expanded, the element name, value, and attributes will be displayed (Figure 12.18).

FIGURE 12.18:

You can display all the nodes of an XmlDocument using a recursive method.

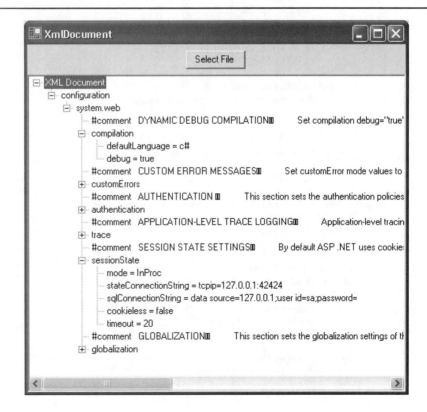

Listing 12.12   Displaying the Nodes of an XML Document Using DOM

```
using System.Xml;
...
TreeNode tn;
XmlNode xn;
XmlTextReader xr;

private void btnFile_Click(object sender, System.EventArgs e) {
    string theFile;
    openFileDialog1.InitialDirectory = Application.ExecutablePath;
    openFileDialog1.DefaultExt = "xml";
    openFileDialog1.Filter = "XML Files (*.xml)|*.xml|All Files (*.*) | *.*";
    if (openFileDialog1.ShowDialog() == DialogResult.OK){
        theFile = openFileDialog1.FileName;
        try {
            tView.Nodes.Clear();
            this.Cursor = Cursors.WaitCursor;
            xr = new XmlTextReader(theFile);
            xr.WhitespaceHandling = WhitespaceHandling.None;
            XmlDocument xDoc = new XmlDocument();
            xDoc.Load (xr);
            tn = new TreeNode("XML Document");
            tView.Nodes.Add(tn);
            xn = xDoc.DocumentElement;
            WalkTheTree (xn, tn);
        }
        catch (Exception excep) {
            MessageBox.Show (excep.Message);
        }
        finally {
            xr.Close();
            this.Cursor = Cursors.Default;
        }
    }
}
private void WalkTheTree(XmlNode xn, TreeNode tn){
    XmlNode tmpXn;
    TreeNode tmpTn;
    TreeNode tmpTnAttr;
    tmpTn = new TreeNode (xn.Name + " " + xn.Value);
    tn.Nodes.Add(tmpTn);
    if (xn.NodeType == XmlNodeType.Element){
        foreach (XmlNode xnAttr in xn.Attributes){
            tmpTnAttr = new TreeNode(xnAttr.Name + " = " + xnAttr.Value);
            tmpTn.Nodes.Add(tmpTnAttr);
        }
    }
    if (xn.HasChildNodes){
        tmpXn = xn.FirstChild;
```

```
        while (tmpXn != null){
            WalkTheTree(tmpXn, tmpTn);
            tmpXn = tmpXn.NextSibling;
        }
    }
}
```

XSL Transformations

The purpose of Extensible Stylesheet Language Transformations (XSLT) is to convert the form (or structure) of an XML document to a different format or structure. Probably the most common use of this is to transform XML into HTML so it can be displayed in a web page, but there are many other possible uses of XSLT (for instance, a document could be transformed so that it contained only the fields required by an application).

You'll find classes related to XSLT in the System.Xml, System.Xml.XPath, and System .Xml.Xsl namespaces. Some of the classes and interfaces most commonly used with XSLT in these namespaces are shown in Table 12.4.

TABLE 12.4: Classes and Interfaces Commonly Used with XSLT

Class or Interface	What It Is Used For
XPathNavigator	Provides an API that provides a cursor-style model for navigating an XML data source.
IXPathNavigable	Interface that provides a CreateNavigator method, which is used to create an XPathNavigator.
XmlDocument	Enables editing and parsing of an XML document. See previous section for more information.
XmlDataDocument	Derived from XmlDocument and allows XSLT transformations to be performed on relational data retrieved from a database. For more information, see "Synchronizing a DataSet with an XmlDataDocument" in online help.
XPathDocument	Provides read-only XML document processing with an XSLT transformation.
XPathNodeIterator	Provides an iterator over a set of nodes in an XPathDocument.
XslTransform	Transforms XML data using an XSLT style sheet.

Once again, XSLT is a topic far too big for a small portion of a chapter. At its best, XSLT is an extraordinary tool for separating form—the appearance of the thing—from structure.

For a simple example of how this works, open a new ASP.NET Web Application. Add an XML file, shown in Listing 12.13, and a file containing an XSLT transformation, shown in Listing 12.14, to the project.

Listing 12.13   The XML File

```xml
<?xml version="1.0" encoding="utf-8" ?>
<NewDataSet>
    <Product>
        <Name>Kite</Name>
        <Desc>It flies</Desc>
        <SubPart>wings</SubPart>
    </Product>
    <Product>
        <Name>Sour Ball</Name>
        <Desc>Tastes good</Desc>
        <SubPart>n/a</SubPart>
    </Product>
    <Product>
        <Name>RoboDog</Name>
        <Desc>Does tricks</Desc>
        <SubPart>CPU</SubPart>
    </Product>
</NewDataSet>
```

Listing 12.14   The XSLT Transformation

```xml
<?xml version='1.0'?>
<xsl:stylesheet xmlns:xsl="http://www.w3.org/1999/XSL/Transform" version="1.0">
    <xsl:template match="/">
        <html>
          <body>
            <table cellspacing="3" cellpadding="8">
                <tr bgcolor="#AAAAAA">
                    <td class="heading"><B>Name</B></td>
                    <td class="heading"><B>Description</B></td>
                    <td class="heading"><B>SubPart</B></td>
                </tr>
                <xsl:for-each select="NewDataSet/Product">
                    <tr bgcolor="#DDDDDD">
                        <td valign="top">
                            <b><xsl:value-of select="Name"/></b>
                        </td>
                        <td valign="top">
                            <b><xsl:value-of select="Desc"/></b>
                        </td>
                        <td valign="top">
                            <b><xsl:value-of select="SubPart"/></b>
                        </td>
                    </tr>
                </xsl:for-each>
            </table>
          </body>
```

```
      </html>
    </xsl:template>
  </xsl:stylesheet>
```

I've called the XML file shown in Listing 12.13 `Many_Prod.xml`. The XSLT file shown in Listing 12.14 is called `Trans_Prod.xsl`. You can add these files to the project in one of several ways: by adding empty XML and XSLT files using the Add New Item dialog, or by creating the files in an external editor and then selecting Project ➢ Add Existing Item. Once the files have been added to the project, they will appear in Solution Explorer.

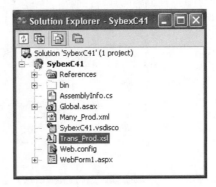

The XML file shown in Listing 12.13 is clearly straightforward, but let's have a little closer look at the XSLT transformation shown in Listing 12.14. This listing combines HTML with tags specified in the `http://www.w3.org/1999/XSL/Transform` namespace that are replaced with values from the XML file to be transformed. You can identify these replacements in Listing 12.14 because the tags begin with `xsl:`.

With the project's WebForm open, use the Toolbox to locate the Xml control (on the Web Forms tab). Add an Xml control to the project, right-click it, and select Properties from the context menu. The Properties window will open, with the Xml control selected in it (Figure 12.19).

FIGURE 12.19:

You can set the XML file to be transformed, and the XSLT transformation to use, with the properties of the Xml control.

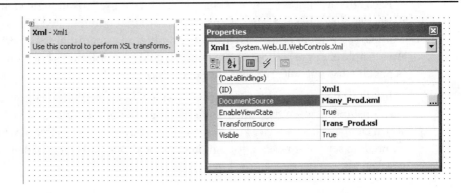

In the Properties window, set the DocumentSource to Many_Prod.xml (shown in Listing 12.13) and the TransformSource to Trans_Prod.xsl (shown in Listing 12.14). Run the project. The data in the XML file will appear in your browser window as formatted by the XSLT file (Figure 12.20).

FIGURE 12.20:

The XML file supplies the data, and the XSLT file formats it.

Database Basics

It's true that you can create database applications in C# .NET without needing to program and without possessing a deep understanding of databases. (Obviously, willingness to program and having a sophisticated understanding of databases does help!)

You do need to know that databases are organized in tables. Each table contains rows and columns, called *fields*, of information. A row across a table is called a *record*.

Each table usually contains a primary key, which is used to uniquely identify records. In other words, within a table, the value of a primary key cannot be duplicated across records. For example, a primary key might be a Social Security number, an e-mail address, or other unique identifier. An example of a poorly chosen primary key would be a customer's last name, because duplication is possible (two people can have the same last name).

In addition to primary keys, *foreign keys*, which do not need to be unique, are used to establish relationships between the data in tables. For example, suppose you have a Customers table in which cust_ID is the primary key. You could also have an Orders table in which the same cust_ID showed up several times as a foreign key (because one customer made multiple orders). This is called a *one-to-many* relationship.

Data organized in this fashion in independent tables is called *relational*. The software used to contain it is, logically, a relational database. Structured Query Language (SQL) is the common language used to manipulate and retrieve information stored in relational databases. High-powered databases are organized as servers and are referred to as a *database management system* (DBMS). (You'll also see the term *relational database management system*, RDBMS.) In effect, the access layer of a C# .NET program is a client of the database server (in the same sense that an Internet browser is the client of a web server).

Good architecture of databases often funnels access through special programs internal to the database, written in an internal, database-specific language intended for this purpose, and are called *stored procedures*. While stored procedures are far beyond the scope of this chapter, you should know that, from the viewpoint of a C# .NET program, what you want to do to a database is either execute SQL statements against it or run a stored procedure in the database intended for access purposes (in large part, the stored procedure itself executes SQL).

NOTE   In production applications, running stored procedures is generally far more scalable and secure than executing ad hoc SQL statements against a DBMS.

ADO.NET

For many developers today, input/output means working with a database. For those in the Microsoft environment, this likely means SQL Server.

Each new version of Microsoft's programming languages has shipped with a new model for the data connectivity layer, and .NET is, of course, no exception. The latest incarnation is, of course, ADO.NET.

Since space in this chapter is limited, I'll forgo historical discussion and concentrate on how ADO.NET provides data access to C# programs—and how to use the tools that Visual Studio provides to make connectivity easier.

Working with Managed Providers

The .NET Data components are supplied as a separate set of four components for each data source. Each set of objects, targeted at a particular data source, is known as a *managed provider*.

Currently, the only managed providers that ship with .NET are a set for Microsoft's SQL Server DBMS and a set that works with any OLE database (OLE DB) source (in other words, a managed provider for all the rest). An ODBC managed provider is also currently available for download. To download it, or for further information, go to http://msdn.microsoft.com, and search for **ODBC .NET Data Provider**.

The two sets of Data components (one set for SQL Server and one set for OLE DB) are functionally identical. The purpose of each of the components is shown in Table 12.5.

TABLE 12.5: ADO.NET Data Components Available on the Toolbox

Component(s)	Purpose
OleDbDataAdapter and SqlDataAdapter	Contains and controls Command objects (see Table 12.6).
OleDbConnection and SqlConnection	Provides a connection to a database server (or source).
OleDbCommand and SqlCommand	Executes SQL statements (or stored procedures). ExecuteReader method of the Command object used to create a DataReader object (to be discussed shortly).
DataSet	An in-memory cache of data (sometimes called a *data store*) made up of one or more tables. This fundamental ADO.NET object is filled using one or more managed provider data adapters.
DataView	Controls can be bound to a DataView, which contains filtered and sorted data based on a DataSet.

The Data components belong to the System.Data namespace. SQL Server components are part of System.Data.SQLClient, and OLE DB components belong to System.Data.OleDB.

You should also know about one other object, the DataReader. The OleDbDataReader and OleSqlDataReader allow you to return read-only result sets from a database. If you need to quickly cycle through all the values in a field but have no need to update or change the values, then the DataReader is probably the easiest route. DataReader objects are created in code using the ExecuteReader method of either the OleDbCommand or SqlCommand objects (see the example in the next section).

The examples in this chapter use the SqlDataAdapter provider with the sample Northwind database tables that ship with Microsoft's SQL Server 2000.

NOTE   Don't worry if you don't have SQL Server running. You almost certainly have some version of the Northwind database, probably in Access format, on your system. The specific location (and name) of the Northwind.mdb sample database will depend on your system and the software that you have installed on it. For example, if you have Office XP installed in the default location, you can find a copy of the database at C:\Program Files\Microsoft Office\Office10\ 1033\FPNWind.mdb. Those with older versions of Office may find it at C:\Program Files\ Microsoft Office\Office\Samples\Northwind.mdb. In addition, you will need to use the OleDbDataAdapter provider rather than the SQL Server provider.

Displaying Data with a *DataReader*

Before we get down to more specifics about how to use the ADO.NET Data components, it may help you to get a feeling for how these components work to run through a simple code example.

The task is to display the company names in the CompanyName field of the Suppliers table of the sample Northwind database. As a preliminary, in the web form application used to demonstrate XSLT transformations, add a ListBox named lstData—which will be filled in the WebForm load event with the required data.

The first step in the code module is to add a using directive to the System.Data.SqlClient namespace:

```
using System.Data.SqlClient;
```

NOTE   If you were working with a OLE DB data source and the OleDbDataReader (instead of the SqlDataReader), you'd want to use the System.Data.OleDb namespace instead.

Next, within the WebForm's load event procedure, create the query string and define a new SqlConnection object (for more information about connection strings, see the following section):

```
string mySelectQuery = "SELECT CompanyName FROM Suppliers";
SqlConnection myConnection = new SqlConnection("data source=SQLSERVER;initial" +
    " catalog=Northwind;password=harold;user id=sa");
```

Using the query string and the SqlConnection, create a new SqlCommand:

```
SqlCommand myCommand = new SqlCommand(mySelectQuery, myConnection);
```

Open the connection:

```
myConnection.Open()
```

Declare an SqlDataReader, and use the ExecuteReader method of the SqlCommand to instantiate and populate it:

```
myConnection.Open();
SqlDataReader myReader = myCommand.ExecuteReader();
```

Use the Read method of the SqlDataReader to run through the DataReader and retrieve the desired data, and its GetString method to display it:

```
while (myReader.Read()){
    lstData.Items.Add(myReader.GetString(0));
}
```

Finally, close the SqlDataReader and the SqlConnection:

```
myReader.Close()
myConnection.Close()
```

If you run the project and click the button, the company name information will be displayed in the ListBox when the WebForm loads (Figure 12.21).

FIGURE 12.21:

The DataReader displays the results of the query in the ListBox.

Listing 12.15 shows the complete procedure that uses the ADO.NET components to create an SqlDataReader, and then uses the SqlDataReader to display specified data.

Listing 12.15   Displaying Data with an *SqlDataReader* Component

```
using System.Data.SqlClient;
...
private void WebForm1_Load(object sender, System.EventArgs e) {
    string mySelectQuery = "SELECT CompanyName FROM Suppliers";
    SqlConnection myConnection = new SqlConnection
        ("data source=SQLSERVER;initial" +
        " catalog=Northwind;password=harold;user id=sa");
    SqlCommand myCommand = new SqlCommand(mySelectQuery, myConnection);
    myConnection.Open();
    SqlDataReader myReader = myCommand.ExecuteReader();
    while (myReader.Read()){
        lstData.Items.Add( myReader.GetString(0));
    }
```

```
    myReader.Close();
    myConnection.Close();
}
```

Connection Strings

Many things can go into a connection string—depending, of course, upon the provider and configuration. A typical SQL Server connection string requires at a minimum the data source, the initial catalog, a user ID, and a password (if required for the user).

> **WARNING** As you are likely aware, the connection string shown in Listing 12.15 uses a plain-text password, a bad idea in the real world from a security viewpoint. It compounds this sin that the user shown in the connection string, "sa", is by convention a database administrator (DBA), presumably with a great deal of access.

You may well need help in finding the various values that go into creating a connection string for a particular connection. One way to find this information is to inspect the properties of the Connection object, discussed a little later in this chapter. Alternatively, assuming that a data connection has already been made, you can open Server Explorer by selecting View ➢ Server Explorer. Next, select the server connection you are interested in and choose Properties from the context menu. You can now view the connection string that interests you in the Properties window (Figure 12.22).

FIGURE 12.22:

The properties of servers shown in Server Explorer can be browsed to determine connection strings.

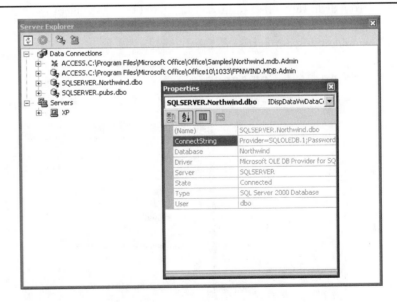

You may also be interested to know that if you save an empty text document in Windows Explorer, rename it to change its file extension to .udl, and double-click on the file in Windows Explorer, the ubiquitous Data Link Properties dialog will open (Figure 12.23).

FIGURE 12.23:

Opening a .udl file
allows you to set
data link properties.

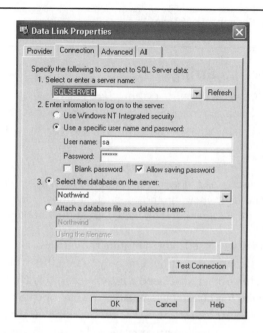

Provided that you are connected to a data source, the Data Link Properties dialog—which will be revisited in the next section—should allow you to choose a database server and database from drop-down lists of those available. Once you've completed the entries on the Provider and Connection tabs of this dialog and clicked OK, you'll find the connection string corresponding to your entries in the underlying text file.

Adding Data Components

The Data components are found on the Data tab of the Toolbox.

To use a Data component, drag it from the Toolbox to a form. Like the other nonvisual components, Data components sit on the tray beneath the form.

> **NOTE** Of course, if you prefer, you can also instantiate these components in code without using the visual interface provided by dragging and dropping.

Setting *DataAdapter* Properties

ADO.NET DataAdapter components (OleDbDataAdapter and SqlDataAdapter) each support four properties, which are Command objects of type OleDbCommand or SqlCommand, respectively, as shown in Table 12.6.

TABLE 12.6: Command-Object Properties of *OleDbDataAdapter / SqlDataAdapter*

Object	Purpose
SelectCommand	Retrieves data from a database
InsertCommand	Inserts data into a database
UpdateCommand	Updates data in a database
DeleteCommand	Deletes data in a database

Datasets

A *dataset* is one or more tables of data. The data connectivity layer "pulls" data from a database and uses it to create a dataset. Items in the tables in the dataset are manipulated to perform the actions required by the program and, in some cases, are saved back to the database.

Although they're very powerful, datasets are disconnected tables of data. This has great performance advantages, because processing can now be done on the client side without consuming database server resources. In some cases, however, you may need to be continuously connected to a database—in which case you will need to use the legacy ADO COM objects.

The first step toward creating a dataset is to add a DataAdapter component.

Adding a *DataAdapter* Component

With a form open in its designer, add an SqlDataAdapter to the form by double-clicking the SqlDataAdapter component on the Data tab of the Toolbox. The Data Adapter Configuration Wizard will open; click Next to start the wizard. The second panel, shown in Figure 12.24, allows you to choose a data connection from the existing data connections or to create a new connection.

FIGURE 12.24:

FIGURE 12.24:

You can choose a data connection from the list of current data connections or create a new connection.

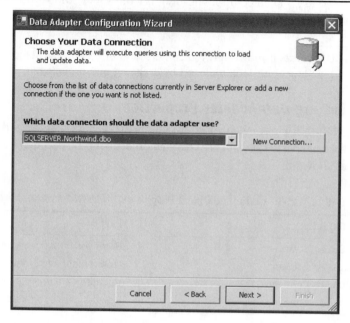

Creating a New Data Connection

To create a new connection, follow these steps:

1. Click the New Connection button in the Data Adapter Configuration Wizard. The Data Link Properties dialog will open, as shown in Figure 12.25, with the Connection tab active.

FIGURE 12.25:

The Data Link Properties dialog allows you to create a new data connection.

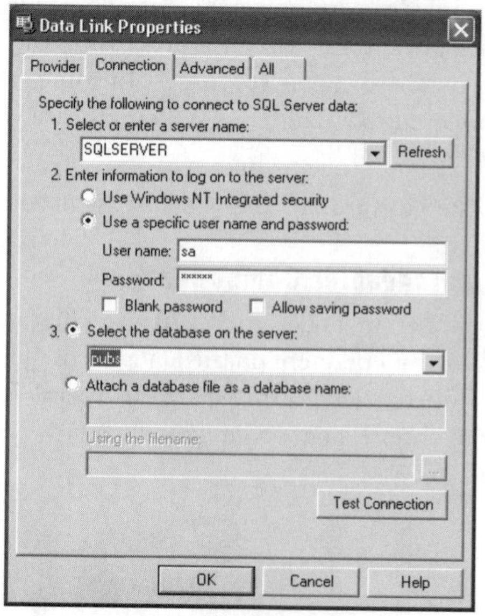

2. The first step in using the Data Link Properties dialog is to select the OLE DB provider you want to use to connect to the data. Click the Provider tab and select your provider. Figure 12.26 shows the Provider tab with the Microsoft OLE DB Provider for SQL Server selected.

FIGURE 12.26:

The Provider tab is used to select an OLE DB provider.

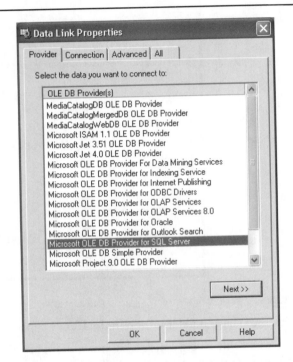

3. Click Next. The Connection tab will reopen. Use this tab to select the database you are connected to, either by typing in a database name or by browsing for it in a drop-down list. (In the case of a flat file Access connection, you can browse for the file using an Open file dialog.)

NOTE   Depending on the provider you selected, the Connection tab is also used when a user-name and password are required for accessing a database server, to specify file types and connection strings, and to supply other information that may be required to success-fully connect. For more information, see "Connection Strings" earlier in this chapter.

4. Click OK. You will be asked whether you want to use SQL statements or stored procedures.

Building a Query

The next Data Adapter Configuration Wizard panel, shown in Figure 12.27, asks you to enter an SQL statement that will be used to create the dataset. Many people find it easier to use a visual tool to create their SQL statement rather than entering one by hand.

FIGURE 12.27:

An SQL statement is
used to determine which
data will be used to
create the dataset.

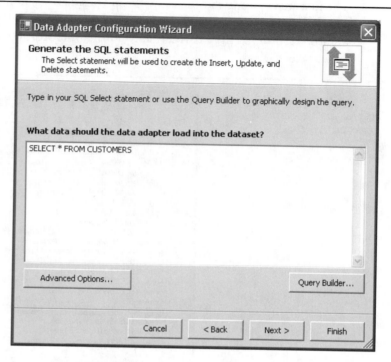

To visually generate a query, follow these steps:

1. Click the Query Builder button in the Data Adapter Configuration Wizard.

2. The Add Table dialog appears, as shown in Figure 12.28. The Query Builder lets you add a table or view. Select a table and click Add.

FIGURE 12.28:

You can add tables and
views using the Query
Builder.

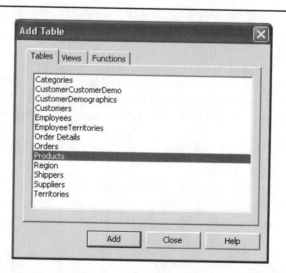

3. Once you have added a table, select the fields you would like to include.

The primary key for the table is shown in bold in the Query Builder.

4. You can add multiple tables to your query by right-clicking in the upper pane and selecting Add Table from the context menu. In the new tables that you added, select the fields you would like to include, as shown in Figure 12.29.

FIGURE 12.29:

Queries built in the Query Builder can include multiple tables.

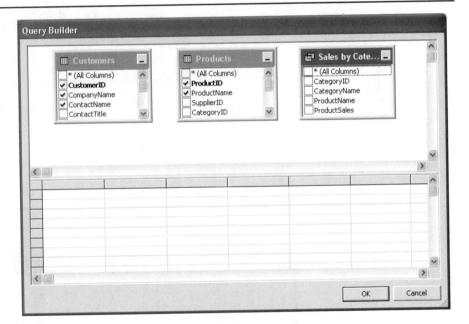

5. When you are satisfied with your query, click OK. The SQL statement will appear in the Data Adapter Configuration Wizard, as shown in Figure 12.30.

NOTE   Figure 12.30 shows a relatively complex SELECT query. For the example that follows, I'll use the simple query SELECT * FROM PRODUCTS.

FIGURE 12.30:

SQL generated by the Query Builder appears in the Data Adapter Configuration Wizard.

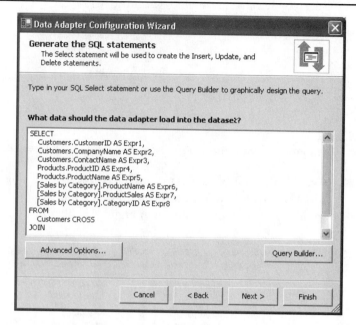

6. Click Next. The final panel of the wizard will list the tasks that the wizard has performed and give you warnings about anything left to do.

7. Click Finish. The wizard will complete its work.

Working with the Data Adapter

After you've added the DataAdapter component, you'll notice that an SqlConnection component has been added to the tray beneath your form and synchronized with the SqlDataAdapter's connection string.

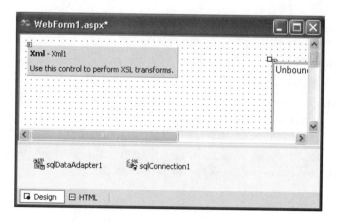

NOTE If you need to reconfigure the DataAdapter, you can restart the wizard by right-clicking the SqlDataAdapter and selecting Configure Data Adapter.

Note that the properties of the SqlDataAdapter are accessible in the normal fashion in the Properties window. For example, if you've forgotten what your SQL query was (or wish to modify it), you can look at the CommandText property of the SqlDataAdapter's SelectCommand.

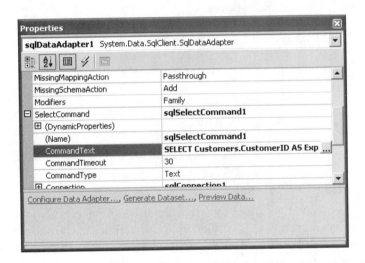

NOTE Clicking the button in the right column of the Properties window of the CommandText property opens the Query Builder interface.

Previewing the Dataset

Your next step will likely be to preview the dataset. To preview the dataset, choose Data ➢ Preview Data from the Visual Studio menus (or use the SqlDataAdapter's context menu). The Data Adapter Preview dialog, shown in Figure 12.31, will open.

In this dialog, make sure that sqlDataAdapter1 is selected in the Data Adapters drop-down list. Next, click Fill Dataset. The Results panel will preview the dataset.

FIGURE 12.31:

The Data Adapter
Preview dialog allows
you to preview the
dataset.

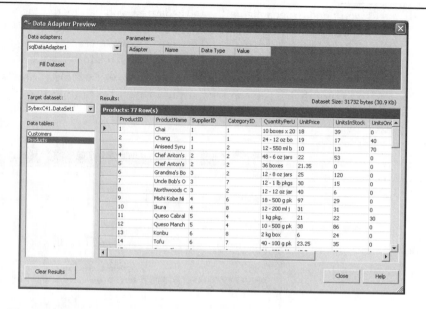

Generating the Dataset

Finally, generate the dataset by selecting Data ➤ Generate Dataset (or use the SqlData-
Adapter's context menu). The Generate Dataset dialog, shown in Figure 12.32, will open.
Select New, and give the dataset a name (for example, DataSet1). Make sure the tables you
want are selected. Also, make sure that the Add This Dataset to the Designer check box is
checked. Click OK. The DataSet component will be added to the tray beneath your form
(so there are now three components on the tray).

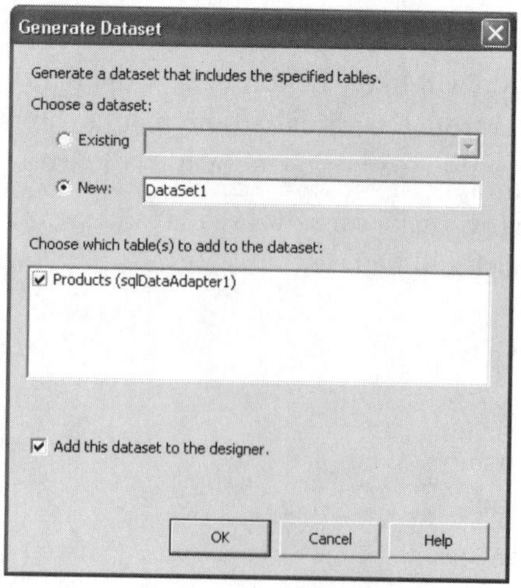

FIGURE 12.32:

The Generate Dataset
dialog adds a DataSet
component to your form.

You can also generate a dataset by adding a DataSet component from the Toolbox to your form.

Bingo! If you guessed that a DataSet is an XSD schema specifying the data elements that it represents as XML, you are exactly right. You can open the DataSet in its designer in the usual ways you'd suspect: for example, it appears as an .xsd file in Solution Explorer.

With the DataSet open as an XML schema in its designer, you can view it in tabular form or as "straight" XML (Figure 12.33).

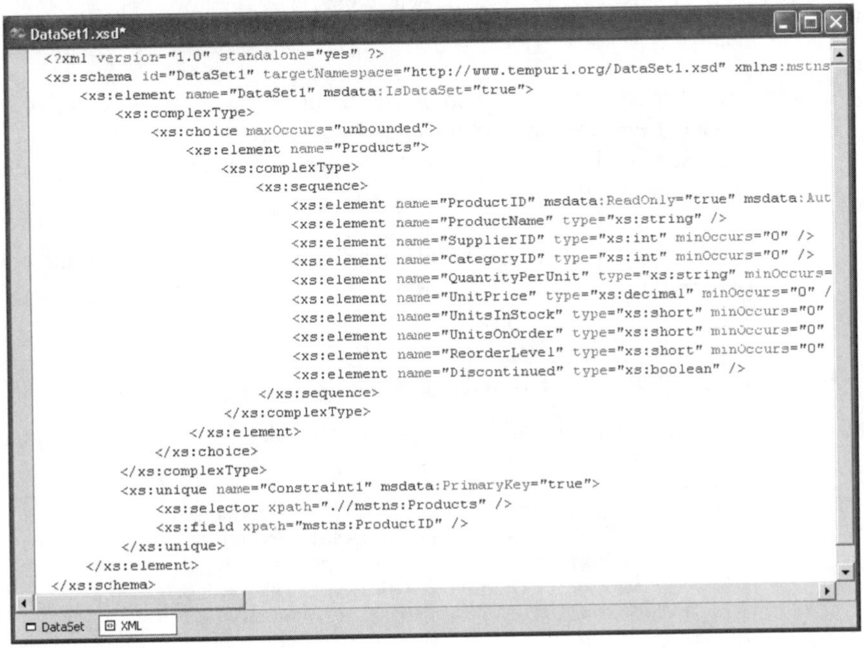

FIGURE 12.33:

A generated DataSet is an XSD schema.

```
DataSet1.xsd*
<?xml version="1.0" standalone="yes" ?>
<xs:schema id="DataSet1" targetNamespace="http://www.tempuri.org/DataSet1.xsd" xmlns:mstns
    <xs:element name="DataSet1" msdata:IsDataSet="true">
        <xs:complexType>
            <xs:choice maxOccurs="unbounded">
                <xs:element name="Products">
                    <xs:complexType>
                        <xs:sequence>
                            <xs:element name="ProductID" msdata:ReadOnly="true" msdata:Aut
                            <xs:element name="ProductName" type="xs:string" />
                            <xs:element name="SupplierID" type="xs:int" minOccurs="0" />
                            <xs:element name="CategoryID" type="xs:int" minOccurs="0" />
                            <xs:element name="QuantityPerUnit" type="xs:string" minOccurs=
                            <xs:element name="UnitPrice" type="xs:decimal" minOccurs="0" /
                            <xs:element name="UnitsInStock" type="xs:short" minOccurs="0"
                            <xs:element name="UnitsOnOrder" type="xs:short" minOccurs="0"
                            <xs:element name="ReorderLevel" type="xs:short" minOccurs="0"
                            <xs:element name="Discontinued" type="xs:boolean" />
                        </xs:sequence>
                    </xs:complexType>
                </xs:element>
            </xs:choice>
        </xs:complexType>
        <xs:unique name="Constraint1" msdata:PrimaryKey="true">
            <xs:selector xpath=".//mstns:Products" />
            <xs:field xpath="mstns:ProductID" />
        </xs:unique>
    </xs:element>
</xs:schema>

□ DataSet  ⊞ XML
```

Binding Controls to a Dataset

Now that we have our Data components in place, it's time to do something with them. As a simple example, I'll show you how to feed the ProductName and ProductID fields from the Northwind Products table into two ListBoxes. For this example, the query SELECT * FROM PRODUCTS was used to create the dataset.

Binding to a ListBox

Add two ListBoxes to the form. Also add a Button control, named btnFill, with the text "Fill".

Within btnFill's click event, the first step is to fill the DataSet using the SqlDataAdapter's Fill method:

```
sqlDataAdapter1.Fill (dataSet1, "Products");
```

Next, set the DataSource property for each ListBox to the Products table, as in this example:

```
listBox1.DataSource = dataSet1.Products;
```

Next, set the DisplayMember property of each ListBox to the field you would like it to display:

```
listBox1.DisplayMember = "ProductName";
listBox2.DisplayMember = "ProductID";
```

NOTE   You can set these properties using the Properties window rather than in code, if you prefer.

WARNING You'll need to change the properties of the SqlConnection component to reflect your own connectivity situation, or this code will not run. As a general matter, code that relies on database connectivity should always employ exception handling (in case there is a connectivity problem).

The complete click event code for filling the two ListBoxes, including rudimentary exception handling, is shown in Listing 12.16.

Listing 12.16   **Filling ListBoxes with Fields from a Database**

```
private void btnFill_Click(object sender, System.EventArgs e) {
    Cursor = Cursors.WaitCursor;
    try {
        sqlDataAdapter1.Fill (dataSet1,"Products");
        listBox1.DataSource = dataSet1.Products;
        listBox1.DisplayMember = "ProductName";
        listBox2.DataSource = dataSet1.Products;
        listBox2.DisplayMember = "ProductID";
    }
    catch (System.Data.SqlClient.SqlException) {
        MessageBox.Show ("Please check your SQL Server connection " +
            "and verify the connection string.");
    }
    catch (Exception excep){
        MessageBox.Show (excep.Message);
    }
    finally {
        Cursor = Cursors.Default;
    }
}
```

Run the project and click Fill. The two ListBoxes will display data from the appropriate fields (Figure 12.34).

FIGURE 12.34:

ListBoxes that have been connected to a DataSet can be set to display fields in a table.

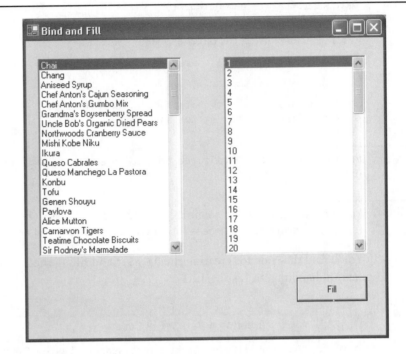

Creating a Dataset in Code

Obviously, there is a great deal to the Visual Studio .NET data objects' interfaces. This interface complexity being what it is, you will probably be pleasantly surprised to learn that you can easily build and use datasets and related data objects in code, without using the interface Microsoft provides. You may, in fact, find this a great deal simpler way to go about things.

As an example, let's load the CompanyName data from the Northwind Customers table into a third ListBox.

Within the event procedure that will fill the ListBox, declare variables and assign them the connection string and SQL command:

```
string mySelectQuery = "SELECT * FROM Customers";
SqlConnection myConnection = new SqlConnection("data source=SQLSERVER;" +
    "initial catalog=Northwind;password=harold;user id=sa");
```

Next, instantiate the DataSet and set up the DataAdapter, using the connection string and SQL command:

```
DataSet theData = new DataSet();
SqlDataAdapter theAdapter = new SqlDataAdapter(mySelectQuery, myConnection);
```

Fill the DataSet using the DataAdapter:

```
theAdapter.Fill(theData, "Customers");
```

Load the ListBox as before:

```
listBox3.DataSource = theData.Tables["Customers"];
listBox3.DisplayMember = "CompanyName";
```

> **NOTE** In this example, the DataSource property is set using the Tables collection of the DataSet.

> **WARNING** You'll need to change the connection string used in the SqlConnection constructor to reflect your own circumstances—or, of course, this code will not run.

You'll find the code for creating the DataSet and filling the ListBox, including basic exception handling, in Listing 12.17.

Listing 12.17   **Creating a *DataSet* in Code**

```
private void btnFillCode_Click(object sender, System.EventArgs e) {
    Cursor = Cursors.WaitCursor;
    try {
        string mySelectQuery = "SELECT * FROM Customers";
        SqlConnection myConnection = new SqlConnection("data source=SQLSERVER;" +
            "initial catalog=Northwind;password=harold;user id=sa");
        DataSet theData = new DataSet();
        SqlDataAdapter theAdapter = new SqlDataAdapter(mySelectQuery,
            myConnection);
        theAdapter.Fill(theData, "Customers");
        listBox3.DataSource = theData.Tables["Customers"];
        listBox3.DisplayMember = "CompanyName";
    }
    catch (System.Data.SqlClient.SqlException) {
        MessageBox.Show ("Please check your SQL Server connection " +
            "and verify the connection string.");
    }
    catch (Exception excep){
        MessageBox.Show (excep.Message);
    }
```

```
    finally {
        Cursor = Cursors.Default;
    }
}
```

If you run the project and click the Fill Code button, the customer names will appear in the ListBox (Figure 12.35).

It's possibly to manage data connectivity entirely programmatically.

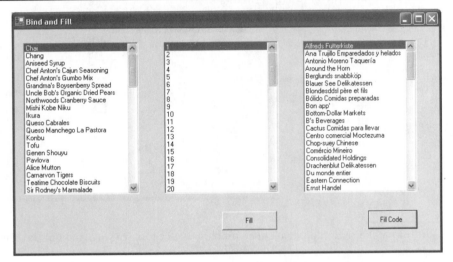

Binding to a *DataGrid* and Updating a Database

DataGrids are wonderful controls for displaying tabular data and for allowing the user to interact with that data. In this section, I'll show you how to bind a DataGrid to a DataSet, fill the DataSet (and thereby fill the grid), and update the database with changes that the user has made within the grid.

First, add a DataGrid control to the form. Then add two buttons: one to load the form and one to update the database.

Next, bind the DataGrid to the existing DataSet, which—as you'll recall—contains the Northwind Products table. To do this, with the DataGrid selected, open the Properties window (Figure 12.36). Set the DataSource property of the DataGrid to dataSet1. Next, set the DataMember property to Products (the drop-down arrow will show you all the tables within the DataSet).

Bind the DataGrid to the
DataSet by setting the
appropriate properties of
the DataGrid.

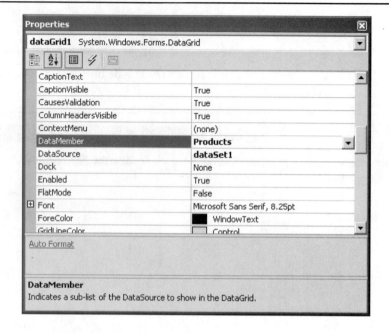

WARNING   Make sure the DataSource property is set to dataSet1 and not dataSet1.Products.

The DataGrid has now been bound to the DataSet, but the DataSet still needs to be filled.
Within the Fill button's Click procedure, add a line of code using the SqlDataAdapter's Fill
method to fill the DataSet:

```
private void btnFillGrid_Click(object sender, System.EventArgs e) {
    sqlDataAdapter1.Fill (dataSet1);
}
```

Run the project and click Fill. The grid will be populated with data from the Products table,
as seen in Figure 12.37.

FIGURE 12.37:

Our grid is populated with the contents of Products.

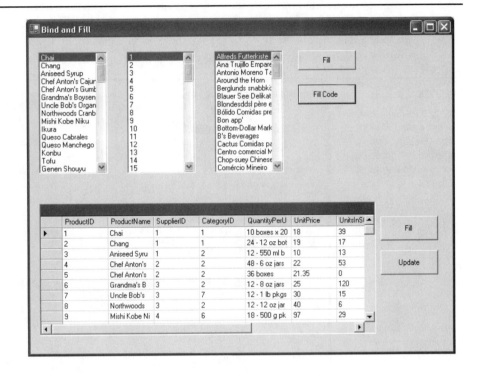

Of course, a variation on this would be to fill a grid automatically without user intervention— for example, in the form constructor.

I started this chapter by noting that a DataSet is a miniature database stored in memory. This being the case, the changes that a user makes within the grid only impact the DataSet—until the Update method of the DataAdapter is invoked. The Update method writes back and reconciles the changes that have been made in the DataSet to the database.

To set this up, add the code to the Update button's Click event that writes any changes made by the user back to the database using the Update method of the SqlDataAdapter:

```
private void btnUpdate_Click(object sender, System.EventArgs e) {
    sqlDataAdapter1.Update (dataSet1, "Products");
}
```

Run the project again, load the data into the grid, and make some changes (for example, to the Product Name data). When you click Update, changes made in the grid are instantly reflected in controls that are bound to the same DataSet, for example, the ListBox in the upper left of the form. Figure 12.38 shows the addition of comments about Harold Davis and his liking for food added to the `ProductName` column. This happens without updating the database, since both the ListBox and the grid are taking their data from the same `DataSet`. However, these changes are also written to the database, as you can verify by taking the sample application down and up, and then re-filling the `DataSet`.

FIGURE 12.38:

Changes made in the grid are instantly made to the `DataSet` and written to the database when the Update button is clicked.

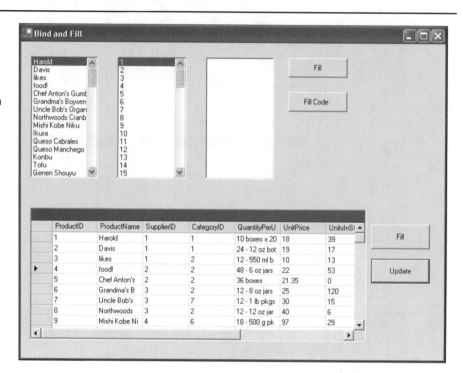

Conclusion

This chapter has touched on some very big topics: XML in .NET and ADO.NET database connectivity. The bad news is that either topic alone—let alone both together—is way too vast to be covered in a single chapter. But no two applications are the same. The good news is the material in this chapter will help point you in the right directions for your own applications. You certainly need to know about connecting to databases. And the extensive and flexible use of XML both above and below the covers in .NET should certainly get you thinking creatively about how you can best use XML in your own applications.

This book started by showing you how to create relatively simple web services. At that point, no knowledge of C# or of the classes in the .NET Framework was assumed. Well, you've come a long way. The next—and final—chapter wraps it all up with an exploration of what you can do with web services now that you have a sophisticated understanding of .NET and a considerable amount of C# programming under your belt.

CHAPTER 13

Web Services as Architecture

- Managing session and state in a web service

- Exposing data and returning a *DataSet* from a web service

- Transaction management

- Exposing a message queue as a web service

- Using the TerraService web service to display aerial photos and topographic maps his book started by showing you how easy it is to create ASP.NET web services—and to consume those services. I moved from there to the nuts and bolts of the C# language, and how to utilize many of the important classes of the .NET Framework.

This chapter revisits the material presented in the beginning of the book. In fact, you may wish to have a look at Chapter 1, "Creating a Web Service," for a refresher on the basics of creating a web service. But we've come a long way in knowledge about .NET and C# since then. The question this chapter looks at is: if you were to use web services as part of "serious" application architecture, what kinds of techniques would you need?

Since life is too short to always be serious, and it's good to end with a bang rather than a whimper, I'll show you as the final example how to consume one of the niftiest, most ambitious, and most fun web services out there: Microsoft's TerraService. The demo program explained in this chapter will display aerial photos or topographic maps of almost any place in the United States, in a variety of scales.

Managing Session and State

Most common web services—including the ones demonstrated toward the beginning of this book—provide methods that are stateless. A stateless method knows nothing about the calling code. For example, it does not know whether this particular code has ever invoked it before—or, in fact, how many times it has been invoked by any client code. Generally, this kind of stateless method does some kind of complicated calculation, or retrieves something, and returns the appropriate object or value, without reference to anything that came before or will come after the method's invocation.

There's no reason to sneer at a stateless method. Using one can be very convenient. And, generally, a stateless method (such as a stateless web service) is used because it is more convenient (and less trouble) than writing the method as part of an application—particularly since, much of the time, someone else has provided the web service and methods.

But normally applications do need to keep track of state information. So if web services are to play an important part of an application's architecture, then they would be much more useful if they, too, could track state information.

When Should You Use a Web Service?

Back in Chapter 1, I noted that web services "are by no means the only architectural technology used for component-based distributed computing." Table 1.1 in that chapter summarizes information about some of these other technologies—which in many cases may have better performance characteristics than web services.

Continued on next page

Web services have two huge pluses, which is why they have generated so much interest:

- They are cross-platform: I can consume a web service equally well from a Unix and a Windows application.

- Web services travel on standard HTTP: they do not require creating custom ports (also called "holes") in firewalls for access.

When should you definitely *not* use web services? If a method is only going to be invoked by one application, it's hard to imagine a good reason for wrapping the method in a web service (you'll save the performance hit by putting the method in a DLL instead).

If you expect all clients to be .NET applications (so you are writing .NET to .NET), consider using .NET remoting instead of web services (for .NET remoting's performance and its rich set of APIs). For more information, look up the topic ".NET Remoting Overview" in online help.

Finally, if extreme security is required, no form of distributed architecture (including web services) should be used.

As it turns out, web services that are created using ASP.NET can use the ASP.NET mechanisms for storing session and state information. When the EnableSession attribute is applied to a web service method, the ASP.NET HttpSessionState object can be used to store and retrieve session and application information. Marking a web service method with the WebMethod attribute EnableSession = true gives the method access to the ASP.NET HttpApplication Application and Session objects for the web service. For example:

```
[WebMethod (Description = "Starts the stateful service", EnableSession = true)]
```

NOTE   In addition to the server side, you also need a mechanism for tracking the state information on the client side. Generally, as you'll see in the example, cookies are used with the Application and Session objects to track information. This is a potential source of problems when the client is a browser and the user has turned cookies off.

Building a Stateful Web Service

This section demonstrates a stateful web service that provides four methods:

StartMe   Starts an individual session and also globally initializes the stateful service.

GetSession   Increments the counter tracking both individual session usage and the global number of sessions, and returns the usage count for the individual session.

GetTotalUsage   Returns the global usage count.

ResetGlobal   Resets an individual session counter and the global application counter to zero.

Each individual session must have a name—and, other than tracking state, returning that name is all it does.

To get started with this, open a new ASP.NET Web Service project. Delete the default and commented-out code provided in the .Asmx module and add a class declaration like this one:

```
[WebService(Namespace="http://bearhome.com/webservices/")]
public class Ss : System.Web.Services.WebService
{
...
```

NOTE   I named the class Ss—short for "stateful service."

Next, start adding the web methods. The first, StartMe, is shown in Listing 13.1. It checks that a name was passed in. Next, the application counter is started or incremented. Finally, the session counter is engaged and the session name saved.

Listing 13.1   **Initializing Session and Application Tracking**

```
[WebMethod (Description = "Starts the stateful service", EnableSession = true)]
public string StartMe(string theName) {
   if (theName == String.Empty) {
      return "You must enter a name to start the service!";
   }
   else {
      if (Application["totalUse"] == null){
         Application["totalUse"] = 1;
      }
      else {
         Application["totalUse"] = (int) Application["totalUse"] + 1;
      }
      Session["numSession"] = 1;
      Session["userName"] = theName;
      return theName + ", your session has started!";
   }
}
```

The next web service, GetSession, shown in Listing 13.2, verifies that the name passed in matches the name of the session. If it does, the application and session counters are incremented, and the session counter value is passed back.

NOTE   The values contained in the Application and Session objects must be explicitly cast to string or integer (as appropriate).

Listing 13.2   Incrementing the Session and Application Counters

```
[WebMethod (Description = "Iterates the stateful service",
   EnableSession = true)]
public int GetSession (string theName) {
    if (theName != (string) Session["userName"]){
       return 0;
    }
    else {
       if (Application["totalUse"] == null){
          Application["totalUse"] = 1;
       }
       else {
          Application["totalUse"] = (int) Application["totalUse"] + 1;
       }
       int numSession = (int) Session["numSession"];
       numSession ++;
       Session["numSession"] = numSession;
       return numSession;
    }
}
```

It's easy to use to get the total usage for the application by just returning the "totalUse" value stored in the Application object, cast to integer type (Listing 13.3).

Listing 13.3   Tracking Total Application Usage

```
[WebMethod (Description = "Tracks total service usage", EnableSession = true)]
public int GetTotalUsage () {
   return (int) Application["totalUse"];
}
```

Resetting values to zero means simply assigning 0 to the "totalUse" value stored in the Application object and to the "numSession" value stored in a Session object (Listing 13.4).

Listing 13.4   Resetting Application Usage

```
[WebMethod (Description = "Reset Global", EnableSession = true)]
public void ResetGlobal () {
   Application["totalUse"] = 0;
   Session["numSession"] = 0;
}
```

With the methods in place, run the project. Visual Studio will generate the "table of contents" WSDL page for the ASP.NET web service (Figure 13.1).

FIGURE 13.1:

The service's methods are listed in the generated pages.

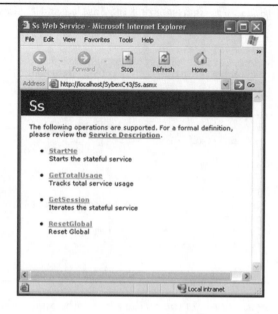

You can click the StartMe link to see the generated test page for that particular method (Figure 13.2). Enter a name, and click Invoke to test the method.

FIGURE 13.2:

You can test a service using the Invoke button.

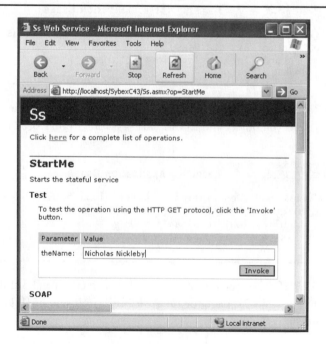

As you can see in the XML returned by the method (shown in Figure 13.3), the method is at least nominally working—it has returned a string indicating it received a name as input.

FIGURE 13.3:

The XML shows the
return value from
the tested method.

Consuming the Stateful Web Service

The rubber meets the road in the client applications that will use the stateful service. Figure 13.4 shows the demonstration client, a Windows forms application, which includes a TextBox for the name of each session, and buttons to start the session (and application), to increment the session counter, and to reset the application.

FIGURE 13.4:

The service requires
that the user input a
name before session
tracking begins.

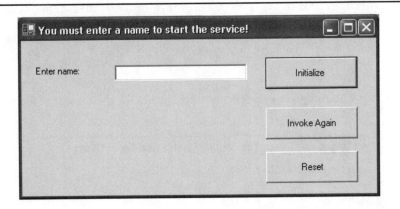

Before you can get started coding the client, you need to add the Stateful Service as a web reference to the client project (Project ≻ Add Web Reference). (You can change the name of the web reference to anything you'd like, so I changed it to "StateService.") You also need to add to the form a using directive that includes the System.Net namespace:

```
using System.Net;
```

Next, in the form constructor, instantiate a `StateService` object and a `CookieContainer`, and connect the two:

```
ss = new StateService.Ss();
CookieContainer cookiePot = new CookieContainer();
ss.CookieContainer = cookiePot;
```

The *StateService* variable is declared at the form level so it is accessible to all the methods in the form class:

```
StateService.Ss ss;
```

To start the service, invoke the `StartMe` web service method:

```
this.Text = ss.StartMe(txtName.Text);
```

It's likewise not very difficult to increment a session and display the session and application counts using the `GetSession` and `GetTotalUsage` web service methods:

```
private void btnAgain_Click(object sender, System.EventArgs e) {
    int numSessions = ss.GetSession (txtName.Text);
    int numApps = ss.GetTotalUsage();
    if (numSessions < 1){
        this.Text = "Sorry, I don't recognize you, stranger!";
    }
    else {
        this.Text = "Welcome back, " + txtName.Text + "!";
        label1.Text = "Number of times for this named session is " +
            numSessions.ToString();
        label2.Text = "Total named usage of application is " +
            numApps.ToString();
    }
}
```

The complete web service–related code for the form module is shown in Listing 13.5.

Listing 13.5   **The Client Application Form Code**

```
using System.Net;
...
public Form1() {
    ...
    // in the form constructor
    ss = new StateService.Ss();
    CookieContainer cookiePot = new CookieContainer();
    ss.CookieContainer = cookiePot;
}
...
StateService.Ss ss;
private void btnStart_Click(object sender, System.EventArgs e) {
```

```
    this.Text = ss.StartMe(txtName.Text);
    label1.Text = String.Empty;
}
private void btnAgain_Click(object sender, System.EventArgs e) {
    int numSessions = ss.GetSession (txtName.Text);
    int numApps = ss.GetTotalUsage();
    if (numSessions < 1){
        this.Text = "Sorry, I don't recognize you, stranger!";
    }
    else {
        this.Text = "Welcome back, " + txtName.Text + "!";
        label1.Text = "Number of times for this named session is " +
            numSessions.ToString();
        label2.Text = "Total named usage of application is " +
            numApps.ToString();
    }
}
private void btnReset_Click(object sender, System.EventArgs e) {
    ss.ResetGlobal();
    label1.Text = String.Empty;
    label2.Text = String.Empty;
}
...
```

To try this out, run the client project. Enter a name in the TextBox, and click Initialize. The session has now started (Figure 13.5).

FIGURE 13.5:

Once the user has entered a name, the service initializes session tracking.

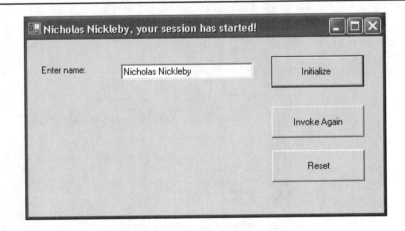

Next, click Invoke Again. It's easy to see that the session number is incrementing (Figure 13.6).

FIGURE 13.6:

Each time the Invoke Again button is clicked, the session is restarted and the tracking counter incremented.

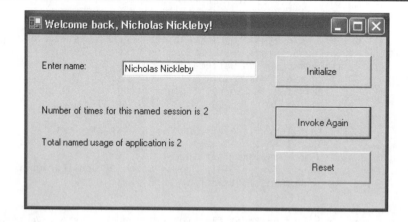

Now it's time to fire up a whole bunch of instances of the client application. You can easily verify that, in addition to the individual session counters, the global application counter is working—and is tracking the total number of times the service has been accessed by any client (Figure 13.7).

FIGURE 13.7:

Session tracking tracks individual sessions, while application tracking records the total number of times the service has been invoked (by any client).

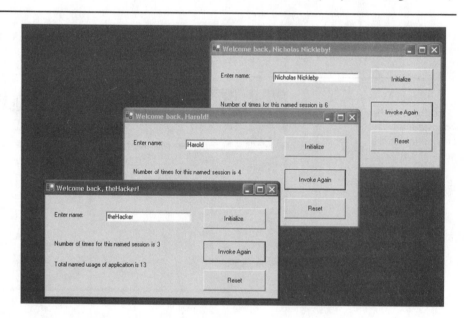

Exposing Data Using a Web Service

As I explained in Chapter 12, "Working with XML and ADO.NET," a DataSet is a kind of miniature database that resides in memory—it can include relationships, tables, and a substantial amount of data. This means that the simple act of exposing a DataSet using a web service can be quite powerful; it provides remote (and cross-platform) access to the potentially extensive contents of the DataSet. Furthermore, it can make this access available to users who are not otherwise connected to the database.

The example I'll show you uses an ASP.NET web application as the client for the web service. This implies that a browser-based application, from anywhere on the Internet, can access the data in a DataSet if it is exposed by a web service. While the sample application just fills a grid with the data in a table supplied by the DataSet, it's easy to see how you can use this technique to create data-driven web applications.

Once again, we'll use the sample Northwind database that ships with SQL Server; this time the DataSet will return the Suppliers table in that database (shown in Server Explorer in Figure 13.8).

FIGURE 13.8:

You can use Server Explorer to find the tables and fields in the Northwind database.

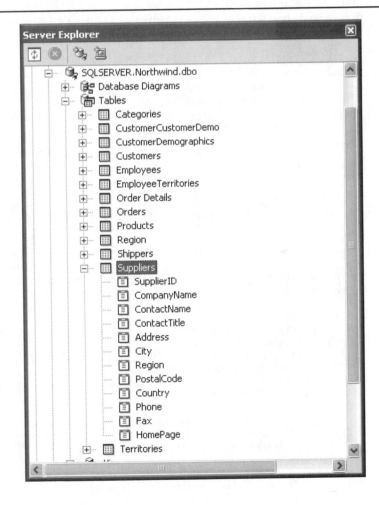

NOTE   If you aren't connected to SQL Server, don't worry! You probably have an Access version of the Northwind database that you can use in its place (a copy ships with most versions of Microsoft Office). See Chapter 12 for details.

The first step is to add a new ASP.NET Web Service project. Within the web service module, add a using directive to System.Data.SqlClient. Next, name the web service class ExposeData.

The GetSuppliers web method should return a DataSet, so here's its declaration:

```
public DataSet GetSuppliers() {
...
}
```

Within the web method, create a SqlConnection, a DataSet, and a SqlDataAdapter. Call the SqlDataAdapter's constructor with the SQL query to be performed and the SqlConnection object, and then use the SqlDataAdapter's Fill method to load the Suppliers table into the DataSet:

```
string mySelectQuery = "SELECT * FROM Suppliers";
SqlConnection myConnection = new SqlConnection ("data source=SQLSERVER;" +
    "initial catalog=Northwind;password=harold;user id=sa");
DataSet theData = new DataSet();
SqlDataAdapter theAdapter = new SqlDataAdapter (mySelectQuery, myConnection);
theAdapter.Fill(theData, "Suppliers");
```

Close the SqlConnection, and return the DataSet. The code for the web method is shown in Listing 13.6.

Listing 13.6   **Using a Web Service to Expose a *DataSet***

```
...
using System.Data.SqlClient;
...
[WebService(Namespace="http://bearhome.com/webservices/")]
public class ExposeData : System.Web.Services.WebService {
...
[WebMethod
    (Description = "Returns DataSet containing Northwinds Suppliers table")]
public DataSet GetSuppliers() {
    string mySelectQuery = "SELECT * FROM Suppliers";
    SqlConnection myConnection = new SqlConnection("data source=SQLSERVER;" +
        "initial catalog=Northwind;password=harold;user id=sa");
    DataSet theData = new DataSet();
    try {
        SqlDataAdapter theAdapter = new SqlDataAdapter
            (mySelectQuery, myConnection);
        theAdapter.Fill(theData, "Suppliers");
    }
    catch {
        // Add exception handling and logging
    }
```

```
        finally {
            if (myConnection.State == ConnectionState.Open) myConnection.Close();
        }
        return theData;
    }
    ...
```

NOTE   For a more complete explanation of the code filling the DataSet, see Chapter 12, where I showed you that you can use the Data components to visually create a DataSet using the Properties window, as an alternative to the technique here of creating it in code.

WARNING   My connection string is not your connection string. For this code to run on your system, you must modify the connection string to your circumstances. For more about connection strings, see Chapter 12.

If you run this project, you'll see the familiar generated test pages for the web service, and if you click the GetSuppliers link, the invocation test page for the method will be displayed (Figure 13.9).

FIGURE 13.9:

The Invoke button starts the web method.

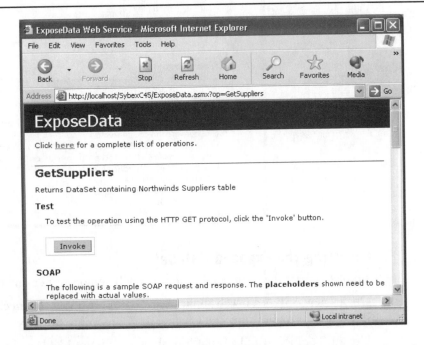

Click Invoke. The DataSet is returned as XML, starting with the XSD schema representing the Suppliers table, and continuing through the data in the table (Figure 13.10). Note that the schema structure shown in Figure 13.10 mirrors the fields shown in tabular form in the Server Explorer window shown back in Figure 13.8.

FIGURE 13.10:

The XML returned by
the method includes
both a schema
and data.

Consuming the Exposed *DataSet*

It's time to create the client application that will demonstrate using this web service.

Open a new ASP.NET web application. (For more about the mechanics of working with ASP.NET web applications, see Chapter 2, "Consuming the Service on the Web.")

Use the Toolbox to add a DataGrid (shown in Figure 13.11) and a Label to the Web Form Designer. Set the label's Visible property to False (it will be used for exception handling messages, so we don't need it yet).

FIGURE 13.11:

A DataGrid added to a WebForm can be used to display the DataSet returned by the service.

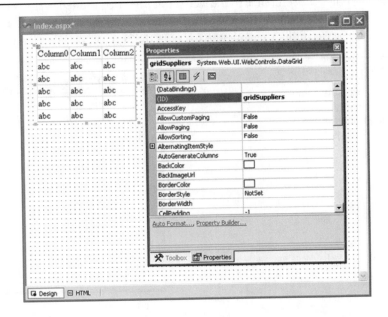

Add a reference to the web service in the normal fashion, by selecting Project ➤ Add Web Reference. In the Add Web Reference dialog, enter the URL for the web service in the Address box at the top (Figure 13.12), and click Add Reference.

FIGURE 13.12:

A reference is added to the web service using its URL.

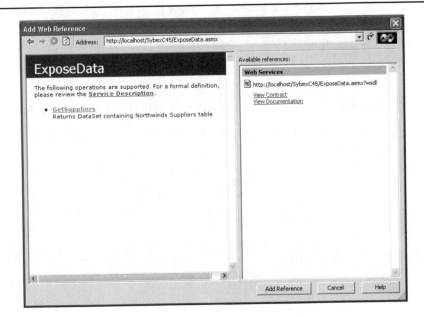

Once the reference to the web service has been added to the project, you'll recall that you can change its name in Solution Explorer to anything you'd like. To keep the coding of this client transparent, let's change the name of the service to "WebService" (Figure 13.13).

FIGURE 13.13:

You can change the name of the web service using Solution Explorer in the interests of clarity.

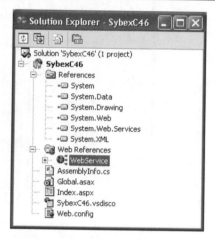

It's easy now to add code to the Page Load event of the web form that instantiates the web method and binds the Suppliers table to the DataGrid:

```
SybexC46.WebService.ExposeData ed = new SybexC46.WebService.ExposeData();
DataSet theData = ed.GetSuppliers();
gridSuppliers.DataSource = theData.Tables[0].DefaultView;
gridSuppliers.DataBind();
```

The complete code for the Page Load event, including exception handling, is shown in Listing 13.7.

Listing 13.7   Using the Exposed Data in an ASP.NET WebForm

```
private void Page_Load(object sender, System.EventArgs e) {
    if (!Page.IsPostBack){
        try {
            SybexC46.WebService.ExposeData ed = new
                SybexC46.WebService.ExposeData();
            DataSet theData = ed.GetSuppliers();
            gridSuppliers.DataSource = theData.Tables[0].DefaultView;
            gridSuppliers.DataBind();
        }
        catch (System.Data.SqlClient.SqlException) {
            lblExcep.Text = "Please check your SQL Server connection " +
                "and verify the connection string.";
            lblExcep.Visible = true;
        }
```

```
catch(IndexOutOfRangeException) {
    lblExcep.Text = "Please check your SQL Server connection " +
        "and verify the connection string.";
    lblExcep.Visible = true;
}
catch (Exception excep){
    lblExcep.Text = excep.Message;
    lblExcep.Visible = true;
}
    }
}
```

If you run the ASP.NET client application, provided you can connect to SQL Server and the Northwind sample database is loaded, the returned DataSet will fill the DataGrid (Figure 13.14).

FIGURE 13.14:

The returned DataSet fills the DataGrid.

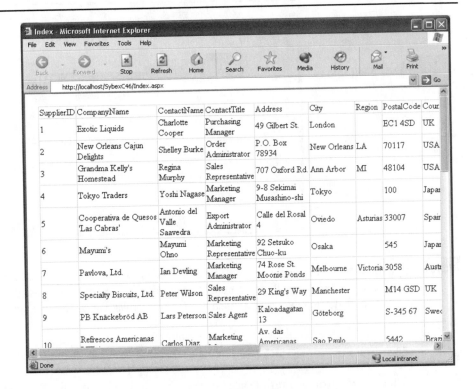

NOTE   If you rewrite the code in the web service to return a strongly typed DataSet (rather than just a DataSet), you'll then be able to take advantage of IntelliSense member completion in the Code Editor.

Handling Exceptions

It's important to include exception handling in the client application, because all kinds of issues can come up with database access. For example, as noted earlier in this section, unless you change the connection string in the web method, it will not run on your system as written. Since the MessageBox method is not available in a web forms application, one way to display exception messages is in a label (Figure 13.15).

FIGURE 13.15:

It's important to include exception handling in the client application if the web service involves database connectivity.

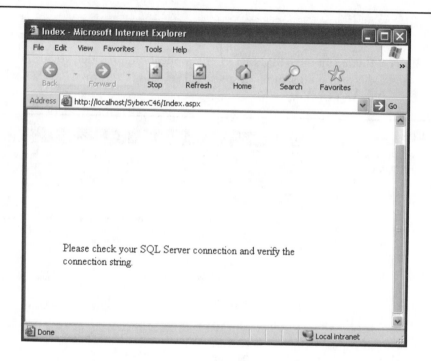

> **NOTE**   If the web service cannot connect to a database for whatever reason, it is written to still return a DataSet (but one with no content). In this case, the most likely exception to be thrown is IndexOutOfRangeException (because Tables[0] will not be found in the DataSet).

Managing Transactions

A *transaction* groups multiple actions together. In its simplest form, a transaction, also sometimes called a "two-stage commit," makes sure that all the actions take place—or none of them do. If one of the actions succeeds, and the next one fails, then both actions are "rolled back."

In the context of the enterprise, transactions are important. The example in this section explores a scenario in which you want to be sure that a log file is written to if the related primary table is altered. But there are many situations in which you need to make sure that an entire transaction—or none of its components—succeeds. One example that is becoming increasingly common in enterprise applications that operate across operating systems and data repositories is a transaction that needs to perform operations using several data sources. A single transaction might need to check inventory on an Oracle server, write order records to SQL Server, and write customer information to a DB2 database.

So if web services are to be part of a scalable, enterprise architecture, they must support transactions. Fortunately, ASP.NET web services do support transactions. As you'll see in the substantially oversimplified—but not entirely unrealistic—example in this chapter, implementing transactions is essentially an issue of turning on a switch.

> **WARNING** The example in this section does not implement exception handling—which, of course, you should in the real world. Also, to get the example to work, you'll need to create the database that is described in SQL Server. In addition, once again my connection string is not your connection string. You must alter the connection string to suit your circumstances.

The idea is this: there's a database, Deposits, with two tables, MoneyIn and MoneyLog. These tables are shown using the Diagram feature of SQL Server in Figure 13.16.

FIGURE 13.16:

The two tables in the Deposits database are shown in a Diagram in SQL Server Enterprise Manager.

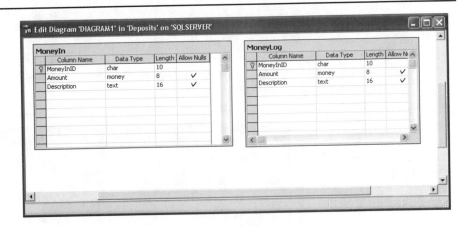

I'd like a web method that inserts a deposit amount, along with an ID and a description, in both tables. The transaction problem is that I want to be sure that the deposit information is inserted in both tables—or rolled back so that it is inserted in neither.

> **NOTE** As a preliminary, to get this example to work, you need to create the tables shown in Figure 13.16.

Implementing a Web Service that Supports Transactions

To start with, make sure that Distributed Transaction Coordinator is running in SQL Server. You can do this from the Services applet in Administrative tools, or by using SQL Server's

Enterprise Manager. In Enterprise Manager, expand the `Support Services` folder (see Figure 13.17), and right-click Distributed Transaction Coordinator to start it (if it isn't already).

FIGURE 13.17:

If it isn't already running, start Distributed Transaction Coordinator.

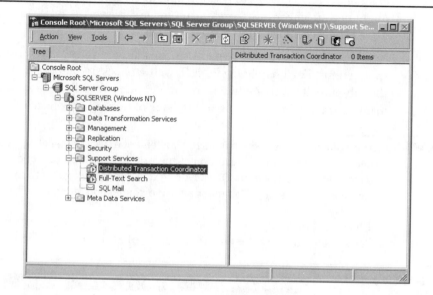

Next, start a new ASP.NET Web Service project. Select Project ➢ Add Reference to open the Add Reference dialog, and use the dialog to add the `System.EnterpriseServices` library to the project (Figure 13.18).

FIGURE 13.18:

Use the Add Reference dialog to add the `System` `.EnterpriseServices` library to the project.

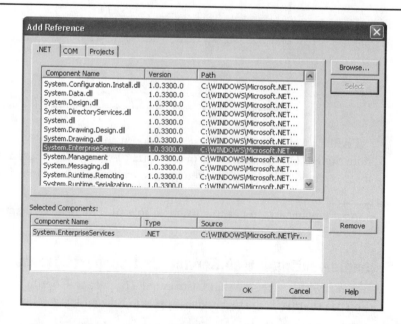

In the web service's class module, add using directives to the System.Data.SqlClient and System.EnterpriseServices namespaces. Change the name of the class to Transaction. Add two private methods, InsertMoneyIn and InsertMoneyLog, which insert into the respective tables.

Next, add a web method, UpDateTables, that invokes both private methods:

```
public void UpDateTables(string inID, float amount, string desc) {
    InsertMoneyIn (inID, amount, desc);
    InsertMoneyLog (inID, amount, desc);
}
```

Mark this web method with an attribute, TransactionOption, set to TransactionOption .RequiresNew:

```
[WebMethod (Description = "Demonstrates two-stage commit",
    TransactionOption = TransactionOption.RequiresNew)]
```

The TransactionOption web method attribute nominally has several possible values, but really only two relevant ones: TransactionOption.Disabled, which is the default, is equivalent to omitting the attribute and means that transaction management has been turned off; and TransactionOption.RequiresNew, which turns on transaction management.

The code for the web service is shown in Listing 13.8.

Listing 13.8   Inserting Two Tables within a Transaction

```
using System.Data.SqlClient;
using System.EnterpriseServices;
...
[WebService(Namespace="http://bearhome.com/webservices/")]
public class Transaction : System.Web.Services.WebService {
...
[WebMethod (Description = "Demonstrates two-stage commit",
    TransactionOption = TransactionOption.RequiresNew)]
public void UpDateTables(string inID, float amount, string desc) {
    InsertMoneyIn (inID, amount, desc);
    InsertMoneyLog (inID, amount, desc);
}
private void InsertMoneyIn (string inID, float amount, string desc) {
    string sqlStr = "INSERT MoneyIn (MoneyInID, Amount, Description) " +
        "VALUES (' + inID + "', " + amount.ToString() + ", '" + desc + "')";
    SqlConnection myConnection = new SqlConnection("data source=SQLSERVER;" +
        "initial catalog=Deposits;password=harold;user id=sa");
    myConnection.Open();
    SqlCommand insert = new SqlCommand(sqlStr, myConnection);
    insert.ExecuteNonQuery();
    if (myConnection.State == ConnectionState.Open)
        myConnection.Close();
}

private void InsertMoneyLog (string inID, float amount, string desc) {
    string sqlStr = "INSERT MoneyLog (MoneyInID, Amount, Description)" +
        " VALUES (' + inID + "', " + amount.ToString() + ", '" + desc + "')";
```

```
    SqlConnection myConnection = new SqlConnection("data source=SQLSERVER;" +
        "initial catalog=Deposits;password=harold;user id=sa");
    myConnection.Open();
    SqlCommand insert = new SqlCommand(sqlStr, myConnection);
    insert.ExecuteNonQuery();
    if (myConnection.State == ConnectionState.Open)
        myConnection.Close();
}
...
```

If you run the web service, the test page generated for it shows, as one would expect, a single web service (Figure 13.19).

FIGURE 13.19:

The generated test page for the web service shows one method.

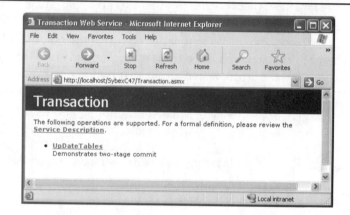

Use the test pages to enter some values (Figure 13.20) and click Invoke.

FIGURE 13.20:

To test the service, enter values and click Invoke.

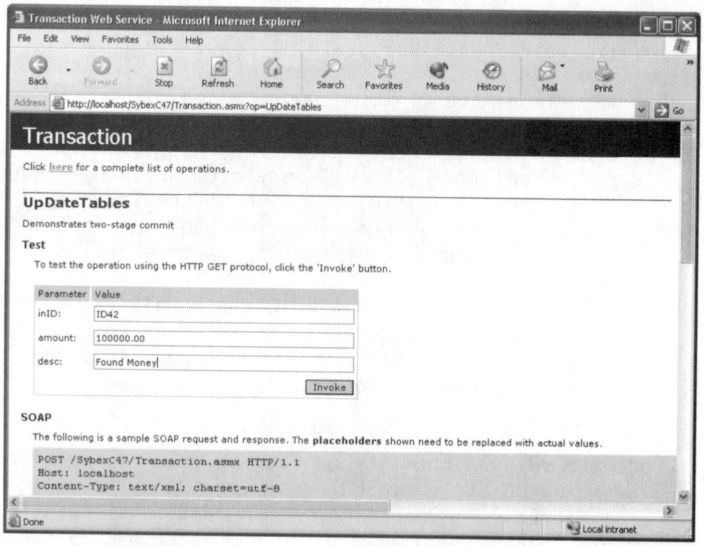

You should verify that the test data has been added to the database tables (as shown in Figure 13.21 in Server Explorer)—demonstrating that both private methods that insert data into the tables are working.

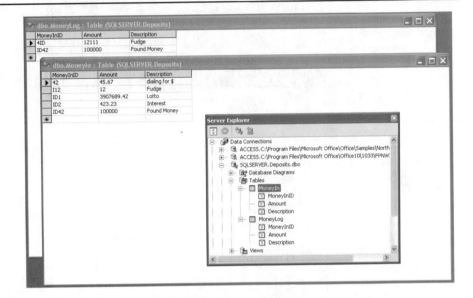

Testing the Transaction Web Service

Now let's see whether transaction management is really working! Modify the second private method in the web service, the one that inserts into the MoneyLog table, so that it throws an exception (and no longer works), as shown in Listing 13.9.

Listing 13.9   Throwing an Exception in the Second Insert

```
private void InsertMoneyLog (string inID, float amount, string desc) {
    string sqlStr = "INSERT MoneyLog (MoneyInID, Amount, Description)" +
        " VALUES (' + inID + "', " + amount.ToString() + ", '" + desc + "')";
    SqlConnection myConnection = new SqlConnection("data source=SQLSERVER;" +
        "initial catalog=Deposits;password=harold;user id=sa");
    myConnection.Open();
    SqlCommand insert = new SqlCommand(sqlStr, myConnection);
    try {}
    finally {
        throw new Exception ("This is a nasty exception!");
    }
    insert.ExecuteNonQuery();
    if (myConnection.State == ConnectionState.Open)
        myConnection.Close();
}
```

With the code that sabotages the second insert in place, run the project's test pages again, and enter some more data (Figure 13.22).

FIGURE 13.22:

With the code that throws the exception in the second insert in place, try it with new data.

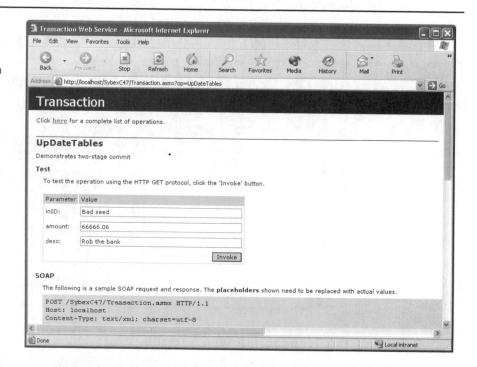

Click Invoke. If all goes according to plan, an exception will be thrown, and you'll get a message that looks something like this (I've excerpted parts):

```
System.Web.HttpException: Exception of type System.Web.HttpException was
thrown. ---> System.Reflection.TargetInvocationException: Exception has
been thrown by the target of an invocation. ---> System.Exception: This
is a nasty exception! at SybexC47.Transaction.InsertMoneyLog(String
inID, Single amount, String desc) in
c:\inetpub\wwwroot\sybexc47\transaction.asmx.cs:line 78 at
SybexC47.Transaction.UpDateTables(String inID, Single amount, String
desc) in c:\inetpub\wwwroot\sybexc47\transaction.asmx.cs:line 55  ---
End of inner exception stack trace ---
...
at System.Web.Util.TransactedInvocation.ExecuteTransactedCode()
--- End of inner exception stack trace ---
at
System.Web.Util.Transactions.InvokeTransacted(TransactedCallback
callback, TransactionOption mode, Boolean& transactionAborted)
```

```
at System.Web.Util.Transactions.InvokeTransacted(TransactedCallback
callback, TransactionOption mode)
at System.Web.Services.Protocols.WebServiceHandler.InvokeTransacted()
at System.Web.Services.Protocols.WebServiceHandler.CoreProcessRequest()
```

The key things to note are the methods I've placed in bold type, which indicate that transaction management was started, a transaction aborted, and the transaction rolled back. You should also verify that the test data has not actually been added to the first table, MoneyIn (Figure 13.23).

FIGURE 13.23:

You can verify that the test data has not been inserted into either table.

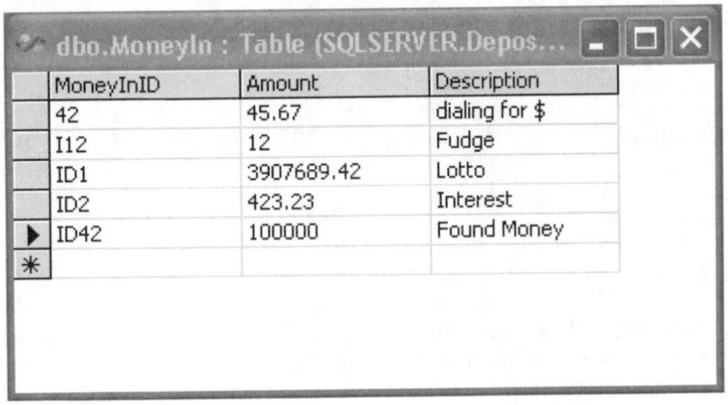

dbo.MoneyIn : Table (SQLSERVER.Depos...		
MoneyInID	Amount	Description
42	45.67	dialing for $
I12	12	Fudge
ID1	3907689.42	Lotto
ID2	423.23	Interest
ID42	100000	Found Money

NOTE   One of the steps in the transaction doesn't have to do something as drastic as throwing an exception to cause the step (and the transaction) to fail. For example, an attempt to use a duplicate primary key will cause the first insertion to fail, even if the primary key used in the second insertion is not a duplicate—thus rolling back the entire transaction.

Exposing a Private Message Queue Using a Web Service

In Chapter 11, "Messaging," I showed you how to use message queues to create distributed applications. These distributed applications could start—and stop—activities by themselves sending and receiving messages.

I did note in Chapter 11 that a drawback to using the messaging application included with Windows as part of an application's architecture is that it limits distributed applications to those running on Windows. This objection can easily be overcome by exposing messaging as a web service. In fact, as the example in the section shows, it's extremely easy to expose private—or public—message queues as a web service.

To start, create a new ASP.NET Web Service project. Name the web service class Mq, and add two web methods. These web methods will operate on a private queue named "WebServices." SendMessage pushes a message onto the queue, and GetMessage pops the message queue. The code for the web service is shown in Listing 13.10 (for a more complete explanation of programming message queues, please refer to Chapter 11).

Listing 13.10   Exposing a Message Queue as a Web Service

```
using System.Messaging;
...
[WebService(Namespace="http://bearhome.com/webservices/")]
public class Mq : System.Web.Services.WebService {
...
[WebMethod (Description = "Pushes a message on the queue")]
public void SendMessage(string theText, string subject){
   string qpath = @".\Private$\WebServices";
   if (!MessageQueue.Exists(qpath))
      MessageQueue.Create (qpath);
   MessageQueue theQ = new MessageQueue(qpath);
   theQ.Formatter = new BinaryMessageFormatter();
   theQ.Send (theText, subject);
}
[WebMethod (Description = "Pops a message off the queue")]
public string GetMessage(){
   string qpath = @".\Private$\WebServices";
   if (!MessageQueue.Exists(qpath))
      MessageQueue.Create (qpath);
   MessageQueue theQ = new MessageQueue(qpath);
   theQ.Formatter = new BinaryMessageFormatter();
   System.Messaging.Message msg = theQ.Receive(new TimeSpan (0,0,10));
   return msg.Label + ": " + msg.Body.ToString();
}
...
```

If you run the project, you can use the generated test pages to see whether the SendMessage web method actually places a message on the queue (Figure 13.24).

FIGURE 13.24:

The generated test pages allow you to test pushing a message on the queue.

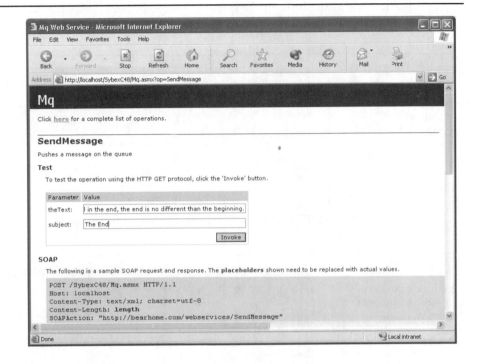

You can open Server Explorer and expand the message queuing nodes to verify that the message was placed on the queue by the web method:

It's also worth running the test page for the GetMessage web method to verify that the message is popped off the front of the queue. As you can see in Figure 13.25, the return string from the web method is the subject concatenated with the body of the message.

Nothing could be simpler than writing a client app that uses the web service to implement messaging (you need, of course, to include as usual a reference to the web service).

The code shown in Listing 13.11 uses the message-queuing web service to place a message on the queue when the Send button is clicked. When the Receive button is clicked, the message that is currently at the head of the queue is popped off and displayed in the title bar of the application (Figure 13.26).

The generated test pages let you check that you can pop messages off the queue.

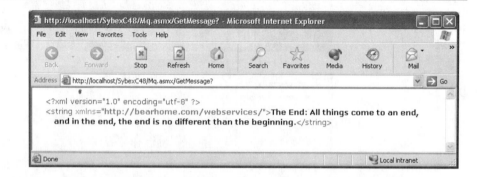

It's easy to use the web service to access the private message queue.

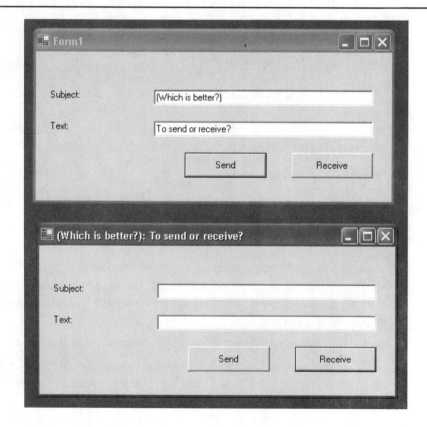

| Listing 13.11 | Consuming the Message Queue Service |

```
private void btnSend_Click(object sender, System.EventArgs e) {
    webservice.Mq ws = new webservice.Mq();
    ws.SendMessage (txtText.Text, txtSubject.Text);
}
private void btnReceive_Click(object sender, System.EventArgs e) {
    webservice.Mq ws = new webservice.Mq();
    this.Text = ws.GetMessage();
}
```

Getting the Picture with TerraService

Microsoft's TerraServer database is partially intended to demonstrate the scalability of Microsoft's database products, since it contains terabytes of aerial and satellite image data supplied by the United States Geological Survey (USGS) and others. The site www.terraserver.com (Figure 13.27) is a portal primarily intended to enable subscription access to this data.

FIGURE 13.27:

TerraServer.com is a "vortal," or vertical portal, primarily offering subscription access to satellite and topographic imagery.

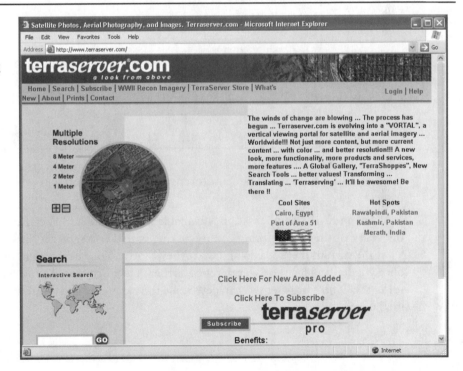

In addition to the TerraServer portal, much of the data—meaning aerial photographs, relief maps, and topographic maps—is available as a free web service. You can add a web reference to the TerraService web service to one of your projects, by choosing Project ≻ Add Web Reference. In the Add Web Reference dialog, if you enter the URL http://terraservice.net/ TerraService.asmx, the WSDL "table of contents"—showing the web methods available— will be displayed (Figure 13.28).

FIGURE 13.28:

The web service WSDL page shows the TerraService methods available and provides access to XML documentation.

Click Add Reference to add a reference to the TerraService web service in your project.

Although XML documentation is available through the Add Web Reference dialog, it is still the case that the hardest thing about working with TerraServer is discovery—figuring out what the various methods do and what they return. Your best tool in this discovery process, once you have added the web reference, is the Object Browser. As you can see in Figure 13.29, using the Object Browser you can determine the parameter and return types of all available web methods.

FIGURE 13.29:

The Object Browser is the best tool in our arsenal for figuring out how the members of the TerraService work.

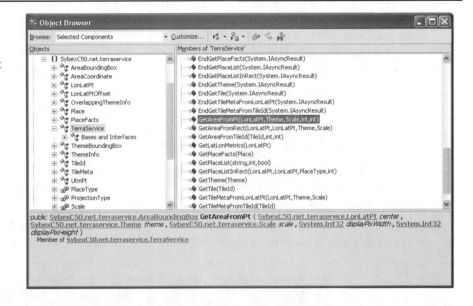

The user interface for the sample TerraService client application—with an aerial view of downtown Seattle—is shown in Figure 13.30.

FIGURE 13.30:

The drama of Seattle's lake-and-ocean setting becomes apparent from this aerial view.

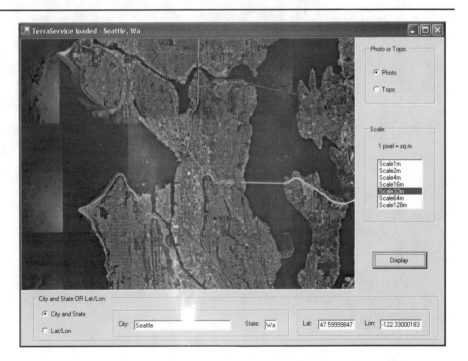

This interface lets the user choose a map by city and state or by lat/lon (latitude and longitude) coordinate pairs. "But wait just a second," you may be saying to yourself right about now. "I'd like to see my house from above. I know the address and ZIP code, but how do I find its lat/lon coordinates?"

As you'll see in a bit, in order to display a city map, the TerraService methods must be used to calculate the lat/lon value of the city center. I've set the user interface of this sample application to display those lat/lon values—so one way you can go about it is to enter your city, read the lat/lon values for the city, and interpolate from there.

It's probably both more precise and easier to go to MapBlast (www.mapblast.com) and enter your address. Create a map based on the address, and then click the button to print the map, and view a printable version of the map. Lat/lon coordinates will be displayed at the bottom of the printable map.

Whichever way you do it, it's easy to use the TerraService client to display aerial views of places you care about (my home is at the center of the aerial photo shown in Figure 13.31).

FIGURE 13.31:

Using latitude/longitude coordinates, you can zoom in on areas of particular interest (this photo is centered on the author's home).

In addition to *where*, the user gets to choose whether an aerial photograph or a topographic map is displayed. Figure 13.32 shows the client application displaying a topographic map.

FIGURE 13.32:

The TerraService returns topographic maps as an alternative to aerial photos.

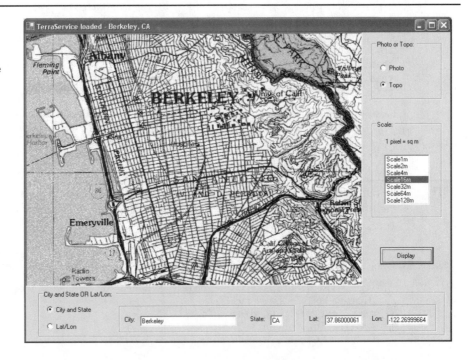

As a preliminary to implementing the TerraService client application as a Windows forms project, you should include using directives to System.IO and System.Drawing.Imaging in the form class module:

```
using System.Drawing.Imaging;
using System.IO;
```

I used a PictureBox control to display the image returned by the TerraServer web service, so the issue is setting the Image property of the PictureBox control. Listing 13.12 shows the portion of the code that manages the user interface, gathers user choices, calls the display method, and handles exceptions. You should know that in addition to the code shown in Listing 13.12, I entered the possible string values for the Scale ListBox into its Items collection using the Properties window. This means that these values are part of the "hidden" form code (see Chapter 3, "Windows Uses Web Services, Too!," for more of a discussion of hidden form code). If you expand the hidden area, the ListBox initialization code will look something like this:

```
this.lstScale.Items.AddRange(new object[] {
                                            "Scale1m",
                                            "Scale2m",
                                            "Scale4m",
                                            "Scale16m",
```

```
                                              "Scale32m",
                                              "Scale64m",
                                              "Scale128m"});
    this.lstScale.Location = new System.Drawing.Point(24, 64);
    this.lstScale.Name = "lstScale";
    this.lstScale.Size = new System.Drawing.Size(88, 95);
    this.lstScale.TabIndex = 0;
```

I also wanted to make sure that an item in the Scale ListBox collection was initially selected, so I added the following code in the form constructor:

```
    this.lstScale.SelectedItem = this.lstScale.Items[2];
```

NOTE   If I had put this in the hidden ListBox initialization code, it would quite likely be removed the next time the project was recompiled by the form auto-generator.

Listing 13.12   Consuming the TerraService (Part I, Getting User Preferences)

```
private void btnDisplay_Click(object sender, System.EventArgs e) {
    pictureBox1.Image = null;
    this.Text = "...Loading...";
    Application.DoEvents();
    Cursor = Cursors.WaitCursor;
    try {
        net.terraservice.Theme Theme;
        if (rdoPhoto.Checked == true) {
            Theme = net.terraservice.Theme.Photo;
        }
        else {
            Theme = net.terraservice.Theme.Topo;
        }
        net.terraservice.LonLatPt point;
        if (rdoCityandState.Checked == true){
            net.terraservice.TerraService ts =
                new net.terraservice.TerraService ();
            // Get the latitude and longitude of the requested city
            net.terraservice.Place place = new net.terraservice.Place ();
            // No empty cities or states
            if (txtCity.Text == String.Empty || txtState.Text == String.Empty){
                txtCity.Text = "San Francisco";
                txtState.Text = "Ca";
            }
            place.City = txtCity.Text;
            place.State = txtState.Text;
            place.Country = "USA";
            point = ts.ConvertPlaceToLonLatPt (place);
            // Display the lat/lon used for the city
            txtLat.Text = point.Lat.ToString();
```

```
            txtLon.Text = point.Lon.ToString();
    }
    else {
        // by lat/lon
        point = new net.terraservice.LonLatPt();
        point.Lat = Convert.ToDouble(txtLat.Text);
        point.Lon = Convert.ToDouble(txtLon.Text);
    }
    net.terraservice.Scale theScale = net.terraservice.Scale.Scale4m;
    // Get the scale picked by user
    switch (lstScale.SelectedItem.ToString()){
        case "Scale1m":
            theScale = net.terraservice.Scale.Scale1m;
            break;
        case "Scale2m":
            theScale = net.terraservice.Scale.Scale2m;
            break;
        case "Scale4m":
            theScale = net.terraservice.Scale.Scale4m;
            break;
        case "Scale8m":
            theScale = net.terraservice.Scale.Scale8m;
            break;
        case "Scale16m":
            theScale = net.terraservice.Scale.Scale16m;
            break;
        case "Scale32m":
            theScale = net.terraservice.Scale.Scale32m;
            break;
        case "Scale64m":
            theScale = net.terraservice.Scale.Scale64m;
            break;
        case "Scale128m":
            theScale = net.terraservice.Scale.Scale128m;
            break;
        default:
            theScale = net.terraservice.Scale.Scale4m;
            break;
    }
    // Time to rock and roll - let's get the picture
    pictureBox1.Image = GetTiledImage (point, theScale,Theme, 640, 480);
}
catch (System.Web.Services.Protocols.SoapException){
    MessageBox.Show ("Unable to return requested map or photo",
        "TerraService", MessageBoxButtons.OK, MessageBoxIcon.Information);
}
catch (Exception excep){
    MessageBox.Show (excep.Message, "TerraService",
        MessageBoxButtons.OK, MessageBoxIcon.Exclamation);
}
finally {
    Cursor = Cursors.Default;
```

```
        if (rdoCityandState.Checked == true){
            this.Text = "TerraService loaded - " + txtCity.Text +
                ", " + txtState.Text;
        }
        else {
            this.Text = "TerraService loaded - Lat: " + txtLat.Text +
                "; Lon: " + txtLon.Text;
        }
    }
}
```

Note that in Listing 12.12, if the user elects to see a photo or map by city and state, the web service method ConvertPlaceToLonLatPt is called to convert the city center to a lat/lon point:

```
point = ts.ConvertPlaceToLonLatPt (place);
// Display the lat/lon used for the city
txtLat.Text = point.Lat.ToString();
txtLon.Text = point.Lon.ToString();
```

As you can see, I took advantage of having this information to display it back to the user.

In Listing 12.12, once all the user choices have been gathered and the city (if selected) has been converted to a lat/lon point, the private method GetTiledImage is called:

```
pictureBox1.Image = GetTiledImage (point, theScale, Theme, 640, 480);
```

GetTiledImage is passed a lat/lon point, a scale constant, a theme constant (e.g., photo or map), and a size in pixels. The return value of this method, which does the actual dirty work of retrieving imagery from the TerraService web service, is loaded into the Image property of the PictureBox. As you can see in Listing 13.13, the tricky part about this is that TerraService GetTile method returns a 200×200 pixel image—too small to be much good. An iteration routine is needed to piece together an image of the proper size, using the AreaBoundingBox structure returned earlier by the web service to determine the corner coordinates for the required image.

Listing 13.13   Consuming the TerraServer (Part II, Obtaining the Tiled Image)

```
private Bitmap GetTiledImage (net.terraservice.LonLatPt point,
    net.terraservice.Scale Scale, net.terraservice.Theme Theme,
    int cx, int cy) {
    // Instantiate the TerraServer proxy class
    net.terraservice.TerraService ts = new net.terraservice.TerraService ();
    // Compute the parameters for a bounding box
    net.terraservice.AreaBoundingBox abb =
        ts.GetAreaFromPt (point, Theme, Scale, cx, cy);
    // Create an image to fit the bounding box
    PixelFormat pf = PixelFormat.Format32bppRgb;
    Bitmap bitmap = new Bitmap (cx, cy, pf);
    Graphics g = Graphics.FromImage (bitmap);

    int x1 = abb.NorthWest.TileMeta.Id.X;
```

```
int y1 = abb.NorthWest.TileMeta.Id.Y;
int x2 = abb.NorthEast.TileMeta.Id.X;
int y2 = abb.SouthWest.TileMeta.Id.Y;

for (int x = x1; x <= x2; x++) {
    for (int y = y1; y >= y2; y--) {
        net.terraservice.TileId tid = abb.NorthWest.TileMeta.Id;
        tid.X = x;
        tid.Y = y;
        Image tile = Image.FromStream (new MemoryStream (ts.GetTile (tid)));
        g.DrawImage (tile,
            (x - x1) * tile.Width - (Int32) abb.NorthWest.Offset.XOffset,
            (y1 - y) * tile.Height - (Int32) abb.NorthWest.Offset.YOffset,
            tile.Width, tile.Height);
        tile.Dispose();
    }
}
// Return the resulting image
return bitmap;
}
```

The TerraServer web service is amazing, and lots of fun too! You can use the application that I've shown you in this section as a starting place, and add aerial photos and maps as appropriate to your own applications.

Conclusion

May the circle be unbroken! May the last note be as sweet and elegant as the first note! C# is a powerful, intelligent, and easy-to-use language—as I hope you've seen in this book. In the beginning, in the first part of this book, the prelude, we created a simple ASP.NET web service, then we got to know ASP.NET web forms applications and learned how to consume the web service.

In the next part, the allemande, as things strode forward, we created Windows user interfaces and started our exploration of the .NET Framework's class libraries.

The dance really heated up in the third part, the courante. We explored the C# language in detail and looked at arrays and collections of objects—and then looked more at objects in C#, and observed life from a string's-eye view.

In the final part, the gigue, we started to close the circle. Files and streams, messaging, XML, and ADO.NET were discussed. In this chapter, we headed back to web services for a last visit. The end is not quite the same as the beginning: the primary concern in this chapter was how web services fit in as part of a larger picture—in the case of the TerraServer web service, a very large picture, indeed!

I hope you've enjoyed my book, and that it helps you to build beautiful, literate, and elegant .NET applications using C#.

Using C# .NET's Help System

No matter how experienced a programmer you are, sometimes you need help understanding a concept or term or figuring out how a feature works. The auto-completion features of the Code Editor make it less likely that you'll need help with basic language syntax or with knowing the members of an object. But it is still the case that nobody knows everything, and one of the most important skills in an environment as complex as C# .NET is being able to find help when you need it.

The help system available to C# might be dubbed "the good, the big, and the ugly," because it includes documentation for the entire .NET Framework as well as the C# language. Along with the precious documentation gems that will help you solve your real-world problems, it also contains myriad "kitchen sink" topics you will never need. In other words, C# .NET's help system is comprehensive, overwhelming, and not always well organized. For a programmer with limited time, adrift in a vast sea of information, the trick is to efficiently find the buried nuggets of information—which this appendix will help you to do.

The help system is so complex to use that you may find yourself referring to the "Help on Help" topic to understand how the various features work. (To access this topic, choose Help ➤ Help on Help.) In addition, often the only way to find what you're looking for is to browse through a great many topics. The good news is that one innovative feature, Dynamic Help, can make life a great deal easier.

This appendix briefly explains the mechanics of how to use the Dynamic Help, Contents, Index, Search, and filtering features of the C# .NET help system.

Dynamic Help and F1

Dynamic Help is a form of context-sensitive help in which a window provides links to help topics, depending on the selection in the development environment. To activate Dynamic Help, select Help ➤ Dynamic Help or press Ctrl+F1 on the keyboard. The Dynamic Help window will open.

NOTE   Depending on how you have your Visual Studio environment set up, Dynamic Help may appear as a tab in another window, such as the Properties window, rather than in a separate window.

As you can see in Figure A.1, which shows the links in the Dynamic Help window when the MainMenu control is selected in the Toolbox, the Dynamic Help window provides information about whatever is currently active in the environment—which can be very helpful, indeed!

There's no doubt that running with Dynamic Help turned on slows down the Visual Studio development environment. If this is a significant concern because you are running on older (and slower) hardware, it is likely that you will want to work with Dynamic Help turned off to gain an extra bit of speed.

FIGURE A.1:

When the MainMenu control is selected, Dynamic Help shows topics related to the MainMenu.

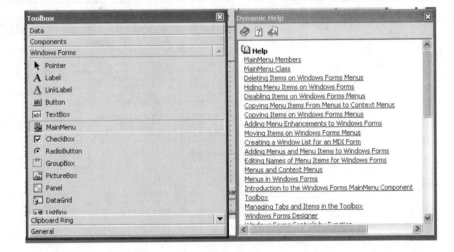

If you are working with Dynamic Help turned off, you should probably bear in mind that the F1 key still provides "good, old-fashioned" context-sensitive help. When you press F1, a help topic relevant to the current active object in the IDE opens in a window.

Contents

The Contents window is used to drill down to find information using nodes and links. To open the Contents window, select Help ➤ Contents. The Contents window will open with a few top nodes showing, as in Figure A.2. Click the nodes to expand them to show further nodes and topics.

FIGURE A.2:

The Contents window: its highest level (left) and some expanded nodes (right).

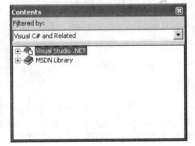
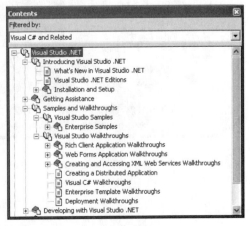

Select a topic to display it. Undoubtedly, it will show further links. Figure A.3 shows an example of the Visual Studio .NET topic page.

FIGURE A.3:

Selecting a topic in
the Contents window
takes you to the
topic's help page.

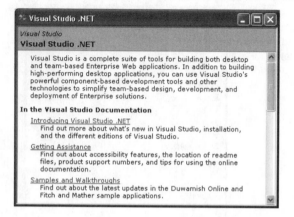

The Contents window, like the Index and Search windows, can be filtered by topic, so that it will show only the information related to the filter. Use the Filtered By drop-down list at the top of the window to choose a filter. You'll most likely want to filter information using the Visual C# or Visual C# And Related settings. For more information, see the "Filtering" section later in this appendix.

Navigational Aids within a Help Topic Window

Many help topics have additional features that can be accessed using icons found at the upper-left of the help topic window. Since these icons are not available for all topics, don't be surprised if you do not see them (they are most commonly associated with help topic items that have been filtered by ".NET Framework SDK").

From left to right, the icons enable you to access the following features:

See Also   Represented by a squiggly up arrow; helpful for finding other help topic articles that are relevant.

Requirements   Represented by a check mark; details platform requirements for the item featured in the help topic—not very useful.

Language Filter   Represented by something like a curved letter *T*. This is actually quite convenient— if you are coding in C#, why should you want to see the VB code, and vice versa?

Index

The Index window allows you to look for specific information. To open the Index window, select Help ➤ Index. With the Index window open, enter the term you are searching for in the Look For box.

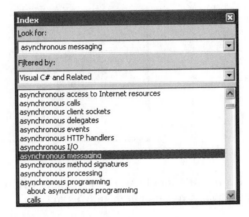

A list of indexed terms, based on the phrase you entered, will appear in the bottom pane of the Index window. If you select a term in the bottom pane, the Index Results window will open, showing all the indexed listings for the term.

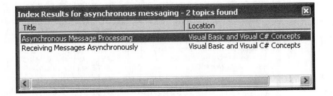

If you double-click a listing in the Index Results window, the topic will open for viewing.

NOTE   If there is only one topic indexed for a given search phrase, it will open immediately when you select it in the Index window (rather than opening the Index Results window).

You can open the Index Results window directly once you have already done a search, by selecting Help ➤ Index Results.

Search

The Search window works like the Index window, except that it produces more "hits" because it searches within help documents, not just on the indexed titles.

To open the Search window, select Help ➢ Search. The Search window offers four options:

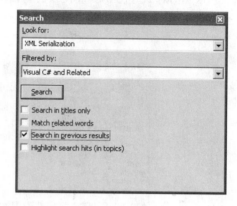

TIP	The Search window is the tool I use most frequently to find things. I find the ability to search through previous results particularly useful.

As opposed to the Index Results window, the Search Results window is likely to show a great many hits—possibly in the hundreds, as you can see in Figure A.4.

FIGURE A.4:

Search Results can be very extensive.

Title	Location	Rank
Class Library	.NET Framework Class Library	1
.NET Samples - ASP.NET Server Control Reference	.NET Framework QuickStarts	2
.NET Samples - How To: XML Data	.NET Framework QuickStarts	3
Classes and Mapping in CLI and WMI	.NET Framework Developer's Guide	4
Inheritance	.NET Framework Developer's Guide	5
.NET Samples - How To: Networking	.NET Framework QuickStarts	6
.NET Samples - How To: Data and ADO.NET	.NET Framework QuickStarts	7
.NET Samples - ASP.NET Data Grid	.NET Framework QuickStarts	8
Base Class Usage Guidelines	.NET Framework General Reference	9
Design Goals for XML in the .NET Framework	.NET Framework Developer's Guide	10
Polymorphism in Components	Visual Basic and Visual C# Concepts	11
Type.GetNestedTypes Method	.NET Framework Class Library	12
Type.GetNestedTypes Method (BindingFlags)	.NET Framework Class Library	13
Heterogeneous Distributed Transaction Impleme...	Visual Studio Samples: Fitch and Mather 7.0	14
Introducing XML Serialization	.NET Framework Developer's Guide	15
Basic File I/O	.NET Framework Developer's Guide	16
System.Windows.Forms Namespace	.NET Framework Class Library	17
Recommendations for Abstract Classes vs. Inter...	Visual Basic and Visual C# Concepts	18
Overview of the .NET Framework	.NET Framework Developer's Guide	19
.NET Samples - ASP.NET Control Authoring	.NET Framework QuickStarts	20
XmlSerializer Class	.NET Framework Class Library	21
Schemas	.NET Framework Developer's Guide	22
.NET Samples - Windows Forms: Control Refere...	.NET Framework QuickStarts	23
Nested Classes in Components	Visual Basic and Visual C# Concepts	24

Search Results for Classes - 500 topics found

You can open the Search Results window directly once you have already done a search, by selecting Help ➢ Search Results.

The Help Toolbar

Many of the topics that result from searches are sections of larger articles. For example, you see "Caching Versions of a Page" show up in the search results. It's part of a larger topic called "ASP.NET Caching Features," but how would you know that?

When you have a topic open, you can click the Sync Contents icon—a horizontal double-headed arrow—in the toolbar, and it will show you where the topic fits in the grand scheme of help information (by displaying the topic's location in the Contents window).

You'll also find the Previous Topic and Next Topic features helpful. These appear in the toolbar as an up arrow (Previous topic) and a down arrow (Next topic). These let you scan the help in the order of the help contents.

Filtering Help Results

As I noted in the section on the Contents window, help results can be filtered using the Filtered By drop-down list in the Contents, Index, or Search window.

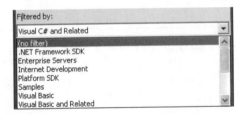

To turn filtering off, select "(no filter)" in this drop-down list. However, it is likely that you will wish to filter by Visual C# or Visual C# And Related, simply to keep your help searches manageable.

TIP   .NET Framework SDK is another very useful filter.

NOTE   You can also set the help filter on your Start page. To do this, show your Start page by selecting Help ➢ Show Start Page. With the Start page open, select My Profile, and set the Help Filter using the drop-down box.

It is an interesting fact that you can customize filters and create new filters using Boolean criteria, as though you were writing the WHERE clause of a SQL query (which is likely exactly what you are doing under the covers!).

To open the Edit Help Filters window, select Help ➢ Edit Filters. Using this window, you can edit the definition of a current filter or select New from the menu bar to create a new filter.

To edit a filter, first select it in the Filter drop-down list. Figure A.5 shows an example of the Edit Help Filters window with the Visual C# And Related filter selected.

FIGURE A.5:

You can use the Edit Help Filters window to customize help filters using a Boolean syntax.

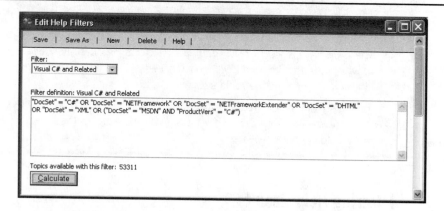

At the bottom of the Edit Help Filters window, you'll find a list of the available attributes that can be used together with Boolean operators to create a filter definition. Figure A.6 shows an excerpt from this list.

FIGURE A.6:

Use the attribute list to edit your filter definitions.

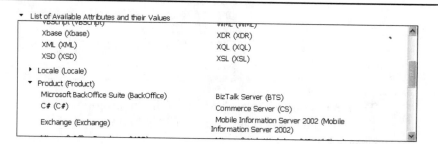

To find out how many topics are included in a given filter, click the Calculate button in the Edit Help Filters window. For example, you may find it relevant to know that the Visual C# filter has 8,093 topics, and the Visual C# And Related filter has 53,311 topics. This gives you an idea of the comparative breadth of each topic (both totals are slightly less than those yielded by the comparable VB .NET filter).

Index

Note to the Reader: Page numbers in **bold** indicate the principal discussion of a topic or the definition of a term. Page numbers in *italics* indicate illustrations.

B

C

N

O

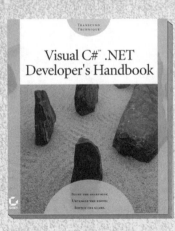 

The quotation on the bottom of the front cover is taken from the thirty-fifth chapter of Lao Tzu's Tao Te Ching, *the classic work of Taoist philosophy. This particular verse is from the translation by D. C. Lau (copyright 1963) and communicates a theme explored throughout the book: true knowledge transcends the ordinary senses.*

It is traditionally held that Lao Tzu lived in the fifth century B.C. in China, during the Chou dynasty, but it is unclear whether he was actually a historical figure. It is said that he was a teacher of Confucius. The concepts embodied in the Tao Te Ching *influenced religious thinking in the Far East, including Zen Buddhism in Japan. Many in the West, however, have wrongly understood the* Tao Te Ching *to be primarily a mystical work; in fact, much of the advice in the book is grounded in a practical moral philosophy governing personal conduct.*